With a Critical Eye

With a Critical Eye

An Intellectual and His Times

By Arthur J. Vidich

Edited and introduced by Robert Jackall

Newfound Press
THE UNIVERSITY OF TENNESSEE LIBRARIES, KNOXVILLE

Newfound Press
University of Tennessee Libraries
1015 Volunteer Boulevard
Knoxville, TN 37996-1000
www.newfoundpress.utk.edu

ISBN-13: 978-0-9797292-4-9
ISBN-10: 0-9797292-4-6

Vidich, Arthur J.
       With a critical eye : an intellectual and his times / by Arthur J. Vidich ; edited and introduced by Robert Jackall.
       x, 491 p. : digital, PDF file.
       1. Vidich, Arthur J. — Career in anthropology. 2. Vidich, Arthur J.— Anecdotes. 3. Anthropologists — United States— History— 20th century— Biography. I. Jackall, Robert. II. Title.
       GN21 .V53 2009

Book design by Jayne Rogers
Cover design by Jayne Rogers, Martha Rudolph, Alana Hawkins

For My Children & My Grandchildren

Contents

Author's Acknowledgments

I began this autobiography some years ago as a personal memoir not knowing who its readers might be. I intended it as a set of recollections of a boy of immigrant Slovenian parents who tried to make his way in the brawling reality that is America that I have spent my life trying to understand. The early chapters of the book reflect on my origins. As I continued to write, the book became a record of my intellectual development and my reflections on it. I offer it to readers as the story of an intellectual who grappled with the problems of his times.

My thanks to William Form for his helpful suggestions about ethnicity and to Franco Ferrarotti for his help in making the International Veblen Association a presence in Europe. Thanks too to Sonia Salas of the Graduate Faculty at The New School for Social Research for helping me find documents indispensable for the chapters on The New School. And special thanks to Donna L. Chenail of Williams College for her invaluable assistance in coordinating production work on several editions of the manuscript.

My great appreciation to Michael Hughey, Larry Carney, Charlotte O'Kelly, Guy Oakes, and Duffy Graham for their extensive editorial work on this book. And I am especially grateful to Robert Jackall both for his editorial work and for guiding the project through to completion.

Many other people have helped bring this work to fruition. My thanks to my children Charles Vidich, Paul Vidich, Andrew Vidich, Joseph Vidich, Max Gregoric and Rosilind Gutterson, and to my grandsons, Jamie, for his close copy editing, and to Joshua, for his engaging dialogue. I am very happy to dedicate this work to all my children and grandchildren.

Editor's Acknowledgments

A great many people worked hard on different parts of this project. My thanks to: Marilyn Bensman, Larry Carney, Donna Chenail, Rufi Cole, Godehard Czernik, Duffy Graham, Carmen Hendershott, Janice Hirota, Mike Hughey, Christine Ménard, Ina Liu, Guy Oakes, Lyn Macgregor, Charlotte O'Kelly, Laurin Raikin, Sonia Salas, Charlie Vidich, Jamie Vidich, Joe Vidich, Josh Vidich, Paul Vidich, and Josh Wakeham.

Special thanks to Harry Dahms, who brought the project to the board of Newfound Press, to Casie Fedukovich for her masterful editing of the manuscript, to Jayne Rogers for her design work, and to Marie Garrett and Linda Phillips for their careful attention to the book through all the stages of production. Finally, my deep thanks to Peter Willmott and to the Willmott Family Professorship at Williams College for supporting my work over the years.

RJ
New York City
October 2009

Introduction

On Marginality and Creativity
Robert Jackall

Art Vidich began to write this memoir in the late 1990s "as a set of recollections of a boy of immigrant Slovenian parents who tried to make his way in the brawling reality that is America that [he spent his] life trying to understand." It became not only a remarkable record of an immigrant childhood and boyhood, but a self-portrait of a singularly important anthropologist/sociologist of the twentieth century. This essay focuses on Vidich's stance as an outsider, a habit of mind initially fostered by his family's social situation and later embraced by him as essential for the kind of understanding he wished to achieve and impart to others. I begin in the middle of the story.

Small Town in Mass Society
Arthur J. Vidich and Joseph Bensman published *Small Town in Mass Society* in 1958. The book describes in close detail the social and cultural situation of "Springdale," a rural, mid-century American small town in upstate New York, complete with telling portraits of Springdale's class structure, its myths and ideologies, and of some key individuals charged or self-appointed with maintaining the town's moral cosmos. The book moves freely between an analysis of Springdale's social structure and the social psychology of its several groups. Such a close examination revealed how deeply a number of structural trends had penetrated even the furthest

My thanks to Janice M. Hirota Yuriko Jackall, and Duffy Graham for their careful critiques of earlier versions of this essay.

reaches of American society. These trends included the following: the growing dominance of large organizations; the concomitant bureaucratization of every key occupational group; the ascendance of the new middle class of managers and professionals attached to the big organizations; the decline of the old middle class of free professionals, small entrepreneurs, artisans, and farmers; and the glaring discrepancy between small town ideologies extolling a glorious, home-made past and the hard cultural reality of a mass society that continually recycles second- and third-hand images of community and self from the metropolis back to the provinces. Springdalers' images of their town's past were largely fictive; the town's future was controlled by forces outside its influence. But many Springdalers, including gatekeepers of the larger society who resided in or near the town, preferred to live with comforting self-images and illusions fabricated either by distant experts with symbols who, though they did not know Springdale itself, knew a hundred towns like it, or by local boosters who constructed and propagated the town's upbeat self-presentation.

Every major structural trend that Vidich and Bensman discerned in Springdale has accelerated. Work is more bureaucratized. Power is more centralized. Old theodicies provide even less private comfort or public guidance than they did fifty-plus years ago, and, despite ingeniously manufactured fictive public realities, our contemporary communities are rarely holistic, well-knit social organisms, but instead they resemble patchworks of common interest, need, and desire stitched together as circumstances require. Our social psychological ambivalence about almost everything is a typical cast of mind for many people, at least in the middle classes. Moreover, our civic culture and public discourse are both dominated by the perspectives, techniques, and ethics of public relations. As substantive expertise in every arena of our society becomes more specialized and more arcane, our society comes to resemble a checkerboard with impassable moats around each square. What happens in one square is, for the most part, unintelligible to those in other squares. But, in fact, as the substantive expertise that underpins our civilization proliferates, so too does the demand for interpretive expertise to fashion the verbal and visual images of complex, substantive realities that can resonate with broader audiences and thus recreate the legitimacy substantive expertise needs to flourish. Once fashioned, images assume a life and reality of their own. And once internalized, in an increasingly specialized society, they often become the only realities that matter. When sociologists probe behind public masks to find out how social reality is really put together, as Vidich and Bensman did in *Small Town*, they almost always encounter hostility not only from those who wear the masks, but perhaps especially from those who have been fooled by the performance.

Small Town in Mass Society is a classic work precisely because it penetrates the placid, banal surfaces of everyday life and reveals powerful undercurrents in American society. Moreover, its framework emerges directly out of its presentation of concrete details gleaned in intensive fieldwork. The 1968 edition of the book contains a series of illuminating papers about fieldwork, and the relationship of theory to field data, some of which were written before the book's original publication. These essays are not only the best in the literature on the virtues and dilemmas of fieldwork itself, but they also provide the key to understanding how *Small Town* penetrated the myths of Springdale so well. At the core of these essays is an insistence on cultivating a stance of intellectual marginality—the ability to stand at the edge of social situations and observe and report both routine and chaos with dispassion—as the prerequisite for sociological understanding.

The Roots of Marginality

Vidich's autobiography provides rich material to understand his ability to adopt an outsider's stance to the social world. This habit of mind came only slowly and by fits and starts, beginning with growing up as a first-generation child of an ethnic immigrant family in an industrial suburb of Milwaukee in the 1920s and 1930s. His book recounts in full detail the cultural puzzles he and his family faced in bridging the old world and the new, but with none of the sentimentality and laments that mark much of the ethnic coming-of-age genre. The early chapters of his book are filled with examples of the resourcefulness and caginess of his and his family's attempts to apprehend the opportunities that American society offered to its newcomers and their success in seizing them.

Indeed, Vidich's initial response to his station of origin was to seek success in America on its own terms and in a vigorous way. His tales of his boyhood recount his developing leadership skills. His outgoing and engaging personality made him exceptional in his cohort. Later, in college, he plunged into student politics and became a big man on campus at the University of Wisconsin. He aspired to become Wisconsin's governor or one of that state's United States senators. He was prepared to tailor himself in any way necessary to achieve these goals.

But immediately after Pearl Harbor, he joined the Marine Corps, a commitment that he later called his last patriotic act. Ironically, before being sent to the Pacific Theater, the Marine Corps gave him the opportunity, in ways he did not fully understand at the time, to develop habits of mind that became defining intellectual characteristics. In his Marine uniform, he took courses at the University of Michigan in piano and in anthropology. He struck up a friendship with the anthropologist Leslie White and read, for the first time, a great deal of ethnography, particularly the work of the great British social anthropologists. That tradition stresses immersing oneself in the social worlds that others construct. By coming to know others from the inside out, one comes to know aspects of oneself that might never be glimpsed if one attends only to the self-rationalization requisite for worldly success.

Vidich was a good and faithful Marine. He rose to the rank of lieutenant (though he mustered out as a sergeant because he did not re-enlist), but he never internalized that institution's semper fidelis ethos. He became a scrounger in the American occupying forces in Kyushu, the southernmost island of Japan, a role that gave him the opportunity to explore the island's depleted resources and housing for incoming brass. As such, he went on his first "field trip," one that foreshadowed later interests. He commandeered a jeep to drive up to Kagoshima Bay to see the small town of Suya Mura because, at Leslie White's suggestion, he had read the ethnography of the town written by John Embree, a Yale anthropologist. He also commandeered a small craft to fly over the city of Nagasaki where he took a remarkable photograph (available on this book's website), one that documents the devastation of the city by "Fat Man" on August 9, 1945. The experience made him an opponent of nuclear weapons for the rest of his life. He left the Marines with pride, but without the nostalgia for camaraderie and action that characterizes many of the organization's veterans.

After returning to Wisconsin, Vidich got involved in an extended field project in Viroqua, a small town in western Wisconsin. His part of the study, which later became his master's thesis, was a sobering examination of the mobility aspirations of young men between the ages of twenty and thirty. He discovered that, by the age of thirty, men are acutely aware of doors that they once thought entirely open being slammed shut. While engaged in the study, he met and interviewed Gerald L. K. Smith, a native of Viroqua who achieved some fame as an American fascist during the 1930s. Vidich asked the controversial Smith some very blunt questions and discovered, much to his surprise, that, in our era, one can ask other people almost anything. The ethos of self-promotion so pervades our society that most people rarely get asked questions about themselves. The chief limitation to good field research, he learned, is the fieldworker's self-consciousness and consequent self-doubt. These produce an anxiety about possible social rejection that inhibits deep inquiry. The researcher who has made himself marginal, by contrast, is free to seek the truth without internally imposed constraints.

Vidich then got involved in a research project called the Micronesian Investigation that took him to Palau, an island nation in the South Pacific. There, he did eight months of anthropological fieldwork, a defining experience in his intellectual life. He studied in particular Modekngie, an "indigenous resistance movement that cut across clan loyalties and was a result of the revolutionary economic and social changes introduced by ... colonizers."

Vidich returned to Wisconsin, where he studied with Hans Gerth. Although Gerth influenced Vidich in myriad ways, he remembered with particular vividness a seminar in which Gerth taught his students how to deconstruct public statements to discern the interests of competing groups, that is, how to recognize that virtually all public reality in a competitive, pluralistic society is a form of propaganda. Later, at Harvard, Vidich's fieldwork in Palau became the basis of his doctoral dissertation called The Political Impact of Colonial Administration. The work describes how different Palauan groups responded to the successive colonial administrations of the Spanish, the Germans, the Japanese, and the Americans. It is a detailed portrait of colonial strategies for domination, of Palauans' collaboration with and resistance to that rule, and of resulting political factionalism. The dissertation grounds this analysis in a social psychological appraisal of the deep anxiety, diffuse hostility, and marked competitiveness of native Palauan society that prevented the emergence of a widespread and unified national resistance to colonialism. Vidich was one of the first anthropologists to abandon the romantic myths and occupational ideologies typical of much American anthropology as a discipline celebrating the primitive as the antithesis to modernity. He always insisted that the focus of anthropological work should be precisely on the nexus of the old world and the new, a stance that, he discovered, made him marginal to professional anthropology, ironically one of the most provincial of disciplines.* His fieldwork in Palau, and his subsequent analysis of his experiences there, became a template for his later understanding of what was at work in Springdale.

It was, however, only in the course of and especially in the aftermath of the Springdale study that Vidich developed a fully self-conscious outsider stance. The Springdale study was part of a gigantic bureaucratic operation that involved scores of researchers from Cornell University. By its nature, as Vidich and Bensman explain

---

*   I once interviewed a candidate from Stanford University for a job in the anthropology wing of the joint anthropology and sociology department at Williams College. She had done her fieldwork in the Pacific. I asked her if she knew a 1953 anthropological dissertation on the archipelago of Palau written by Arthur J. Vidich. Not only did the young woman know the Harvard thesis, she exclaimed, but she considered it the single best anthropological work on the Pacific. Then she added: "But Vidich never wrote anything else." Like many other anthropologists, this young scholar had mastered an exotic language and subjected herself to a long period of isolation and personal privation to become an expert on a very small world.

in the 1968 edition of *Small Town*, bureaucratically organized research standardizes not only its own staff functions but its collection of data. The data that such organizations generate are uniform, but invariably formal, and often sterile. Once the research organization becomes committed to such formal types of information, however, it becomes unable to absorb other kinds of data. Moreover, project staff inevitably have contrasting images of the community being investigated, requiring the project managers to develop a consensus fictive image of the community so that the project's work can proceed. Such an image often bears little relation to reality, except that, for purely practical reasons, it usually conforms closely to the image of the community constructed by local vested interests. Finally, bureaucratically organized research rarely produces work of lasting value and frequently does not produce any work at all except for the inevitable "final report." This is quite often ghostwritten for the project directors by a "salvage expert" who puts together fragmented bits and pieces of work into a jerry-built framework without any central organizing problem. It is worth noting in this regard that, apart from *Small Town*, the Cornell project, despite the expenditure of a great deal of money, never produced even a single scholarly paper, let alone a monograph. In short, bureaucratically organized research is frequently little more than a type of public relations, the main object of which is to get funds for the next research project in order to maintain the organization that one has assembled.

Reflections on Fieldwork

The kind of fieldwork Vidich did in Palau, Viroqua, and Springdale contrasts sharply with such bureaucratized research. Here are the main themes of his thinking about fieldwork, based on scores of conversations with him over the years, along with my reflections on my own fieldwork influenced by him.

1.   Fieldwork begins with framing a significant intellectual problem that, appropriately re-framed as necessary, is amenable to empirical research. For instance, in *Moral Mazes*, the big question was: How does bureaucracy shape moral consciousness? I re-framed this into a problem that I could address empirically: What are the occupational moral rules-in-use of corporate managers? Deep into my fieldwork, I realized that I could get at almost every important issue by asking: Who gets ahead around here? But at every turn in one's fieldwork, one keeps one's eyes on the big question.

2.   Fieldwork demands good eyes, good ears, and especially the willingness to enter into other people's worlds and understand them and the world they have constructed from the inside out. One has to listen patiently to descriptions of events, usually told in fits and starts, to accounts and explanations of decisions made or roads not taken, to appraisals of other people's abilities and motivations, and especially to stories, the meaning of which is often puzzling to the subjects who recount them. Good fieldworkers possess the adeptness at easy informal conversation that invites others' disclosures.

3.   Fieldwork depends on certain assumptions about human action and society and how to study them, including the fundamental premise that the

basic unit of human society is meaningful action by individuals. The meta-problem of all social analysis is how, in what ways, and why have particular individuals combined to construct particular social worlds and concomitant worldviews? The fieldworker develops therefore a deep interest in individuals' personal biographies, how these intersect with the biographies of other people, and the mapping of both against the historical trajectory and convergence of trends that produce particular social structures. The fieldworker nurtures an appreciation of the multiple levels of consciousness possessed by every individual and instituted in every social situation. One develops the relentless curiosity necessary to plumb those levels of consciousness until others' commonsense worlds become clear. And while one pays close attention to what one's subjects say because words are deeds, one always remembers that deeds are also deeds.

4.   Fieldwork requires the intellectual openness to allow the concepts, terms of reference, and the very organization of one's analysis to emerge directly out of one's carefully recorded and organized field materials. It demands the discipline to let one's field materials ground, guide, and limit one's interpretations.

5.   It also requires the recognition that concealment, secrecy, fakery, and deception are constituent parts of all social realities, perhaps particularly modern social realities. This is coupled with the

cultivated awareness that allows one to penetrate individuals' and organizations' public faces and recognize the differences between publicly-held and privately-held views. Even as the fieldworker "let[s] the data speak," he is mindful of the many sources of error that they may contain: slanted or dramatized information; over-information from zealous local reformers; outright deception or stonewalling; accounts for untoward behavior; information manipulated to further personal ambitions; or rehearsed information based on advance rumor. He strives over time to develop the self-confidence necessary to recognize that the verbal responses of his subjects may cloak deeper levels of meaning that only a dynamic, intuitive assessment of many sources of information can reveal.

6.   Fieldwork so conceived and practiced is the antithesis of survey research, at least the kind that dips into the swirling eddies of public opinion and refutes or confirms a predetermined hypothesis. But it is also the antithesis of much of what passes for fieldwork today in anthropology and sociology and in other disciplines that have borrowed aspects of the methodology. A short list of bastard notions of fieldwork includes fieldwork that cherry picks examples to illustrate already worked-out theses or ideologically driven frameworks, whether Marxist, feminist, third-world-revolutionary, or reactionary ones; fieldwork that disguises social cause advocacy as scientific work; fieldwork that one undertakes to

work out troubling personal concerns to confirm or refute some narrow disciplinary issue; or the post-modern rummaging through personal experiences or others' field data for exotic materials to display in the unmoored speculation that now passes for theory.

7.   Fieldwork done right shapes the self of the fieldworker in decisive ways. The fieldworker is the quintessential observer, the comprehensive docu-menter, the man or woman who is content to re-cord and try to understand the accomplishments, triumphs, failures, and foibles of others. The field-worker is a bystander in and a witness to the world of affairs, not an advocate, apologist, or adversary. To do his work properly and well, he satisfies himself with the conviction that nothing is more necessary and compelling than seeing the world as it is and reporting it accurately.

Vidich's understanding of these aspects of fieldwork, along with his identification of himself as a fieldworker, reached maturity dur-ing the Springdale project. Through his extensive conversations with Joe Bensman as his work proceeded, and especially after the field-work for the project ended, he extricated himself from the deep ties he had forged in Springdale and from his necessary conformance to the social norms of the community, as well as from those of the research organization. One cannot do fieldwork without gaining the social acceptance of one's subjects, but that acceptance sometimes re-quires the researcher to make himself over in ways that subsequently prevent the cultivation of the marginal attitude toward the objects of study that alone yields fruitful knowledge. Similarly, professional ties, such as those in Cornell's research organization, are important for one's identity as a professional and for one's subsequent career, but they can also narrow one's vision of the world.

The self-objectification required to work out the substantive themes of *Small Town* inevitably led Vidich to distance himself further intellectually from Springdalers as well as from many of his professional peers committed to bureaucratized research. The firestorm of reaction from both town and gown when *Small Town* was finally published underlined Vidich's chosen role of outsider. The analysis of Springdale offended local town leaders and members of Cornell's research team. It was also taken as an affront by powerful figures in the field of sociology who saw the social uproar that *Small Town* caused in both the town and the university as an unwelcome embarrassment as they strove to secure social respectability for the discipline. Not many sociologists can look back on the memory of being hung in effigy from the back of a manure spreader during a Fourth of July parade and, simultaneously, of being the object of an organized professional attack, not only out of Ithaca, but out of Cambridge and New York City as well.

The last point is particularly important. Intellectual marginality is a difficult stance to maintain not least because the whole social organization of most professions is antithetical to it. This is certainly true of academic disciplines, not least both anthropology and sociology. Both disciplines, like others across the academy, have centers of power, intricate networks that control the allocation of patronage and prizes, and elaborate rituals of deference. Moreover, these networks are very successful in declaring certain lines of inquiry *de rigueur*, out of date, or completely off limits. Within such a framework, the scholarly quest for truth often gets subordinated to the exigencies of self-promotion. By contrast, one chooses a stance of being an outsider only when the center of one's professional life is intellectual work itself. Fieldwork is only one of many possible paths to such marginality; the essential attributes of the stance, however, are a dispassionate openness to the astonishing varieties of human experience and the independence to report what one sees despite the possibility of ruffled sensibilities or outrage or even the loss of friends and colleagues, with the intellectual isolation and existential self-doubt that these bring.

Vidich went on to a distinguished career at the Graduate Faculty of Political and Social Science at the New School for Social Research, which began its existence as the University in Exile, a haven for European scholars who escaped Nazi-dominated Europe. He was initially an outsider there as well, an American among mostly German-speaking exiles. But, largely because of his remarkable gifts of personality and his rejection of narrow disciplinary concerns, he became the bridge between the European tradition of theoretical appraisals of major world trends and the American emphasis on concrete empirical examinations of particular social realities. His focus on fieldwork that explores paradigmatic social situations with big structural implications married the two. For decades, Vidich taught the dissertation seminar for advanced students, helping generations of young men and women frame their intellectual problems. He also brought back to life the Graduate Faculty's famous General Seminar, the interdisciplinary forum for faculty work and debate begun in the earliest days of the University in Exile. Vidich brought scores of scholars from all over the world to the New School for lively presentations and discussions. With Stanford Lyman, he led the defense of the New School's unique sociology department against a coordinated assault by luminaries of the discipline who, under the aegis of a New York State commission, were determined to destroy it. Later, Vidich and Lyman wrote *American Sociology: Worldly Rejections of Religion and Their Directions*, a book that sharply critiques mainstream sociology. The idea for the book came to the two authors in the midst of the successful fight to preserve the heterodox New School department. Still later, Vidich and Guy Oakes wrote *Collaboration, Reputation, and Ethics in American Intellectual Life: Hans H. Gerth and C. Wright Mills*, an eye-opening account of a tormented relationship marked by Mills's ruthlessly ambitious drive to be seen as a "secular prophet" at Gerth's expense. The critique of the sainted Mills, a hero to those young sociologists who see themselves on the barricades, distanced Vidich even further from the profession.

What is the fruit of being an outsider? Vidich and Bensman provide their own assessment when they write: "Only the individual scholar working alone—even in the midst of a bureaucratic setting—has the possibility to raise himself above the routine and mechanics of research.... The work of the individual scholar, no matter where he is located, and no matter how he is financed, organized, constrained, or aided, is perhaps the sole source of creativity." The readers, students, colleagues, and friends of Arthur Vidich, as well as the disciplines of anthropology and sociology despite themselves, have been the beneficiaries of such creativity.

1

Recollections of a Slovene Boyhood in America

From the Julian Alps to the Mesabi Range: Some Tales

Before my father came to America, he was a smith. He learned his craft in Kropa, a small Alpine village located in the vicinity of iron ore deposits. Then part of the Austro-Hungarian Empire, Kropa was set in the Julian Alps in the province of Carniola, an area that spans southwestern Austria and northern Slovenia. After completing his apprenticeship, he was inducted into the Empire's Army where he served as an orderly to a Viennese officer. Having seen the larger world, pounding iron into nails in an isolated mountain village at the end of the road was no longer to his taste. Pictures of him as a member of Kropa's band show that he was tall and handsome. Like other youths in the area, he was well versed in the arts of gardening, vinting wine, brewing beer, and distilling the 100-proof plum brandy known in Slovenia as *slivovica*. He was typical of the South Slav immigrant to America at the turn of the twentieth century.

His father and grandfather had been smiths before him. In the sixteenth century, their ancestors, who had been small farmers, migrated to Kropa from Srednja Dobrava, a village two miles distant from Kropa. In their day, iron working was a respectable occupation that carried with it a measure of honor in the community. Industrial workers were town dwellers, owning no land but possessing usufruct rights to the collection of firewood on communal timberland. The house in which my father grew up with a brother and two sisters was a large three-story building with small windows and walls measuring two feet thick. I saw this building for the first time in 1951 when, as a Fulbright Scholar at the University of London, I took an opportunity to visit the town of my parents' birth. The house was then occupied by my father's younger sister, my aunt. I learned from her that as the only surviving male in my father's descent line, I could inherit the property, a right I had no wish to exercise, having no desire to establish roots in the place my parents had left. The house still stands as a symbol of a prosperity long vanished.

Before leaving for America in 1910 at the age of twenty-four, my father, Josef Vidic, made an agreement with his fiancée, Pavlina Pesjak, to have her follow him in a year. A native Kropa family, the Pesjaks were influential in the original creation of the ironworks and in its cultural history. Pavlina was a daughter of a local merchant wealthy enough to have had her educated at Klagenfurt, a city close to the Austrian border heavily influenced by German language and culture. In Klagenfurt, she learned to speak German and play Strauss waltzes on the piano. When I was a school child and became aware that my parents were immigrants, I began to inquire about my ethnic roots. In response to my inquiries, my mother advised me that our family was Austrian. Since Slovenia had been integrated into the Austro-Hungarian Empire, this identification might have been technically correct in 1911, but after the Treaty of Versailles in 1918, Slovenia had become a province in the newly created Kingdom of Yugoslavia. My mother downplayed her Slovene roots, presumably because of the Slavophobia engendered by the peace treaty. She identified with Austria because Carniola, despite being peopled primarily by Slovenes, was part of Austria at the time she emigrated. The region includes Bled, Klagenfurt, and Maribor as well as settlements south of Graz in Austria. From this perspective, Carniola is as much Austrian as it is Slovene. This gave her the option of choosing her nationality.

My mother's attitude toward her national identification instilled in me a feeling that Slovenia had fewer claims to cultural status in America than Austria. However, I could not fully accept her claim because it contradicted what I saw at home and experienced among my school friends. At home, my mother recited the poetry of Slovenia's national poet, France Prešerem, spoke Slovene, served a Slovene cuisine, and belonged to the Slovene National Benefit Society.

The ethnicities of my school friends were, among others, Croatian, Serbian, Italian, Dalmatian, Irish, and Polish, but none were Austrian. While I bravely tried to identify myself as Austrian, I knew that this cover story was not wholly true. It left me with some ambiguities about how I should identify myself, Carniola being a term that I had heard mentioned at home, but which meant nothing to me geographically or linguistically.

Only later did I discover that my mother's ethnic claims were related to her family's status in Kropa and the difference between its status and that of my father's family. Her father was the local merchant, and, by local standards, her family's status was above that of industrial workers. Like herself, her siblings were educated, and her parents preferred to think of themselves as Europeans rather than Slavs.

The attraction between my mother and father transcended the social differences between their families. In her later years, after it was no longer necessary to defend her choice of marriage partner, she told me a story to illustrate this status difference. Her father had followed the practice of selling merchandise on credit (poof in her terms) to poor families. When a particular family's credit was overdrawn, it was her duty as an eldest child to act as a collection agent, calling on the family and demanding payment. The Vidic family was one such customer, always in arrears, capable of making only small token payments on an accumulating bill. The complexities of their romantic relationship were intertwined with the disparity in social and economic standing. In fact, my aunt Lojzka, my mother's younger sister, told me years later that the romantic relationship between them was not sanctioned by my mother's family and would not have led to marriage if the couple had stayed in Kropa. Emigration freed the couple from the constraints of local matrimonial norms.

The violation of these norms made possible by emigration had long-run consequences for the marriage. In America, my mother aimed to achieve a status equivalent to that she had enjoyed in her past. My father had no such aims. My mother's cultural identification with Austria and my father's acquiescence to being a working immigrant in America symbolized the conflict in their married life.

Kropa had a long history of iron making. The village straddles the Kroparica, a fast moving mountain stream that provided the power for the bellows needed to achieve the high temperature necessary for producing wrought iron. By the fourteenth century, a smelter known as the Slovene furnace was erected in upper Kropa and later, in 1442, another was built in lower Kropa. In its day, the iron-working technology represented the state of the art. A single smelting required eighteen to twenty tip loads of charcoal and iron ore, and once smelted, the iron was worked under a sledge weighing 1,000 pounds. Kropa once had the distinction of being one of Europe's early industrial towns.

In bondage to feudal overlords, Kropa and its iron industry were rigidly controlled by outside overseers who specified work requirements and production schedules. In 1550, Kropa and neighboring iron-working towns were freed of bondage and taxes except for payments for mining and land rights held under hereditary ownership. Over successive generations, the manufacture of pronged hooks transported by mule to Triestian shipbuilders gave way to the production of nails for hobnailed boots, railway spikes, and ornamental wrought iron products. At the end of World War II, the federal government rewarded the town with a factory in return for its role in the defense against the German invaders. Local militia held down, at great cost, units far superior to their own. In recognition of these heroic defensive efforts, central planners allocated to the town a new factory for the production of cold-pressed nuts and bolts. This factory, using electricity rather than water as a power source, imported its raw materials from the United States. Even its ornamental iron and copper products were fabricated from imported raw materials. The old smithies that now line the banks of the Kroparica are preserved as tourist attractions.

When my father left for America, the old homes, once occupied by traders, housed the citizens of an under-populated and depressed community; between 1850 and 1931, the population had dropped from 1240 to 578. New low-cost technologies of iron and steel production, especially as developed in the United States, deprived local industry of its markets and economic function. In 1894, in an attempt to revive its iron-working industry, local businessmen created a nail and hardware cooperative designed to include the manufacture of ornamental iron and copper products. To Catholic Church authorities, however, the idea of a cooperative meant socialism, so the effort led to ideological friction between the church and the cooperative's organizers, one of whom was my maternal grandfather.

This conflict created a lasting schism between the Pesjak family and the church. My mother suggested to me that it might also have included a threat to excommunicate my grandfather, a story I wanted to believe because I liked the word "excommunication." She carried her father's socialism with her to America. Like untold numbers of other Europeans with similar beliefs and few hopes for the future, she was the bearer of a political dream for a better world.

My father left for America in steerage via Hamburg. His point of entry was Ellis Island. It was there that his name was changed from "Vidic" to "Vidich," with the hard "ch" sound rather than the soft Slovene "ts." Such fine linguistic distinctions were unknown to American immigration officials, who added the "h" to any name ending in "c," even if it lacked the diacritical mark.

When he reached Manhattan, he was met by Agnes, a person whom we always called "Aunt Agnes," although she was not his sister. She was either a distant cousin or a ward of my father's family from Jamnik, a small settlement further up the mountain. As a young woman, perhaps a teenager, she was stigmatized by the birth of an illegitimate child. Taken in by my father's family, she managed a passage to America, leaving her son behind. According to local practice, her choice was either to remain unwed for the rest of her life, carrying alone the burden of raising her child, or to leave the country. Choosing the latter, she had preceded my father to New York and had married an Austrian watchmaker, Carl Fritz. These putative relatives, my aunt and uncle, were the only relatives I ever knew until I visited Slovenia.

My father settled on East 6th Street in New York, in an area populated by immigrant Poles, Lithuanians, Ukrainians, Croatians, Serbs, Slovenes, and Russians. Peter Cooper, one of New York's early philanthropists, had already built and endowed Cooper Union in the same area. The chance juxtaposition of the names "Cooper" and "Vidich" in the same geographic area did not become meaningful until two generations later when my eldest son married a lineal descendent of Peter Cooper. Though he began as a cooper rather than as a smith in Kropa, Peter Cooper had become wealthy.

Named in honor of Slovenia's patron saint, Saint Cyril's Church, located at 62 St. Mark's Place, is the only remaining monument to the Slovene presence in the East Village. As an archeological artifact of immigrant history, it is still the religious hub of a Slovene community dispersed throughout the metropolitan area. I was surprised, when I later came to live in New York, to receive an invitation to buy lottery tickets for a Saint Cyril's Church raffle. I never saw my father enter a church, except for the marriages of his daughters, but given the aggressiveness of Slovene Catholicism, he might have been a parishioner. All of my memories, however, are of my parents' anticlericalism. My father never mentioned Saint Cyril's in his accounts of his life in the East Village. His most salient memory was of the affluence of New York City, where sausages and bread were served free of charge in bars so long as the customer continued to drink and pay for beer. His attitude toward life was material, not spiritual.

True to the craft into which he had been born, my father's first job in the New World was as a smith. At the time of his arrival, the municipal government had mandated the construction of fire escapes on the city's tenements. This was steady work that produced the income required to underwrite the passage of his future bride. My Aunt Lojzka, aged six at the time my mother left, remembered her departure as a day of sadness and family crisis. She left Kropa in 1911 at the age of nineteen, never to return.

In the same year, 1911, and perhaps at the same time, her brother France and my father's brother Florjan, also left for New York. Agnes, France, Florjan, and my parents were Kropa's only émigrés to America in that generation. Their presence in New York is seen in pictures taken at Coney Island, posing as a group, dressed in their finest attire. These pictures are now part of a family archive and can also be seen in Kropa where they commemorate lost sons and daughters.

My mother took a job as a German-speaking governess to the children of the Ruppert Brewery family. She lived with the family on Central Park South, vacationing with them summers at Edgartown on Martha's Vineyard. Loyal to her widowed mother in Kropa, she regularly remitted part of her earnings to her. But she considered her work as a governess beneath her status, and I remember her making only one reference to it in my lifetime, when she remarked upon the stern discipline the Rupperts imposed upon her. She had no intention of following a career as a domestic servant; her ambition was to enter business on her own.

In the years following the great industrial expansion after the Civil War and before World War I, the best opportunities for immigrants were in the industrial cities of the Northeast and in the mining regions of Pennsylvania, Illinois, and Minnesota. Slovene networks supported by newspapers already existed in Cleveland, Chicago, and Pittsburgh, and in the mining regions of Minnesota. I do not know why they chose Minnesota. Most likely they knew Slovenes who had already gone there and were attracted by the promise of good jobs and high wages offered by mining companies in need of laborers. It is also possible that the iron working traditions of Kropa led them to believe that they could market their skills on Minnesota's Mesabi, Cayuna, and Vermillion ranges. In retrospect, their choice seemed to be a logical one. France, Florjan, and my parents left for Minnesota in 1913.

On the hope for the future offered by the mines, my parents were married in 1913 in Virginia, Minnesota. In their formal wedding picture, they are seated in front of Florjan and France, who witnessed the ceremony.

In 1915, their first child, Pauline, was born. In rapid succession at intervals of two years, four more children appeared: Joseph, 1916; Olga, 1918; Elizabeth, 1920; and me, 1922. Joseph died at the age of three as a result of a household accident. He suffered fatal burns when he pulled a pot of boiling water off the stove onto himself; medical care in the remote mining region was inadequate. Not much was ever said of this family tragedy. My parents had one picture of him, taken in a photographer's studio sitting on a carriage with my sister. Throughout my youth, this picture was prominently displayed in our living room. The image of it is cut into my mind, but I never asked for nor was given details about this tragic episode in my parents' lives. In 1972, at the suggestion of my second wife, Mary, while on a trip through Minnesota, I visited Joseph's gravesite on the upper reaches of the Mississippi River. We found the gravestone and took a picture of it with my son, Joseph, his uncle's namesake, seated next to it. The inscription on the lifeless marker is the only concrete evidence I have of my brother's existence.

My parents' optimism, as expressed by their rapidly expanding family, was not shared by France and Florjan. France returned to Kropa before World War I began. I met him there for the first time in 1951 where he was living in the family home. Florjan left for California where he died in a mining accident in 1933. He never fulfilled the promise he had made to the wife and child he left behind: that one day they would join him in America. His daughter, Ludmilla

Umberton, settled in Carrières-sur-Seine, France. Like almost every other little town in Europe, Kropa acquired its own international extensions.

Years later, when my father learned that I had taken a teaching position in New York City, he asked me to visit and look after Aunt Agnes, who by then lived in Queens. She was eighty years old and arthritic. After her husband had died, she could no longer care for herself and wished to be placed in a nursing home. In collaboration with her local priest, I made arrangements for her admission to Madonna Residence in Brooklyn, located across the street from Grand Army Plaza and Prospect Park. The question arose of what to do with the money she received from the sale of her house. I advised her to give it to her son and grandchildren in Slovenia, but she would hear none of this. Though she could have been kept as a charge of the county, she preferred to give a small amount of the proceeds to her church and retain the rest to pay her keep at the Residence. She regarded the acceptance of charity as beneath her honor and wished to be a paying resident who wrote her own check for her monthly bill. In her new life, this assertion of her independent means was her claim to self-respect. I visited her many times and the nuns always greeted me warmly, but traveling to Brooklyn was always a chore. I took every opportunity to recruit Mary, our children, and any visiting sisters to take the subway ride to Grand Army Plaza with me. Learning about Brooklyn is what I still owe to Agnes.

Conversations with Agnes focused on a ritual repetition of three subjects. She invariably began with her complaint that the Hungarian nuns were prejudiced against Slovene Catholics. Their treatment of her was not in accord with her status as a paying resident. She always asked that I report this fact to the Mother Superior. Second, she recited the names of residents who were older than she, a list that dwindled as the years passed. Third, she announced her position in the rank order of age of her competitors; over the years she had become one of the oldest residents. Besides her faith in God, she had a powerful motivation for giving meaning to her life: outliving her oldest competitors. She lived in the Residence for fourteen years, to the age of ninety-four, not relieving me of my duties until 1975. By that time, I had met her son and grandchildren in Slovenia, but I did not tell them of her indifference toward them. We never talked about her son, grandchildren, Kropa, or Slovenia.

Before the beginning of World War II, I had no interest in Slovenia, nor had I any curiosity about relatives I may have had in a country far removed from my concerns as the son of immigrant parents trying to make their way in their new country. I do remember, however, the day in 1936 when my mother received word of her mother's death. This news made her cry and led me to understand for the first time that I had had a grandmother, but it did not lead me to inquire about the possibility of surviving grandfathers. Only when the war began in Europe did I begin to hear about the fate of relatives in Slovenia. After the war, when we sent an endless flow of care packages to Kropa, I began to realize that my parents had lived in a world apart from mine. I only discovered that part of their world when I went to Slovenia myself in 1951.

Male Child Born in Minnesota

My birth certificate lists my name as "Vidich (Male child)," born in the village of Manganese, Crow Wing County, Minnesota, to Joe Vidich born in Slovania [sic] and Polina Peszek [sic] born in Slovania [sic]. After discharging me into the world, my mother fell sick and was hospitalized, leaving the registration of my arrival to my father. Apparently, no name had been chosen beforehand, so I legally remained "Male child" until later when my parents gave me the unregistered name of Arthur Joseph.

The choice of the middle name Joseph was in keeping with traditional naming practices. My older, deceased brother was named Joseph for my father, but in my case, a different Christian name was required in order to avoid identification with a dead brother. Arthur is a name that cannot be found in Slovenia, nor in any other Slavic country. My sisters' names were Slovene cognates: Pauline for Paulina, Olga, and Elizabeth (or Betty) for Betka. The choice of Arthur marked a linguistic break with Old World traditions. Giving me a quintessentially English name, despite the auditory dissonance between it and the Slavic Vidich, symbolized the family's turn toward Americanization. I was to be an American, even if the last name had been changed from Vidic to Vidich, a change in spelling that forever irked my mother and for which she laid the blame on my father's ineptitude for failing to correct the clerk at Ellis Island. As a result, I acquired the name Arthur and a last name that was to be pronounced not with the soft Slovenian "c" (ts), but with yet another form that my mother invented. In her effort to retrieve the original pronunciation, she replaced the hard "ch" sound with the "k" sound, as if the name were spelled "Vidick," but the k was not an exact substitute for the "ts" sound as in "Vidits." Hence, though we had the name Vidich which was in fact a variation on the original pronunciation, we wished others to pronounce it "Vidick." Other speakers, however, automatically gave our name the hard "ch" as might be expected from the ending. Whenever our name was "mispronounced" by innocent speakers, my sisters and I were required to inform them of the correct pronunciation. This has been an endless task for the immediate members of the family and also for my wives, children, their spouses, and their children. Making the correction has always been such a nuisance that I stopped doing it, accepting any pronunciation unless explicitly asked how my name is pronounced. Otherwise, I have learned to accept "Vidich," "Vidick," and "Vidits," secure in my appreciation of my mother's efforts to right the wrong done to our family name on Ellis Island in 1910. With an English first name and a corrupted Slovene last name, it is no wonder that my mother's efforts to make me an Austrian were not successful. I could easily add a chapter to Louis Adamic's book, *What's in a Name?*

In addition to having only a last name, there was another oddity coincident with my birth. My mother told me later that, at the time, the family was estranged from the priest who cared for the Slovene flock in Manganese. His incessant demands for money—"all the church ever wanted was money, money" was a refrain I heard many times—and my mother's refusal to meet the priest's demands led to a break with the congregation. Being a daughter from a family back in Kropa that was anti-clerical had already provided her with the attitude she needed to resist the priest. The relevance of this episode for Male child Vidich is that he never made it to the baptismal font. At no time in my later life was the lack of a baptismal certificate corrected. From the point of view of the Christian church, I remain uncertified. So far, this has not had discernible negative consequences, and I remain secure in my inalienable right that no *a priori* religious commitments had been made for me.

Except for one dramatic incident, I have no direct memories of my life in Minnesota. When I was no more than two years old, my father took me for an automobile ride. After a short drive, he stopped the car at the edge of a bridge where he was to do an errand. I understood that this was no ordinary errand when he told me to stand on the front seat of the car, a 1922 Overland, and to shout to him while he was gone if I should see another car coming from either direction.

I was to be his lookout in an act of conspiracy that apparently frightened me enough to make the event unforgettable. He unloaded gallon jugs of whiskey from the back seat of the car and buried them under the bridge. The mission was completed without incident, and we returned home. The whiskey, made at home, was secreted away to remove it from the premises in case a federal inspector paid a call. The image of using the underside of a bridge for this unique purpose has always remained somewhere in my mind. It vividly returned to me many years later when I came across Anatole France's remark that "At this task they must labour in the face of the majestic equality of the laws, which forbid rich and poor alike to sleep under the bridges, to beg in the streets, and to steal their bread."[1] Despite the law, I have taken endless satisfaction for the role I played for my father in his own independent discovery of this use for the underside of a bridge.

Slovene-American Affinities: The Liquor Business

From family stories I have heard about the iron ranges, it is evident that life in Minnesota was difficult. Workers were poorly paid. To their own benefit, employers fomented ethnic tensions among the complex mix of Finnish, Hungarian, Anglo-Saxon, and Slavic milers. Workers suffering job-related injuries received no compensation or health benefits. My father was one such case. When he hurt his knee while working in the pits, the prospect for economic advancement as a wage laborer on the frontier of the mining region evaporated. There was little hope left of fulfilling the immigrants' dream of economic success. America, in myth as much as in reality, promised opportunity for those willing to work. Failure in America was not an

---

[1] Anatole France, *The Red Lily*, 95.

option my parents could accept. Seeing no future for themselves in Kropa, the act of emigration was a public statement to those they left behind that they would do better elsewhere; to accept anything other than economic success would have negated the wisdom of the act of migration itself. Even more important, such economic gain as might be achieved could be used to return remittances, certifying to those left behind one's success as well as the wisdom of the choice to migrate. Considering the differences in economic and social status of my parents' families in Kropa, and my mother's defiance of her family's wishes, it was a matter of personal pride and a moral imperative to succeed. My parents quickly learned that working in the iron pits was not the way to achieve their goal.

The alternative they chose was consistent with the skills each brought to the marriage and rational with respect to market opportunities in the region. Young men in Kropa knew the art of distilling hard spirits. As a matter of course, every household owned a still and produced its own slivovica. To this day, the still is a standard item in any Slovene hardware store. My mother's training was in the skills of marketing and bookkeeping. Combining their production and sales skills, my parents entered the liquor business in a market area where consumers for their product were hard working, frequently unmarried, iron ore miners.

From a cultural point of view, there was nothing reprehensible in immigrants like my parents producing and selling beer, wine, and whiskey. Drinking alcoholic beverages in Catholic Mediterranean countries was and still is associated with religious ceremonials and commensalism. To the Protestant asceticism of the dominant culture in America, however, the consumption of alcoholic beverages for any purpose was morally reprehensible. By force of circumstance, their venture into the business was necessarily clandestine.

Before the beginning of Prohibition in 1918, the production of hard spirits for domestic consumption was legal, protected by the constitutional right prohibiting search and seizure. Selling liquor without a license on the open market was not legal. In order to evade the law, my parents produced their product at home and used the same place as their distribution center. Theirs was a cottage industry in the great American tradition of free market entrepreneurial enterprise.

By all accounts, the business was successful. On the strength of its profits, it was possible for them to own a house and an automobile even before Prohibition began. After 1918, when the sale of all liquor became illegal, the business became even more lucrative. Since they already had a product in the pipeline, as it were, Prohibition gave my parents both a price and a marketing advantage over newcomers to production and distribution. The business was also more risky because it came under surveillance of not only the Bureau of Alcohol, Tobacco, and Firearms, but also of neighbors and disgruntled customers who could become informers. Weighing the value of profits against the risks, my parents chose to remain in business despite Prohibition.

My father continued to work in the mines while he served the needs of his local clientele. Managing the business fell to my mother, who, in spite of needing to care for a growing family, understood the critical importance of capital accumulation. Conscious of her exceptional opportunity, she serviced a growing market despite the risks it entailed. The risks included arrest and imprisonment; my father served a term of three months in jail. For my mother, the risks included overwork. I was her fifth child in eight years, and as I said earlier, she fell ill and was hospitalized at the time of my birth. Because the local doctor was unable to diagnose her condition, she nearly died and survived only because she was transferred to the Mayo Clinic where she was diagnosed as suffering from exhaustion. During the period of my mother's convalescence, Pauline, my eldest sister, age seven, cared for Male child Vidich, and she became the surrogate mother for all of us children, a role she was not to escape until much later in her life. Even then, she had been so thoroughly trained in her role that at the age of eighty-five she continued to show a maternal concern for me, remembering my birthday, each year without fail, with a card and a twenty-dollar bill.

The immigrant's successful pursuit of economic opportunity in America was a function of finding a fit between the rules of the old culture and those of the new. It entailed learning a new language, conflicts with the law, a desire to become Americanized, and, above all, a readiness to make the sacrifices necessary to achieve a level of economic success greater than would have been possible in the Old Country. Only after I visited Kropa did I learn how significant their own parents and siblings were to my parents. It was from them rather than from their new American neighbors and friends that my parents sought to claim status and respect. Success required a display of affluence; remittances were the tangible proof of it. An illegal but prosperous business justified success and rewarded them both with elevated status in Kropa, as well as the external symbols of their affluence in Minnesota.

When my parents spoke of their Minnesota days, I heard names such as Hibbing, Crosby, and Ely, and I learned about Manganese when I needed a birth certificate to apply for a passport. Hibbing was northeast of Crosby and sat squarely on the Mesabi Range. For my parents, those were days of deprivation, of moving from one town to another, of being treated with disdain by school officials, and of linguistic insecurity in their dealings with employers, the law, doctors, hospitals, and elected officials. Their success in business overcame these hardships and provided our family with the wherewithal to leave life on the ranges behind. The Mesabi, in the area of the headwaters of the Mississippi River, was the equivalent in our family's history of Plymouth Rock.

Another Migration: To West Allis

In spring 1924, house sold, cash in hand, automobile loaded with camping equipment, the family began a one-week trek to West Allis, an industrial suburb of Milwaukee named for Allis of Allis Chalmers, a producer of turbines, tractors, and other heavy equipment. I have no memory of the trip being eventful. If anything, I remember it as my first camping trip, feeling completely secure that neither risks nor dangers were involved. Only later, when reflecting on this event in conversations with my sisters, did it begin to dawn on me the enormity of this exodus. With four young children, carrying all their worldly assets in cash, my parents had pulled up stakes in order to begin life anew in parts unknown.

A Slovene community already existed in and around Milwaukee. The Slovenska Narodna Podporodna Janota (SNPJ), an ethnic benefit society, had a branch in West Allis. Slovene language newspapers, published in Chicago and Cleveland, were available. My parents preferred the secular Cleveland publication, *Prosveta*, to the Catholic-oriented Chicago newspaper. The benefit society provided a ready-made, centrally organized network for its members, and the two newspapers carried information about Slovene settlements across the country. In America, regional distinctions that had existed in Slovenia collapsed into a conception of a generic Slovene. The work of literary and journalistic intellectuals preserved the language that they used to create a Slovene national community and culture within the larger society. The culture included itinerant speakers as well as Slovene language essayists and book authors. Louis Adamic stands out in my memory as a writer and socialist political activist who was one of my family's exemplars.

Fifteen years of living in the United States had provided my parents with the networks and contacts they needed to prepare for the move to West Allis. In my childhood, I knew none of this, nor did my parents make any effort to inform me of it. By community and culture, they knew they were Slovenes in America, but they did not wish this to be the fate of their children. We children were taught neither to read nor speak Slovene, a language my parents used only when they wished to speak of things they did not want us to understand. The excision of the Slovene language was meant to encourage our Americanization. It meant also excising my parents' culture, something that my mother was also trying to exorcise from herself. Being suspended between two worlds took its toll on all of us. It left us children with the ability to understand but not to speak the household Slovene that my parents spoke, and, since my parents spoke English with a Slovene syntax, we frequently used that syntax when speaking and writing English, leaving us with neither a proper Slovene nor a proper English. In the critical early stages of language acquisition, we were all stunted because we were on the margins between two linguistic worlds.

The worlds of parents remain impenetrable to their children, and vice versa. In the immigrant family, positioned between two cultures, the barriers to any chance of mutual understanding are all the greater. I have never known the reasons that led my parents to leave Minnesota or why, of all places, they chose West Allis as a destination, nor have I ever been privy to the world of the Slovene immigrant in America.

Even before arriving in West Allis, arrangements had been made for a place to stay. It was neither a house nor a hotel, but a single-story building otherwise designed to be a small store located in the 5800 block of West National Avenue. We camped in this building for a short time before moving to a large building two doors to the east: 5808 West National Avenue, where I lived until I went to college. The building housed two commercial establishments on the ground floor: an A&P market and a butcher shop. Above the shops, one half of the building was an apartment containing four bedrooms, a small kitchen, a dining room, a living room, and a bath. The building sat on a lot the size of a quarter of a football field. I never heard that my parents took a mortgage on the property.

Once we were installed in this building, events began to move rapidly. My father took a job at Allis Chalmers, but he remained there for only a short time. Within months, my parents entered into a business partnership with another Slovene couple in downtown Milwaukee. They rented a building at 115 Clinton Street, now known as First Street, located north of National Avenue at a bend where Clinton Street terminates at the edge of the Milwaukee River. This was not part of the elegant downtown area on Wisconsin Avenue where Gimbels, the Boston Store, the Wisconsin Theater, the railway station, and Milwaukee's famous German restaurants were situated. Nor was it where the local elite lived along the shores of nearby Lake Michigan. It was, however, in walking distance of all these places. Clinton Street was, so to speak, on the wrong edge of the river. Its vicinity included rooming houses, small grocery stores, and restaurants, all of which served as fronts for the sale of hard spirits.

The residents of the area were hard-working, single, immigrant men. They were employed as stevedores, gandydancers, and bridge snakes. The neighborhood was Milwaukee's equivalent of

New York City's Bowery, that is, an area that the sociological literature has dubbed "Skid Row" in cities such as Minneapolis, Chicago, and Kansas City. The term may have originated in Seattle where a steep incline was set up off the waterfront to distribute and load timber onto shipping vessels. The enormous logs were dumped at the top of the incline and "skidded" to the bottom. The incline was called "Skid Row." The more familiar use of the term developed from that, referring to the rough-and-tumble culture surrounding the work site.[2] A good description of "Skid Row" culture appears in *The Hobo: The Sociology of the Homeless Man*, by Nels Anderson, a Chicago-trained sociologist, one of Robert E. Park's students, and someone whose work I celebrated in a paper I read at a sociology meeting in Boston in 1979. He knew what he spoke about because he had been a hobo himself. And his description certainly fit some of the local residents in the vicinity of my parents' business, men who were seasonal workers on the frontier. The gandydancers repaired railroad tracks. In order to transport themselves along the rail line, they used a two-man cart called a gandy that was propelled by the hand power of the two men riding it; hence, the men came to be known as dancers on the gandy. Many of the residents never married, either because of unfavorable sex ratios or because they did not offer women good economic prospects; others had wives and children waiting in the Old Country.

The building at 115 Clinton Street had two stories. The ground floor front was equipped with a vintage bar and barstools that faced a mirrored wall behind the bar. It also had other accoutrements that have lately become fashionable in upscale bars that try to recreate the

---

[2] I'm indebted to Duffy Graham for this historical note.

ambiance of the saloons of the 1920s era; it had a nickelodeon that for ten cents played automated music and, for an additional five cents, came with violin accompaniment. The center ground floor room was the dining area with the kitchen in the rear. Behind the kitchen was a shed that housed the equipment required to make home brew, a "near beer" whose production conformed to the law; hence, it could act as a partial front to legitimate the business. Behind the shed lay the elevated tracks for the Chicago-Milwaukee rail line that ended in downtown Milwaukee at a point just short of Wisconsin Avenue. My mother did the cooking. Meals were served on a long table, home style. Charlie Smrdu, another Slovene, was her dishwasher. My father tended the bar, supervised his children in the manufacture and bottling of the beer, made sure there was always an ample inventory of liquor, and acted as a bouncer when inebriated customers grew truculent. It was a family-oriented small business.

A pair of full-size double doors marked the entry to the establishment. These were followed by half-size swinging gates like those seen in Hollywood's version of a western cow-town saloon. On either side of the exterior doors were half-size plate-glass windows that prevented a direct view into the area of the bar. On one window appeared the sign "Joe's Place," printed inconspicuously so as not to call undue attention to the building. The structure was one of a number of similar buildings on the block occupied by proprietors engaged in variations of the same business.

By evidence available even to one as innocent as myself, Joe's Place was phenomenally successful, at least by the standards of an immigrant family. Within a few years, even before 1929, the year of the stock market crash, my parents had remodeled the house in West Allis, added a rental apartment to the second floor, replaced the exterior stucco finish with brick, and built a four-car garage with an appendage on one end containing a chicken coop, a smokehouse, and an enclosed garbage area. Apple, plum, and cherry trees were planted on the back half of the empty lot, and space was reserved for a garden plot. The smokehouse, chicken coop, fruit trees, and garden were like those that can be found in any Slovenian village. When Henry Ford's first Model A Fords rolled off the assembly line in Detroit, my parents replaced the Overland with a four-door model. In 1931, we became a two-car family. In the midst of the great crash, they paid $3,000 cash for an eight-cylinder maroon Nash touring car, complete with running boards, exterior trunk in the rear, and a spare tire that was housed in the front fender. It was as elegant an automobile as was then mass-produced in America.

Neither the construction projects nor the cars were mortgaged. My mother believed in "cash and carry"—"neither a borrower nor a lender be"—in the same spirit as the self-sufficient individualism of the shrewd, suspicious Yankee trader. She did not trust banks and had little trouble adapting the financial practices she learned in Kropa to the prevailing norm of American business. She worked hard, saved, invested, and always hedged against the future uncertainties of the markets by holding substantial amounts of cash on hand (in a trunk in her bedroom). The Slovenes, it has been said, are the Calvinists of the former Yugoslavia.

During the Depression, my parents kept the business until 1936, despite high unemployment and reduced wages. Between 1933 and 1936, during the era of the federal government's Works Progress Administration (WPA), employment opportunities for wage earners were created; money continued to circulate among the core clientele of Joe's Place. More than ever spirits were needed to lift the spirits of the victims of the debacle on Wall Street. Without America's saloon keepers, dissidence and dissatisfaction among America's deprived might have been greater than it was. The bootleg industry helped to sustain the peace during the social crisis. This patriotic contribution to maintaining the political stability of the government and its ruling groups remains unacknowledged. Insufficiently acknowledged also is the wisdom of our political leaders who in lifting Prohibition rejected the idiocy of trying to legislate the cultural norms of a hard-drinking population. My parents welcomed the end of Prohibition because it made their product legal; the government welcomed it because it provided a new source of taxation, cutting into the profits of legitimate producers. However, I have no memory that my parents paid taxes on the manufacture or sale of their product. The business dried up and was sold in 1936, the worst year of the Depression, when my father was fifty. Clinton Street, which had been vital to the family fortunes and to our way of life during the critical years of our youth, came to an end.

In the booming and roaring twenties, the manufacture and sale of illegal spirits became a vastly profitable industry across the entire nation. It was commonplace in the Midwest for immigrant Jewish and Italian entrepreneurs to choose this business (known as "bootlegging") as a means to their economic Americanization. Elite patrons in the cities were the prime consumers of all that could be produced by immigrant manufacturers, thus forging a link, usually in a speakeasy, between the respectable and the disrespected. In Chicago, Al Capone was a notorious case because he used violent means to obtain and protect his markets, thus giving the entire industry a bad name. The Bronfman family, also operating out of Chicago, was more successful. When Prohibition ended in 1933, the Bronfmans became legal purveyors of Schenley's Whiskey. They later converted capital originally acquired from bootlegging into major holdings in the chemical and entertainment industries. The unspoken failure of my parents was that, when Prohibition ended in 1933, they did not convert their cottage industry into a large-scale legitimate business.

Two Worlds

Those twelve years in the saloon business left a mark on the four siblings that remained a badge of their identities for the rest of their lives. We were schooled in West Allis and had a second life on Clinton Street, where we frequently ate our dinners and returned home with our parents when the business closed late in the evening. The two worlds contrasted sharply with each other: in West Allis the family presented an image of itself as prosperous restaurateurs in downtown Milwaukee and the owner of two automobiles and a substantial property producing three rental incomes. Our economic standard was equal to that of any of West Allis's businessmen and professionals, but socially it was that of an immigrant family. While the lack of money never seemed to be a problem, parsimony was still a virtue. Investments were made in utilities. Cost was never a factor when it came to medical or dental bills; my mother had her surgeries done at the Mayo Clinic in Rochester, Minnesota. Summer months were allocated for out-of-town, lakefront vacations. We were clothed from the racks of the Boston Store or Gimbels, setting us apart from our friends whose fathers worked in factories or were railway conductors, street car trolley men, construction workers, or petty white-collar civil servants. Our comparatively better economic status was conspicuously evident in school, not only by our style of dress, but also in a measure of economic differentiation encouraged by school officials. It was the practice of school authorities to issue each student a bank savings book on behalf of a local bank. On Mondays, the students brought a sum of money ranging from a penny to a dime to class to be deposited in his or her bank account.

The amount deposited was also posted on the blackboard after each student's name. Deposit of a ten-cent piece earned a gold star; lesser amounts earned a silver star. Those who could not bring even a penny were given a black mark. Teachers responded favorably to gold-star students, regarding them as upholders of the virtues of saving, parsimony, and good citizenship. From the children's point of view, the rankings on the blackboard were a testimony to acceptance as a worthy citizen. My sisters and I never failed to bring the dime, certifying that our parents cared about our education and conformed to what was then a cardinal American virtue. Unfailingly bringing in the weekly deposit meant parental concern for the child. Despite her distrust of banks, my mother never forgot to send us to school with our bank deposits, knowing that the family's social status was at stake. My mother never met any of my teachers and would have felt ill at ease speaking with them in her accented English.

The reality of our lifestyle in West Allis, however, included more than its appearances. Conducting the business was a family affair that frequently required everyone's presence on Clinton Street. Early every morning, my father left home to open shop. My mother remained home in order to feed us breakfast and get us off to school. Before taking the trolley downtown to join my father, she prepared our lunch; schools did not yet have lunch programs. My eldest sister walked us to elementary school, supervised our lunch, and returned us to school. That my mother was not home to serve us lunch made me feel different from the other children whose mothers I assumed did not work. Even though no one need know that I was not normal in this respect, it was a source of embarrassment to me until, on one occasion when class reassembled after lunch, my teacher asked each of the students what we had had for lunch. When it was my turn to speak, I could do no more than tell the truth: "a baked apple and a baked potato." To my surprise, I received special praise for my healthful diet. Those were the days when "an apple a day kept the doctor away." The praise that I received redeemed my mother and left me with the feeling that our family was not so abnormal after all.

After school, under my oldest sister's supervision, we played with our friends in West Allis until we boarded the trolley for the trek downtown where we ate our dinners, returning home late in the evening at whatever hour the business was shut down for the night. On Clinton Street, we played with other children whose parents had similar businesses on the street. Our associations with adults included the saloon's customers who were stevedores, railway workers, transients, drunkards, and what my mother referred to as "bums," a designation on which she was wrong. Technically, they were hobos whose honor and respectability depended upon refusing charity, rejecting begging, and insisting upon working for whatever they received. Except when drunk, these men had a strong sense of personal dignity; because they were at the bottom of the social heap, their only claim to status was the economic independence that enabled them to avoid the dole. Sober or drunk, they never molested children. When flush with money they gave us their small change, enjoying being philanthropists to grateful children. They were the immigrant labor force that helped to create America's economic and physical infrastructure, despite being treated as status inferiors by their employers and those who were already Americanized.

Every business faces the problem of timely replenishment of its inventory. Finding wholesale supplies of whiskey during Prohibition was an art form of its own, based on the skill of surreptitiousness. My parents had two sources of supply. One was a Slovene friend who manufactured his own product and delivered it in his motorcycle sidecar. His timing was always perfect. The other was whiskey distilled at our home in West Allis and delivered personally by my father.

In making safe deliveries, it helped that the police were in collusion with my father. In exchange for providing the cop on the beat with meals and drinks, the law looked the other way. Small-scale bribery was an intrinsic feature of business practice on Clinton Street. Those were the days of your friendly, Irish-Catholic cop—Pat O'Brian—made famous as a role model by Hollywood. Yet the risks were always present and threatened our claims to respectability in West Allis.

The family's appearance of affluence and respectability in West Allis could be sustained so long as the fiction concerning the nature and location of the business could be upheld. Maintaining the fiction was necessary because everyone in the family with the likely exception of my father regarded the saloon business as disreputable even while respectability in West Allis depended upon it. To uphold the fiction, my mother developed a strategic plan and told us to execute it.

To explain our father's occupation to our school friends, we were instructed to say, if asked, that we owned "a restaurant downtown," but not to specify its location. Up to 1933, the end of the golden years and the beginning of the worst years of the Depression, our frequent trips to Clinton Street were a source of our West Allis school friends' curiosity. In answer to questions about where and why we were going, our response was to be limited to "downtown."

In reality, we had another set of playmates on Clinton Street, some of whom remained friends for many years. With these friends, among other things, we made and sold lemonade on the street, put pennies on the railway tracks to have them flattened by the wheels of a passing train, and went to Sunday afternoon movies on Wisconsin Avenue. Our friends in one place were not to be part of our lives in the other place despite the intensity of our associations with both groups. Sometimes the "Maginot Line" we tried to construct was penetrated. Once, for example, a friend from West Allis noticed me on the street, called my name from a car, and waved to me. I returned the wave, but turned away, making every effort to minimize the significance of the incident. In another case, years later when I was in high school, our football team played against opponents from a Milwaukee school. The opponents' fullback had been a Clinton Street friend. To the surprise of my schoolmates, I visited the fullback on the opposing bench, raising the query of how I had come to know him. Not knowing when these two worlds might intersect by chance induced a feeling of lightness-of-being enhanced by both the ambiguities of my ethnic identity and the ever-present need for secrecy about the nature of my parents' business. Coping with life under these conditions provided me with my initial training in cultivating that essential sociological attitude of detached marginality.

The word "downtown," as used in the expression "going downtown," had a magic quality. It provided a universal explanation to account for where I was when not in West Allis. The first time I heard Petula Clark sing "Downtown" on my Volkswagen radio in the 1960s while I was commuting from Storrs, Connecticut, to The New School in New York City, it cast a spell over me, evoking sharp images of my own "downtown."

This Bowery-like neighborhood of Clinton Street was where I spent some of the more memorable days of my childhood. In later years, I revisited the Milwaukee waterfront and began to appreciate that this was where I made my first sociological observations about American society. By then, the old days were over and, as one might expect, the area had become gentrified. Micro-breweries had replaced the saloons, restaurants were upscale, and the gay and lesbian coalition had its headquarters on the street. The area had become a miniature version of New York's Greenwich Village. A part of my past had been obliterated.

Education of an Intractable Child

As Pauline remembers it, she was responsible for getting us to and from school and for safely delivering us to Clinton Street after school. This responsibility was not always easy to discharge as she was acting as a surrogate who had no direct recourse to parental authority. Yet I remember only one occasion when, under duress, she reported my fractious behavior to my mother. When I was in kindergarten and on a class trip, a friend and I successfully ditched the group and went off on our own. However, once we had gained our freedom we then faced the problem of what to do with it. Having no objective other than the escape itself, we tardily returned to the classroom where our teacher, regarding our behavior as a major crime, punished us by making us stand face to the wall in the corner of the cloakroom. Pauline, then in sixth grade, was summoned to the kindergarten room to observe my humiliation and to report my misconduct to my parents. That was only one incident in my career as a young delinquent.

Acceptance of authority did not come easily to me. Corralling me for the trolley trip downtown was one of Pauline's constant problems. Clutching me by the collar as I resisted, she often had to forcibly pull me all the way to the trolley car. Pauline understood that she could not compromise her authority when dealing with me. Testing her limits, I once demanded that she give me a nickel, threatening to jump out of a second story window if she refused to give it to me. I went so far as to open the window and poise to make the jump. She steadfastly held her ground until I retreated in defeat.

My mother had her own problems with my youthful intractability. While still no more than five or six years old, I chanced to look into the housing of the piano located in the living room. To my surprise, I found a bag of ten and twenty dollar gold pieces. At the time, it was not illegal to hoard gold—it was after the bank moratorium in 1933. Owning gold was consistent with my parents' suspicions of banks and paper currency; it was the Old World form of insurance against political instability. Spotting the cache, I seized my opportunity and took my treasure to the garage where I hid it in a tool chest, the place where I also kept my marbles. A few days later when its disappearance was discovered, my parents asked, "Who took it?" Silence. No confessions. I was not prepared to reveal my secret so easily, nor was I prepared to hand over my new possession. Now realizing I had acquired something of great value, my instinct was to check immediately to assure that it was still safely hidden.

It seems that I had been the prime suspect from the beginning because my mother followed me and was standing behind me at the moment I opened the chest. Caught with the evidence and humiliated, my reaction was to run out to the yard and up the street, leaving the bag of gold behind. My mother followed me and chased me around the block until she caught me. What followed was not a spanking but a moral lecture on the difference between right and wrong. Nothing was ever again said about this incident, and I am the only one who prefers to remember and talk about it. I have found it useful to recount the incident to my children, stepchildren, and grandchildren who have invariably identified with the thief. My hunch is that many children have similar thoughts about their parents' money, and in hearing the story, they are relieved of any potential guilt they may have about harboring similar intentions.

Except for one fact, the details of my first-grade education elude me. The indication that I had problems during that year is that my teacher and the principal agreed that I should be flunked and required to repeat the year. The problem seems to have been that I did not carry out my assignments and refused to learn to read. The report card mandating my failure shocked my mother and sisters and called for immediate and drastic measures. This was the beginning of the end of the freedom I had enjoyed because of my parents' preoccupation with work.

First, if the school could not teach me to read, I would be taught at home. Therapy at home consisted of sitting me on a high stool, back to the wall and book in hand, being tutored relentlessly until I grasped the idea of reading. Second, the school, and especially the principal, Miss Hoole, were blamed for my failure that was not only considered a blot on the family's reputation, but left me one half year "behind" the class in which I should have been. Miss Hoole was blamed for committing a discriminatory act against the family. We took revenge by referring to her as "Miss Hooligan." Despite my mediocre academic performance and my continuing incorrigibility, Miss Hoole nevertheless remained my mother's enemy. Removing the blot of my failure became for my mother something of a long-term project—a mission to have it corrected. This mission was only accomplished many years later when I was in high school, where I took extra classes and extended summer school to "make up" the "lost" semester, enabling me to graduate with my rightful classmates. No matter how long it took, restoration of family honor and vindication of my talent was like a crusade. There is no need to recount further incidents such as fights in the school yard during recess and unruly behavior in the classroom. The school still had the primary responsibility for correcting my delinquency even while domestic pressure and surveillance intensified when I showed few signs of improvement.

Among the boyhood friends I had in elementary school it was held that any of us who did not resist conformity to the rules of classroom conduct was a sissy. My friends—Al Pinter, Al Teshnik, Art Demshar, Bob Babich, Micky Krueger, Jimmy Thompson, Alex Alexander, and Bill Mantyh—made insubordination a manly virtue. Since we denied ourselves such recognition as we might have gained from academic performance, we established our own in-group standards for making claims to self-esteem. Our criteria for the measurement of self-worth focused on sports and games. Baseball was the sport of the day; we played it, followed the rankings of the major league teams, and hoped to become professional players like Phil Cavaretta and Gabby Hartnet of the Chicago Cubs. Among the winter sports, there was ice skating at the county park in West Allis, where speed skating was our ideal. Our heroes were the older skaters like Al Luchini, who could take a jumping leap over ten barrels lined up in a row while skating at full speed. We were at the two-barrel stage and full of faith that practice and growing older would lead to fame. Skiing, sledding, and tobogganing were our choice of sports in the cold snowy winters of the Midwest. A few blocks to the south of 58th Street we had access to a large, park-like area established as a soldiers' home for disabled World War I veterans. It contained a forty-five-foot ski jump, a baseball diamond (later developed into a stadium for the Milwaukee Brewers), and a hill known to us as "Devil's Dive." We ski-jumped on barrel staves and regarded Devil's Dive to be the ultimate test of risk-taking courageousness. In these activities, cuts, bruises, and broken teeth—in my case, two fractured lower incisors remain as permanent testimony—were badges of fearlessness. Disregard for personal injury was a form of heroism.

In other seasons we played games: hide and seek, tug of war, and eeney-eeney-eyeover are some that I recall. Shooting marbles and flipping baseball cards were more businesslike ventures, where winning or losing could lead to joy or grief. In the case of marbles, the object of the competition was to win the best kind. One class of marbles is known as "mibs," small round clay-like objects about three-eighths of an inch in diameter. They are breakable and hence are played on soft ground. Two other classes are glass beads anywhere from one-half to one inch in diameter. If a bead is pure red in color, it is known as a "Kaneely." "Steelies," nothing more than ball bearings retrieved from wheel bearing casings in automobile junk yards, also came in several sizes. A large number of games can be played with this combination of marbles. For one example, a glass bead is used to knock out mibs from a circle drawn in dirt that contains a quantity of each player's stock. Each player shoots his marble (either knuckles down or from the air, depending on prior agreement) until he fails to knock a mib from the circle, thus forfeiting the turn to his opponent. The players can break even, or one can win some of the opponent's mibs. The same game can be played with steelies, or with steelies against steelies, or with combinations of glass beads and steelies. The rules for flipping baseball cards are much simpler. Like tossing two pennies simultaneously, the cards can land either odd or even. Each player alternates in making the call. If the call is even and both cards land face up or face down, the caller wins and picks up both cards— and so on and on.

The objective in playing both marbles and cards is to win those of the opposing player. It was common practice for the players to brag to each other of the number of cards or marbles in their stock. All the players in the group were expected to tell the others the correct number in their possession. It was usually the case that all players in the group knew who had how many marbles or cards. On a day-to-day basis, everyone thought they knew their relative standing in relation to the others, but, as might be expected, deception and ambiguity were part of the game. The value of a single card could count as two or even three, depending upon its rarity or the reputation of the baseball player pictured on it, leading to claims and counter-claims about the overall value of a collection. Claims could be adjudicated by third parties, but their judgments need not be accepted by the parties to the quarrel. One case that still sticks in my mind involved deception about who owned the most marbles. All except one in the group reported accurately the number of marbles he possessed. The exception reported a number less than he actually possessed, leaving the others confident of their relative standing until one day this person made an extravagant claim for the possession of a number far exceeding all others. To certify this claim required an open count of the claimant's stock. Sure enough, Bill had concealed his winnings until he had more than the others, enabling him to sandbag and defeat the rest of us. He had won, but in the losers' terms, at the price of engaging in unethical conduct. Yet he had won, so all we could do was call him a liar. At that age, we were all incipient lawyers.

Relative standings could also be altered by new acquisitions purchased in the marketplace or by a visit to the junkyard. Since baseball cards were packaged with bubble gum, the stock of cards grew with the volume of bubble gum chewed. New acquisitions featured the pictures of new baseball players, thus stimulating the desire to flip more cards; each friend had his own favorite baseball heroes and knew who had cards he would like to win. Not all cards had equal value to all players. This introduced card trading (sometimes two for one) as a variation on the game of flipping. Those who possessed the greatest numbers of any variety, or of specific items, were sought out as premium players; diminishing their stock was something to brag about. These were engaging and ego-inflating games that we regarded as more important than the things we did in the classroom, regardless of what our teachers or parents may have had in mind for us.

In elementary school, I was unreceptive to the idea of being a student. I can remember the names of friends and the games we played, but not my teachers' names or what I might have learned in the classroom. It cannot be said that my teachers made no efforts on my behalf. Though I appeared to have learned the basic skills of reading, writing, and arithmetic and was exposed to the higher cultural arts of music and drawing, none of the latter left an imprint on me. When I tried to sing in a school choir, I learned that I could not carry a tune. My mother, who was musical, thought I should learn to play the violin. Encouraged by the new violin she bought for me, I took a few lessons, but lacked discipline and motivation. Despite my appreciation of the sounds produced by this instrument, my fingers were attuned to baseball, not the fingerboard. When I later learned to appreciate violin concertos, I regretted this failure, another of life's lost opportunities. I fared no better with lessons in public speaking, which consisted, in second or third grade, of standing before the class and telling a joke. For my performance, my joke was, "What's the difference between a salesman and a baby? A salesman goes from city to city and a baby goes from titty to titty." The boys laughed, the girls were embarrassed, and the teacher reprimanded me for my vulgar taste. My first experience as a public speaker gained me no academic standing and reinforced my reputation as a troublemaker. During the first five years of my elementary school career, I rejected the norms of approved conduct and refused to compete for their rewards. Instead, I competed for the recognition of my friends, who in my imagination were my gang among whom I sought to be *primus inter pares*. In order to accomplish this end, I used the means available to me, including telling a risqué joke, owning the most baseball cards, or being the fastest speed skater. This was not always an easy pose to sustain successfully, and the pressures to desist imposed by school and family were not only great, they became insurmountable.

I am not sure how my conversion happened, but I know it took place in the sixth grade while I was in Mrs. Jerabek's class. Under Dorothy Jerabek's administration, my proven methods of getting attention and distracting teachers no longer succeeded. She had methods for ignoring my disruptive behavior and thus isolating me from the rest of the class. Or she ridiculed my efforts to focus the attention of the class on myself; even my closest boyfriends enjoyed the defeats she inflicted upon me. My negative attention-getting devices were quickly and decisively neutralized, leaving me no other option than to replace them with the terms she set. If I were to defend my honor, I would have to do so academically.

By taking me on and defeating me as a troublemaker, Mrs. Jerabek also showed that she cared for me. It helped that she was beautiful, but, even apart from that, I fell in love with her. She had a fine figure, soft and delicate facial features, English in complexion and descent, and fulsome breasts. It is no wonder that she became my ideal, my third mother.

I read the books, did the geography lessons—one wall of the classroom was covered with a map of the world—and never failed to submit assignments on time. When I contracted scarlet fever and was quarantined to my home for six weeks, she sent my assignments to my home, corrected them, and had them returned to me by my classmates whom she appointed as couriers. By receiving this attention, I was distinguished from other students and became known as teacher's pet.

Mrs. Jerabek had other pets as well. One of these was Betty Meyer, who in being my female counterpart, also became my sixth-grade girlfriend, as if I were appropriating my competitor for Mrs. Jerabek's affections. I worked to gain Mrs. Jerabek's exclusive affection and resented those who did not respect her. For example, one of her duties was to answer the telephone in Miss Hoole's office adjacent to our classroom when the principal was out of the office. Running out of the classroom to answer it, her large breasts rhythmically and conspicuously bounced, drawing the attention of the entire class of boys and girls who reacted with twitters and subdued smiles, at which I took umbrage, regarding myself as her sole defender.

Twice in the course of the sixth year, Mrs. Jerabek invited Betty and me and our closest friends, Mickey Krueger and Jean Lucas, to have Sunday afternoon tea at her finely-furnished brick two-story house at 2350 South 58th Street. This was the first time I had ever heard of drinking tea on Sunday afternoon. These were momentous occasions not only for the special recognition they accorded us, but also because this was the first time I had been inside of what I imagined was a truly American household. My own was unconventional and certainly not American. Whatever I thought that that might have been, Mrs. Jerabek gave me my first hint of how real Americans lived.

Mrs. Jerabek was a teacher who thought of teaching as a personal relationship between teacher and student and that her classroom had no boundaries. Years later, I learned that I was not as select as I thought I had been and as I wanted to believe. When I returned to

West Allis for a high school reunion, I discovered that other class-mates had had similar experiences in the sixth grade. In 1980, I also learned that Mrs. Jerabek was alive and well, still living on 58th Street. I renewed my relationship with her—and, as I learned, so did Betty Meyer. I corresponded with her and visited her, gave her copies of my books, and, apart from a moral obligation, wanted to hear the story of her career and life. Shortly after she had taught my class, she became pregnant, and under municipal rules then in effect, she was required to resign her position. After the birth of her son, she mar-ried a Czech musician, a cultivated man, and was hired to teach at Saint Rita's parochial school, where she continued to teach until she was 90. She died, still beautiful, at the age of 93 in 1997.

Had it not been for her personal attention, my intellectual curi-osity might never have been stimulated. When later in life I finally recognized this, I understood that learning about life cannot be sep-arated from the moral example given by the teacher.

Some Boyhood Discoveries

In his narrowly circumscribed universe of family, playmates, and school, this child led a protected existence. The youngest sibling and only son, he was indulged by a mother who had high aspirations for his future in America. By the time the boy was born, his father, then thirty-six years of age, had already submitted to the authority of his wife, to whom he deferred in both familial and business affairs. Mat-ters of family policy pertaining to the boy were held firmly in the hands of his mother, who made her husband her administrative as-sistant in her son's care and training. His three older sisters treated him as their kid brother whose welfare was their responsibility. He was, after all, an only son, all the more favored because his family also projected onto him the hopes and aspirations they had held for

the firstborn son and brother, now dead. In this protected and femi-
nine universe, it was easy for the boy to believe that he was the family's center of attention in a world that existed for him. Yet it was
inevitable that this illusion proved to be unsustainable.

The Depression

While still only seven years old, and even before I had seen the maps
of the world on Mrs. Jerabek's classroom wall, the stock market crash
in the autumn of 1929 abruptly ended my shielded life.

I learned that my mother owned stocks in utilities and that what
had been thought to be the American way to economic fortune
proved to be illusory. Highly speculative utility stocks fell precipitously on November's Black Thursday, and they continued to fall until 1933. The Chicago utilities tycoon Samuel Insull, an Englishman,
had leveraged his position on the market with other people's money
and finally went bankrupt, teaching the family a lesson in the practice of American business. The Crash gave me my first lesson in economics. I did not then read the *New York Times* Industrial Index, but
I quickly learned that there was a stock market and that it could not
be trusted. Only much later did I learn that fortunes could be made
on the downside of a market. Bernard Baruch, who sold heavily just
before the Crash, bought back when prices were low and became, by
the time I was fourteen, an economic advisor to President Roosevelt.
His prescient and lucky decision to sell was enough to make him a
wealthy man, and when coupled with contributions to Roosevelt's
political campaign, to validate his political acumen, confirming the
old American adage that "money talks." The Crash and the extended
Depression that followed left a permanent scar on several generations
of Americans who have not forgotten that it could happen again. Its
meaning for me was mostly personal.

Before the Crash, I had been depositing my money in the Wisconsin Savings State Bank. I had thought that my money was securely held in the huge, impressive bank safe located where National and Greenfield Avenues intersect at 62nd Street, just a comfortable four blocks from where we lived on 58th. When the bank failed—perhaps having lent my money to Samuel Insull, enabling him to hold up his marginal positions until the bitter end—it locked its doors, sealed its accounts, and left me with my valueless bank book. As if by magic, my money had disappeared. Only later in 1933, when President Roosevelt lifted the bank moratorium was my money returned to me, but now its value was discounted, something like twenty percent of its original value. My money had not only earned no interest, it had almost disappeared. At the age of eleven, I learned the meaning of currency devaluation. The adage I had been taught at school about the virtues of "saving for a rainy day," and, moreover, that your "money would work for you," now meant that an Englishman would take your savings from you. In my lexicon, the name Insull still has pejorative connotations.

The Depression, even more than the rise of Nazism and the Spanish Civil War, was the critical event of my boyhood. Despite high unemployment, the lag in downward price adjustments, and an all-pervasive economic pessimism, Herbert Hoover could only offer promises for a better future, that "prosperity was just around the corner" and that there would then be a "chicken in everyone's pot for Sunday dinner." Though the national economic crisis did not jeopardize our family's economic well-being—my mother had hedged her market position with reserve cash stashed in the trunk in her bedroom—I recall a pervasive uncertainty about the future. People in the neighborhood and on Clinton Street reached for any straw that promised a better future. All eyes focused on the federal government waiting expectantly for Hoover's assurances reported in the press and on radio from Washington. When Hitler was appointed Germany's Chancellor in 1933 and Father Coughlin began his radio broadcasts from Detroit, my father, for the first time in my memory, took an interest in politics. Together we listened to Hitler's speeches rebroadcast in translation on Sunday afternoons. What Hitler said was usually described as propaganda, but my mother used the term more broadly to cover the speeches of our own political leaders as well as political reporting in the press. In a very short time, the world had become larger, but it was a world that seemed intractable to human intervention. The Depression brought the world into my life at home on 58th Street and National Avenue, where a comfortable, secure existence could no longer be taken for granted.

Religion and God

As my mother saw it, the Catholic Church was primarily business, an attitude born on the iron ranges of Minnesota where the Slovenian priest had summarily dunned—perhaps even taxed—parishioners for contributions, disregarding their volition or ability to pay. It was not in my mother's nature to succumb to the priest's dictates, and regarding them unacceptable, she left the congregation. As a result, eschewing the church had become a family tradition, so that when we reached West Allis, not only was I never sent to church, I was led to believe that the priests were essentially corrupt, an opinion justified for me by a rumor that the local priest in the Slovenian Catholic Church on 61st Street had fathered the child of one of his parishioners. The priest, and by extension the Church itself, was morally tainted and therefore irredeemable. I was not given a church and, in my view, I did not have a religion. When my playmates asked me if and where I went to church, it was easy for me to tell them "I don't go to church" because I was confident in the correctness of my mother's image of the church as an economic institution. The connection between economic ethics and religious faith meant nothing to me until much later when I read Max Weber's *The Protestant Ethic and the Spirit of Capitalism*. In my youth, I understood this nexus in much simpler terms.

When, however, my friends asked the next logical question, "Do you believe in God?" I did not have a ready answer. I had certainly heard the phrase "God damn" used by my father and was familiar with his frequent use of the Slovenian word hell (*hudic*), but this knowledge did not help to answer the fundamental question. Not having an answer, I refused to answer it, taking what is now known as a Fifth Amendment right against self-incrimination. This position, however, still left me in doubt about whether I did or did not believe in God. Finding myself in this indeterminate position and lacking an authority that could give me an answer, I reasoned that the choice was my own. But, though the choice was left to me, I did not know how to make it.

Looking for a solution to my dilemma, I took my problem back to my parents, asking them directly, "Do we believe in God?" The answer I received was equivocal. "Yes," my mother said, "there *must* be a God, but it's not necessary to go to church." I do not remember my father saying anything, implicitly agreeing with my mother by his silence. I understood that there was no family policy with regard to God and that the choice was truly mine. This did not, however, solve my problem; it only left me free to find my own solution.

Further questions about the meaning of my existence arose in early adolescence. The issue was not so much a belief in God, but rather how might religion provide me with something I could now call a philosophy of life: What was the meaning of life, and specifically, why was I born and what would happen to me afterwards? I knew I needed help to answer these questions. Since I was already convinced that a priest in the Catholic Church would be of no help, I tried the Presbyterians. They were located only a block and a half away, on the corner of National Avenue and 60th Street, where some of my friends with whom I had played basketball in the church's basement gymnasium were members. Believing that one church was as good as another and having no knowledge of the theological differences among Protestant churches, proximity and my friends made the Presbyterians a logical choice. I went to a Sunday service hoping to talk to the minister, but learned that he was a substitute who was not otherwise available. Having no luck with the Presbyterians, I turned to the Lutherans.

This determination was certified for me by my sister Olga's best friend, Dorothy Runkel, a Lutheran, whom I admired for her charm and delicate beauty. Her church was located on Layton Boulevard in Milwaukee, a few miles from home. Dorothy made the appointment for me to see her minister at the church, an imposing stone edifice, where I met a young cleric fully outfitted in vestments. This was an important occasion for both of us, but our ideas differed about why. I wanted to discuss my immediate existential problems. The minister's objective became clear when, after a short interview, he presented me with a Lutheran catechism that he asked me to study before returning for a second visit. I left with the catechism and tried to read it, but my efforts only proved to me that it did not contain the answers I needed. My search was for direct answers to my immediate questions about the origin of life and why I was here. The catechism introduced me to the terms under which I could accept a faith, the dogma peculiar to Lutheranism. In asking me to accept their faith, they made me an object of their mission rather than the other way around. In any case, the biblical and theological terminologies were beyond my skills of comprehension and meant nothing to me. I never returned for a second visit and drew the conclusion that I could not expect much help from the Protestant churches, leaving me, at the age of thirteen, with no further choices within Christendom.

Later, when I was eighteen and a counselor at the YMCA Camp Manitowish at Boulder Junction in northern Wisconsin, I was thrust into a religious setting again. At the camp, Catholics, Protestants, and Jews mixed together under a watered-down YMCA version of Christianity. Catholic campers had the option of attending mass in the nearby city of Woodruff; the Jews, however, had no such choice in upstate Wisconsin. Camp policy required attendance at a Sunday morning service held on the campground's outdoor chapel in an atmosphere that evoked the supernaturalism of nature itself. I also took my turn at delivering the Sunday "sermon." I remember this as a homily on good sportsmanship, emphasizing character-building over winning, rather than the muscular spirit of the Gospel. It was the practice at camp to pray before meals and at evening fireside gatherings, but these ceremonies were a multicultural version of Protestantism; as the counselor of my dining table, I took my place in a rotation and had no trouble giving a prayer for our daily bread. That I was qualified to officiate in these ceremonies did not enhance my respect for Protestantism. The YMCA version of Protestantism was limited to a few prayers of thanks and a demand for goodwill and love toward others. It was a benign faith that made no particular demands for sacrifice on its believers and could be accepted easily.

My search in the Christian church for solutions to my existential questions ended at about that time, but my encounters with Protestant cultural agencies did not.

When I was an undergraduate at the University of Wisconsin, Dean of Men Rudisili chose me to be a Danforth Fellow to attend Camp Minnewanka on Lake Michigan near Travers City, established by the Danforth family, owners of Ralston Purina in St. Louis. Located in an exotic setting on the shores of the lake and provisioned with tennis courts, ball fields, and game rooms, the purpose of the retreat was to enhance a spirit of Christian brotherhood and sisterhood. My only lasting memory of it is that of the co-ed with whom I took to playing tennis and walking the beach. It surprises me that all other images of it have vanished. My next encounter with Protestantism was in the Marine Corps at Parris Island, where a fundamentalist Southern Baptist minister addressed the platoon on the virtues of motherhood, patriotism, God, country, and winning the war, but not sobriety. Because as boots we were already intimidated into the acceptance of discipline and obedience, we listened respectfully to this strange, bloodthirsty Christian message. Having acquired from these experiences the belief that Christianity was a superficial religion, I assumed that the Christians expected no more from their faith than I. Later, when I married a Congregational minister's daughter, I learned otherwise.

Without knowing it, I was more of a Catholic than I realized. Fragments of Catholic rituals were integrated into the family's lifestyle. My mother observed the rule of serving fish on Fridays and accepted the dietary sacrifices required by Lent. Easter, if not so much an occasion for the observance of the Resurrection, still required special dishes and collective drinking of specially selected red wines. Easter dinner stood apart from ordinary weekly meals. We conformed to a Catholic calendar but did not need an affiliation with the church to do it.

Our family had its own secular theodicy, designed to explain the ways of the world to my sisters and me. I was taught to have sympathy for the poor and that mendicancy was neither a crime nor preordained. The family dictum was that there were good and bad people in all groups and that it was wrong to have prejudices against a group as a whole. Without putting it in explicit Catholic terms, we were all God's children, but in our case, we were taught that all were free to believe as they wished, that one religion was no better than another, nor were missionary efforts to convert others consistent with independence of mind. In its simplest terms, it was the Golden Rule of "Do unto others as you would have others do unto you." We never said prayers at mealtime, nor did I ever take Communion in the Catholic Church. The family culture was Catholic, but more out of habit than zeal. Our "Catholicism" had more to do with adherence to a Slovenian cultural tradition than to a faith or theology. The irksome question of the meaning of my existence—of a philosophy of life—never disappeared and has always reappeared at unexpected times, but its immediate salience in my boyhood was mitigated by my daily round of life in family, among playmates, at school, and by my ambition to be successful in America.

Family Solidarity as Religion

The success of our "restaurant" business on Clinton Street presupposed a tightly organized familial solidarity. By force of the logic of conducting a family business, my mother functioned as a chief executive who determined and executed policy, making husband and children part of a collective project larger than ourselves. Coordinating our different schedules at school and getting us to and from the school were only part of it. Each of us had our own chores: my earliest duty was to submit to the supervision of my sister Pauline. By the time I was ten years old, the task of washing dishes and cleaning the kitchen after meals had already descended from the older sisters to Betty and me and remained with us until Betty graduated from high school, leaving me to do these chores alone when she went to college. To this day, any member of any of my families can vouch for my skill as a busboy and dishwasher. Ordinary tasks such as weeding the garden, picking the fruit, mowing the lawn, shoveling the snow, tending to the garbage, caring for the dog, and shopping for groceries were tasks routinely assigned to me. On Sunday mornings, it was the children's duty at 115 Clinton Street to bottle the coming week's supply of near beer. Our mini-brewery was in a ramshackle, rain-proof, wooden shed located between the kitchen and the Chicago, Milwaukee, and St. Paul railway tracks. Each week, my father prepared the necessary ingredients for the beer and placed them in a twenty-five-gallon copper vat elevated a foot off the floor. After a week of fermentation, his crew bottled the mixture. The job was simple enough, but it required some care and coordination. Drawing the beer from the vat to the bottles was done with a siphon hose inserted not too deeply into the vat. Drawing on the hose caused the beer to flow and required the immediate insertion of the hose into a clean beer bottle, washed in advance by the same crew. When the bottle was full, the hose was nipped and inserted into the next bottle in line until it too was full, and so on. Each full bottle in this assembly-line process was passed to the capper who placed the cap on the bottle and passed it to the presser who, with a hand-powered press, slammed the cork-lined cap airtight onto the bottle. This primitive industrial activity produced about eight cases of beer ready for sale to waiting customers. In its own way, this Sunday morning practice was our substitute for attending church; tasting the beer as we did was a sacramental activity.

After our "service," we were permitted to attend the Sunday matinee at the Wisconsin Theater on Wisconsin Avenue in downtown Milwaukee. Working together in our micro-brewery was our equivalent of praying together in church; our reward, however, was immediate and material.

While I was still a boy, the justification for life on a day-to-day basis was implicit in the family as a collective enterprise. That we needed each other was its own justification. Situated in a kind of limbo between West Allis and Milwaukee and without an extended family, we accepted our mutual dependencies. Acting as a corporate joint holding company and living by our own rules, there seemed to be no need for outside support, let alone a church or religion. We supplied our own rituals and justification of the ways of the family in this world rather than the next.

Boyhood Rituals and Secrets: My World in the Basement

The basement of our house in West Allis was a small universe of its own. It was large, covering the full area of the house. Above it was the butcher shop and an A&P Grocery Store, and above them were our living quarters. The ground floor entrance to our home opened to both a stairway that led to the second floor and to a hallway that led to the basement. The basement could also be entered through an external hatchway that in addition served as the sleeping quarters for my dog. It was in the basement where I learned some prosaic facts of life and where my nascent political ambitions were initially cultivated.

The basement's key areas were a butcher's area, the wine cellar, exterior hatchway, interior basement access, storage space/clubroom, and coal bin. Its installations included the butcher's hot water vat and the home heating center, including the furnace, klinker bin, and the Iron Fireman, and the laundry complex, including gas stove, sink, and Maytag washing machine. At least until my father retired from the saloon business in 1936, this was where I performed my household tasks and enjoyed freedom from parental scrutiny.

The house was heated with a coal-burning furnace that required regular replenishments of fuel during the long, cold midwestern winters. Feeding anthracite coal to the furnace was accomplished by the Iron Fireman, the trade name of a machine that was then the state of the art in heating systems. Consisting of a hopper capable of containing a supply of fuel, it fed coal on thermostatic demand directly into the base of the furnace. Twice daily, its hopper had to be filled, and the ashes and "klinkers" produced by the combustion needed to be removed from the base of the fire. The Fireman needed little attention, but human assistance was critical to its proper functioning. I provided this service before I went to school and when I returned in the afternoon. Shovel by shovel, I transferred the anthracite from the coal bin to the hopper; the coal was delivered in a size the Fireman's rotor could digest. Klinkers that formed at the base of the fire, if not removed, impeded the automatic feeding of the fuel into the furnace. Without the removal of the klinkers and ashes, the Iron Fireman was a helpless robot. Probing the fire pit to locate the red-hot klinkers, I removed them with long-handled tongs and placed them in the klinker bin to cool.

Remembering this procedure years later when I read in one of Eugene O'Neill's plays a portrait of a ship's stoker, I have always been able to identify with those men, including my father in his original career as a blacksmith, who work in the intense heat of coal-fed boilers or molten steel. The easier task of removing the ashes re-mained after removing the klinkers. A slight shake of the furnace's grate with a crank connected to a protruding bar brought the ashes to the bottom; opening the cast iron door at the furnace's base, I could easily remove them with a shovel. But again, if not removed on schedule, their accumulation impeded the proper combustion of the coal. Even before I was brought under control by family and school, I was disciplined by the machine. When I read Thorstein Veblen's *The Instinct of Workmanship* about the social-psychological consequenc-es of machine discipline on the worker's mentality, I could under-stand what he meant when he said that the machine process induces a rational bent of mind in those who are subjected to it.

Once a week, I was assistant to my mother on laundry day. An electrically powered Maytag washing machine stood on a raised platform. Adjacent to the platform sat a two-burner gas stove used to heat the water for washing—and on other occasions to provide my father the heat needed when he distilled his private reserve slivovica. Though electrically powered, the Maytag was not connected to a wa-ter supply. Hot water for washes and cold water for rinses were sup-plied manually in buckets: hot water from the stove and cold water from the sink. In those days, water metered by the city was an expen-sive commodity to be used sparingly, not only in the laundry room but also for purposes of bathing; we took our baths once a week, on Fridays, the four siblings using only two bath waters. Managing the Maytag's water consumption required the use of several holding buckets. The hot water used for the first wash was drained and set aside in buckets while the wash was rinsed in cold water. The same hot water was then reused for the second wash. The cold rinse water was also saved and used as the rinse for the next wash. After the cold water rinse, the wash was pressed through an electrically powered wringer. Not until all water had been wrung out was the cold water removed and saved to be used for another rinse.

Four or five loads of clothing sorted in piles according to color were processed in this way. A complete change of new water, hot and cold, was done at the halfway mark, the last washes being reserved for dark garments. Only then was the water discarded. The laundry operation, like that of Friday night bathing, was premised on the parsimonious use of water. The idea of conserving water was part of a general belief in the virtue of saving that also included the sparing use of electricity and the telephone: light switches were always to be turned off when not needed and phone calls kept short and to the point. In our world, waste was to be avoided, and each was responsible for observing these economies. I still turn off light switches.

The butcher had his own corner of the basement. It contained a large gas-heated vat and various counters used to cut up carcasses. Shipments of live chickens were received on Fridays to be slaughtered and prepared for sale on the weekend. There were no frozen chickens then. Preparation of a dressed chicken for the market was still the work of a craftsman, a skill not yet transformed into a large-scale, scientifically orchestrated factory operation capable of slaughtering millions of chickens daily. After slitting the chicken's jugular, the butcher threw the carcass into a barrel where it remained until its blood had drained. He then dunked the bloodless but completely bloody carcass into the vat containing the hot water, withdrawing it when it was ready to be plucked. The carcass was then gutted and prepared for sale. This was an operation I saw many times, and I recalled it easily when, in the early 1950s, I took a job at Cornell University that required me to live in a farmhouse and play the part of a local small-town resident. The farmhouse had a chicken coop. This gave me the idea of acting out this role by raising a flock of my own. When the time arrived to butcher them, I followed the procedure I had observed so many times, but I learned that doing was not the same as watching. A live chicken does not easily submit to having its throat slit; I had difficulty holding the struggling chicken while trying to find its jugular. Every craft is an art in its own right, the practice of which is best left to those who have been trained for it. In my case, a doctorate in anthropology was no help.

The wine cellar was an enclosed, windowless area that could be entered through a door that was never locked. It contained a large wine press, twice as high as I, and made up of at least six thirty-one gallon oak-staved barrels—enough capacity for a full year's supply for domestic use. The barrels were reused from year to year, and each was cleaned when emptied of its contents. If wine is to ferment properly, clean barrels are an absolute necessity. Wine barrels were made of wooden staves held in place with metal hoops designed to clamp the finely edged staves together. The barrel's base and top cover are tongued disks made to fit the grooved staves and are held in place by the metal hoops. After a barrel was emptied, it required a thorough brushing of the inner side of the staves, base, and cover. Removing a hoop releases the cover, giving access to the inside of the barrel. One of my jobs was to clean the empty barrels and prepare them for use in the following season. In the wine cellar, I was my father's assistant.

Each year in the early fall, a truckload of Concorde and Muscat grapes arrived from vineyards located along the sandy eastern shores of Lake Michigan. Wine-making season began when we unloaded a shipment of boxed red and white grapes and carried them into the basement through the cellar hatchway. That same day, and late into the night, my sister Betty and I pressed grapes until the whole shipment was converted into "must," the grape juice combined with the pulp and skins. Looking back, the press seemed to be six feet tall and was capable of holding two bushels of grapes at a pressing. The press squeezed the grapes downward under the weight of a steel plate operated by a crank connected to a set of gears. The press's downward action on the grapes released the juice from the pulp and skins, allowing the liquid to drain into a tray at the base of the press. My job was to operate the crank while my father managed the operation as a whole until all the barrels were filled with the proper amounts of juice and must. Once filled and capped with a cover, the barrels were laid on their sides. At the top of the center stave, a bung hole was opened and left open during the fermentation process. A wooden spigot inserted in the face of each barrel was used later to drain the wine. I do not remember any of this wine ever being bottled. Both the red and the white were decanted directly from the barrel, but only after the fermentation had been completed and the bung hole capped. The whole process required several months and marked the fall as a special season. For my father, making the family's wine was the same thing he would have been doing if he were still in Kropa, following a seasonal ritual repeated year after year. For me, it was a chore in which I had little interest; only later did I regret not learning the craft, another missed opportunity in my life. My father did not think to instruct me, perhaps thinking I would automatically learn it as he had in his youth. Another feature of Kropa's culture was lost in America.

There were, however, important rewards for this work. One of them was immediate: drinking the delicious juice from the freshly pressed grapes. Even greater rewards followed as the wine matured. What my father called "young wine," whose alcohol content was still low, was a heady grape juice that could be drained and drunk directly from the spigot. Wine was an integral part of the family's cuisine; even as young children we were served small portions with dinner on Sundays and festive holidays. The real treat came on New Year's Eve when the family drank a special preparation of mulled wine served with freshly made bread. We dipped it into the warm wine in a sacramental ceremony to commemorate the new wine and the new year. Even now, I dip my bread into red wine, and it still evokes for me the authentic flavor of that mulled wine, a personal ritual that transports me back to the house in West Allis where I had my first taste of it. Such are the remnants of an ethnic-American way of life.

The wine cellar had a special meaning for me because it was there that I surreptitiously took my friends to treat them to private wine tastings of my father's best. I thought of the cellar as a perfectly respectable part of the house. You could be proud of the Iron Fireman, then an ultra-modern piece of equipment. Not all families could afford a Maytag washing machine, and to have a butchering area in the basement was a novelty. I kept my dog in the hatchway to the basement where he slept and ate. Because of my dog, my friends knew the hatchway very well, so it was almost inevitable that I should take the next step and invite them into the basement I knew so well. Serving them my father's wine directly from the spigot supported my claim to be the audacious leader of what I called my gang.

Those invited to the basement were only my most trusted friends. We were four little boys (German, Polish, Irish, and Slovene) who were looking for affirmation in each other. Our activities were secretive and imbued us with a conspiratorial attitude that tightened our fraternal bonds. I don't remember the exact steps that led to the creation of our club, but we took to making the storage room the place

WITH A CRITICAL EYE

where we held meetings. The first thing we learned was that there was no point in having a secret club unless others knew of its existence, raising the question of its purpose. We engaged in no charitable work, harassed no enemies, and did not have plans to steal. Telling our friends about the club informed them of their exclusion. We had learned to appropriate a social status by the simple process of excluding some of our playmates, arousing their curiosity and desire to learn more about what we were doing; Groucho Marx rejected such notions of appropriated status when he said that any elite club that invited him to join was not good enough for him. By accepting our claim to exclusivity, our friends validated our existence, but secret meetings in our hiding place were not enough to justify ourselves as a self-selected elite. We solved this problem of purpose by creating titles for ourselves—president, vice-president, secretary, and treasurer. Since we met in *my* basement and drank *my* father's wine, there could be only one candidate for president. When I asked, "Who should be president?" it was agreed by consensus that it should be me. That is how I became a president for the first time. The club had no purpose other than our own celebration, but that was enough to set us apart from the others and make a claim to our exclusivity.

Much later, at the University of Wisconsin at Madison, I was similarly honored as president of the Student Union by being admitted to an exclusive club for campus leaders. Each spring, five or ten junior class leaders were inducted into the Iron Cross Society; each new group had its names engraved in a large metal plaque. Late in the darkness of an evening, the novices carried the plaque and chained it to the foot of the statue of Abraham Lincoln located at the top of the Bascom Hill. Removed later, the plaque was then installed on a wall in the Student Union Rathskeller where it remains to this day. We were a self-appointed, self-perpetuating elite that had no function other than to bestow this honor on those like ourselves. My political career, begun in the basement and successfully pursued in high school and in college, ended when I later realized that self-promotion was an essential qualification for a political career.

Exorcising the Slovene Roots

I do not remember the time when I became aware that there was a difference between being a Slovene and being an American. More plausibly, it seems that this was not a sudden discovery, but rather more like a gradual awakening that there might be a species "Americana." My immediate neighborhood and circle of friends included Italians, Croatians, Germans, Swedes, Serbs, Hungarians, Poles, Irish, Slovenes, and Scots, but there were no Jews or Negroes, as the latter were then called. This diversity of origins left me with the impression that my world was composed of a multitude of nationalities, each taking as his own the nation of his parents; we designated ourselves according to nation, not ethnicity as is the current practice.

However, within this mix of nationalities, there was also the imputation that some nationalities were more worthy than others. Germans, with names like Meyer, Krueger, Bietzel, Rehberger, and Kiefer, who were the largest group in our neighborhood, were already second generation, and had parents who spoke English without an accent. In my estimation, this itself elevated the status of Germans above that of other nationalities. That my mother proudly spoke German and claimed an Austrian nationality helped to confirm this impression. When my eldest sister entered high school and was required to study a foreign language, my mother insisted that it be German, giving the Germans another increment of status. But in my scheme of things, this did not mean the Germans were American. It only made them better than other nationalities. At the bottom of my ranking were the Poles. This was, first, because my elementary school teachers had more difficulty pronouncing Polish names than those of other nationalities; a teacher's stumbling over a student's name could make a classroom at least snicker if not laugh out loud. Besides, all Polish names ended in "ski," as if one were indistinguishable from another. Second, and even more telling, my father had worked with Poles and had learned to speak their language, but whenever he made the claim that he possessed this skill, my mother derided him not only for the worthlessness of the language, but even for the claim that he knew it. Somewhere in between on this scale of prejudices were the Italians, whom I associated with both the Mafia and the discovery of America, and the Irish, who were poor, noisy, and had too many children. Scandinavians were invariably blond, had high foreheads and pronounceable names like Hanson and Samuelson, and ranked next to Germans or, on the basis of appearance, even higher. Scandinavians were already second-generation immigrants, giving them a greater claim to status than latecomers such as the Slavs, Hungarians, and Poles. Time of arrival and country of origin were the ready-made criteria I used to locate myself in my hierarchical ordering of nationalities.

Despite my mother's efforts to make me an Austrian, in practical terms, this was a label that I could not appropriate. To make the claim, as I did on occasion when my friends and I discussed our parents' countries of origin, placed me in a strange category, separating me from other Slovenes whose names were similar to mine. How could I be Austrian if my name was Slovene like those of my friends Stupic, Potocnik, Teshnik, Pagocnik, Pintar, and Tratar? In the neighborhood, I not only knew I was a Slovene, but I also knew that my mother's claim to Austrian-ness made us superior. Despite the falseness of this claim to national superiority, it nevertheless had the consequences she desired: to exorcise our Slovene roots.

In the aftermath of World War I, Slovenia had become a part of the newly formed kingdom of Yugoslavia, now designated as a Slavic region. In this new map of Southern and Central Europe drawn by the Allied Powers, Slovenia had lost its status as a part of the Austro-Hungarian Empire, posing the problems not only of how to identify Slovenia, but also of how to prove that it existed at all. It was a small territory with a small population whose emigrants, when they came to this country, moved primarily to steel-producing cities and iron-mining regions. Except for the émigrés themselves, most people in the United States had no idea where Slovenia was. Austria had the double advantage of being both known and a European country, as if that gave us a better status claim in America.

My parents took every opportunity to denigrate the country they had left. "Slovene," they said, "is a language not worth knowing." "The old country is corrupted, and they are always killing each other in wars." "Slovenia is a poor, destitute country controlled by the rich and the church." "In Slovenia, you couldn't get ahead," and "In the Austro-Hungarian Army, a soldier was paid only a few dollars a month." It is no wonder that my parents never returned to Kropa for a visit and had no desire to do so. By contrast, in this country, "If you study hard, you'll succeed." "Everybody who is ambitious has a chance." "In America everybody is equal—there are good and bad people in all religions and nationalities," but despite this ideology there was a slight carryover of a traditional Old World prejudice against Croatians. We were to become Americans despite our immigrant status and despite my father's preference for reading Slovene newspapers rather than the *Milwaukee Journal*. It was implicitly understood that I was to absorb the values and norms thought to be American. On the other hand, there was no question that within the family we lived differently from others.

The way of life in our household was more typical of life in Kropa than that which I imagined to be American. I knew of no other family that produced *potica*, a holiday-season pastry (of Austrian origin) or that followed an annual fall ritual of buying halves of porkers and steers to be made into smoked sausages, hams, and *prcut* in a backyard smokehouse. Our hand-cranked sausage-making machine produced a year's supply of hearty, heavily garlicked *kranjski kilbase* links. Blood sausages were made from a mixture of rice and pork blood and, when made, left the kitchen smelling the way I imagined a kitchen in Kropa might smell. I did not wish to share any of this part of my life with my friends. Considering that I already felt stigmatized by the saloon business, the heterodox industries associated with our West Allis household added to my belief that we were not, strictly speaking, *bona fide* Americans. On the other hand, when facing the outside world, my parents urged me to be an American. They were carriers of the old-world culture that had been bred into them, but they urged me to be American even as they bequeathed to me the old world that they did not want me to accept. I lived a split life.

In our children's world, despite our consciousness of each other person's national origins, spatial proximity rather than nationality determined our choice of friends. My childhood territory was circumscribed by a few contiguous blocks between 58th and 60th Streets on the north side of National Avenue, a commercial street and trolley car route that was also the dividing line for elementary school districts. I did not associate with children in the adjacent school district on the other side of the trolley tracks until I went to junior high school. That I was Slovene did not seem to matter to others, and I reciprocated in kind. For my friends and me, our neighborhood was a multi-ethnic enclave whose cultural diversity remained invisible to us because we met each other on the streets and not in each other's homes. I never saw the living rooms of any of my friends' homes, just as they never entered our apartment; possibly everyone had something to hide. Meeting on the streets, we rarely saw each other's parents. It came as a shock when a friend suddenly announced that his mother had given birth to a baby sister; no one had known his mother was pregnant. The announcement shocked us because we could not conceive that our parents would or could have sexual relations. The baby had arrived ten years after the mother's preceding child. This event could only evoke images of the friend's mother and father having intercourse, something that parents no longer did. By our Puritanical standard, the event violated our norm of respectability. When the reality had to be faced, the family's collective front was penetrated. The privacy of the home was a community norm and not something peculiar to our family. We therefore were never apprised of the national, cultural, and lifestyle differences among us. We knew the national origins of each other's parents, but on the streets, in our relations with each other, we invented an American culture of our own.

I learned a significant part of that culture because I had three elder sisters, each of whom had boyfriends. As part of their approach to their girlfriends, the boyfriends indulged me with their attention, leading me in my self-centered world to believe they were my friends as well. Pauline's boyfriend, Del Budde, was seven years older than I, yet despite the age difference, he talked to me man-to-man and treated me with respect. Al Luchini, Olga's friend, who was my idol on the baseball field also, became my speed-skating instructor. Under no circumstances, except for his interest in Olga, would he have paid any attention to me at all. That it did him little good with Olga made me the beneficiary of his efforts to win her attention. Betty's friends, who were only two years older than I, became my friends as well and incorporated me into their lives. Gordon and Howard Samuelson were cases in point. Howard helped me to organize my own Little League team and showed me how to finance the purchase of baseball equipment by buying Campbell's Soup wholesale and selling it to our friends' mothers; when we ran short of funds, I was taught how to steal baseballs from the five-and-dime. This was a fairly simple job involving no more than letting the contraband fall through the hole in the pocket of my knickers where it rested invisibly at the base of the knee-high pantaloon. Shoplifting, a truly American custom that I learned at an early age, is now a twenty-five billion dollar industry across the country despite all methods of electronic surveillance. We played several full seasons of self-organized Little League ball at the Soldiers' Home, an area that until recently was the home of the Milwaukee Braves. I can remember the score of our first game, a long one, with a final tally of 54 to 57. Despite being older than me, Gordon befriended me, and later when I entered the University of Wisconsin, he was already there and became my mentor. He had aspirations for making me the governor of the state and had World War II not come along, I might have had a political career inspired in good measure by Gordon. Learning what it meant to be an American was a process that occurred by osmosis, and, without knowing it, one we helped to define by our own actions.

Critical examples of middle-class Americanism were provided for me by my elementary school teachers. Because they were teachers, they were by definition American. In that day, they were all women and none had foreign names. They spoke English without an accent and showed a preference for students who came to school with clean fingernails and hands, hair combed and brushed, and dressed in freshly washed clothing. Never being tardy and having perfect attendance were standards that were reinforced by my sisters and my mother, but that I did not always fulfill. Nevertheless, they were standards by which I was measured. However, it was not until the day I've already mentioned when Dorothy Jerabek invited Betty, Jean, Mickey, and me to her home for Sunday afternoon tea that I saw something I could imagine to be American.

Without a conscious awareness, I learned that there was not much to be gained by thinking of myself as a Slovene. Since I could not be an Austrian either, I came to accept my mother's advice that in America anyone who studied and worked hard could be successful. In this land of opportunity, nationality did not count against you.

By the time I entered junior high school in the seventh grade, I had become a competitive student, determined to succeed on "their" terms. In order to accomplish this objective, I made it my task to expand the size of my English vocabulary. By systematically studying my dictionary, I supposed that if I learned three new words each day, I could learn all the words there were to know. My method was to look up words at random and write them along with their definitions on cards that I posted on the wall of my bedroom, replacing old ones with new ones and including some words I might have encountered in books. I followed this practice more or less regularly until I finished high school. The dictionary was to be my admission ticket to a successful career.

My parents left Slovenia because it was too poor to give them a decent living and because the New World promised them a different kind of future. My mother was committed to the values of education and social and economic mobility. In her effort to achieve in America a social status relatively equivalent to that of her family in

Kropa, she went to school to study English and ideologically aligned herself in action and word with American socialism. She made it clear to her children that we were to have college educations. My father appreciated his opportunities for steady work and an income that exceeded any of his earlier expectations, but his heritage did not include aspirations for social mobility; when I graduated from high school, he suggested I secure a steady job at Allis Chalmers. Despite my family's lifestyle and its multiple associations with Slovene culture, it cannot be said that I suffered prejudice or discrimination in either the ethnic or Anglo world. In retrospect, the problems I felt about being the son of Slovene immigrants were not projected onto me by others. I created them myself.

2

Coming of Age in West Allis

West Allis was one of Milwaukee's industrial suburbs. It shared with Milwaukee the cultural dominance of early German settlers as well as the political and economic control of Germans, who owned the machine tool industries and the breweries for which the region was famous. The area had been chosen as a place of settlement by a rising bourgeoisie who opposed Germany's 1848 Restoration and who hoped to realize their socialistic ideals on the shores of Lake Michigan. Theirs was not the socialism of Karl Marx that I later learned about at the University of Wisconsin when I read the *Communist Manifesto* in Selig Perlman's course, "Capitalism, Socialism, and Democracy." It was the paternalistic socialism of local elites who took it upon themselves to make Milwaukee a civic-minded, orderly, class-stratified community whose inhabitants were expected to have an enlightened appreciation for culture and learning. As if to point to their city as an example of the acme of civilization, the town fathers had established one of the country's early municipal anthropological museums. As a child on school trips, I saw life-size dioramas of the "pre-civilized" ways of life from places around the world and understood that life in West Allis was on the highest evolutionary plane. Socialism in Milwaukee was administered under the sufferance of an enlightened commercial and industrial bourgeoisie who were self-appointed guardians of public morality and civic virtue. During my time, Dan Hoan was Milwaukee's socialist mayor.

My mother was also a socialist, a political identification she had inherited from her father who had socialized the iron works in Kropa. Socialism in West Allis did not, however, include the political control of the means of production. Instead, in keeping with the spirit of a benevolent industrial bourgeoisie, West Allis acquired its name from Allis Chalmers, the town's dominant business enterprise, the makers of farm equipment and turbines. However, the owners and managers of Allis Chalmers, as well as those of its other machine tool industries, were absentee owners who left no trace of philanthropic stewardship on the town. There was no Allis Chalmers's library, college, or hospital. In West Allis, as in Milwaukee, under a socialist ideology that presupposed governmental responsibility for social welfare, civic benevolence fell under the purview of public administration. The well-being of the mass of workers and small merchants was to be aided and abetted by enlightened social policy. Milwaukee's socialism was a moral and civic socialism created by Lutheran capitalists. When I was growing up, a socialistic infrastructure—including schools, playgrounds, parks, and a reformatory—was already in place.

Washington Park, a short walk from home, had tennis courts, horseshoe pits, a wading pool, and ball fields that were converted into skating and hockey rinks in winter. It had its own clubhouse where athletic equipment could be signed out for temporary use. A Soldiers Home for disabled World War I veterans was located a few blocks from where I lived. It had open spaces, playing fields, and innumerable disabled veterans who welcomed the presence of children in their otherwise segregated enclave. Greenfield Park, a county facility on the western edge of West Allis, contained a full-size swimming pool and a golf course. The City of Milwaukee had public beaches on Lake Michigan, a central library, a historical and anthropological museum that included its own curator, a zoo, and botanical gardens displaying the vegetation of all the world's climates. It also had its own arcade, The Plankinton, in emulation of the Parisian originals studied by Walter Benjamin. In West Allis, we had a Carnegie Library, the only public facility in my memory (except for the Pabst Theater in Milwaukee) that carried the name of a benefactor. We had a farmers' market where I could see and talk with real farmers, and we also had a state fairground where I saw my first cows, hogs, sheep, and farm equipment. In the shadow of this world of ready-made recreational and cultural opportunities, the presence of the reform school acted as a powerful moral constraint.

The State Fairground was located on Greenfield Avenue above and to the north of 76th Street in an area larger than that occupied by Allis Chalmers and was big enough to accommodate speed-car racing, a roller coaster, side shows, animal barns, horse racing, and a football stadium where the Chicago Bears and Green Bay Packers played their games in the 1930s. In one memorable game between the Packers and the Bears, with the Bears leading 18 to 6 in the final three minutes of play, Don Hutson won the game single-handedly with an interception he ran for a touchdown, a punt return of a touchdown, and a running drop kick for a three-point field goal. That was the sort of miracle that could happen at the fairground. I sampled Wisconsin cheeses with names I had never heard before and looked forward from year to year to relishing the taste of a Wisconsin State Fair Cream Puff made with a secret formula. Acting as a magnet that drew visitors from everywhere in the state, the Fair introduced me to the names of towns like Sheboygan, Two Rivers, Racine, Appleton, Fondulac, and Portage. The fairground was even more important to our provincial town than Allis Chalmers.

Milwaukee's civic institutions were within easy reach of West Allis. The Milwaukee public museum and library were introduced to us on school-sponsored excursions designed to expose us to the larger culture. Afterwards, my sisters and I went by ourselves to attend Saturday morning programs on astronomy, evolution, and the early history of Wisconsin. The Milwaukee Zoo, located to the north of West Allis, was less than an hour's walk if we took shortcuts off the main streets. En route to the zoo, we inspected an abandoned quarry, long-since flooded, and stopped to throw rocks into the water to see them splash and to speculate on the number of dead bodies that might lay at its bottom; that the quarry was posted off limits did not deter us. A visit to the zoo gave an opportunity to take the visitors' tour of the Pabst Brewery, also conveniently located along the way. After repeated visits, this tour became boring, but we took it anyway because at its end, each visitor was given a stein of beer. Our ages did not matter. This was Milwaukee where beer was a form of wholesome food. To us youngsters from West Allis, the animals—polar bears, giraffes, monkeys, lions, alligators—were like a world tour. When we used the expression "monkey sees as monkey does" to describe a "copycat," we acknowledged the primates as our genealogical ancestors.

The farmers' market was an important community institution for both the townspeople, many of whom had a rural past in the old country, and for the truck farmers whose farms were located at the western edge of urban development. For us children, it had other meanings. It was there that we could meet farmers who needed weeders and pickers willing to work for twenty-five cents per hour. Upon finishing work, we repaired to the Greenfield Park golf course and played eighteen holes. We played with clubs purchased at pawn shops adjacent to Milwaukee's modest little red-light district on Wells Street between 5th and 6th Streets in the downtown area off Wisconsin Avenue.

Amid the clutter of exotic objects available in the pawn shops, one could buy a driver, putter, and a couple of irons, and still have enough money left over to pay for admission to the nearby striptease parlors to watch a midday performance. The women wore high heels, pasties on their breasts, and small coverings over the pubic area while prancing on an elevated platform. For my golfing buddies and me, this seemed to be the ultimate in manly sophistication, but its commercial crudity and the audience of depraved old men destroyed the high expectations of anticipatory excitement. We were still too young to be exposed to sleazy, mundane eroticism that contradicted our romanticized images of our girlfriends. The farmers' market was our territory. Late on a Saturday night, a bushel of tomatoes at the edge of their life expectancy could be bought for fifty cents from our employers. For ten cents apiece, five of us could buy a bushel and have a "tomato war," throwing them at each other as if they were snowballs, a form of recreation not sanctioned by the town fathers. When I was growing up, this civic arena was my world. Compared to what my parents told me about Kropa, I knew I was better off in West Allis.

My Political Education

When I was ten years old, in 1932, early in the Depression, my mother took me to a political rally in honor of Norman Thomas, then a candidate for President of the United States. His opponents in the election were Herbert Hoover and Franklin D. Roosevelt. Our family, like those of other Milwaukee socialists, had contributed to Thomas's campaign and was invited to a reception in his honor. Taking me to this event was part of my mother's effort to give me a political education. I have no memory of what Norman Thomas said in his speech, but I recall being introduced to him. He seemed exceptionally tall and very friendly, even friendlier than I thought he should be, considering he had no idea who we were; what was this man doing talking to my mother as if he knew her? When my mother introduced me, he patted me on the head, treating me like a little boy, a paternalistic gesture that offended my sense of importance as a participant in what I thought was a family affair of great political significance. It did not take me long to learn that Thomas, despite my having met him, would never be President. My mother later changed her mind about him and from 1936 onward voted for Roosevelt and continued to vote for Democrats the rest of her life. Nevertheless, this experience was one of the causes of my later efforts to try to understand socialism.

Family discussion at the dinner table centered on the world economic crisis and the paths possible to its political solution. Roosevelt's election led to high hopes for a quick recovery that did not materialize until years later, and then only as a result of military preparations for World War II. It was common to compare America's economic policies with those of Germany and the Soviet Union and also to compare the Soviet Union's with those of Germany after the rise of Hitler. In 1932, early in the Depression, communism and fascism were seriously considered as alternatives to capitalism. Some of my friends' parents who were German were sympathetic to Hitler because he had solved the problem of unemployment. Others—including Finns, Scandinavians, and Eastern Europeans—who were or had been socialists became communists or Soviet sympathizers; underpaid and underemployed Allis Chalmers workers were radicalized.

Among people on the dole there was little sympathy for "Big Business": Big Businessmen were either "plutocrats" or "economic royalists," labels then commonly used in the press. The long depression held my family and my friends' families in thrall for a decade.

It activated my father's political consciousness. With the repeal of Prohibition in 1933, his business had crumbled. When he sold it in 1936, he was forty-eight years old, unemployed, and without prospects for another career until my mother and he bought two rooming houses on Knapp Street in downtown Milwaukee, of which my father became superintendent. But before that, he lived for two years in a household managed by his wife. It was under the circumstances of idleness and frustration that he turned to drinking as a source of support and to the radio for access to the outside world. His was a plight well described in E. Wight Bakke's book *The Unemployed Worker.* Our RCA Victor with turntable attached occupied a conspicuous corner in the living room. Besides listening to Jack Benny and Rochester (sponsored by Jell-O) and Eddie Cantor, he and I listened to the news reports and analyses of domestic and world events including those programmed on Sunday afternoons by the University of Chicago Round Table Forum, whose discussants included Robert Hutchins (president of the university and self-defined educator of the public); Frank Knight (economist and translator of Max Weber's economic lectures); and Harry Gideonse (social scientist, anticommunist, and after World War II, president of Brooklyn College, and still later, my colleague when he was appointed Chancellor of The New School for Social Research). On Sunday afternoons, the Chicago Forum recapped and interpreted the week's economic and political events; I could have gotten a good education from the Forum had I been prepared to receive it.

The radio also carried Hitler's speeches in simultaneous translation, and Father Coughlin's homiletics, delivered from his pulpit in Detroit, in which he advocated a form of Christian fascism resembling that being applied in Germany. Charles Lindbergh, the "Lone Eagle," who had visited German aircraft factories and saw a future for air warfare in which the United States could not match the quality of Germany's air force, admired Hitler and Goering. Henry Ford, one of Roosevelt's bitterest enemies even to the point of resisting Roosevelt's early efforts to rearm the country, supported with his philanthropy both Father Coughlin and Gerald L. K. Smith, publisher of *The Cross and the Flag* and a Protestant Christian advocate of an American fascism. In those days, the country was deeply divided on issues of economics and on intervention versus nonintervention in the affairs of Europe. Only later, under conditions of wartime propaganda, did Germany become an implacable enemy. Listening to the radio with my father taught me that there were no easy solutions to complicated political problems. Competing political appeals and discussions about them were just that, not a means to the resolution of the social problems caused by the Depression.

Nevertheless, the 1930s bred many political messiahs. A case in point was Philip LaFollette, then the Governor of Wisconsin, who in 1938 tried to launch the National Progressives of America in an effort to seize the presidency at the University of Wisconsin's football stadium, using the technique of the mass rally to dramatize the announcement of his candidacy. Delivering his speech from a platform decorated with larger-than-life portrait posters of himself, he borrowed some of the techniques of mass propaganda invented by Goebbels. The state of Wisconsin, an incipient welfare state that regulated the commodities and labor markets, had already played a role as God's surrogate to create a just state.

Roosevelt had used the idea of the mass rally when he gave a political speech in Chicago, but LaFollette's approach had an added evangelical quality to it, reminiscent of a Christian call to arms. LaFollette was predisposed to outdo Roosevelt on his own terms. He emulated Hitler's Nuremberg rallies with their combination of elaborate mass choreography, dramatic lighting, martial music, and politics as theater. He presented himself as a leader who could deliver his audience out of the abyss. If this new political style was a descendant of evangelical calls for religious renewal and revival, then both Hitler and LaFollette had simply adopted and perfected the techniques of Protestant revivalism. In the peak years of the Depression, people were looking for leaders and there were many self-proclaimed, self-confident candidates anxious to lead.

In the mid-1930s, Paul Robeson came to Milwaukee to perform the lead in "Othello." He was known for his Soviet sympathies and had recently made a much heralded tour through the Union. Taking advantage of an opportunity to expose me to another political and cultural figure, my mother took me to see his performance at the Pabst Theater on the corner of Water and Wells Streets, a place otherwise thought to be for the cultural elite of the city. Without my realizing it at the time, I was being groomed to think that politics and the higher cultural life were things to which I could aspire.

Some Social Training

My mother's tutelage included a watchful eye for my physical appearance. My clothing was selected for me on shopping trips with my sisters to Wisconsin Avenue's Gimbels and the Boston Store, which the women in the family thought were purveyors of the latest fashions. We did not shop at the clothing stores in West Allis. My first suits had knicker pants, but as I grew older, and especially when

I entered high school, I was dressed in herringbone tweeds with long pants. Pauline knitted my sweaters from fashionably correct designs printed in knitting magazines. They were conversation pieces that caught the attention of the girls. On one occasion, I decided to shop for myself. With my own money earned from my newspaper route, I purchased a pair of working man's shoes at a haberdashery on Greenfield Avenue just north of Allis Chalmers on 71st Street, owned by the father of Leon Schur, my high school friend (later to become a dean at the University of Wisconsin in Milwaukee), who was then tending the store. When I brought them home, I was criticized for my bad taste. Humiliated, I never wore them. Nor, however, could I return them and face the further humiliation of having to explain my error. My standards for appropriate attire were set by the women in my family, leaving me free to pretend that my appearance was of no concern to me, while enjoying the admiration and attention I received for it from my friends.

When I was fourteen or fifteen, in the ninth grade, at about the time dancing events began to be held at school, the committee of women determined that I be enrolled in the Arthur Murray School of Dance, located on Greenfield Avenue at 62nd Street in a second-floor space adjacent to the Paradise Theater. The only dancing I had done before this was at the Turner Hall on 4th Street and National, where my parents' Slovenian Club held its social events and dinners on occasional Sunday afternoons. On those festive occasions, adults danced the polka. We children imitated awkwardly and exaggeratedly to the music of accordions. But I thought of the polka as a foreign thing, at least not American, and therefore not a dance at all. Arthur Murray specialized in the two-step, waltzes, the fox trot, and, not only that, the instructor was an attractive woman who held you close to her while teaching the steps. I liked it and knew it gave me an advantage with the girls that my friends did not have. I am not exaggerating the care and attention given to my training in the social graces. By the time I willingly went to dances—the high school prom, for example—I knew that the orchid was something you had to bring to your date, as she was then called. When I was preparing for my departure to attend my first year at the University of Wisconsin, my mother took me to be fitted for a tuxedo, a garment she thought was essential for a young man who was beginning his university career. I accepted such attention to my wardrobe and training in the social graces as if, naturally, that is the way a boy could expect to be trained, never thinking what my sisters thought of the disproportionate attention given to me.

Schoolboy Entrepreneur

My mother believed that in addition to appearances, the requirements for success included hard work, education, and determination. As a successful entrepreneur herself, she encouraged my efforts to make my own money, but I had my own reasons for wanting to be a newsboy.

From the age of eight or nine, going to the Paradise Theater Saturday matinee to see serialized episodes of "Rin-Tin-Tin" or "The Lone Ranger," a movie, and the Pathe News, was something I could do only with parental permission and their money. I would plead with my mother, who could hold her ground despite my badgering and entreating her for the price of admission to the theater. Being denied without recourse taught me the limits of persuasion. When I was still in grade school and without money, I was not averse to stealing a nickel or dime from my mother's purse that was always stuffed with coins. It was easy enough to get into and out of her purse without being caught (and she never caught me, nor apparently did she discover that anything was missing), but it was a risky practice and I only did it because I lacked another means to my end. I already understood that honesty was the better policy. Even then, however, I did not like to ask my parents for money because I thought it made me dependent upon them. My income from the paper route solved my money problems and put my career as a thief behind me.

When I became a newsboy, I had my own pocket money and what I thought was financial independence from my parents; we did not then know of the custom sometimes followed in middle-class families of a regular weekly allowance. My conception of independence and self-sufficiency pertained mainly to paying my own way to the movies, having money to go on dates, buying my own bicycle, and having money in my pocket when I wanted a candy bar or ice cream. My parents encouraged both my efforts at being independent and my entrepreneurial activities.

When I was not yet twelve, I took my first job as a legally underage newspaper boy for the *Milwaukee Journal*. My task was hawking newspapers on a street corner on 48th Street and National Avenue, an intersection just east of the Soldiers Home, where cars were required to stop when the light was red. A corner boy wore a green *Milwaukee Journal* apron with four change pockets and was required to stand on the curb and flash the paper to potential customers in passing cars. To be caught sitting at any time during the two-hour rush period was harshly disapproved by my manager, who, I discovered when I entered Horace Mann Junior High School in September, was engaged to my seventh-grade teacher Lenore Fidler, a discovery that taught me the meaning of a network. The price of a copy of the *Milwaukee Journal* was three cents, two of which I gave to my manager and one of which I kept. On any one day I could sell thirty papers, thus netting thirty cents, not counting an occasional tip. For the six-day week, I usually netted more than two dollars. Part of my job as a street vendor was to commit the casual buyer to a subscription for home delivery. Lining up enough home delivery customers meant a promotion to a home delivery route with fifty to seventy-five customers. By the end of the summer, I had my own route and had saved enough to buy a bicycle on sale at Gimbels for twenty-six dollars, which gave me the transportation I needed to pedal the route.

A route carrier delivered both the daily and Sunday editions; the latter cost ten cents and netted two cents for the carrier. Collections were made weekly at the rate of twenty-eight cents; a route of fifty customers netted four dollars per week for the carrier, not counting tips. Without exception, home delivery customers were sympathetic to the newsboy, usually giving a two-cent tip and rarely failing to pay on time. In the eyes of the customer, the newsboy was an exemplar of the ambitious American boy, committed to the ideal of work and service, diligently delivering the newspaper every day of the year. This image was in part fostered by the manager who monitored the carriers' appearance and use of language, frowning on profanity and insisting upon punctuality and politeness in dealing with the customers. The place where we picked up our daily allotment of papers was also a kind of finishing school in newsboys' etiquette. For central management, our training was linked to maintaining and increasing subscriber lists: a carrier could forfeit his route if he lost subscribers. Advertising rates, the key to profits in the newspaper business, were largely dependent upon the number of home delivery subscriptions and thus upon the initiative and salesmanship of route carriers. Central management regularly held subscription drives in which carriers could compete for prizes, awarding those who met quotas for soliciting new home delivery customers. I won several prizes, including a *Milwaukee Journal* four-wheel coaster wagon (which I could haul my papers in when connected to my bike) and a week's stay at a *Milwaukee Journal* summer camp (my first camping experience). I liked making money and winning prizes and, as a further reward, my parents were proud of me.

My success as a salesboy for selling new subscriptions was based upon earning the potential customer's sympathy for my cause. To achieve this end, I used one method with two variations—my sales pitch always worked better if the "lady of the house" answered the door because it was easiest to elicit sympathy from women. I told my "mark" that I was working for a prize and that I could win it if she would sign on as a daily and Sunday subscriber for a period of at least two months. If that did not work and more pressure was required, I added that I needed only one more subscriber to win my prize, putting my mark in the position of depriving this sincere, wholesome boy of his reward. My method worked even in cases where the economic hardship of a family should have led to a refusal: I can almost hear the wife explaining to her husband, "But he's such a nice boy." In my ruthless innocence, I had learned a fundamental technique of the American "con man," gaining the sympathetic confidence of the mark so thoroughly described in all its variations by Herman Melville in *The Confidence Man*.

In late August of each year, during the week of the Wisconsin State Fair, the *Journal* required all of its West Allis carriers, while wearing the green apron, to hawk papers at the fairground. Although few fairgoers, except for some exhibitors, cared to read newspapers, the *Journal* wanted itself advertised to the statewide audience. My carrier colleagues and I walked the fairground for seven days, in effect as walking billboards for the paper's advertising department, carrying an armload of papers that few wished to buy. We spent our days, from nine in the morning until three in the afternoon when we delivered our routes, exploring the fair, selling a few papers, discarding some to keep up appearances, and paying for them ourselves. We believed that the fairground was a place where it was easy to find money on the ground. If you kept your eyes open, you could sometimes find coins or even a dollar bill someone had lost; our code was, "Losers weepers, finders keepers." The fairground was a place where you did not want to encounter girlfriends while wearing the apron; otherwise, it was the worldly place to be.

I peddled papers throughout the years of junior and senior high school. My last *Journal* route had seventy-five customers and was located between National and Greenfield Avenues on the east side of 74th Street and the west side of 75th, a small area with a dense middle-class *Journal* readership including several of my teachers and the principal Ralph West. The route could be delivered in less than half an hour. I had reached the zenith of the carrier's career only to discover that my route interfered with my after-school extracurricular activities. With regrets, I sold the lucrative *Journal* route and began delivering the *Sentinel*, a morning paper then considered inferior to the *Journal* and a step down in the newspaper status hierarchy, but I could deliver it before school.

One of my *Sentinel* customers, the proprietor of a dry cleaning establishment, hired me to fire up his steam boiler each morning for an additional two dollars per week. This meant that he trusted me to enter his establishment when he was not present, a situation that on one occasion tested my honesty. One morning, I found a dollar bill lying on the floor. Should I take it or not? I decided not to take it on the grounds that the owner may have deliberately planted the money in order to test my honesty. What would I say if I were to take the money, and he had known it was there? I chose not to risk being caught and established myself as an honest person at the cost of one dollar.

With my newspaper earnings, I opened another account in the Wisconsin State Savings Bank, thinking of my savings as the money I needed to finance my college education. This was independence. I saw no distinction between it and my dependence on my parents for clothing, food, and housing. Illusion that it was, my parents never challenged it, but rather encouraged it as if understanding that I had to make my own way as they had when they abandoned Slovenia and came to America.

School Boy

My mother regarded my report cards as important documents, so much so that she saved them until she died. For her, they were a measure of my progress and the successful attainment of her aspirations. Her faith in the importance of the report card was determined by the note to parents that the superintendent had included on it:

> This report is an attempt to give you a condensed picture of your child's activities in school. This report on these activities covers regular school subjects and also the varied extra-curricular activities in which the pupil is engaged....Your child is also acquiring habits of life. Parents are asked to review these reports carefully and to cooperate with the principal and teachers in the guidance of the pupil.... Special reports are sometimes mailed when students are not making satisfactory progress.

I brought home a report card three times each semester. On it, in addition to grades, teachers' marginal comments were included.

For example, Ms. Margaretha Meyne, 12A, "Government Problems," wrote, "Test and recitation A-, but notebook organization not up to par." Other notations on the card included days absent and times tardy. My mother took careful note of information like this and required satisfactory explanations for what she regarded as delinquencies. Since I had to get my parents' signatures (actually, my mother signed for herself and forged my father's signature) before returning the card to my homeroom teacher, I was careful to contrive excuses and explanations in advance, rehearsing my answers ahead of time on my way home. The signing of the card remains etched in my mind as a ceremonial occasion.

The report served multiple functions, but not the same ones for my parents as for me. Besides being a measure of academic performance, it also assured my parents that I was in good standing with school officials. Lacking firsthand experience with the American school system—the larger milieu of extra-curricular activities, boy-girl relations, friends unknown to them—the report gave them assurances of my good behavior. It meant that I could be trusted to do the right thing.

It did not take me long to understand that it was to my advantage to bring home a good report. In order to get acceptable grades, I mastered the techniques required to get them. I made myself conspicuous to my teachers by participating in class discussions. I learned to read the assignments on time and to cram before exams. Studying the dictionary and coming up with new words always helped: in a class recitation I once used the word "irregardless" only to be told by my teacher that this usage was "redundant, 'regardless' would be sufficient," but the mere attempt to punctuate my remarks with an unexpected word left a good impression. Efforts like these paid off. They not only produced good reports, but they also inflated my academic self-confidence. From the point of view of my parents, they confirmed my diligence and gave me a substantial degree of autonomy from parental supervision.

My report card earned me the key to the house and the freedom to come and go as I pleased. Even when I wanted to use one of the cars and asked permission to have it, my problem was not obtaining its use, but rather whom to ask. I usually asked my mother first. She advised me to ask my father. When I asked my father, he said: "Ask your ma." I went back to my mother saying, "Pa said to ask you." My mother seemed to want to involve my father in decisions concerning me, but he knew he had already lost his authority, and, moreover, had no basis for making a decision, knowing even less about my affairs than my mother. This buck-passing ritual never entailed a refusal. For my parents it may have meant that neither of them wanted to take the responsibility in case something happened. For me, it was a ritual I had to go through in order to use the car when I needed it, no questions asked.

One snowy night, on returning home from a school dance, I wrecked the family DeSoto in an attempt to avoid hitting another car. Given the autonomy granted to me by a father who understood almost nothing of my world and a mother who in blind faith invested so much in me, it was no surprise that the incident was treated matter-of-factly, without a scolding, as if this were something that might be expected. Their only demand was that I use my bank savings to replace the damaged vehicle, a punishment that freed me of guilt. This treatment was consistent with the unqualified approval my actions were usually given. That my parents never withdrew their trust and support strikes me as the ultimate sacrifice immigrant parents make for their children. Thorstein Veblen, also a son of immigrant parents, called it "the parental bent," the responsibility that the preceding generation has for those who follow.

Reflecting on my schooling in West Allis, I have difficulty remembering what I learned or some of the subjects I studied. In Horace Mann Junior High School on 62nd Street, boys were required to study printing, woodworking, electricity, and metalworking, basic skills that might lead to a job as an apprentice; what I know about carpentry and electrical circuitry, I owe to Horace Mann Junior High. In our metalworking class, I made a mold of Abraham Lincoln's profile and cast it in molten metal. This was a solid object I could take home and show my parents. In print shop, I sat on a high stool facing a large tray of type to be placed, letter by letter, word by word, properly spaced and printed on a manually inked and operated printer. I tried joining the school band as a trombonist, but just as I had failed as a violinist in grade school, so I failed as a trombonist. I did no better in my art class. I remember it only because the class collectively made a mural that ran the length of three walls. There were also English, history, and science classes. For my research project in science, I chose to do a report on an article I had found in a science magazine in the school library. The subject was lymph nodes. Working closely with my "primary source," I described the location of nodes and their functions. My teacher, who probably knew as little about the subject as I, was impressed with my report and effusive in her compliments. I was less impressed than she because I had done no more than digest and summarize the contents of the one article, not a creative task. Yet because the exercise required a close reading and comprehension, I have never forgotten where my lymph nodes are. If there was a social studies class, I have no memory of it, but I do remember an inexplicably low grade from my English teacher only to discover, when I asked for an explanation of it, that he had made a clerical error in recording my mark and changed it before I took the report home. I try to explain to myself why I cannot evoke sharp images of the substance of what I might have learned at Horace Mann, but no explanation is forthcoming. I suppose that those experiences have been crowded out and layered over by the overpowering residues of later ones.

Official educational doctrine with regard to sex was premised on the Protestant Ethic of suppressing and controlling all erotic impulses. Social life in junior high school had less to do with girls than it had in grade school where we boys already had a healthy interest in what girls had and we did not, and where I considered Betty Meyer to be my girlfriend. In junior high, girls were taller and more physically advanced than I, still small, and not gaining my full height until I entered college. While the erotic impulses did not abate, segregation of the sexes was enhanced. Girls were placed in home economics classes and boys in the manual arts as if to teach us that girls were mothers and homemakers and boys were fathers and breadwinners. Gym classes were rigorously segregated, and girls wore uniforms that disguised their individuality. Girls became Girl Scouts and boys Boy Scouts, associations that the school sponsored, providing a teacher as a leader. Scouts programs were after-school activities, but they were not highly organized. We had neither uniforms nor the training exercises required to win badges on the way to becoming Eagle Scouts. When our troop met, we pledged allegiance and wrestled and punched each other for a few hours, but we never went on hikes or overnight camping trips. Scouting was a way to segregate boys and girls and to keep us off the streets for a few hours. Despite the segregation of the sexes, sex was in our minds but remained at the level of innocent curiosity. I had kissed Betty Meyer when I was in the sixth grade but did not kiss a girl again until I was in high school. In junior high school, sex went underground and was restrained. Some of the restraints were self-imposed, like limiting discussions of it to the subject of classifying girls according to their looks and the size of their breasts. Inhibitions had set in, but this did not prevent some of the more aggressive boys from attempting to peek into the girls' dressing room. We lived at a time when one never saw a man and woman in bed together in a Hollywood movie. In my day, the older Puritanical prohibitions of public displays of eroticism were still in effect.

In the sexually wholesome corridors of Horace Mann, in the eighth grade, our cultural tastes were satisfied by a class production of "Hansel and Gretel," performed for admiring parents in the school auditorium. As I saw it, "Hansel and Gretel" was a story about the ancient past, having no relevance to my immediate life. If my mother had not saved the playbill for the May 24, 1935, performance in which I was a member of the chorus, I would have no memory of this event. I learned from another playbill for "Treasure Island," performed by my class a year later, that I played the lead role as Jim in a production directed by Miss Aurelius. There in the playbill are the names of my teachers and of my classmates, revealing the ethnic diversity so characteristic of West Allis. As mnemonics, the playbills led me to remembrances of a lost past. As Emily Dickinson once said, "The past is not a package one can lay away."

Despite the singing I may have done when acting as Jim, music was not my forte. I wanted to be on the Student Council and to become class president. In the ninth grade, I achieved both of these ambitions, convincing myself that I could be a leader and assured that I was popular. Of course, holding offices like this did not entail much more than seeking and getting them. From a pedagogical point of view, however, selecting candidates and holding elections were supposed to be exercises in the American democratic practice. We were being taught electoral procedures and how to run for political offices, a kind of lesson in civics that I viewed as a popularity contest. As president of the class in the ninth grade, I planned and executed the class's school-wide fundraising project, a drive to collect saleable wastepaper and metal objects (empty metal toothpaste tubes, not the plastic ones we have now, were a big item) to be sold to the proprietor of the local junkyard owned by the Jewish scrap dealer, known to us as the "Sheenie." Those were the Depression years when nothing was wasted, let alone sent to the dump, our form of a civic-minded recycling and waste-management system. By generating sufficient student enthusiasm and under skilled management, the scrap drive could net the class more than one hundred dollars. It was my job as class president to mobilize the student body for the drive. I exhorted them at general assembly meetings and conducted a poster campaign. Since everything had to be collected in one day, the idea was to get students to think and talk about scrap, so that on the assigned day they would remember to bring their contributions and place them in the bins provided by the dealer. If students forgot to bring the scrap in the morning, they had a second chance in the afternoon when they went home for lunch. My assistants spotted forgetful students and urged them to return with contributions in the afternoon. The drive was successful, and the class could take pride in its collective communal effort for a job well done, providing us with a sense that we had accomplished something. We took it for granted that our class was the best ever and in our chauvinism believed our successors could not surpass us. This was a blind faith in our superiority attributable to the self-centered innocence of fifteen-year-old children. I was a self-confident believer and promulgator of this faith.

Full of my apparent success as an organizer and advertiser, my reaction was to do it again. My suggestion to my teachers that we have another drive the next semester was rejected. Despite their disapproval, I decided to do it on my own authority, a brash act on which I staked my reputation. Over my teachers' objections, I set a date, arranged for the bins, and took on the job of advertising the event. Under fire to succeed and vindicate myself to my teachers, I spread a rumor among classmates telling them to expect to hear an important announcement, telling no one of my project. A week before the drive, I posted nine-inch-by-twelve-inch sheets of paper in the school's corridors, inconspicuous signs announcing the new drive. In large red letters, I printed the word "announcement" and drew an arrow from it to the bottom of the page where the day of the second drive was specified in small type, along with the words, "We can do it again," signed Art Vidich. My assumption was that students had already been trained to respond, but this time did not need—or perhaps want—exhortation but might want to regain the feeling of communal unity and accomplishment. The scrap was collected and we earned seventy dollars—half the amount we netted in the first campaign, but still enough to be considered a face-saving success. I took pleasure in proving to my teachers that I could do it. Without knowing it, I had learned my first lesson in the Machiavellian exploitation of mass psychology, and I liked it.

That my teachers tolerated my effrontery, or at least did not exact a price for flaunting their authority, may have been because they thought they were cultivating a political leader. They gave me all the authority I usurped and, like indulgent parents, let me test my limits.

It was as if they were surrogate parents guiding us not only in academic subjects but preparing us, the children of immigrants, to take our place in a world for which our parents could not prepare us.

It was almost natural to think of my teachers as surrogate parents for, in fact, many of them did not have children of their own and made their students the beneficiaries of their maternal and paternal impulses. Miss Martha Neprud, my high school English teacher, entertained her students in her apartment on the lakefront in downtown Milwaukee. In addition to teaching grammar, she told me what she thought of my choice of girlfriends and that I was "fickle" when I changed from one to another: I knew that Miss Neprud was watching over me. Peter Warner, director of the High School YMCA Club (Hi-Y), invited club members to his home on Layton Boulevard where he lived with his widowed mother. Hi-Y was his passion, and he took its motto, "The Quest for the Best," as his personal mandate. If ushers were needed for school events, Mr. Warner provided Hi-Y members. He held weekly club meetings on Mondays at 7:30 in Room 148, where speakers, each representing a different occupation, told us about career possibilities—Warner's version of guidance counseling. He supervised the elaborate annual performance of the "Hi-Y Minstrel and Vaudeville Show," designed to raise money for club members' scholarships. When members graduated, Mr. Warner followed their careers as a father might do. It was easy to think of Peter Warner as a father figure or an older brother and a teacher because he made no distinction between his private and occupational lives.

Many of my teachers lived within walking distance of their classrooms. Three of them, including the high school principal whose daughter was my girlfriend, were customers on my paper route on streets adjacent to the school. Mr. John Plichta, my high school American history teacher, and Ms. Dorothy Jarabek, my sixth-grade teacher, lived in my immediate neighborhood. In West Allis, you could unexpectedly meet your teachers on the streets or in shopping areas. Teachers walked to school just as the students did. There were no parking lots at this school: you either took the trolley or went on foot. The ubiquity of the teachers meant that there were no anonymous students at West Allis High.

In part, such student-teacher relations were a phenomenon peculiar to the Depression decade. Teachers' jobs were both scarce and well paid compared to the prevailing wage rates in white-collar occupations. The market for teaching jobs was competitive. To secure a job at West Allis High School required at least a master's degree, and my teachers had MA or MS degrees from schools such as Columbia, Chicago, Wisconsin, Iowa, Minnesota, and Indiana. The structure of the labor market was conducive to making the career of a teacher a way of life, a vocation dedicated to students and the community, even at the sacrifice of personal freedom. That teachers were *in loco parentis* was something real.

Some Contradictions in My Education

High school was a place where all possibilities seemed to be open. Having mastered the techniques for keeping up my grade average, I turned my energies to extra-curricular activities. I joined the debating team, played on the tennis squad, and became a library helper. In Latin class, Tony Tratar and I published, partly in Latin with the help of a pony, the *Roman Gazette* under the *noms de plumes* Antonio Tratario and Arturo Vidicchio and by-lined our articles "Associated Press." I joined the Hi-Y Club and became its president and co-master of ceremonies at its annual "Minstrel and Vaudeville Show," was elected a member of the Student Council, became president of the senior class, and delivered the "President's Address" at the Senior Honor Assembly Program. I remember all these facts because my mother preserved all the documents that certify them. When I was in high school, I liked to be at the center of things and to collect as many presidencies as I could. Largely under Peter Warner's guidance, I was well on my way to becoming a certified Rotarian. High school was the place where my plan to pursue a political career was born.

School authorities aided my ambitions by selecting me to participate in Badger Boys State, a one-week camp dedicated to the propagation of the ideals of American democratic political practice. Boys like me, selected from schools throughout Wisconsin, were brought together for the sole purpose of conducting a mock political campaign for the selection of candidates and the election of officers for state government positions: governor, lieutenant governor, secretary of state, and attorney general. Campaigning began the evening of the first day. I decided on that day to run for governor and began to recruit staff and followers, including a campaign manager and workers to make posters ("Art Vidich for Governor") from materials allocated equally to all aspirants. Platforms were concocted in a hurry and campaign speeches readied for delivery. Needless to say there were plenty of candidates—almost as many as there were voters. In order to reduce the number of candidates, opposing groups combined and made trades, votes for offices, and amalgamations of political platforms. The point of the exercise was to teach a lesson in the arts of pragmatic political compromise and by that means to be a winner. For idealistic and ambitious youth, it was an edifying experience in political realism, and it was the first election I lost—and the last in which I ran for governor.

In contrast to the Boys' State political ethic of winning for the rewards of winning, the Young Men's Christian Association (YMCA), the parent organization of Hi-Y, fostered the ideals of sportsmanship and brotherhood. As a member of the Hi-Y Club, I was automatically affiliated with the YMCA in downtown Milwaukee. There I could sign up for swimming lessons and play on another baseball team and meet boys from other schools including those from Milwaukee's North Shore. This gave me an opportunity to measure myself against competitors from the upper-middle classes of Shorewood and Whitefish Bay, whom I thought of as the "real Americans," but I was a good ballplayer and could see that they were no better than I. The YMCA stood for the idea of social uplift and equality, and I was a ready-made recipient for it.

As part of his paternal project, Peter Warner managed the Hi-Y Club to make successes and socially responsible citizens of "his boys." At each week's meeting he presented us with civic-minded speakers who spoke about themselves and their careers as if to offer us examples from which to choose our own careers. One impressive speaker, a Harvard graduate and lawyer who left a lasting impression on me, was Carter Wells. He was handsome, self-confident, elegant, and sophisticated; to my eyes, he was worldly in every respect, someone whom I wanted to be like. My friend John Gustafson and I spoke with him after his speech and continued our conversation with him in his car when he offered to drive us home. The subject was what we (unconnected sons of immigrants) could do with our lives. I confided in him about my plans to enter politics, perhaps beginning by running in West Allis for the area's congressional seat. His advice shocked me. He advised against a political career and thought it more important to make money, suggesting that if he had it to do over again, he would go into cosmetics where the real money was—"cosmetics are 98 percent water." Making real money was not a possibility I had thought of, and my admiration for this elegant Harvard graduate was suddenly tinged with ambivalence about his integrity even while I could understand that my own ambitions were equally self-serving.

Hi-Y was a club that fostered an adventuresome spirit. Having suffered no real defeats—at least none that I was prepared to acknowledge—in my high school career, and gaining confidence in my ability to make my way in the world, I had the idea that I wanted to go to New York to see the World's Fair of 1939. This was during the summer after completing my junior year. In league with my friend John Gustafson, we determined to get there by bicycle, the same means we used to explore Milwaukee's environs. We persisted in our plan in the face of parental objections, until finally my parents offered us the use of our 1930 eight-cylinder maroon Nash touring car, complete with running boards, trunk, and spare tire mounted on the front fender. This was an unexpected windfall that led us to elaborate our plans into a much larger project. Recruiting our fellow *Milwaukee Journal* route carriers and classmates Clint Warwick and Oiva Maki, we projected a trip through Canada and the eastern United States with stopovers in New York City and Washington, DC, where I hoped to meet John C. Schafer, the Congressman representing West Allis. At a cost of sixty dollars per person, we projected a six-week trip following a route that included as many of our collective relatives as we could induce to accept and entertain us; to the extent possible, we hoped to hop from relative to relative. Our plan was to operate within a budget of $240 by mooching, sleeping in the car, carrying food in the car's trunk, and paying ten cents per gallon for gas. It never occurred to us that we might telephone home for additional funds if we fell short; that would have been the equivalent of admitting failure. We worked with a finite budget and intended to make do with it.

Leaving Milwaukee on Highway 41 bound for Chicago en route to Detroit, our destination the first day was the home of friends my parents had known in Slovenia. In fact, I had met them before when they had visited us in West Allis. On that visit, the family had brought along their son who was about the same age as my oldest sister Pauline, and there was the implication that the parents were trying to make a match. Nothing came of it, but the idea that parents might have such plans left me with a bad taste about these friends—not only that they might have such intentions, but that my parents might think that Pauline should marry a Slovene, not exactly an American thing to do. However, when my parents suggested that we stop to see these friends in Detroit, I had a sudden change of heart about them because they gave us a place to eat and sleep on our first day of travel. As might be expected, the cuisine and beverages were like home and served generously to the four of us. These friends and their friends were workers in the automotive factories of Detroit at a time when the industry, except for Ford, was just beginning to gear up in preparation for war. The industrial plants in Detroit were enormous compared to Allis-Chalmers in West Allis. In Detroit, everything was about cars and what was not about cars was about Slovenia.

John Gustafson's Swedish Aunt Emma Peterson lived on a farm in Galeton, Pennsylvania, our second stop. She was John's mother's sister, a farmer's widow, with a school-teacher daughter, cousin Doris. Going from the heart of industrial America to a bucolic setting, complete with swimming hole and an exotic Scandinavian cuisine, led us to extend our visit for three or four days—every extra day was calculated as a way of saving money. Our next stop was Buffalo with John's cousin Hilder, where we stayed in a tiny apartment, all four of us gratefully sleeping on the floor in exchange for the opportunity to see Niagara Falls, one of America's great natural wonders, something to talk about when we returned home.

After that, we cruised through Canada to Quebec (my first experience in a place where French is spoken). There we bought soft drinks on the verandah of a hotel overlooking the city—my lasting memory of Quebec, a city to which I have never returned. We then continued down along the coast of Maine to Boston, Plymouth Rock, Beacon Hill, and Bunker Hill, Paul Revere's ride, and Harvard Yard's statue of John Harvard. From there, we forged on directly to New Haven and Yale to complete our scrutiny of what Damon Runyan called "the Harvards and the Yales." None of us had relatives in New England, nor did we sign into any tourist cabins, as motels were then known. Instead, we slept in the car, drove long hours, carried our own water, and stopped at the roadside to relieve ourselves. We drove in as straight a line as possible to my Aunt Agnes's place at 22-44 42nd Street, Queens, New York, where we stayed as honored guests for a full week.

With Agnes as chaperone and tour guide, we saw the wonders of the future on display at the World's Fair. We saw our first television, models of autos yet to be produced, and household products designed for the homes of America the Beautiful. The Fair loudly proclaimed that the Depression was over, and for New York at least, this seemed to be the case. Robert Moses had been hard at work on construction projects that revitalized the city and the region. Exuding optimism, Agnes proudly gave us a tour of Moses's Triborough Bridge and a day at Jones Beach to which we drove via the Southern State Parkway and over Robert Moses's causeway. Four young, impressionable boys got a taste of the Big City and ate it up. This was something to write home about, but we had no time for that.

Clint Warwick, the only one among us with an English name, had family friends in Washington. Theirs was another small apartment with sleeping accommodations on the floor. Apart from the monuments, the big thing in Washington was the Federal Bureau of Investigation and J. Edgar Hoover's campaign against the likes of John Dillinger, Pretty Boy Floyd, and other desperadoes. The FBI was set up for innocent tourists like us, and we willingly had our fingerprints taken for the newly created national fingerprint archive. We also visited the mint where we saw thousands of sheets of currency of various denominations being printed on the presses at an astounding rate. We learned how money was made, but we had to wonder who would dispose of it and what would be done with it. It was the year of the 76th Congress in 1939, and I was determined to visit the office of my congressman, John Schafer, from whose office I received a Members' Pass to the Visitors' Gallery of the House of Representatives. I cannot remember if the Congress was in session or if I went, but I still have the pass dated July 19, 1939. No doubt I was thinking that I too might one day issue such passes.

We left Washington bound for Augusta, Georgia, where Oiva's relatives lived on a farm. The coastal route south took us through towns that contrasted with anything we had seen before. This was the Deep South of cotton and tobacco towns, where unemployed black men were sitting on street corners and the drinking fountains and restaurants were designated "for whites only." We four parochial boys had never seen anything like this in West Allis, nor in Milwaukee, where we knew that blacks lived on Walnut Street, although we had never been there. My image of the South was that of *Gone with the Wind*, which I saw with Evelyn Jensen when we skipped school one afternoon to attend a showing at a theater in downtown Milwaukee. Our reaction to the segregation of the South was to break the barrier by talking with the unemployed men sitting on the street corners. Such injustice, we thought, could be corrected by challenging the barrier. These older men were amused by our noble efforts, understanding that nothing could come of them but indulgently tolerating our sincerity. Like other Northerners, our discovery of the Southern caste system, despite our revulsion to it, was something with which we learned to live. Oiva's relatives, who were themselves immigrants, had not only already learned to live with it, but did so with a stridency that exceeded that of old-time Southerners, as if the immigrant needed a social inferior.

On their farm on the outskirts of Augusta, in the midst of the Deep South, Oiva's relatives had recreated a Finnish cultural atmosphere complete with a sauna—the heat of the tropical summers notwithstanding. Suddenly we were in Oiva's Finnish-speaking community, and because we spoke no Finnish, we were excluded from it. Oiva, however, became so embedded in it that he became homesick and decided to take a bus home by himself. While waiting at the bus station, he changed his mind. We remained together to finish our trip as a group.

After Augusta, there were no more relatives. We were on our own, but this was the South where it was warm and sleeping outdoors was easy. We were off to Daytona Beach, site of the famous car races and the place where we spent our first night sleeping on sand under the open sky. Arriving on the beach early in the evening, we swam and ate our dinner of sandwiches at seaside, ready for bed at dusk. Suddenly, the mosquitoes arrived. Not just a few, but hundreds, attacking us from all sides. Our only recourse was to pack up and walk to a nearby beach hotel where the proprietor had been expecting us, knowing that we could not survive the night without mosquito netting.

Our trip plan called for a drive through Miami and onward to Key West. On discovering that this would add three days to our journey, and weary of sleeping in the car, we decided against going to the southernmost tip of the United States; we had wanted to be able to claim that we had traveled the full length of the East Coast. Not going meant that we could not make that claim—a failure as we saw it. We were disappointed, but we found a solution: we entered into a conspiracy to claim that we had made the trip even though we had not. Relieved after finding this solution to uphold our honor, we headed home on the last leg of our journey, a three-day drive via Louisville. On the all-night drive to that city, Clint ran the car off the road at a railway crossing and flattened a tire. Luckily, the owner of a restaurant in Louisville not only helped us move the car off the tracks, but offered us a meal at his restaurant the next day, a kindness to be remembered forever. We arrived home with less than a dollar in our treasury and spent it on four milkshakes before going our separate ways home after a tour that covered six thousand miles. I gave a report on the trip to my social studies class and thought better than to mention Key West—let alone our conspiracy. The trip was the biggest event in the lives of four *Milwaukee Journal* route carriers in West Allis—confirmed as such many years later at our twenty-fifth-year high school class reunion.

At one of our Hi-Y meetings in 1940, our speaker was Mr. Mervin Ott, an officer of Milwaukee's YMCA and Director of the Association's camp located at Boulder Junction in upstate Wisconsin. As president of the club, I sat with Mr. Ott at the speaker's table and introduced him to the group. It seems that Peter Warner had in mind that Mr. Ott should inspect me as a candidate for a summer job at the camp. A few days after the event, I was offered a job as the camp's truck driver. Apparently my trip around the country had established my qualifications as a driver. What do you do the summer before going to college? I needed the job and was grateful to the YMCA for thinking of me as being worthy of it. The Hi-Y combined the functions of social service, an uplifting boys' association, and guidance counseling at a time when these functions had not yet become separated and specialized in the public schools. It was easy to commit myself to the values of the YMCA. After all, Warner had granted me a scholarship of ten dollars per month for my first year in college and wrote me a graduation card inscribed, "Art, you did a swell job."

On the other hand, winning the American Legion Certificate of School Award from the Tanner-Paull Post 120 of the Department of Wisconsin posed another contradiction in my education. On June 6, 1940, the American Legion certified "That Arthur J. Vidich of West Allis High School is selected for this award because he is found to possess *among others* [emphasis added] those high qualities of character—honor, courage, scholarship, leadership, and service—which are necessary to the preservation of the fundamental institutions of our government and the advancement of society." The award was on embossed paper with the blue and gold seal of the American Legion. When I finished my acceptance speech at the awards ceremony, I was handed a check for $100. That was big money, but I had reservations about the excessive claims made about my character and about the organization that was the source of my award. These were veterans who had survived World War I intact. I knew that there were other veterans living in the Soldiers Home whose lives had been destroyed by the war—traumatized, shell-shocked, gassed, without arms or legs, living incomplete lives on a reservation. I cashed the check but knew that this was an act of hypocritical opportunism. I identified with the maimed men who were spectators at our summer ball games at the Soldiers Home and could not accept the approbation of these lucky survivors. In my scheme of things, the Legion could not justify its assertion of the virtues it attributed to me.

When I grew up, World War I was still an event people talked about. The use of gas and the gruesome reality of trench warfare were thought of as a violation of the rules of war. *All Quiet on the Western Front*, the movie made from Erich Maria Remarque's book, dramatized the costs and futility of "the war to end all wars." Things I was learning by going to the movies contradicted the Rotarian spirit of my high-school world. What I saw at the Paradise Theater gave me a different and less "wholesome" reflection on society. My Hollywood teachers—Harold Lloyd, Buster Keaton, the Marx Brothers, and Charlie Chaplin—were specialists in irreverent humor and slapstick comedy. They punctured pomposity, rent the veil of respectability, and above all violated conventional norms. The Marx Brothers and Charlie Chaplin tore the mask off the world of appearances exposing its cant, propriety, and conformity. Breaking the world apart by turning it upside down and inside out, they showed how not to be part of it. I identified with their self-defined marginality even as I was trying to overcome my own.

Chaplin gave me my first exposure to serious social criticism in *City Lights* and *The Gold Rush*. The Tramp's kindness toward a blind flower girl in *City Lights* evokes the human tenderness of the unwashed masses, while *The Gold Rush* illustrates the ferocious greed that the opportunity to make quick money arouses. Scenes from *Modern Times* remain with me to this day—the industrial worker with a wrench in each hand whose job it is to tighten two bolts simultaneously while they move along an assembly line the pace of which is governed by the machine. Another machine automatically serves the worker his lunch, dispensing the food with a large spoon that, however, is not precisely coordinated with Chaplin's mouth and misses the mark. After the botched lunch, the line speeds up. In his heroic efforts to keep pace with it, Chaplin follows the line as it moves upward into a set of enormous gears through which he passes and disappears. This was the defeat of the individual by the machine in technological society. Another vivid memory is the New York City urban scene in which masses of people, like a flock of sheep, march dumbly together, descending in lock-step into the bowels of a subway station as if marching to their dehumanization and annihilation. One Chaplin short film that spoke directly to me was *The Immigrant*. The Tramp seeks asylum in both the United States and Mexico. Neither country wants him. The final scene finds him running at breakneck speed along the US-Mexico border with one foot alternately in the US and the other in Mexico. When his foot touches the Mexican side, the Mexican border guards shoot at him. When his foot touches on US territory, immigration agents try to arrest him. The episode ends with the Tramp running into infinity, one foot in, one foot out, condemned for eternity to homelessness and marginality. I could see my parents still living like Slovenians but not being Slovenian, living in America but not being American. The Tramp taught me about my legacy and my difficulties in finding my resolution for it. By undermining the conventional values and norms that I strove to emulate, I was confronted with their unconventional opposites. But I did not yet face the implications of these contradictions.

3

Two Universities:
Wisconsin and Michigan
1940-1943

As I noted earlier, I started my academic career by failing the first grade. Ms. Hoole, the principal at Roosevelt Elementary School, had held me back one semester, putting me in a class that would graduate from high school in January 1941. In order to satisfy my mother's wish that I graduate with my rightful group in June 1940, I took extra classes in high school, including a geometry course during a summer session. As a result, I graduated ahead of those who had been my classmates throughout elementary, junior, and high school. I thereby vindicated my mother's grudge against Ms. Hoole and erased what she regarded as a blot on the family's reputation. I began college in September 1940, with my "rightful" cohort.

From the time I became a serious student, I knew I would go to college. My sister Pauline had gone to art school; Olga and Betty went to Marquette in Milwaukee. My mother wanted me to go to Marquette and live at home while studying to become a lawyer. Consulting no one, I chose the University of Wisconsin because I did not want to attend a Catholic school, the more so after I happened to read Betty's biology text for her nursing course and discovered that it rejected the theory of evolution into which I had already been indoctrinated. Although the combination of my public school education and my activities in the Young Men's Christian Association made me less of a Catholic than other members of my family, that was not the real reason I chose not to go there. My sisters had left the nest, and I was the last child living at home. My parents' relationship to each other was not always pleasant. They had taken to bickering and frequently appealed to me to side with one or the other in their quarrels. I did not want to live at home while going to college.

It was uncommon for graduates of West Allis High to go to college. The Depression wasn't over. Wisconsin's tuition of fifty dollars per semester put it out of reach for many students. Out of my class of over five hundred students, only a few went on to college, mostly to the University of Wisconsin extension in Milwaukee or to one of the religiously affiliated liberal arts colleges located in the region. A handful of my graduating class went to the University in Madison.

Wisconsin was the only school to which I applied. It never occurred to me that I might not be accepted, nor did I visit the campus beforehand. On freshman orientation day, my parents drove me in our 1930 Nash to the Badger Club, a university accredited, privately managed dormitory where I was to work as a part-time waiter in exchange for a reduction in the costs of my room and board. I contracted for the job as part of my plan to be a self-supporting student, self-sufficient and independent of parental support. I wanted to be on my own, and to that end, I applied for and received a job working for a research professor in the Department of Education tabulating numbers for a federally supported project, a program that would now be called "work-study." It did not take me long to discover that I could not support myself and be a full-time student. Without making an issue of it, my parents paid the balance of my room and board for the year and sent me fifty dollars per month in cash—old bills, vintage 1930s, taken straight out of my mother's cash holdings that she kept in a trunk in her bedroom. I learned to like those bills. They also gave me a new appreciation for how they were acquired at 115 Clinton Street in Milwaukee.

The Badger Club consisted of two frame dwellings located a short distance off State Street on a side alley not far from the Wisconsin State Historical Library, Bascom Hill, the University Club, and Langdon Street. In its earlier incarnation, its two frame buildings had been private residences. Now the parlor was used as a common room furnished with a piano, and the rest of the space had been converted into dormitory rooms with bunk beds and desks. The members of the Badger Club, twenty-four of us, were supervised by an elderly couple. The wife was our cook and the husband, a stern and humorless man, collected the rent and watched for any signs of moral turpitude among his charges. The club was home away from home.

Some members were upperclassmen, who, acting as tutors for the less experienced freshmen, took it upon themselves to socialize the greenhorns. We were told that no women were permitted in the building. As it happens, such a thought never would have occurred to me—I had never even brought a girlfriend home to meet my parents. We waiters were further admonished that we could lose our jobs if we checked in late. Those were the basic ground rules of the Badger Club game.

Members were from different towns in the state, all as undistinguished as West Allis, but the two from New York made the place seem exotic. For a kid from West Allis, this was an eye-opening experience. Russell Austin, my roommate, was from Albany, New York. He was a student of literature who had been accepted into a special seminar being taught by Sinclair Lewis. Here was I, sharing the same room with a member of a widely publicized "Author in Residence Seminar," established to put the University of Wisconsin on the cultural map. After several sessions, however, Lewis abruptly quit his own seminar, explaining in a public statement that he could not tolerate the stifling atmosphere of a university campus; he broke his contract and left town. How could such an affront to my chosen university be explained? As might be expected, the publicists saved face for both Lewis and the university by attributing his departure to a creative writer's desire to do his own writing; no one was to blame. Though Russell missed out on that class, he became a writer and had a long career as a journalist for the *Milwaukee Journal*, the same paper I had worked for as a route carrier. Brownie Beyers, a journalism student who believed you could not be a journalist unless you could hold your liquor, expected to return to a small upstate town to take over his father's newspaper. Another Badger Club member from New York planned to make the study of the League of Nations his life's work. The big issue then being debated at the League in Switzerland was the Abyssynian question and the fate of Haile Silassie in the face of Mussolini's occupation of that country. In deadly serious monotones, he talked of nothing else, as if the future of the world depended upon those debates that we learned shortly thereafter were a charade. One of the upperclassmen studied music and played the piano beautifully right there in our parlor; I had never been that close to a person who played so well. The Badger Club was my new community away from home. I kept my eyes open, listened, and learned.

When I received my letter of acceptance from the university, it informed me that Harold Taylor would be my academic advisor. It also instructed me to read one book of my choice before arriving and to be prepared to discuss it with him during my first counseling session in the fall. The book I chose was Mortimer Adler's *How to Read a Book*. Adler was associated with Robert Hutchins at the University of Chicago and was promoting his ideas about Great Books, always spelled in capital letters. *How to Read a Book* was designed to show that there was a specific way in which to read one. When I told Taylor, who was a member of Max Otto's pragmatically oriented philosophy department, that I had selected Adler's book, I knew immediately from his facial expression that I had read the wrong book. No one, Taylor admonished, could tell someone how to read a book, not even Adler. I had never before heard the word "pragmatism," and did not know what it meant, but Taylor made clear the pragmatist point that the same book was different things to different readers. Adler was merely telling people how he wanted books to be read. For Taylor, you read the book you were ready to read at the time you read it, and if you read it again later, it could become a different book, depending on what the reader had learned in the meantime. Moreover, how a book is read has no necessary relationship to the author's intentions. This was my first pedagogical lesson at the University of Wisconsin.

During my freshman year, I had the mistaken notion that there was nothing I could not do if only I were to lead my life on a pre-cisely organized timetable; without knowing it, I was following the methodically organized life prescribed by Benjamin Franklin and analyzed by Max Weber in *The Protestant Ethic and the Spirit of Capitalism*. I calculated my daily activities, including sleep, hour by hour, and thought by this means that I could control my life and experience everything the university had to offer. In addition to waiting tables for the dinner meal, I signed up to take flying lessons that the federal government was offering free of charge to univer-sity students. The course consisted of a class meeting on Thursday evenings and flying lessons twice each week in the early morning before breakfast and my first class. I rose at five a.m., hitchhiked to the airport for a six o'clock flight lesson, and returned in time to attend Professor William Kiekhofer's "Introduction to Economics." After a month of flying lessons and some close calls during landing exercises, I decided I was not meant to be a pilot, no matter how glamorous the idea had seemed.

In "Introduction to Economics," I joined a mass of five hundred students who, when Kiekhofer entered the stage, shouted a cheer, "Ziz Boom Bah, Wild Bill," a greeting transmitted from one student generation to the next. Each year, Kiekhofer delivered his emotionally charged lecture on the "Silver Question," a nineteenth-century issue that he was still fighting. Fully costumed in a string-like black bow tie and a mane of flowing white hair, he repeated the same lectures year after year, and the students loved it, stomping their feet in affirmation. Kiekhofer lectured more like a theatrical performer than an economist. No matter how early I woke up, I could not possibly fall asleep in beginning economics.

Undeterred and eager to find new things to do, I responded to an ad in the *Daily Cardinal* announcing tryouts for positions as announcers on the university radio station. Asked to read a script that included French phrases and foreign names, I stumbled badly and was not asked to return. Freshmen were obliged to sign up for the Reserve Officers Training Corps (ROTC) or gym class. I chose the latter. Over the course of the year, this required instruction in four sports of my choice. I signed up for boxing, tennis, badminton, and ice hockey. Since tennis had been my sport in high school, I tried out for the freshman tennis team only to be eliminated in the first draw. In the winter months, I played intramural hockey with a pick-up team of friends. It did not take me long to engage in student politics and to see that the Student Union was the place to go for this purpose. At the Union, I met the political radicals and fraternity boys who invited me to parties where I was presumably being judged as a candidate for membership. The heavy drinking at these parties repelled me as did the pseudo-sophistication that I could not emulate. I decided against joining even before I learned what a membership might cost. Instead, I declared myself an "Independent," a representative of the political bloc standing in opposition to the "Fraternities." This division was roughly equivalent to that of the Democrats and Republicans, or the masses and the rich. Fraternity boys entered their fathers' businesses when they graduated while political Independents became lawyers, politicians, and journalists. Being an Independent put me on the side of the morally virtuous and was the means I chose to enter campus politics.

In my first year, I tried to do more things than I could handle, but despite my failures, I was not humbled. Others had made choices for me by rejecting me and thwarting my efforts. But that still left me with other opportunities. I learned, however, that I could not live my life according to a strict schedule. There were limits to being a fully self-rationalized student.

Wisconsin's Academic and Political Milieu

Of the Big Ten Universities, Wisconsin was known for its academic and political liberalism. The university and the state were then sponsoring Alexander Mickeljohn's residential college, a program featuring a pragmatic philosophical orientation designed to produce socially responsible citizens. The state legislature was known for protective social legislation toward farmers, labor, children, the poor, and higher education. Richard T. Ely and John R. Commons were nationally recognized "institutional economists" who were influential in formulating legislative programs for the state. These early economists were committed to the Christianization of the social sciences as part of an effort to use social scientists on behalf of a rationally administered state. Paul Rauschenbusch, the son of the Social-Gospel Baptist minister Walter Rauschenbusch, was an eastern liberal and an important official in the state labor bureaucracy. He had come from Boston with his wife Elizabeth Brandeis. She, along with the labor historian Selig Perlman, was among the few Jewish professors in a university that took pride in its ethnic and religious diversity. Pragmatism and liberalism contributed to the image of Wisconsin as a progressive, socially conscious school. Some businessmen and the conservative press criticized it for being too progressive, maybe even communistic.

Wisconsin had the making of a quasi-welfare state (without the Keynesianism) even before the beginning of Roosevelt's New Deal. Patterned after legislation they had already written for the state, professors of economics Morton, Witte, and Groves wrote similar legislation for Roosevelt. In 1940 and 1941, Walter W. Heller, already a Keynesian and later a presidential economics advisor, was added to the faculty of the economics department. John Gauss, later appointed to a position at Harvard, was a professor of political science who specialized in public administration and social planning. He was one of a new generation of thinkers who recognized the organizational implications of the new federal and state bureaucracies spawned by the crisis of the depression. In Wisconsin's this-worldly Scandinavian and German Lutheran traditions, the government was thought to have a moral responsibility for its citizens, not only to look after them, but also to watch over their public and private morality. Wisconsin was an incipient welfare state, taking into its hands the regulation of the free market and acting as God's surrogate to create a just state.[1]

This was the social and political milieu in which I found myself as a beginning university student. Since I planned to be a politician, I needed a law degree and at the recommendation of my advisor chose a course of study called "American Institutions," a program designed specifically for pre-law majors. The requirements included studies in economics, political science, American history, and a smattering of courses in science and literature, but not sociology or anthropology. The courses I remember most vividly were Selig Perlman's "Capitalism, Socialism, and Democracy," Elizabeth Brandeis's course on "Early New England Economic History," and "The Civil War," taught by Hesseltine. I remember my astronomy class because I sat next to an attractive female student and received an F. I also remember an English course in which I read Shakespeare, Lord Byron, and Milton for the first time in my life and was shocked to discover that it was easy to read these great writers. "Music Appreciation" was taught by Gunnar Johansen, the University Pianist in Residence. He played piano and ad-libbed for five hundred students, leaving me with no greater appreciation for music. At the Student Union, I visited the art gallery, attended dance programs and the theater, and listened to the speeches of itinerant lecturers. My eyes were opened to new possibilities for cultural consumption the likes of which I could not have dreamed of in West Allis.

---

[1] See the extended treatment of this subject in Vidich and Lyman, *American Sociology*, 151-167.

I didn't want to return to West Allis. With each passing semester, my sense of distance and alienation from that milieu became more acute. When I went back for visits, I didn't contact old friends and never thought to visit my teachers. My family was my only reason to return, mainly out of a sense of duty, but also because I couldn't cut the umbilical cord of economic dependence. On one such visit, while sitting on the trolley car that took me via Reed Street and National Avenue from Milwaukee's train station to West Allis, passing en route through the neighborhood of my father's old saloon, I suffered an acute case of melancholia. My boyhood world no longer had meaning, but I had found no secure substitute for it. I was in limbo and alone. My recourse was to commit myself totally to my life on the Madison campus.

Politics on the Campus

In my innocence, I wanted to enter campus politics both as a prelude to a conventional political career and to be an activist committed to ideological causes. On the one hand, my pre-law major would prepare me for my career, and on the other, I wanted to learn all I could from the ideological contention then raging over communism, socialism, the Hitler-Stalin Pact of 1939, and the America First movement. I had difficulties digesting these contrasting commitments.

During my first year, I made myself noticed in committee work at the Student Union. I learned that leaders of the campus Independents lived in the YMCA dormitory situated immediately adjacent to the Student Union, and I moved there in my second year. Bob Lampman, later an economics professor at the university, Nate Hefferman, later a member of the State Supreme Court, and Bob Avery, who in my eyes was *the* "Big Man on Campus," also lived there, as did Stan Glowacki, who, in that same year, became the editor of the

Daily Cardinal, the campus newspaper. Like the YMCA Camp Manitowish where I had worked during the preceding summer, the Y was considered a place where serious and wholesome students lived. Bob Schumpert was its diffident and trusting director, and Ed Nestigen, the assistant director, had a missionary's zeal to aid and assist anyone in trouble. Carl Stange, Nestigen's assistant, in fact hoped to become a missionary. Some of the residents were Nigerians and Ghanese, sponsored by mission schools in Africa. Kwame Nkrumah was a frequent visitor, and, like him, the African residents later became leaders in the independence movements of their countries. Julius Margolis, a first-year graduate student who had never taken an economics course, was Walter W. Heller's assistant in his courses on Keynesianism. John Gustafson, my friend from West Allis, was a first-year student and my roommate on the third floor across the passageway from Stan Glowacki. I could not have been in a better place to make my way into campus politics.

In order to acquire the sophistication required of a Big Man on Campus, I bought several pipes, one with a curved stem, and began to smoke, getting sick when I inhaled. In the spring, in collaboration with two aspiring classmates, I bought a sailboat for twenty dollars from a graduating upperclassman. It was a partially rotted C-boat, a class of vessels I had learned how to sail at Camp Manitowish. It already had the reputation of being a campus institution and had the outrageous name "Sea Bitch." The boat, moored on Lake Mendota behind the Y, was a status symbol and a sign that I was integrated into campus life. To add patina to my reputation, I drank beer at Lohmeyer's on State Street and played pool and billiards on one of the four tables that dominated the lobby of the YMCA. On Saturday nights, when our moral supervisors were off duty, we Independents had drunken beer parties just like the fraternities but without the "coeds," as female students were then called. It was, however, an unwritten rule to respect the prerogative of the upperclassmen to take their girlfriends to their rooms. These Saturday night affairs were ceremonially ended by dropping the empty beer keg out the third-floor window and watching it hit the ground. The Y provided me with the ambiance for establishing my credentials as a campus persona and promising campus leader.

The Big Men on Campus had in mind careers as lawyers, state legislators, senators, judges, or maybe even presidents of the United States. Their concerns were with making connections with each other and searching out a political base. Each of us could imagine where we would begin our careers and who would be the predecessors whom we would succeed. Of those in my generation, for example, Gaylord Nelson became a US Senator and Melvin Laird a congressman (a fellow counselor at Camp Manitowish who inherited his father's seat in Wausau) and later Secretary of the Armed Forces in Richard Nixon's administration. According to the logic of state politics, I would return to a base in West Allis. Far removed from this mundane universe of political careers were the burning and unresolved issues generated by the Depression of the 1930s.

Learning more about socialism was still on my agenda and drew me to political forums that were held in the Student Union. This was still before Pearl Harbor, but the Hitler-Stalin Pact had recast the debate over socialism, communism, and fascism. When Roosevelt made the Lend-Lease deal with Winston Churchill, he not only committed the United States to war, but aroused the ire of anti-interventionists in the US, and by doing so, connected domestic and international politics. America Firsters, led by Colonel McCormick of the *Chicago Tribune* with the assistance of such proto-fascists as Gerald L. K. Smith, editor of *The Cross and Flag*, Father Coughlin, a parish priest in Detroit, and Charles Lindbergh, were all sympathetic to German and Italian fascism. The campus and the country were deeply divided on ideological grounds. It was in this political climate that communists, Trotskyists, Young Socialists, anarchists, and America Firsters held their forums in the Student Union and clashed with each other.

The campus carriers of left-wing ideologies were returned Spanish Civil War veterans of the Lincoln Brigade, in-state students of German, Norwegian, Swedish, Finnish, and Slovene descent whose parents had imported ideas about socialism and revolution from Europe, and Jewish students from Brooklyn and the Bronx. Of the eight thousand students enrolled at Wisconsin, it appeared to me that as many as twenty percent of Wisconsin's students were Jews, but clearly this was only an appearance attributable to their overwhelming presence in radical groups and to my first exposure to Jewish students from New York. They had come to the university because educational opportunities for them in New York State were limited. New York did not then have a state university system and City College, already almost exclusively Jewish, was not everyone's choice. Midwestern state schools, however, were eager to admit out-of-state students because they paid higher tuition. The high value that Jews placed on learning could be accommodated at the University of Wisconsin, which, in any case, was the school most favored by Easterners because of its reputation for academic and political liberalism. In my entire class at West Allis High School, only two or three students might have been Jews, but they in no way resembled the assertive, articulate, politically sophisticated students from Brooklyn and the Bronx who had been raised in New York City's ghettoes. When they made speeches, they spoke with passion and conviction. In a single forum, pro and con speakers were equally sure of their positions and seemed to be convinced that what they said would save the world from its folly. Politically precocious and impressive as these Eastern activists were, I was unable to understand how they could be so sure of themselves. Yet the emotional commitment and worldliness of these Easterners attracted me. Because I went to these forums and associated with them, I was called a "Jew-lover" by another group of students. I was startled by this designation. After all, I had learned at home that there are "good and bad in all groups," and I did not choose my friends by ethnic or religious standards. My education in anti-Semitism began somewhat abruptly at the Student Union. After a while I discovered I could not be both a political activist and a campus politician. I chose the latter.

When I returned to Madison for my sophomore year, I learned that Dick Oberly, the president of the Student Council board, had used student-funded treasury monies for personal entertainment purposes, namely to pay for a fraternity party. I had just begun to live at the Y and found myself occupying a room adjacent to Stan Glowacki, editor of the *Daily Cardinal*. I took the story to Glowacki who, at my behest, broke it in the *Cardinal*. Taking the high ethical road against leisure-loving, corrupt fraternity boys, we played out a political drama that had as one of its purposes the furtherance of my own political career. This was a stroke of luck.

The story ran for a few issues of the *Cardinal*, but misuse of public money by those who were to become Wisconsin's political leaders and judges was not part of the image the university wished to convey to its state constituencies; faculty advisors stepped in and called for journalistic moderation. The damage had been done, however, and my career was enhanced. Having established my ethical credentials, I was appointed President of the Student Union in my junior year, a position that carried a stipend of sixty dollars per month and eating privileges in the Union's exclusive dining halls. I felt that I had been rewarded for upholding the ethical standards of campus politics. I also knew that the standards were only appearances. I had succeeded, but I was also left with the knowledge of my own motives. I learned more about myself and politics than I was prepared to digest.

Campus politics teaches both the value of political moralism and its uses for self-enhancement. Socialization into this ethic had begun for me even before I entered college. My Badger Boys State experience taught me to organize political parties and manage political campaigns for the purpose of winning political offices. These Boys States were a national institution designed to pre-socialize youth into the rituals and mechanisms of political parties and to stimulate their political ambitions. William Jefferson Clinton attended Arkansas Boys State where in a famous picture he is shown standing beside John F. Kennedy, a visitor to the camp, whom he chose as the ideal for his own career. Entry into a political career in the United States is not left entirely to chance. A theory of the institutional selection of America's political leaders might take account of their pre-socialization in both the Boys States and on America's college campuses, allowing for variations in styles of political education in state universities and Ivy League colleges. Such a theory might examine how novices learn the arts of deal-making, political and ethical compromise, loyalty and disloyalty, and the rewards of success.

December 1941

Like other American universities, Wisconsin went on a wartime footing on December 8, 1941, committing its resources to the cause of total war. This meant releasing faculty for governmental and military assignments; the biochemistry department moved en masse to Fort Detrick, Maryland, where professors created the dreaded wartime biological warfare program. It also meant that universities accepted military contracts for training students in uniform and cooperating with the intelligence agencies whose duty it was to examine the loyalty of university personnel. Total war meant the rational administration of the nation's material and manpower resources in an age of high technology and professional specialization. The technical resources of American universities commanded the respect of military planners, but the militarization of the campus both violated its past liberalism and, for the duration, provided it with a secure financial base. It also erased the intellectual contentiousness that flourished on the campus before the declaration of war.

Loyalty and patriotism became the order of the day. Enemies within were to be looked for everywhere and discordant voices silenced. Hans Gerth, for example, a German émigré professor of sociology who arrived in the United States in 1937, was classified as an enemy alien and was not permitted to leave the city limits of Madison except with the permission of immigration officials. Moreover, since he lectured on the subject of Germany to uniformed servicemen, his classes were monitored for political correctness: he knew that reports on his lectures were made to the dean. It was not that 1984 had already arrived, but rather that under wartime conditions the university had lost its academic and cultural autonomy.

I was in my sophomore year and well on my way to continuing my high school successes at the university. I discovered with a jolt, however, that the world of the university and its competitive atmosphere were far more demanding than the resources available to me. Despite this realization, I was determined to succeed despite my misgivings. In my junior year, I was invited into Iron Cross, an honorary society of self-selected leaders whose predecessors selected their own successors into an organization that had no other function than its own perpetuation. Harold Taylor and Frederick H. Burkhardt (both pragmatists who later became presidents of Eastern girls' schools, Sarah Lawrence and Bennington) invited me to join a quasi-philosophical religious organization they called Vanguard (Joe Bensman called it "Rearguard"). Vanguard was a variant of Eastern Unitarianism, having had its origins in Ralph Waldo Emerson and the Harvard Divinity School. Its moral and social perspectives were linked to the pragmatism of Wisconsin's philosophy department and were consistent with the watered-down Protestantism to which I had been exposed in the YMCA. With the best of credentials, I was headed for a law degree and ultimately a political career about which I now had doubts.

Despite my outward appearance of self-confidence, I believed that I could not fulfill the future I had set for myself and allowed others to anticipate. My friend from West Allis, Gordon Samuelson, was my political advisor and hoped that he would manage my political career. Taylor, Burckhardt, Dean Rudisili, and Porter Butts, Director of the Student Union, had taken a personal interest in aiding my welfare. Then there was the support my family had given me and the expectations I had led friends to have for my future. How could I betray those who were counting on me, those whom I later learned, when reading George Herbert Mead, were my "significant others"? With deep reservations about myself and my future (would I go back to West Allis?), and under the social pressure of maintaining the appearance of self-confidence, I thought of suicide as a definitive solution to my quandary. On many occasions, my depressions were so deep that as I lay in bed, I thought it would be better to die than to face the day. Yet, despite these depressions I never missed a class. I played the part of a successful campus politician and maintained the public appearances that denied the reality. I told no one about my state of mind. It occurred to me later that keeping this kind of secret to oneself is its own therapy, that is, learning to live with the "unbearable lightness of being," as Milan Kundera put it.

When the Japanese attacked Pearl Harbor, the mood on campus became somber. Reports that the Japanese might be ready to invade California demanded acts of patriotic commitment. When pictures of the destruction of the battleships in Pearl Harbor appeared in the press, war fever on campus ran high. For campus leaders, some of my friends, and me, enlistment was a matter of personal honor. With a light heart and a deep depression, I regarded the Marine Corps as an acceptable alternative to suicide. I enlisted in the Marine Corps Officer Training Program on April 6, 1942. My motives for doing so were mixed. Enlistment was easy and made socially acceptable, even honorable, by the fact that hundreds of students were doing it, including other campus leaders and sports heroes like Elroy "Crazylegs" Hirsch, the University of Wisconsin Badgers' superstar running back.

Within a few months of the declaration of war, professors began to speculate in their classrooms on the war's meaning for my generation of soldiers. I have a vivid memory of a lecture by Professor Quintana, who recounted the story of the lost generation of the World War I English poets, scholars, and intellectuals who eagerly went to the front and lost their lives. Brooding pessimistically, he saw the future of another lost generation, in this case one that included me; his lecture evoked my first doubts about my enlistment in the Marine Corps.

Within a few months, upperclassmen were called for active duty and shipped directly to Parris Island. According to Marine Corps policy, activation to duty was by college class (seniors first) and alphabetical order. For example, since I was a sophomore my class was called after the juniors, and when called, I came after those whose first letters of their last names came before mine; to have a last name beginning with "V" was an advantage. Seniors were called immediately and did not finish the academic year. Nevertheless, some recruits in the first contingent married girlfriends whom they would otherwise have married upon graduation. One such wedding was Rosemarie Carlson's to the basketball star and athletic hero Bill Koch. Her story was a poignant one. Rosemarie had the shock while she was in college of learning that her father had committed suicide. Six months later, she was presented with the news that her husband had been killed in battle on Tarawa. Cases like Rosemarie Carlson's brought the war to the campus on a level of grimness that it had not had before. Now, in addition to my depressed state of mind, the risks of war became an objective reality.

Anticipating being called to active duty and the thought of entering the Pacific war as a Second Lieutenant Infantry Platoon Leader in the Navy's brutal island-hopping campaigns caused a not-too-subtle change in my attitude about life on the campus. I could enjoy being president of the Student Union and sailing the Sea Bitch with girlfriends on Lake Mendota. Burton Waisbren, later to become a doctor in Milwaukee, whom I met in upstate Wisconsin where he worked at a Jewish boys' camp, suggested that we book rooms for the fall semester at the University Club on State Street across from the library; the club was accepting students as tenants in lieu of faculty who had gone to war. This was spacious, well-appointed living that included dinners served in an elegant dining room and access to the comfort of the club's lounge where we met over-draft-age faculty for discussions that continued into the late evening hours. It was there that I met Miles Hanley, English professor and editor of a dictionary of regional dialects in the United States, who also had the habit of walking naked to the bathroom, much to the consternation of the maids who encountered him on his sojourns. I also met Louis Adamic, who stayed at the University Club when he gave a lecture on the war in the Balkans. A group of us—including Warren Paley, John Gustafson, Gordon Samuelson, and others—began playing weekend bridge games beginning on Friday after classes, ending late Sunday evenings, keeping four seats filled the whole time with a revolving set of players. The war and the prospect of my imminent participation in it, along with possibility of an early death, made life worth living.

My class was not called for active duty until the late spring of 1943, a year and a half after I had enlisted and a year before I would have graduated. In the meantime, I had completed three more semesters of course work. In addition, I had had another summer as a camp counselor at Camp Manitowish. When I was inducted, I was sent not to Parris Island, the Marines' dreaded boot camp, but to the University of Michigan. There my contingent, which included Elroy "Crazy Legs" Hirsch and other members of Wisconsin's football and boxing teams, entered the Navy's V-12 program where we continued as students while waiting to be programmed for assignment to boot camp.

To learn what socialism might be was no longer the pressing issue it had been. However, I later learned from the Marine Corps that an impersonal, totalitarian bureaucracy demanded strict obedience in exchange for clothing, feeding, bedding, and arming those over whom it had jurisdiction. The gigantic wartime enterprise—eleven million American troops dispersed throughout the world, supported by a civilian industrial base that fed, clothed, and armed them—was an example of rational social planning that would have impressed Saint Simon. In retrospect, the project known as World War II was an example of militarized socialism to which soldiers and civilians acquiesced with body and soul. I learned that successful social planning was possible and that entire populations and economies could be directed by a central bureaucracy. To accomplish this, all that was required was a clear-cut foreign enemy, a propaganda machine that could mobilize the opinion of noncombatants, and an industrialized military machine manned by troops prepared, if and when necessary, to die.

A Marine at the University of Michigan

At the University of Michigan, I became a uniformed private, outfitted in tailored Marine greens, fore and aft cap with attached Marine emblem in the shape of the globe of the world, and shod in Marine-vintage, oxblood-colored shoes, always polished to a mirror-like shine, ready for inspection at all times. I was in a contingent of several hundred volunteers recruited from the Universities of Wisconsin, Minnesota, and Michigan. We were now brought together and organized into platoons of twenty-seven men each and divided into three equal columns according to height, with the tallest at the head and the shortest at the end of each column. Because of my height and last name I occupied an inconspicuous place in the middle of the rear column. Assigned to dormitories in the West Quad, we were under the supervision of a fatherly reserve officer colonel and his noncommissioned staff of sergeants. Regimented according to the rules of military protocol, we mustered daily at 7:00 a.m. in the quad's parking lot, and at 10:00 p.m. we were inspected for bed check. As if to acknowledge that we were still students, these military routines did not apply on weekends. We were served three meals a day and received privates' pay. Though our noncommissioned officers exercised immediate authority over us, they had come up through the ranks and were overly respectful of those who ultimately would become their supervisors as officers. In the university setting, these sergeants were avuncular, not at all like the sergeants we were to meet later at Parris Island. Apart from the daily observance of a military routine, the main difference between student life at Wisconsin and that of military life at Michigan was room, board, books, and privates' pay.

I discovered that being a Marine alleviated both the responsibilities connected to the practical necessities of life as well as the need to think in long-range terms about it. With the future prospect of becoming an infantry platoon officer leading troops into battle, I could put the future out of my mind and relax.

On weekends, friends and I went to Detroit or Chicago. Traveling in a Marine Corps uniform was a big advantage. The corps public relations specialists promoted Marines as fearless defenders of the nation, and here I was, one of them, ready to take advantage of privileges earned for me by Marines who fought and died in Pacific Islands. In the anonymity of public life, no one need know that I was only a student. The uniform itself was a valuable social commodity that earned perquisites from strangers. Railway conductors, for example, granted free passage to Marines, a privilege customarily reserved to the clergy. When I went home to West Allis via Chicago and Milwaukee on the interurban trolley, I had no trouble renewing friendships with old high school girlfriends; the uniform bestowed an advantage with women on and off the campus.

The Marines prided themselves in their *esprit de corps*, and we were more willing to share in that pride since we were reaping its tangible benefits. Life could be carefree in the way I had imagined it to be for the fraternity boys at the University of Wisconsin.

To be in uniform and to be a collegian on campus were both new experiences. Gambling in the West Quad and "chug-a-lug" beer-drinking at the Pretzel Bell, Ann Arbor's campus beer parlor, filled in the spaces that my extracurricular activities had had for me at the University of Wisconsin. The upper floor of the West Quad was the site of a standing crap game, a form of recreation forbidden by our colonel, whom we teased as if he were a dean by never letting him catch us in the act. Even though the roll of the dice in the cement building reverberated into the colonel's office, and the sergeant on duty knew the game was on, he could not locate it because we stopped playing until our lookout gave us the all-clear signal. When a call came for tryouts for the university's varsity hockey team, I played until I was told I had not made the cut. I was no match for players who learned their game in the small, icebound towns of Upper Michigan. At Wisconsin, my curriculum was crammed with courses in political science, economics, history, and the physical sciences. The corps, on the other hand, imposed few academic requirements on this future pool of officers; I had only to fulfill calculus and introductory physics requirements. Since I had already completed the corps's other requirements at Wisconsin, I was free to indulge in courses that struck my fancy. Needing only a set of unspecified credit requirements for graduation, I took beginning piano, anthropology, a course on Henrik Ibsen's works, biology, and comparative anatomy. As an afterthought, I enrolled in an economics course, thinking that this could complete a major in that field and earn me a BA degree from Michigan. Being a Marine and a student was like being on an academic vacation or in a cafeteria where one could choose whatever dessert one pleased.

Attending classes in a Marine uniform made one a special kind of student for whom professors were prepared to grant concessions. For example, I received the grade of C in calculus. I thought I should have flunked it, but an émigré professor taught the class and passed all Marines. Physics class bordered on the scandalous. In its V-12

contingent of Marines, Michigan had inherited the top football players from Wisconsin and Minnesota, adding them to its already outstanding roster of players. Thus Michigan had the number-one team
in the country. Since football players practiced long hours and traveled extensively during the season, they had no time to study physics,
though they were required to take the course along with everyone
else. No one was scandalized when they openly cheated on the exam.
The players sat with their exams on seats adjacent to a row of windows that reached to the floor and could be opened from the bottom
up. They slipped the exam out the window to a waiting colleague
who returned it by the same means when completed. It might well
have been that our elderly professor was unaware of these clandestine procedures, but not the exam's proctors, who were in collusion
with the cheaters. No one was inclined to blow the whistle, not least
the other Marines for whom such an act amounted to disloyalty. The
logic of the war undermined academic standards. It was thought to
be unpatriotic to hold back a Marine destined to fight to preserve the
very institution being debased by the need to fight the war.

Free to elect whatever courses I wished, I signed up for piano lessons. It had always impressed me that my mother played the piano,
and I thought if she could do it I could too. The Marine Corps gave
me my chance. My piano teacher, a matronly woman, was delighted
to have a Marine for a student. Since the university was on a wartime
footing, instruction in music was not a high priority. She was attracted to the idea of having a young Marine as a student. She treated
me as a serious student and labored to teach me some basics and even
a Chopin étude, but I was a dilettante doing too many other things to
be able to submit to the discipline that playing the piano required.

My course in economics focused on John Maynard Keynes, the
British economist whose theories about investment, savings, and

unspent income have been credited with solving the problems ensu-
ing from the over-production and under-consumption that were, in
part, the root causes of the Great Depression. Keynes reversed the
dogma of the classical economists by making a virtue of consumption rather than saving. He argued that demand could be created by
deficit spending and that such spending stimulated production and
economic growth at regulated rates of inflation, the latter held in
check by continuous growth. Keynes was an eye-opener, but it was
the course in anthropology that had a lasting effect on my life.

Professor Leslie White taught my anthropology course. He was a
dynamic lecturer, a dogmatic evolutionist, and an aggressive atheist
who enjoyed shocking his students with stories about the beliefs and
ways of life of primitives. He was a celebrated character on campus
with a reputation somewhat like that of Kiekhofer at Wisconsin, and
his classes were large. At the time I enrolled, most of his students
were daughters of respectable, middle-class business families from
around the state of Michigan. I was the only Marine and was ready
to receive White's message.

Each week, White gave two bombastic lectures in which he ruthlessly challenged his students' moral and cultural values. In order
to provide cases that illustrated the relativity of values, White used
George Peter Murdock's *Our Primitive Contemporaries* as one of his
texts. It was based on the premise that the primitive cultures of the
world were our evolutionary predecessors whose forms of social organization differed from our own. The textbook contained some fifteen
case studies of cultures arranged in order from the most primitive
hunters and gatherers to the most advanced clan and tribal cultures;
the organizational complexity of the cultures increased with the passage of evolutionary time. Each chapter included the same categories—including kinship, economy, religion, and warfare—giving the

book a mechanical quality that made it dull reading. Ethnographic in its intent, the book made no attempt to explain how these primitive cultures came to be and why they were scattered over the globe as they were. The ethnographies had a lifeless quality as if the carriers of these cultures did not exist. Despite that, the book carried a powerful message of cultural relativism. Why were there so many different religious beliefs and why were there so many different methods of reckoning kinship relations and obligations? If these primitives were our contemporaries, how could they be used to develop a theory of cultural evolution? The relativity of values, norms, and folkways needed an explanation not offered in this book. Nor did White offer one. He used the case studies for the pedagogical purpose of showing his students that their own culture was only one of a number of possible ways of life. His stress on the relativity of values was designed to shake students out of their comfortable, complacent lives in Michigan. Much later, I learned that the relativism implicit in the study of non-Westerners placed anthropologists in a double bind: if their work illustrated relativism, they could not proclaim universal values or even basic human rights. If they proclaimed the latter, they became activists against injustice and tyranny. I wanted to know why these primitives differed from us and believed as they did, but that was not White's problem. His mission was to startle students out of their comfortable customary ways of thinking.

In order to learn what his students thought, White invited us to submit anonymous questions to him in writing. He devoted his Friday class to giving responses to these questions. This pedagogical method provided students with an opportunity to challenge his atheism, evolutionism, and cultural relativism. There were times during his lectures when students were visibly upset by his dogmatic pronouncements, even stomping their feet to express their disagreement.

On Fridays, students had an opportunity to strike back. White read their questions, decoded them, answered them, and never conceded a point. Always deadly serious, humorless, and a true believer, he relentlessly defended his scientific faith (partly Marxist) against conventional folkways and middle-class morality. Without cynicism, he was on a mission to indoctrinate his students into anthropological truths.

I had never before seen or heard a professor with such determination and passionate conviction, and I was impressed. The content of his lectures opened up new intellectual possibilities for me. His challenge to middle-class mores by contrasting them with the ways of primitives allowed me to see differently, for the first time, the values I had internalized as a youth. White gave me another way of looking at the world and an alternative to the career I had rejected. Impressionable amateur that I was, I began to mimic White's ideas and to try them out on my fellow Marines in the dormitory where we lived in West Quad.

During evening bull sessions, I began to argue positions based on the ideas I had learned the day before from White, including strident atheism, then a subject for public discussion because a priest somewhere in the Pacific had declared, "There are no atheists in foxholes." One of my roommates, Harold Peterson, a malaria-ridden veteran of the Guadalcanal campaign who had been transferred to the V-12 program, supported my position. He gave testimony disputing the priest's claim, saying that there was no time to think about anything when in a foxhole under fire. The uncertainty of our futures as Marines made death and its meaning a hot topic of discussion. Holding to my atheism, I went further in my experimentation with my new knowledge and declared all life to be without ultimate meaning, an idea whose full complexity I learned later when I read Max Weber's sociology of religion. If existence itself is an absurdity, what do you do? My answer to this question was to argue from the position of anarchism. I remember making a speech while standing on a chair in the dorm before an audience of, among others, Harold Peterson, Don Thornberry, and Gerald TerHorst (who later resigned as President Gerald Ford's press secretary instead of announcing Ford's pardon of Richard Nixon), arguing for the rejection of all conventional values. Of course, nothing came of the anarchism. Being an anarchist in the Marine Corps that was feeding, clothing, housing, and paying me was a contradiction in terms. Despite the excesses I had learned from White, I decided that the subject of anthropology was something I wanted to study when the war was over. I had not anticipated that my studies at Michigan would have this influence on me. The insights I gained from White's approach to anthropology liberated me from the values to which I had been committed. Anthropology not only gave me a new way of seeing, but also a purpose for wanting to survive the war. Being in the Marine Corps contradicted my new attitude toward life.

This contradiction in my situation became more poignant when I learned of the deaths of some of our predecessors in the V-12 program and when some of the enlisted survivors of the Guadalcanal campaign were admitted into our officer training company. These troops had been in the worst of island warfare and wanted no more of it. They were ridden with malaria and dedicated to a future of noncombat service. Their attitude was one that I came to share, and it led me to formulate a plan to escape the Marine Corps.

By chance, I noticed an announcement posted on a bulletin board outside the colonel's office to the effect that the V-12 Medical Training Program was looking for recruits. I checked out the requirements needed to make the transfer and found that I qualified, having completed courses in biology, comparative anatomy, physics, and calculus. I took this as the opportunity I was looking for and petitioned my colonel to make the transfer. This reservist colonel, who had never seen combat, regarded combat service as a Marine's highest aspiration. In answer to my request, he told me, "You do not want to be a swab jockey," and declared, "You want to be a Marine." He adamantly refused to so much as consider the transfer of a single Marine into service in the Navy. That was the end of my plan to escape the Marine Corps by becoming a medical student.

At the end of the fall term at Michigan, I was shipped off to Parris Island, South Carolina. During the two semesters, the Marine Corps had unwittingly provided me with a respite from academic pressure, an opportunity for a reassessment of my aspirations, and the possibility of a career as an anthropologist. The University of Michigan held a small ceremony exclusively for Marines and awarded me a BA degree in economics, but I have never heard from the Michigan Alumni Association.

The corps had also given me the opportunity to know Professor White. I corresponded with him during the war, thinking that I would see him again and perhaps study with him. Years later, in 1949, I met him when he was a visiting professor at Harvard while I was an anthropology student in the Department of Social Relations. By that time, his evolutionism and Marxism had become even more dogmatic. He had become something of a cult figure for Marxist graduate students at the University of Michigan and also at Columbia University where Julian Steward's Marxist-oriented students adopted some of his ideas. After the bomb dropped on Nagasaki, the effects of which I observed firsthand, White developed a unidimensional "energy theory" of human history in which he posited the evolution of world culture according to an index based on sources and amounts of available energy. This was a time when American businessmen were touting the commercial benefits of nuclear power, something that White regarded as the highest stage in the evolution of humankind. For a moment, he became a public celebrity when the Westinghouse Electric Company had him speak on his new energy theory of civilization on its weekly television program, the Westinghouse Hour. For me, that event marked the end of what was left of my respect for the professor who had introduced me to anthropology. In the light of the bombs and the new nuclear power, his anthropological perspective was out of touch with his own civilization.

4

The Marine Corps,
the Bomb, and Japan

Marine Corps Training

Travel to Parris Island was on an overnight troop train from Ann Arbor to South Carolina. This train made one stop in a rural, nondescript, small southern town where the Marine Corps had a contract with a restaurant that served us breakfast. This restaurant was prepared for our arrival and fed several hundred troops with a southern-style breakfast that included grits topped with a pat of butter. Ever since, that breakfast has had a sacramental meaning for me because it was my last meal before becoming a "boot" and my first taste of southern cuisine. That the corps had a commercial contract to feed troops in transit at a restaurant in a small southern town on a railroad siding led me to a later discovery that the Marine Corps was essentially a southern institution, staffed in its higher noncommissioned ranks by southern military careerists.

The career of a boot on Parris Island began with a degradation ceremony. Our platoon was directed into a barbershop where in a matter of a few minutes the entire group was shaved to the scalp. Next, we were ordered to pack all items of clothing, books, and personal adornment for shipment back home. Shorn of all personal possessions, naked and bald, the platoon was processed through a delousing chamber. Entering nude and exiting deloused from the chamber had the effect of symbolically leveling us to a common

denominator—Parris Island "boots." Deloused, each boot was supplied with socks, underwear, two pairs of marine boots, marine fatigues, a backpack, a pith helmet, and an M1 rifle. Fully dressed in
boot fatigue, we assembled in platoon formation in descending order
of height, all looking alike, except for differences in height; no longer
individuals, we were a look-alike collectivity. The psychological implications of this ceremony left an impression on me sufficiently deep
to reflect upon it and analyze its meaning in an essay.[1] The transformation of boots from individual to collective identity was reinforced
at every stage of boot-camp training by the method of blaming and
punishing the collectivity for rule infractions or misbehavior of the
individual.

Now reconfigured as boots, wearing new boots and carrying approximately sixty pounds of gear, we fell into formation under the
orders of the drill sergeant. The sergeant, dressed in an impeccably
pressed and starched uniform, ramrod straight and with an attitude
that asserted unlimited authority, confronted a rag-tag platoon of
former collegians who the day before had still retained the self-confidence of their individuality. Arranged from tallest to shortest into
three columns, we were introduced to Parris Island's first lesson in
close-order drill. Inasmuch as we had already had drill instruction
at the University of Michigan, we knew the basic orders and movements. However, this training, instead of providing a skill advantage,
was a challenge to the drill instructor (DI) who took it as his mission

---

[1]   Editor's note: See "The Dissolved Identity in Military Life," written with Maurice Stein. The essay appears in Stein, Vidich, and White, eds, *Identity and Anxiety*,
493-506. The following footnote graces the first page: "Portions of the data for this
study were collected by the authors as participants in the U.S. Marine Corps and
the U.S. Army. Our study was part of a larger project called 'World War II.' We
wish to thank the directors of this project for allowing us to use their facilities."

to establish his unqualified authority over his contingent of university-trained officer candidates. On our inaugural afternoon, we were drilled, excoriated for failing to achieve perfection of execution, and marched for hours in an aimless pattern over various drill fields.

The tallest and shortest members of the platoon, most conspicuous in the eyes of the DI, were selected for special harassment, being brought front and center to face the DI one-on-one and given a frightful tongue lashing. During the performance of this ceremony, assistant DIs, of which there were two, looked for signs of relaxation or unacceptable facial expressions—a slight snicker or a smile—in platoon members standing at parade rest. After three hours of being bullied and harassed under the full weight of sixty pounds of gear, we were led, exhausted, to our Quonset huts. Within a period of one afternoon, we had been terrorized into unqualified submission to the authority of a drill sergeant who spoke with a deep southern accent.

The DI had used his first meeting with us recruits to spot members of the platoon who eventually became his disciplinary targets, specifically those who could not "snap to" on a drill order, or who responded slowly to a command or appeared to be slouching while in formation. These unfortunate mates were made scapegoats for whom all were required to suffer. For example, the platoon was expected at any time of day or night to be able to "fall in" to perfect formation within a period of two minutes. During the day or after mealtimes, this was usually possible after one or two attempts. But at times, without warning, the platoon was called to form itself in the early hours of the morning, say, at two or three a.m. Everyone knew it was impossible to get out of bed, dress, grab the rifle, and fall in within two minutes. It was inevitable that this test would be failed. Unable on the first attempt to meet the standard, we were instructed to undress, get back into bed, and wait for another call to formation.

Of course, after three or four failures to meet the standard, we used every method to accelerate our response time, returning to bed fully clothed waiting for the next command to fall in. That command might come in five minutes or in half an hour. In the meantime, we waited tensely and wide awake for the shrill voice of the DI. To achieve collective relief from this torture we helped one another to meet the standard of barrack appearances (beds made, blankets smoothly cornered) and the two-minute deadline.

Though going back to bed fully clothed was a violation of the conditions of the test, the assistant drill instructors colluded with the recruits and overlooked this violation of standards. Everyone understood that it was a charade. This exercise in irrationality had the rational purpose of establishing the right of authority to harass without recourse and to create camaraderie and solidarity among the members of the platoon, making each responsible for the other. In the language of the corps, we were all each other's buddies, mates whose lives depended on loyalty to each other.

During the two months of boot camp, each recruit at some point was tested by the DI. For the most part, I managed to remain inconspicuous by not providing the DI with an opportunity that called attention to me. Once, however, during instruction on the M1 rifle, the parts of which we were expected to know by heart, the DI held up a part of the rifle and asked, pointing to me, "What is its name?" Somewhat unsure of myself and with a slight hint of hesitancy, I said, "The cam shaft." The sergeant boomed, "Are you sure?" Not being confident of my reply, I took a chance and bluffed, answering with a sharp and resounding, "Yes Sir." Luckily I was right. Thereafter, I was never again tested by any of the DIs' repertoire of harassment techniques. I learned the value of the straight-faced bluff from this experience and have had occasion to use it in my academic career in relations with academic administrators who use the same method in their work as drill sergeants—bluff against bluff, so to speak.

The sheer senselessness of the exercise of military authority that seemed to have no rational foundation, such as re-cleaning latrines that had just been cleaned or swabbing decks that had already been swabbed, had as its military purpose the unqualified acceptance of commands. The value of unquestioned obedience was drummed in along with that of unqualified loyalty to one's comrades, a combination of values that when fully inculcated led to the efficient functioning of the military bureaucracy—the submersion of the individual into the collectivity of a totalitarian social order.

Acceptance of the boot camp social order was based on hatred of the DI and hope for revenge against him when you were an officer and he an enlisted man and your paths crossed later somewhere in the Pacific. But neither the hatred nor the hope for revenge survived the completion of boot-camp training. The harassment, the punishment, the senseless demands, and being tested to the limits of endurance for two months were treated upon completion of boot camp not as humiliations but as a personal accomplishment. One had not only survived the ordeal but had done so successfully. Each recruit had proved his own worth to himself and credited the DI for making him a Marine. No longer hating him or hoping for revenge, the DI was now respected and admired—almost loved—for making you the Marine that you thought you had not been capable of being. This reversal of attitude toward the DI and the identification with the Marine Corps as an elite military unit was the objective of the training program and has, as a further consequence for many Marines, led to an aggressive lifelong pride in having once been a Marine.

Nonetheless, not all became gung-ho Marines ready to die for "Corps and Country." There were a number of limitations and

qualifications that stood in the way of achieving the full effectiveness of the objectives of the boot training program. Some recruits
could not meet its standards and were washed out. In our platoon,
wash-outs included gays and recruits with physical limitations; as
negative cases, they served to confirm the accomplishment of those
who succeeded. Another member of the platoon, Sid Toabe, rejected
the officer training program to become an infantry soldier because
he wanted to see combat without delay. In his case, a political motivation superseded any pride that might be derived from being a
Marine officer. However, the decisive factor that worked against acceptance of a gung-ho ideology was the knowledge that infantry second lieutenants were the Marine Corps's special variety of cannon
fodder. The duty of a platoon leader was to lead troops into enemy
fire, and it was common knowledge that the rate of casualties among
platoon leaders exceeded that of any other rank of commissioned or
noncommissioned officer. The prospect of this fate for some of us
undermined the heroic image of the fearless, fighting Marine.

Our officer training program at Quantico, Virginia, was a three-
month reprieve before assignment to active duty. Graduation from
this program was loaded with symbolism. As a *rite de passage* it included the issuance of Marine Corps dress greens, dress khakis tailored to perfection, and second lieutenant's shoulder bars. Attired in
dress greens, each newly commissioned officer was photographed in
a three-quarter body-length shot that placed stress on the tailored
uniform and second lieutenant's shoulder bars. Copies of this photo
were sent to the subject's parents and to his hometown press. In all
its elegance, this photograph seemed to suggest the immortalization
of the image, if not the body of its subject. My parents preserved this
photo until they died, and it is now in the possession of a grandson

who collects World War II memorabilia. The photo captures my youthfulness, but not my attitude toward the corps.

My first assignment was not to a replacement platoon for shipment overseas, but to Camp Lejeune, North Carolina, where I was to become a machine gun instructor. This was in the early fall of 1944, before the Iwo Jima and Okinawa campaigns. However, this stroke of luck was suddenly erased. Within a month, I found myself in a replacement battalion on a troop train bound for Camp Pendleton and immediate shipment overseas to join a convoy headed for the battle of Iwo Jima. This change of fortune resulted from my failure to meet a six o'clock Monday morning platoon muster. In the Marine Corps, missing a muster was a crime for which there was no redemption. I missed this muster because the driver of a car hired for a weekend trip to New York ran out of gas on the return trip.

While still at Quantico and also at Camp Lejeune, my friends and I used our weekend passes to visit Washington or New York City. On one of these trips, while still at Quantico, I met Virginia Wicks, whom I had known while I was still a student at the University of Wisconsin and who was then living with her girlfriends on Charles Street in Greenwich Village. During my first three weeks at Lejeune, I made this trip to New York each weekend, leaving North Carolina by car on a Friday afternoon, arriving in New York at midnight and leaving for the return trip late Sunday evening to arrive back in time for the 6:00 a.m. muster.

This weekend, the travel plan failed. The car service commissioned to make our round trip was a six-passenger limousine. Its owner-driver was a local entrepreneur who charged fifty dollars per passenger on a fully loaded trip; his rate included gasoline for which he supplied the necessary gas rationing coupons without which gas could not be bought. We knew and the driver acknowledged that his coupons were counterfeit, but for the most part, station operators accepted these coupons from a driver carrying a load of Marines.

On this trip, however, a station operator refused to observe this convention, leaving us with insufficient gas to return. Our driver solved this problem by hustling gas from some farmers on the way, but this was a time-consuming operation that added two hours to our trip, resulting in our failure to meet muster. The action of our commanding officer was swift and decisive. We were immediately assigned to a replacement battalion and within a week assigned a platoon of new recruits just graduated from Parris Island. Within two weeks after a week-long voyage across the country on a World War I vintage troop train, I was on a troop ship bound for Iwo Jima.

Life Overseas

Accommodations on a troop ship, even for an officer, are cramped, and for enlisted men, they border on the intolerable. Bunks for lieutenants are stacked four to a cabin, but enlisted men in the holds are stacked fourteen high on canvas bunks about a foot apart. On the other hand, a troop ship is a low-grade floating hotel; meals and sleeping accommodations are provided, and passengers are a leisure class cared for by the ship's crew. Like any leisure class, rich or poor, boredom is always a potential problem to be solved according to one's tastes.

Immediately on entering San Diego Harbor, the vessel passed through gentle but undulating swells that caused ninety percent of its passengers to become seasick. The stench caused by hundreds of vomiting troops combined with the seasickness almost made me wish I were dead, but after three or four days, troops and officers settled into a routine consisting of platoon musters, calisthenics, three musters for chow, gambling of all kinds, endless gazing at the water, sleeping, smoking, fighting, card-playing, and viewing war-time propaganda movies designed to entertain and to sustain the troops' morale. Every ship carried her own film library and made deals for exchanges on the high seas with other vessels. The prospect of acquiring a new inventory from a passing ship was greeted with hoots and cheers by the assembled troops. Hollywood and its propaganda specialists had an uncanny sense for nourishing the morale of the troops.

Halfway across the Pacific, several days before reaching Eniwetok, my ship broke her propeller. Abandoned by the convoy heading for Iwo Jima, we were left to drift on the open seas. Makeshift repairs enabled the vessel to hobble into the Eniwetok lagoon, where we remained for two weeks until repairs were made. The rest of the convoy went directly to Iwo Jima where some of my college friends and Quantico classmates were wounded or killed. One's fate hinged on these kinds of imponderables. The ship had been built by the Henry Kaiser/Todd Shipbuilding Company, a joint company founded in 1939 and financed by the Bank of America. I've often thought that I owe my survival of World War II to the Kaiser-Todd company's shoddy work standards.

Eniwetok is a small, sandy atoll a few hundred yards wide and about a mile long. Its lagoon, however, could accommodate dozens of large ships and was therefore a major harbor and transfer point in the Pacific war. The atoll was too small to accommodate transients, and its PX supplies were reserved for base personnel; for us, this meant no disembarkation and no beer. During this layover, the game of bridge became a serious pastime. I had become part of a foursome shortly after leaving San Diego Harbor, but up until this time, we played mostly in the evenings and early hours of the morning. The game became a compulsion, and we began playing for a penny a point and continued to play until we reached Guam. After thirty-six days on a transpacific voyage and under the tutelage and endless criticism of the career gunnery sergeant who was my partner, I learned some of the essentials of the game; though I had played bridge in college, sometimes continuously from Friday to Sunday evening, I owe to the Pacific war my ability to count the cards.

The Guam campaign had taken place a few months before our arrival. The island had already been declared secure except for a few Japanese soldiers who had refused to surrender. Early on in the Pacific battles, both sides had abandoned the practice of taking captives. The response of these Japanese soldiers was therefore perfectly rational. Forty years later, the world press reported that the last surviving Japanese soldier on Guam, a Corporal Yokota, had finally surrendered. Yokota returned to Japan to a hero's welcome and many offers of marriage, one of which he accepted, and he started his own successful business.[2]

In a matter of months, Guam was transformed into a major military base. The Sea Bees built roads, tent camps for thousands of replacement troops, a submarine harbor, and an airfield capable of accommodating hundreds of B-29s. Using massive amounts of heavy construction equipment manned by former construction workers and midwestern farm youth recruited for their ability to use heavy equipment, the Sea Bees had made the place a fortress.

The troops in our convoy debarked on landing ships and on shore were loaded into trucks and taken to a Second Division Marine

---

[2]   My thanks to Nobuko Gerth for the information on Corporal Yokota.

Corps tent camp where we remained until the time the Second Division was to be committed to combat. We expected the Division to be committed to the Okinawa campaign, but it was not. Instead, the newly formed Fifth and Sixth Divisions were given this assignment with the Second Division being held in reserve.

Throughout that campaign, we played bridge, chess, gambled in high-stakes poker games, drank beer and whiskey, and sacked out. Poker games with stakes of thousands of dollars were commonplace throughout the island. The best known game was located over the mountains at the submarine base, but getting there and back by hitchhiking was problematic. I made the trip once, but when trying to return was able to hitch a ride only halfway to the top of the mountain, where I spent the rest of the night sleeping half-drunk in a roadside ditch.

It was on Guam that I took up smoking. Our issues of K-rations, besides including crackers and Spam, also contained a pack of three cigarettes. At first, I gave away or traded these cigarettes, but one afternoon, bored and sacked out, I tried one for myself and became hooked. Later, when we no longer had K-rations, we could buy cigarettes at the PX for five cents a pack or fifty cents a carton and might smoke a couple of packs a day. These cheap cigarettes supplied to all American troops throughout the world created a new generation of American cigarette smokers. The cigarette industry, forever alert to creating new markets for its product, could take credit for bolstering the morale of its victims.

On Guam, the only inconvenience we suffered was water rationing. Each trooper was allocated one helmet-full of water per day that was used first to brush the teeth, then to shave, and finally as a bathing douche. Heavily chlorinated drinking water was supplied in centrally located canvas water dispensers. The volume of beer available to the troops exceeded that of water. My mother, a staunch opponent of both smoking and excessive drinking, regarded the Marine Corps as a negative influence on my character.

Guam was a place where it was easy to meet friends from the V-12 Program, boot training, Quantico, or Lejeune. I came across a drill sergeant who had been my superior at the University of Michigan. All ideas of revenge were forgotten at the sight of a familiar face and of shared reminiscences. When I heard that Warren Jollymore, who had been on the boxing team at the University of Wisconsin, was a B-29 pilot, I visited him for an afternoon and came away with his pilot's pistol; second lieutenants in the Marine Corps were issued a Carbine, not a 45-calibre pistol. When I commented on his pistol, Jollymore asked me if I wanted it. He said that he would declare that he had thrown it overboard on a return flight from a fire-bombing exercise over Tokyo. The twenty-four hour round trip from Guam to Tokyo left almost no margin of extra fuel for the return trip. B-29s that had not been shot down over Tokyo or abandoned for lack of fuel while returning to Guam routinely threw their gear overboard in order to gain a few more minutes of flight time: dumping all excess equipment was a permitted practice. In fact, it was a necessary practice. B-29s frequently returned to Guam with almost no fuel, and pilots attempting to land with empty fuel tanks jockeyed with each other for landing position ahead of other planes in similar straits. So Warren gave me his pistol, assuring me he could easily draw another. I carried this pistol the rest of the war and brought it home with me, eventually giving it to Frank Powell, the Chippewa-French Indian who built my log cabin on Northern Lights Lake. I never saw or heard of Jollymore again until years later, when I read his obituary in the *New York Times*; he had had a career as the advertising manager for a Detroit automobile company. He never learned the history of his pistol.

Casualties of the Iwo Jima campaign, where many of my friends fought, were transferred to field hospitals on Guam. I read the casualty lists and learned that quite a few members of my Quantico graduation class were now dead, leaving their parents with only their photographs. I saw Sidney Toabe's name on a list of wounded. He was the man who had dropped out of our officer training class in order to get into combat more quickly. I decided to visit him in the hospital. Toward the end of the campaign, he had taken a bullet in the shoulder and had been evacuated. I mention Toabe again because we remained in touch with each other for half a century, not only sustaining a correspondence but seeing each other in, among other places, California, New York, and London. In a letter in April 2000, he wanted to know how I had found him on Guam while he was in the hospital. That visit had apparently impressed him, and it certainly impressed me because it reminded me of what might have been my own fate.

In the spring of 1945, the Second Division was shipped from Guam to Saipan and began active training for an invasion of South Vietnam's (then French Indo-China) Mekong Delta. Training consisted of a few geography lessons, sandbox simulations of the delta terrain, and field maneuvers designed to coordinate the actions of rifle platoons with those of supporting 50-calibre machine gunners. This was in the summer of 1945, just before the atom bomb was dropped on Hiroshima. Within days after the second bomb had been dropped on August 9th, we were boarding troop ships destined to arrive in Nagasaki on August 18th, just after the Japanese had officially surrendered to General Douglas MacArthur on board a ship in Tokyo harbor.

I had been in the Marine Corps for four and a half years and never fired a shot at an enemy. The only person I saw killed was an enlisted man who, during a hardball game on Saipan between officers and noncommissioned troops, was hit on the chest by a fastball pitched while I was acting as catcher. Assuming he had earned a free base, he dropped his bat and ran to first where he collapsed and, despite the efforts of the doctor who was playing in the game, could not be revived. This was the only death I had seen firsthand during the entire war and, in its senselessness, had as much meaning as those who had died on Iwo Jima or were the victims of the bomb, a subject I will discuss later.

I have always been of the opinion that the taking of Iwo Jima was tactically unnecessary. Unlike General MacArthur, who had bypassed well-defended islands on his return to the Philippines, naval strategists, especially Nimitz, followed the practice of island-hopping because they were committed to using the technological means available to them—troop ships, landing craft, and Marines trained for ship-to-shore invasions. They needed a dramatic act to prove the worth of naval warfare. Okinawa would have served the purpose of providing a land base from which to attack the mainland just as well as Iwo Jima.

The official propaganda claiming Japanese brutality became more strident as the war approached its end. Efforts to convince me of the moral superiority of our actions were no longer creditable. The patriotic enthusiasm of December 8, 1941, had given way to my opinion of war as primarily a demonstration of the superiority of technical means and overwhelming power. I happened to be in the Marine Corps so I accepted as an irrevocable given that over which I had no control: I was told what to do and did it upon command, detaching my own sensibilities from my actions. I did not disobey orders and never thought to reject my status as an officer. I had discovered the depths to which war could dehumanize otherwise ordinary men who gave no thought to the immoral excesses of their military orders. General Curtis LeMay had ordered low-level incendiary bombing flights over Tokyo to increase their efficiency without regard to the inevitable loss of twenty or thirty percent of the planes and their crews. Never having fought, I was not a hero and did not want to be one, especially a dead one. I had had this attitude even before going overseas. My brother-in-law, Frank Olson, who was then an army captain working in biological warfare at Camp Dietrich, Maryland, informed me with pride that half the men in a unit to which he had earlier been attached were killed or wounded in Europe in a single battle. For him, this was heroism, but for me it was not. I did not believe that heavy casualty lists were a sign of bravery or were meant to enhance the pride of survivors. During the Cold War, Olson found himself engaged in other secret applied bacteriological research in North Africa and against former World War II enemies of the United States. He lost his patriotic zeal and, for this, it is alleged that he was killed under suspicious circumstances by his own security handlers. The moral deficits earned by American military and national security policies during World War II and after remain a part of our national heritage.

In World War II, new technological means and new moral standards had been introduced to modern warfare. Neither civilians nor entire urban populations were regarded as noncombatants. Under a professional ideology of modern total war, nothing is sacrosanct, not cultural objects, not the natural terrain, not the hapless individuals who by chance happen to become victims.

The Bomb and Japan

During the summer of 1945, at the age of 23, I was a machine gun platoon leader on the island of Saipan. My platoon and the rest of the Second Division of the Marine Corps were engaged in maneuvers in preparation for an invasion scheduled for November 1st that was now to be Kyushu, Japan's southernmost island. Roosevelt's death in April, just short of VE day on May 8th, had shaken the morale of troops throughout the world, leaving them with a sense of leaderlessness and uncertainty, not helped by the lack of confidence engendered by his successor, Harry Truman. Truman's speech announcing Roosevelt's death to the world was in a high-pitched, mundane, midwestern diction that could not compete with Roosevelt's sonorous, aristocratic voice. In office since 1933, Roosevelt was the only leader the generation of soldiers who fought World War II had ever known. The efficient wartime anti-Japanese propaganda had convinced the troops that combat during an invasion of the mainland would be worse than it had been on Iwo Jima or Okinawa. The Second Division had not been committed during the invasions of Iwo Jima and Okinawa. It was to be the advance force in the invasion of Kyushu, to be followed later by an army attack on the northern Kanto Plains surrounding Tokyo. On August 6, 1945, news reached the world, the Second Division, my platoon, and me, that a super-bomb had been dropped on Hiroshima.

The vaunted power of the new bomb and the fantastic destruction of Hiroshima—endlessly repeated on the radio and in the military press—were for me and the troops cause for jubilation. That devastation was followed three days later, on August 9th, by the second bomb, which annihilated Nagasaki. No one stopped to consider what later came to be the moral issues concerning the use of the bomb and mass killing of civilian populations in two cities. For us, the bomb was a form of salvation not to be questioned, but instead to be thankfully accepted and regarded as justly used against those who would have used it against us had they had it.

When the second bomb was exploded, scuttlebutt had it that the war in Asia would soon be over. In fact, the Japanese surrendered a few days later, and on August 11th or 12th, the Second Division boarded ship not for an invasion but for an occupation of Kyushu. On August 18th, our regiment disembarked in Nagasaki harbor at the same moment that Allied prisoners held in the notorious Japanese prison camp located a few miles southeast of Nagasaki were embarking on a Red Cross ship. Those prisoners had been held for years and were demoralized and embittered. It was only fate (and geography) that prevented their prisoner-of-war camp from being obliterated with the rest of Nagasaki.

By a quirk of geography, Nagasaki harbor, located at the southern tip of the city at a bend in the river, was shielded from the atomic blast. It was here that we disembarked from landing craft, fully armed as if going to battle and scared stiff, expecting we knew not what from the "treacherous Japanese." Doing what infantry organizations do best, our regiment and my platoon, despite fears for our safety, fell into parade formation on a harbor street and waited for further orders. While we waited, a young Japanese woman came out of the house in front of which we stood and began to speak to me in English. She was a Catholic, heir of the efforts of Saint Francis

Xavier's missionary sojourn to southern and central Japan of four hundred years earlier and part of a despised community living in the slums of the only undamaged part of the city. In a few short minutes, she described her terror when the bomb exploded and said that an electrical charge had flashed through the wiring on all the streets and thunderously shook the ground. Within minutes, wounded, skinless, bleeding people, direct victims of the blast, ran through the streets craving the coolness of the water. Acting as a one-person welcoming committee, she treated us not as conquerors but with appreciation that our presence meant the end of the war. This memorable, short encounter was ended by an order to load the troops onto the personnel carriers for the trip to the newly evacuated POW camp that was to become our base. The young woman fit neither the stereotypes impressed on me during the war nor any of the expectations of the reception we had thought we faced when we first landed at the former Nagasaki. A couple of weeks later, I persuaded the pilot of a little piper cub attached to our marine regiment to take me up over the city. I took nine photographs of the devastated city, a very sobering sight.[3]

---

[3] On May 25, 2003, Charles Arthur Vidich, my son, interviewed me in Middletown, Connecticut, about my recollections of these nine photographs. The most important of these pictures is reproduced in the website accompanying this book. In this interview, I said:

[T]he expectation was of course that there would be a tremendous fight. Of course there was no fight whatsoever. Also what they have since argued is that the use of the bomb saved a half million American lives and so forth and so on. That was an ex-post facto justification for the use of them. You know that is one of the great questions that historians have been going after: Was it necessary to use the bombs? Any objective analysis would say it wasn't. That it wasn't from the point of view of causing the end of the war. The Japanese were already negotiating for peace through the Soviet Union—through Moscow. But the Russians refused to let

We traveled to the POW camp in open trucks on dirt roads that passed through several small villages and settled areas. Along the way the roads were lined with Japanese women and children who were our larger welcoming committee, smiling, waving their arms, and shouting "Ohayo (pronounced Ohio) gozaimasu!" (good morning!) to the passing convoy. In response to these cries of "Ohayo," the troops responded by shouting "Tennessee," "New York," "California," and the names of other American states. These exchanges, based on an odd congruence of linguistic usage, convinced us of Japan's acceptance of our conquest and occupation. At the sight of these poorly dressed women and barefoot children—and the absence of any men among them—it was evident that the cost of the war had been borne by the civilian population. Clearly, the civilian population had suffered extreme deprivation and welcomed the end of the war even in defeat.

Our camp was made of flimsy barracks each two stories high, constructed of two-by-fours and four-by-fours, and infested with lice and thousands of huge rats. The daily rat detail collected barrel upon barrel of poisoned rats. The troops, unaccustomed to living

---

Washington know they were negotiating because the Russians were biding time to move their troops from Europe to Asia to make their claims for joint administration of Japan. But you see the Americans wanted to exclude the Soviet Union. This history about the bomb and the end of the war is one that is still inconclusive. ... [The Japanese] hadn't built the bunkers the way they had built them on Iowa Jima. There were no men on the islands between the ages of 15 and 60. They were all overseas. So they had a bunch of kids, and they had a bunch of very old men. With all the cities devastated and no natural resources, they didn't even have the cement to make the bunkers because everything had been invested in their overseas empire. Anyhow, that's a history I've been obsessed with because the bomb was one of the great mistakes of this civilization if I can put it in those dramatic terms.

among rats, took to shooting them from the rafters, spotting them with flashlights at night. I have a special memory of these rats because one of them crawled beneath my neck on the cot where I slept, waking me up with a fearful start and leaving me with a lifelong, recurrent, and ineradicable nightmare about rats crawling under my neck while I sleep. The movie *King Rat* that I saw fifty years later did not capture the rat culture that I had experienced. For those of us who inherited their quarters, the POWs' survival under these conditions (some of the POWs had been incarcerated since the fall of Bataan three years earlier) was beyond comprehension.

The Second Regiment's mission was to demilitarize the Nagasaki region. For a number of weeks, perhaps three or four, I led my machine gun platoon of fifty-four men through the countryside looking for weapons and military installations. My impression was and still is that not only the Nagasaki region but all of Kyushu that we later "demilitarized" was without defenses against an invading force of well-armed, well-supported, and well-fed troops. There was nothing comparable to the kind of bunkers dug in for the defense of the islands, and for that matter, we found nothing that indicated a system of defenses designed to counter an invasion. Our searches for weapons resulted in the collection of a few old rifles and some ordinary Samurai swords, but no heavy weapons or military vehicles. Units that demilitarized the air force found and destroyed maybe a hundred single propeller training planes that, if functional and supplied with gasoline, might only have been useful as kamikazes. There was no gasoline to be found anywhere, and the few vehicles still on the road were propelled by a gas-producing coke fire located on a platform where a gas tank had been. Even after a full year's reconnaissance of the entire island of Kyushu, my estimate was that Japan's resources for continuing to fight the war had been exhausted in the defense of the Pacific islands, its losses of naval and cargo shipping, and the long naval war with a superior American Navy. Late in the war, the sinking of Japan's famous battleship Yamamoto, the largest in the world, had eliminated the Japanese navy as a further threat. While its China and Manchuria armies were still intact, they were needed to protect supply lines from the mainland. Putting these observations together has led me to question the high official estimates of the number of casualties that might have resulted from a full-scale invasion of Kyushu and the Kanto Plain. Japan had been at war on the Asian mainland since 1933 and in costly military confrontations with the allies since 1941. Lacking its own natural resources, it had depleted its stockpiles. Its cities and industrial base had been seriously damaged by aerial bombardments. Wars cannot be fought without petroleum, and Japan was utterly lacking in this decisive commodity as well as the means of war dependent upon it. It became abundantly clear to me, at least, that Japan had not prepared and was not capable of preparing its defenses for an invasion. In the many books I have read about the occupation of Japan and the bomb, my analysis of this lack of preparedness for a defense of the main islands has been confirmed only once. In *The Invasion of Japan: An Alternative to the Bomb*, John Ray Skates describes the elaborate plans for "Ketsu-Go: Defense of the Homeland." These plans were not formulated until fall 1944, and nothing had been accomplished by spring 1945. Skates notes, "The entire construction program lagged behind goals," and that "[s]teel and cement, two critical materials to building fortifications[,] were in short supply."[4] Further, "The motorized vehicles [required for the defense] would be

---

[4]   Skates , *The Invasion of Japan*, 101.

requisitioned from twenty-four thousand civilian cars that were still 'in operating condition.'" "Clearly," continues Skates, "the Japanese logistical plans were based on thin substance and wishful thinking: they would not have sustained a prolonged defense." Commenting on these defenses, Skates writes, "After the war, a Japanese officer remembered that the third mobilization [for Ketsu-Go] 'exhausted practically all of the reserve manpower of Japan and the majority of those called up were either untrained or too old. If Japan had been attacked at this time (June 1945), it would have been impossible to conduct an adequate defense.'"[5] This level of preparedness raises the question not of whether the bomb was needed to end the war, but of the state of America's Japanese intelligence at this stage of the war. The claim that half a million lives of American troops were saved by the use of the bomb appears to me to be an *ex post facto* political and moral rationalization for the use of the bomb.

When the Second Regiment of the Second Division was assigned the mission of demilitarizing the southern and eastern parts of Kyushu, I was relieved from my position as a machine gun platoon leader and appointed assistant to the regimental quartermaster. The regiment, made of about 1,000 troops and detached from Division Headquarters, now had to depend upon itself to secure its own provisions while making its reconnaissance of Kyushu. I was given this job because my personnel file indicated that I had completed a BA degree in economics as a Marine Corps V-12 student stationed at the University of Michigan. That I had studied the economics of John Maynard Keynes was hardly a qualification for this position. Under

---

[5] Skates, *op. cit.*, 106.

field conditions, on-the-job training is the rule. Procurement meant maintaining liaisons with Headquarter's supply base in Sasebo and requisitioning supplies for the regiment. I worked under a major who made me his errand boy and delegated the procurement of Japanese supplies to me. My new job carried with it access to regimental air transport consisting of a pilot and his two-seater Cessna. Most of the senior officers had been using this air wing for observation flights over the former city of Nagasaki, and now it was possible for me to do the same. In early September, I had my first aerial view of the full meaning of the new age of atomic weapons.

The entire city up and down the valley had not only been leveled, but had been cleared by workers of all remaining debris with the exception of a burned out but not completely demolished hospital building. It remained as the only visible sign that there had once been a city on this site. This first visual image remains with me as clear and vivid as the day I saw it and was the beginning of my lifelong obsession with the implications of nuclear bombs and the promotion of nuclear energy as a source of power.

Physicist Glenn T. Seaborg led the power industry's campaign for Atoms for Peace. Not a nuclear physicist, he sold nuclear energy to the power industry and the public as a cheap source of endless low-cost energy. American businessmen saw Atoms for Peace as the opportunity of a lifetime to reap huge profits from low-cost production and combustion of nuclear fuel, without giving a thought, let alone a hard assessment, to the possibility that the invention and development of nuclear power could be the greatest mistake of Western civilization. The atomic age was ushered in with little consideration to the problem of the future disposal of its lethal byproducts.

In 1945, neither the Japanese nor the American troops had been apprised of the dangers of radiation, nor were they privy to the experimental nature of the choice of cities to be bombed. As for the American troops, on an order presumably designed to protect military personnel from exposure to radiation, the area of the former city was declared off limits; nevertheless, this has not prevented veterans of the Nagasaki debarkation from making liability claims against the American government for radiation exposure. In what was surely a sign that Japanese authorities successfully retained disciplined control over the population, thousands of rescue workers were recruited to evacuate the wounded and to clean the Nagasaki site of its remaining debris. Later in 1978, when I revisited Nagasaki at the invitation of a student who had been enrolled in the Kyoto Summer Seminar where I was a Fulbright lecturer, I was told by this student's sister, who was eleven years old in 1945, what she had seen in the days after the bomb exploded. Their home was located east of the city, beyond the reach of the bomb, within view of the railway line on which victims were evacuated. In her memory, trainload after trainload of parched victims with irradiated bodies hanging from open windows passed by endlessly, destined for care that did not exist. No one can know how many new victims were created by the rescue and clean-up operations managed by efficient Japanese bureaucrats.

I learned in 1977, when I was at Doshisha University in Kyoto, that the US Air Force planners had chosen Kyoto as their bomb target of first choice. Destroying Kyoto, Japan's preeminent cultural center and symbolic repository of Japanese history would, they believed, have the maximum psychological impact on crushing Japanese morale. But for the intervention of Truman's Secretary of War, Henry Stimson, who had once visited Kyoto and had developed an

appreciation for that beautiful city, this plan might have been executed. Because of Stimson's objections, other sites were chosen and the
people of Kyoto were saved. The archives at Doshisha University note
this historic reprieve with gratitude. I later reflected on the meaning
of this for those who survived and those who died in a short essay,
"Hiroshima's Legacy: The Theodicy of Man-Made Hazards." As fate
would have it, Hiroshima was the second choice, so its population
substituted, so to speak, for the people of Kyoto. "Why," the survivor
of Hiroshima might ask, "did they choose this city and not Kyoto?"
Can they blame Secretary of State Stimson, and are the people of
Kyoto and their succeeding generations forever beholden to him?

The scientists who had conceived, built, and planned the dropping of the bombs thought to conduct an experiment to give them
information on the bomb's effects when exploded over different geographical formations. Hiroshima was the target of second choice because it was located on a delta—in effect a flat plain. For Hiroshima,
a high-altitude detonation of the bomb would, it was thought, provide a measure of the extent of its destructive power over the widest
possible circumference, unimpeded by natural barriers. Nagasaki
was located in a river valley in a geographical area similar to that of
the Hudson River palisades. Its bomb was detonated at a low altitude
between the hills in order to measure how the concussion spread
up and down the valley. Construction of the bombs and plans for
their delivery had been conducted under a secret program known
as the Manhattan Project. When information about this project was
released to the world, the scientists who had managed it achieved
the status of public icons. On the heels of signing the peace treaty,
physical and social scientists conducted on-site studies of the bomb's
physical damage and human costs in the two former cities. Science

and the scientists had proved their worth to political and military leaders—that science could produce practical political and military results.

Only after viewing the total and efficient destructiveness of the bomb did I begin to reflect on the price Japan paid for pursuing its goal of creating an "Asian Co-Prosperity Sphere," an empire in the Far East. The good fortune of my own survival was shaken by the knowledge that the delivery of a single weapon could erase an entire city. Of course, many others had similar reactions and became equally obsessed with one question: "Was the use of the Bomb on Hiroshima and Nagasaki necessary to achieve the Japanese surrender?" The attempt to answer this question focuses on the issue of whether the bombs were detonated for reasons other than purely military and has generated a publishing industry all its own, much of it linked to the name of Gar Alparovitz, who has devoted a large part of his intellectual life to answering this question. Alparovitz notes that the end of the war in Europe began an incipient competition between the US and the USSR, already moving troops freed from combat in Europe to the Far East with the aim of sharing the occupation of Japan with the US. While the Japanese had earlier initiated a peace overture to end the war via its embassy in Moscow, the USSR withheld the information from the Americans, hoping to have an opportunity to declare war on Japan before the Japanese could surrender. Our use of the bomb was in part Secretary of State James Byrnes's tactic to foil the Soviets' aims by ending the war quickly, thus defeating Soviet claims to participate in the terms of the peace. In addition, pressures to test the bomb and to have the "honor" of delivering it were brought to bear. First, the bomb's creators, the physicists, stood to gain status from their scientific discoveries. Second, Curtis LeMay wanted to demonstrate that air power was decisive in gaining the victory, a prelude to his championing the establishment of the Air Force in 1947. Vice-President Truman, who had not been privy to the existence of the bomb until he became president upon Roosevelt's death in April 1945, was dependent on advisors who feared the Soviets and wanted to use the bomb in order to gain a strategic advantage in a forthcoming confrontation with the USSR. Therefore, the idea of not using the bomb was not an option, nor were the bomb's moral implications or the possibility of a nuclear arms race considered. Political considerations thought to be practical gave birth to the civilizational irrationalities of the nuclear age.

My initial personal reaction to the potential implications of atomic warfare was somewhat innocent. I had thought that all cities could now become atom-bomb targets and that it was prudent to find a retreat or haven invulnerable in an atomic war. In 1946, after leaving the Marine Corps, I acted on this thought by buying an island on Trafalgar Bay of Northern Lights Lake in Western Ontario and building a log cabin. An area one hundred miles west of cities then known as Port Arthur and Fort William, accessible by boat only from the American side, seemed to be the ideal wilderness location. The Soviet Union, already in a cold war with the United Sates, was hard at work building its own bomb, an arms race that led both sides to produce ever more powerful hydrogen and neutron bombs. However, it became clear that if the Soviet Union targeted Chicago for destruction and the bomb intended for it was off its mark by one or two degrees, it would likely wipe out the entire wilderness area where my cabin was located. My realization that no place was invulnerable led me to abandon my illusion that I could control my fate in an atomic war.

For the remainder of my tour of duty in Kyushu, the Second Regiment was stationed for periods, each of a few months, in the southern cities of Miyakonojo in Kagoshima Bay, Kanoya, and Miyazaki in the southeast, and Beppu in Oita prefecture, a resort city on the northeast coast. In each of these small cities, I worked with a Japanese counterpart who informed me of inventories of Japanese resources and their locations. In all instances, these Japanese liaison officers spoke English and had been repatriated from undefeated naval forces in China and the China Sea. They were chosen for their positions because they had not been defeated and therefore could still be proud. They were polite, deferential, and accommodating. They invited me to dinner in their homes and played the part of well disciplined civil servants who had learned their craft as naval officers. Their etiquette fulfilled the Japanese stereotype as portrayed in Yasunari Kawabata's novels.

In addition to regular trips to Sasebo to bring back by train our allotments of beer and whiskey, my normal duties involved procurement of housing, Japanese goods, and materials for regimental use; to the extent possible, the Marine Corps was supposed to appropriate its supplies from Japanese sources. It became clear, however, as we made our way through the secondary cities of Kyushu that there was little to be procured. There were no Japanese surpluses of food, automobiles, gasoline, or alcoholic beverages. According to the legal requirements of the occupation, all items procured were to be itemized and recorded on vouchers supplied by headquarters in Tokyo. I filled out and signed hundreds of these vouchers, each itemizing the goods appropriated. The vouchers' ultimate destination was Tokyo, where they were charged as debits against the American occupation. Each voucher required my signature and that of my Japanese counterpart; for me, signing them became a meaningless ritual of military protocol, but for the terms of the peace, they substantiated the legality of the appropriation.

The troops and officers were housed according to rank in Japanese military installations. The riding horses that had formerly belonged to Japanese officers were procured for higher-ranking US regimental officers, while Samurai swords and rifles were distributed to the troops as war trophies. Creation of an officers' mess was always a high priority accomplished by appropriating tablecloths, cutlery, and other items from military warehouses.

When our unit was in Miyazaki, my colonel called me to his office and said that ranking officers' wives were be permitted to join their husbands in Japan if housing could be found for them. I was instructed to make a housing survey in the southern region of Kyushu. With a jeep and a driver, I visited dozens of towns and cities; Kyushu was then a poor agricultural area with few industries. In each location, I cruised the streets and found dwellings that were well constructed and attractive. In every instance, the dwelling was a Geisha house. My survey, the first in my career as a sociologist, was, in effect, a report on the location of the region's Geisha houses. When I submitted my report to the colonel, he rejected out-of-hand the idea that officers' wives might be billeted in Geisha houses, saying, as I remember exactly, "You wouldn't want ladies from Philadelphia living in Geisha houses, would you?" Though I had been aware before this time that many senior officers in the regiment had been Philadelphians, it only then occurred to me that upon graduation, Annapolis-trained naval officers could opt for service in the Marine Corps, technically part of the Navy. By tradition, higher ranking naval officers were recruited from America's eastern aristocratic families. Though I was proud of the thoroughness of my survey and impressed by the comfort and luxury of the housing I had located, the colonel's standards were those of a Philadelphia gentleman. No ladies from Philadelphia joined their husbands in Kyushu.

Once, when examining the map of Kyushu, I noticed the town of Suye Mura at the northern end of Kagoshima Bay and remembered a book by that title written by the anthropologist John Embree with his Japanese-speaking Russian wife. As I mentioned earlier, I had thought about a career as an anthropologist after taking Leslie White's anthropology course at the University of Michigan. After leaving the University of Michigan for boot camp on Parris Island, I carried on a correspondence with White, from whom I thought there was much to learn. Thinking to study anthropology after the war, I thought that White could later be of help to me. These anthropological ambitions led me to take an unauthorized trip to Suye Mura. This was my first anthropological field trip. I had not the foggiest notion of what to look for; except for a few phrases, I could not speak Japanese. I drove around a few dirt roads, saw a few houses and some pedestrians, and returned to Miyakonojo. However, I felt as if I was more of an anthropologist than I had been before.

Wanting to know more about the history and culture of Japan, I wrote to Virginia Wicks, to whom I was to be married when released from the Marine Corps, and asked her for reading material on Japan. At that time, she was at the University of Wisconsin studying sociology and taking a course with Hans H. Gerth. At the recommendation of Gerth, she sent me a selection of books including Inazo Notobé's *Bushido, the Soul of Japan*; Helen Mears's *Year of the Wild Boar*; G. B. Sansom's *Japan: A Short Cultural History*; and Glen Trewartha's *The Geography of Japan*. The latter left a deep impression on me. Though I had taken "Introduction to Geography" as a freshman at the University of Wisconsin, I had never heard of Trewartha, who was that University's and the geography profession's foremost geographer of Japan. Not knowing this and only learning it in Japan left me with a feeling of intellectual inadequacy bordering on naiveté, even stupidity; why had I not known about this man when I had studied in his department? I read several other books that Virginia sent, but for lack of an academic foundation on the subject of Japan they gave me little appreciation for what I was seeing and experiencing in Kyushu. This was the first time I had heard the name Gerth, the German émigré sociologist who had arrived at the University of Wisconsin in 1940 and who deeply influenced me later.

I returned to the States in May of 1946 and was mustered out of the Marine Corps on July 2nd at the Great Lakes Naval Base. I was handed a letter addressed to First Lieutenant Arthur J. Vidich (041390), USMCR, from Harry S. Truman, the White House: "To you who have answered the call of your country and served in its armed services to bring about the total defeat of the enemy, I extend the heartfelt thanks of a grateful nation. ... We now look to you for leadership and example in further exalting our country in peace." At the same table where I received my discharge papers, a recruitment officer offered to sign me up for the Marine Corps Reserve. My friends and I had discussed the merits and demerits of joining it. Its merits were that one could retain status as an officer and be paid a reservist's monthly income; the pay was a big incentive because we were all being thrown back into civilian life without job or income. Most of my friends joined the reserves, but a few of us did not. In principle, we who did not were eager to sever our ties to the Marine Corps and its slogan *Semper Fidelis* (always faithful). To cement my resolve to make a decisive break with military life, I made a compact with my friend Richard Burns to "never ever again step off with the left foot" (as in close-order drill), a final anti-militarist statement about life in the Marine Corps during World War II.

Due to a legal technicality, our wartime officer commissions had a temporary status. Those of us who rejected reservist duty were discharged as sergeants. I had no regrets and quickly shed my identification with the corps and all its artifacts.

I left all of my Marine Corps uniforms and other paraphernalia, including the combat zone ribbons that the corps was always so eager to award, with my parents. My mother included my uniforms, combat fatigues, great coat, and officer's bars in her care packages to relatives in Kropa in Slovenia: some ex-partisans in Tito's war were the beneficiaries of these goods. I gave my Japanese rifle to Mel Ott, director of YMCA Camp Manitowish at Boulder Junction, Wisconsin, where he hung it on the wall in his office. I cannot remember to whom I gave the Samurai sword. I had fulfilled my compact with Burns, and the Marine Corps has thoughtfully never communicated with me since.

Friends who opted for the reserves were called up at the beginning of the Korean War. Bob Van Amman—who, because his last name began with a "V," had been in my Parris Island and Quantico platoons—was killed there, another friend from Milwaukee who became a victim of chance.

The Marine Corps had inadvertently provided me with a safe passage throughout the Pacific war. I had enlisted at the age of 19 and completed a BA degree in economics at the University of Michigan under a full Marine Corps Scholarship at age 21. It had paid me an officer's salary for two years and discharged me with a bonus of $600. I had survived the war and had money to spare. The injustice done to those who were wounded or died in combat was quickly forgotten except in an abstract patriotic sense. The American soldier who survived the war was a beneficiary of a welfare program sponsored by the government. It was a welfare program designed to insure the loyalty and fighting spirit of an ethnically mixed armed force, supported by wartime taxation, rigid control of civilian consumption, and the new Keynesian economics.

As part of manpower plans for the demobilization of millions of service personnel, the World War II generation of soldiers became the benefactors of another public welfare program. Known as the "GI (Government Issued) Bill of Rights," it guaranteed to each honorably discharged soldier an educational scholarship; for each month of service, a veteran was granted the equivalent of a month of study at government expense. Counted from the day of my enlistment on April 6, 1942, I had earned some 50 months of educational credits. Translated into academic semesters of four months each, this meant I was entitled to an academic scholarship of six years. In fact, I was on this scholarship five years: two years (1946-1948) at the University of Wisconsin; two years (1948- 1950) at Harvard University; and one year (1950-1951) as a Fulbright scholar at the University of London and the London School of Economics. The scholarship included full payment of tuition, a book allowance, and a cost of living stipend adjusted upward for those who were married and had children. Supplemented by a few graduate student scholarships, teaching assistantships, a Fulbright Grant, and summer employment, I had achieved economic independence while being a married graduate student with two children. Five million veterans were recipients of this governmental welfare program.

As part of a national manpower planning program, the GI Bill had several rationales. In the first instance, it provided a large contingent of demobilized veterans with an income and an academic career rather than creating a contingent of unemployed veterans who might become a destabilizing political force. In theory, the veterans, committed to their studies, would not be political and, in fact, they were not. When the AmVets, a politically left (possibly a front) group attempted to organize these veterans on American campuses, they failed. Veterans no longer had the radical impulses they may have had during the depression years before the war. Another rationale was based on the expectation of the future manpower needs of an expanding economy that resulted from a victorious war. This generation of American youth entered the economy at the beginning of the Cold War and remained in it for the rest of the "Golden Age of American Capitalism." We had become a new generation of new middle classes in the burgeoning suburbs of postwar America. The trajectory of our lives had been shaped by the war. We continued to be shaped by it for the rest of our lives.

5

The University of Wisconsin
1946-1948

A Pathway to Anthropology

In the 1930s, Wisconsin was thought to have one of the country's ranking departments of sociology and anthropology. E. A. Ross, the elder Gillen, Howard Becker, and Ralph Linton had been its stars. Becker, then considered Talcott Parsons's competitor, had been considered for an appointment at Harvard. C. Wright Mills, Don Martindale, and Reuben Hill had been graduate students whom Becker had attracted to the department. Hans H. Gerth, the German refugee scholar, was appointed in 1940. After hearing Gerth's first lecture, C. Wright Mills became his admirer and student and collaborated with him in the publication of *From Max Weber: Essays in Sociology* and *Character and Social Structure: The Psychology of Social Institutions*. While I was an undergraduate, I knew none of these professors except Reuben Hill, who had been teaching social work and was an administrator at the Wisconsin Student Union. I met him through my activities as an aspiring BMOC and had impressed him sufficiently to have him recruit me to enroll in his course on social work practice, a workshop designed to instruct us in the art of managing people in committee meetings. We were taught how to set agendas, act as chairmen, and generally control the content and process of committee meetings. It was my first training in bureaucratic technique. One of Hill's techniques was the use of the eye wink. He looked directly at one and winked his right eye. His purpose in doing this was to convey a confidentiality that carried with it the assumption of your implicit assent and agreement with what he was saying, as if this gesture trapped you into agreement with him. I was repulsed by the Machiavellianism of group-work practice. What I learned in the class is that I did not want to be a managerial bureaucrat. This was the full extent of my sociological education before I entered graduate school in Madison.

Except for Leslie White's course in anthropology mentioned earlier, there was nothing in my academic record to support my admission for an MA in anthropology at the University of Wisconsin. The only person in the department whose name I knew was Gerth's and that was only because he had recommended the books on Japan that Virginia had sent me when I was still overseas. Having no specific qualifications, the factor in my favor for gaining admission was the dearth of graduate students immediately after the war. The military draft had depleted graduate school enrollments though a few former graduate students such as, for example, Don Martindale returned to the department after the war. Others, like C. Wright Mills, had completed their degrees and were already teaching elsewhere. Veterans like me and women were the only source of recruitment for a new cohort of graduate students. On the strength of my minimal qualifications, the department admitted me on a provisional basis until such time as I could establish an acceptable academic record. The department had its own standards, but still they needed me as much as I needed them.

The specialties of the anthropologists then in residence at Wisconsin reflected what then was the conventional four-field anthropological curriculum—archaeology, physical anthropology, cultural or social anthropology, and linguistics, for which there was not a faculty.

W. W. Howells, nephew of William Dean Howells and a student of Harvard's Ernest Hooten, taught physical anthropology, evolution, and Oceania. David Barrais, archaeologist and Columbia graduate, taught old and new world archaeology and its research methods; his courses were extended exercises in classifications of stone tools and artifacts, intellectually deadening because there seemed to be no problem other than tracing evolutionary sequences. Scudder Mekeel was the cultural anthropologist who was then teaching a course in culture and personality based on a seminar he attended at Columbia University taught by Abraham Kardiner and Ralph Linton. Linton had left Wisconsin earlier to take an appointment in Columbia's anthropology department. The Kardiner-Linton studies on basic and modal personality types that stressed the overriding influence of early childhood training, as exemplified by Margaret Mead's swaddling hypothesis to explain Russian character and Ruth Benedict's book, *The Chrysanthemum and the Sword*, to explain Japanese character, attributed the formation of character structure and institutions to methods of "toilet training," an approach Gerth referred to in derision as "piss-pot psychology." C. W. M. Hart was the social anthropologist who taught an English version of social anthropology with an emphasis on Emile Durkheim, A. R. Radcliff-Brown, Raymond Firth, Evans Pritchard, and Bronislaw Malinowski, contrasting their studies with the work of the American anthropologists Alfred Kroeber, Ruth Benedict, Margaret Mead, Clyde Kluckhohn, W. Lloyd Warner, and Robert Redfield. Hart was a Canadian and English Commonwealth internationalist who contrasted these sets of writers to make the point that anthropology did not have a determinate set of problems.

John Useem was a recent appointment to the department and, like Hart, bridged the fields of sociology and anthropology; he had just returned from wartime work as a Naval Officer and administrator of native populations in the Pacific Islands. He taught a seminar on social systems, an expression then becoming fashionable, that attracted both sociology and anthropology students because it was thought to be something entirely new. In this seminar, Joseph Bensman and I teamed up to do a report on the works of Margaret Mead and Ruth Benedict, the beginning of a collaboration that continued for many years and came to include our books *Small Town in Mass Society* and *The New American Society*. I had known Bensman from before the war when we had been on the Student Union Forum committee, and he had been enrolled in some of the same economics courses as I. In this seminar, I read all of Mead's writings, including the multi-volume study *The Mountain Arapesh*. In that book, Mead seemed to be trying to establish herself as a theoretician rather than as the journalist she had been when she wrote books on Samoa and New Guinea. My report followed the usual critical style of a graduate student, discovering all her weaknesses and inconsistencies without crediting her for her vast researches or for her invention of a new ethnographic method, that of using the data from exotic societies to attack Puritan sexual prudishness among Americans. Her books *Coming of Age in Samoa* and *Growing Up in New Guinea* became bestsellers and were used extensively as texts in introductory anthropology courses. Their popularity helped to sell anthropology to a new generation of middle-class Americans and stimulated the growth of anthropology as an academic discipline in the postwar period. It was for good reason that she became the preeminent icon of her profession.

My curriculum included the full scope of courses taught by the anthropologists. Hart's course on social anthropology had its starting point in Émile Durkheim's *Elementary Forms of Religious Life* and in Radcliff-Brown's concept of structural functionalism fully elaborated in his posthumously published volume *Structure and Function in Primitive Society*. The English anthropologists, Hart argued, produced monographs concerned with a single tribe, each of its customs fitting together in a consistent whole, stressing the psychological integration of a society in a non-temporal framework. American anthropology, according to Hart, derived in large part from Alfred Kroeber's concept of the superorganic (a concept derived from Herbert Spencer) and on Kroeber's work, "On the Principle of Order in Civilization as Exemplified by Changes in Fashion," and in part from Clark Wissler's studies of American Indians (for instance, *North American Indians of the Plains*) that focused on the presence or absence of particular cultural traits. The Crow have a certain trait while the Navajo do not. This leads to a concern with time sequences. When did the Crow get a particular trait, and how did this trait spread? Wissler's studies of diffusion were essentially historical reconstructions. Hart seemed to have read everything, including the section on Durkheim in Parsons's *Structure of Social Action* that was the first indication I had that Parsons's functionalism had its origins in the work of the British anthropologists whom he had studied while he was in England. Hart reviewed most of the salient work of American anthropologists, including Robert Lowie's *History of Ethnological Theory* (but not *The Method and Theory of Ethnology*, Paul Radin's answer to Lowie's book); W. Lloyd Warner's *Black Civilization*, an account of an Australian tribe; Conrad Arensberg's and Solon Kimball's *Family and Community in Ireland*; Alexander Leighton's *Governing of Men*; Robert Redfield's *The Folk Culture of Yucatan*; and Elton Mayo's *The Human Problems of an Industrial Civilization*. He said nothing, however, about what anthropology's central problems might be. One was left to think that nothing added up, and that each anthropologist had his or her own approach to the discipline.

Because my interests were in social organization or social anthropology, the anthropology curriculum, based as it was on exposing the students to all of its subfields, seemed to be deficient in subjects I wanted to learn about. This led me to audit sociology courses that Joe and Marilyn Bensman and Virginia were taking. It was, after all, a joint department, then an academic norm, in which the lines separating the two fields were blurred; the faculty did not consider it a betrayal to show an interest in sociology or vice-versa. I began auditing lectures by Howard Becker, Don Martindale, and Hans Gerth.

For his introductory course, Becker had made mimeographed copies of his textbook (later published as *Modern Sociological Theory in Continuity and Change*) and sold it at the going textbook rate to his students who found this bit of commerce offensive, especially as the course was required. Even worse, since what he had to say was already in the text, he devoted portions of his lecture to reading the poetry of Scottish authors.

Don Martindale taught the introductory course in social theory that he conceived as a survey of the ideas of major thinkers including Weber, Durkheim, Marx, Ferdinand Tönnies, William Graham Sumner, Franklin Giddings, George Herbert Mead, and so on. Martindale was impressive because he seemed to have read everything and poured out the information systematically with every idea properly placed. He held to the practice of writing his lectures in advance and reading them to his students, so that it was not only easy to take notes, but also nothing unexpected ever happened. I later discovered that his lectures for this course, as well as others, were chapters for books later to be published in almost the same form. See, for example,

his *Sociological Theory and the Problem of Values*. Martindale's pro-
lific productivity was a result of his use of this technique. His course
enabled me to see the connection between Hart's discussion of British anthropology and the ideas of thinkers who were regarded as sociologists; there seemed to be no difference between them except that
most anthropologists studied non-Western societies. The reasons for
this division of labor were not clear to me.

Gerth was teaching George Herbert Mead's social psychology,
Weber, social stratification, public opinion, mass communications,
and a variety of other subjects as well. Since studying with Leslie
White, this was my first encounter with a teacher who left a lasting impression on me; I can still remember Gerth's lectures and
ideas in detail. For example, one evening when teaching his seminar on mass communications, he brought a copy of the *New York
Times* with him to class. In a lead story, the *Times* printed a joint
ecumenical statement released by the World Council of Churches,
then holding its ecumenical meetings in Stockholm. Analyzing this
statement word for word, Gerth proceeded to show why each word
was there as a result of compromises that each faith was required
to make in order to arrive at a joint statement. The lecture retraced
the sectarian schisms within Protestantism from the time of Martin
Luther and the contemporary efforts of the various faiths to hold
to their doctrines while appearing to stress unity. The lecture was a
lesson in how bureaucratic committee work can lead to consensus
at the cost of substance. This was a Gerthian linguistic *tour de force*.
During the war years, Gerth had been translating some of Weber's
writings and made these available to his students. He also translated
and/or distributed portions of Oswald Spengler, John Ruskin, and
Georg Simmel. When Gerth and Mills published *From Max Weber:*

Essays in Sociology in 1946, I bought the book courtesy of my GI Bill of Rights book allowance and still have this annotated copy of the original edition. Reading Weber presented intellectual problems for me because his approach to understanding the world was difficult to square with what I was getting in other courses and books, especially in anthropology. Weber's ability to define a problem and analyze it stood in sharp contrast to the factual, descriptive, classificatory, and ethnographic style of the anthropologists. For example, his book *The Agrarian Sociology of Ancient Civilizations* that I read much later made me understand that I had wasted my time in Barrais's archaeology courses because Barrais didn't consider it his responsibility to explain the implications and meanings of his classifications. Even V. Gordon Child's Marxist archaeology illustrated in *Man Makes Himself*, a book that is a truly synthetic archaeological explanation, does not compare favorably with Weber. While Gerth introduced us to the ideas of European thinkers, he used these ideas and applied them to analyses of American institutions, politics, culture, music, intellectuals, religion, and character. Gerth understood the philosophical foundations of sociology and, as a neo-Kantian, never forgot the complex relationship between material and ideal values, but when he analyzed anything, he always used concrete, empirical reality as his starting point. The breadth of Gerth's historical knowledge, the depth of his erudition, and his analytical skills overwhelmed me and other students who took his example as their own standard for work in the social sciences. One learned from Gerth, as Gerth already knew, that it was not possible to understand the underlying values and the institutions of capitalism and modernity without reference to the great social and economic analysts—those who saw them in the process of formation—of the late nineteenth and early twentieth centuries.

The Socialization of a Graduate Student

Apart from learning the subject matter of a discipline, the graduate student is also privy to the inner workings of the department and its ethical standards. Thrust into close association with professors when acting as their course or research assistants, the student learns the mores and folkways of the sociological profession and enters into a socialization process typical for novices in any craft.

In my case, I felt anointed when W. W. Howells asked me to be his assistant in his course on physical anthropology. I had taken the course the year before and for the first time read Howells's textbook on primate and human evolution, *Mankind So Far*. The terminologies used by physical anthropologists were not entirely unfamiliar to me because at the University of Michigan I had taken a course in comparative anatomy as part of my failed attempt to escape the Marine Corps by transferring into the Navy as a medical school candidate. This knowledge of physical anatomy gave me a slight advantage over other students. It allowed me to impress Howells sufficiently to gain the assistantship and to become an instructor conducting weekly discussions for students taking the course the year after I did. As the instructor, I was required to attend Howells's lectures and read his book for the second time. This, my only formal training for the job, taught me my first lessons about teaching. Though everything I knew about physical evolution I had learned from Howells, it was easy to appear to be an authority on the subject: one did not have to know much if one was a teacher of those who knew even less. The authority of the position and a slight age advantage guaranteed the respect of beginning students and established the distance between student and instructor on which the authority was premised. Much later, when I became a professor, I learned that students, out of awe, respect, fear, boredom, or some other attitude, grant the instructor the authority which, in turn, accounts for a common professorial occupational hazard. That is, that the professor's own intellectual standard can easily be determined by the intellectual level of the students: being new to the professor's subject matter, the student is impressionable, making it easy for the professor to appear to be erudite. My discovery of this hazard was confirmed when I read the chapter, "What Teaching Does to Teachers," in Willard Waller's book, *The Sociology of Teaching*, where Waller notes this to be the cause of much mediocrity in the teaching professions. As a career in teaching grinds on and an instructor realizes that the old notes are still marketable to a new batch of students, a routinization of teaching sets in.

When, as his assistant, I attended Howells's first lecture, it did not surprise me that his lecture was the same as that he had given the previous year; in fact, he read from the same notes. The facts of human physical evolution, it appeared, were well established and unchanging. The repetition also made my job much easier because it meant that the subject's parameters were circumscribed by the textbook and lectures. I was reassured to learn that what I already knew had neither changed nor was problematic. On the other hand, however, it was not reassuring to discover that Muriel Seaburg Howells was enrolled in her husband's course and became a student in my discussion section. Her presence in my class meant that she could report directly to her husband on my performance. Luckily, however, Mrs. Howells was not an academic, had not previously read her husband's book, and as a Bostonian transplanted to a midwestern university town, seemed to be enrolled in the course to alleviate the boredom of life in Madison. In any case, according to her husband who reported to me her reports to him, her reports were positive and Howells was pleased with my work. Under the circumstances, it could not have been otherwise, for Mrs. Howells was reporting my repetition of his own work to her husband; Howells could only be pleased to hear his own work confirmed by his wife. This episode meant that the standing of my reputation with Howells was contingent on his wife's opinion of me, something I could never have imagined could be a determining factor in an academic career. Among other things, Howells's recommendation to Clyde Kluckhohn helped me gain admission to Harvard University. This was only the beginning of my education in the mores and network structures of academia.

My wife Virginia experienced an instance of academic ethical standards, or rather, lack thereof. She had been hired as a research assistant by Marshall Barron Clinard, who was writing a book on price controls and the black market. During World War II, Clinard had worked in Washington in the Office of Price Administration and, while there, had collected his data for a project on white-collar crime. Clinard gave Virginia assignments that amounted to writing drafts of chapters for his book *The Black Market: A Study of White Collar Crime*. Virginia's drafts appeared as chapters in that book in substantially unrevised form. Indisputably, the data were Clinard's and the book's conception was his, but large parts of it were written in draft form by Virginia. Surprisingly, when the book was published, no mention was made of Virginia or of the contribution she had made to it. I learned later that professorial exploitation of graduate students and its reverse, students' exploitation of their professors, was almost an academic norm. In cases I learned of later, students have used the ideas of their professors without acknowledgment, and professors have published their students' papers as if they were their own. In the first case, C. Wright Mills used many of Gerth's ideas without appropriate acknowledgment in his book *White Collar*. Guy

Oakes and I wrote about this in our book, *Collaboration, Reputation and Ethics in American Academia: Hans H. Gerth and C. Wright Mills*. The other is that of a well-known sociologist who had published several of his students' dissertation chapters as his own. When brought before the American Sociological Association's ethics committee to face charges, he defended his right to publish their work and, much to the astonishment of those who knew of the case, was exonerated. As editor of a journal's special issue on Latin America, I had solicited papers from both the professor and the student and received the same paper, word for word, from both. I knew the student had written it because I had been reading other chapters of his work. The university had conducted an extensive investigation of the case, but chose not to make a public issue of it, agreeing instead to accept the professor's resignation. The academic marketplace of intellectual capital is both unregulated and beyond the purview of legal recourse. Claims of theft—that is, plagiarism—are difficult to substantiate legally and can blemish the reputations of both accused and accuser alike. As a result, it's rare to find whistle blowers in the culture of academia.

Intimate and personal relations between professors and graduate students lead to awareness of and exposure to professorial competitiveness, animosities, gossip, and prejudices, positive and negative. Not fully trusting each other, professors air their gripes to their students and sometimes to each other against third parties. In addition, students are enlisted as supporters in the professors' causes and can be rewarded if they inform their mentors of the peccadilloes of other professors. Like any group of individuals brought together in close and sustained proximity, the interpersonal affairs of an academic department—favoritism, rumored conspiracies, back-biting, likes, dislikes, personal antagonisms, betrayals, and intellectual compromises—help to socialize the novice to the culture of academia. After the initial and sometimes disturbing exposure to this culture, the beginner learns to accept it as a fact of career expediency.

My education in such matters was furthered in the summer of 1947 when my wife and I were invited by John Useem and Peter Munch to join their study of the acculturation of Norwegians in a Wisconsin community. During that summer, relations between Useem and Munch deteriorated for both personal and intellectual reasons. Each seeking support for his cause, both independently turned to my wife and me to support their antagonism toward one another. Caught in the middle of this dispute and dependent on both men for our jobs and academic standing in the department, all we could do was to listen to both, criticize neither to the other, and hope to escape from the dilemma at summer's end. However, that summer's research transcended their conflict and became a formative part of my education, for it gave me my first opportunity to do my own field research.

Viroqua's Norwegian Community

Useem and Munch had received a foundation grant to study Norwegian acculturation in the towns of Viroqua and Westby in western Wisconsin, not far from LaCrosse and the Mississippi River, in this heavily Norwegian part of the state. Other than what I had learned in William Sewell's rural sociology course in the College of Agriculture, I knew nothing about small towns. Sewell's course did not teach me much about life in rural communities because it was mainly concerned with statistics about rural demographic patterns, family as distinguished from corporate farming, and so forth. What I remember of Sewell's course were his stories about his youth as a farm boy when he walked barefoot in the mud on his father's farm—he gave a vivid description of "mud oozing between his toes."[1] My academic exposure to rural sociology gave me no preparation for research in Viroqua.

Virginia and I were to do interviews for Useem and Munch, and I was given the opportunity to carry out a research project of my own. I needed material for an MA thesis, and this invitation seemed like a good opportunity for me to learn something about research, a word that had no precise meaning for me. The only research I had ever done was to conduct the one-man survey of the housing market for Marine Corps Officers' families in Kyushu that I mentioned earlier, and that was more an exercise in search than research. Since I had not taken any academic courses in research methods other than statistics, where I learned to do a chi-square and a regression table, I went into the field to learn about research by doing it.

I formulated a problem designed to examine the success aspirations of young men between the ages of twenty and thirty. I wanted to learn the relationship between their aspirations and the objective possibility of their achievement. Based on interviews with fifty-eight men, I discovered that, with advancing age and greater occupational and life experience, aspirations held by men interviewed at age twenty were no longer evident in respondents who had reached the age of thirty. The American dream, the notion that on merit one could succeed in any endeavor if only one worked hard and believed in success, collapsed when confronted with reality. This led to the abandonment

---

[1] Some years later, Sewell became chair of the sociology department in the College of Arts and Sciences, giving it a positivistic orientation and greatly increasing its size during the Cold War years when federal money poured into the Wisconsin campus. Much later, in 1978, Sewell's path crossed with mine again when he was appointed by the Commissioner of Education of the State of New York to chair the Sociology Rating Committee to evaluate graduate departments of sociology throughout the state. For more on this, see "The Re-making of the Graduate Faculty," the last chapter in this book.

of youthful goals. However, while expectations were reduced with increasing age, credence in the success dream remained untarnished: the respondents accommodated their life situation to a new personal standard while continuing to believe in the myth. This study, entitled "The American Success Dilemma," became my MA thesis. Not strangely, the choice of this research topic was connected to my own life situation. Having been socialized to believe that any goal was attainable, I had been disabused of this idea when confronted by the reality of constraints on achieving the goals I had set for myself. My research problem was linked to my own biography. Awareness of this led me to always look for the biographical origins of the research problems investigated by other social scientists. All research, at least in the social sciences, is, at bottom, driven by personal demons.

Unexpectedly, Viroqua had been the birthplace of Gerald L. K. Smith, editor of *The Cross and the Flag*, anti-Semite, and promoter of an indigenous variety of a Christian-based fascism. During that summer, Viroqua was holding its centennial celebration and used this occasion to bestow honors on Smith, its renowned native son. The centennial organizing committee invited Smith to give a speech and planned to award him a diamond ring. But when news of this forthcoming event reached and was assailed by the press in Madison, Milwaukee, La Crosse, and in other towns, the centennial committee came under fire for its decision to choose Smith as its centennial speaker. Embarrassed by the negative reactions of the press, civic leaders revised their plans and downgraded Smith's visit to a private gathering to be held at the home of a local leader. Confident of myself as an interviewer, I decided to try to interview Smith. I had no trouble getting an interview. In fact, when I expressed an interest in knowing more about his political program, I was welcomed to participate in the private ceremony. I learned from the ease with which I secured this interview that both the respondent and the interviewer hope to gain something from an encounter in which both have separate but mutually reinforcing agendas.

Smith arrived on the scene in a new Lincoln Continental, a gift from Henry Ford, Sr., evidence of Ford's support for Smith's political program and, until a few years ago, still a source of embarrassment to the Ford family only partly remedied by its use of philanthropy to erase the anti-Semitism of Henry Ford, Sr. For example, David Riesman, a well-known sociologist, was appointed to Harvard's distinguished Ford professorship, and executives at the Ford Foundation supported research that stressed its political liberalism. I questioned Smith about whom he thought were his supporters, why they supported him, and what he thought were his political prospects. Smith's answers impressed me. He analyzed his appeals with hard-headed realism, noting that his constituents were people in small midwestern towns and agricultural regions and that he was a carrier of populist appeals against eastern cosmopolitanism. He knew why the appeal of *The Cross and the Flag* had been weakened by World War II: internationalism had prevailed over "America First." I knew then that I had met a shrewd and dedicated politician whose internally consistent political ideology, expounded fearlessly despite his critics, rested upon his faith in his righteousness. Smith was a politician who did not compromise his principles for pragmatic political reasons, as did Michigan's Senator Vandenberg at this time, when at the end of the war he joined the ranks of the internationalists.

Later that fall, I learned that Smith was speaking at a political rally in Milwaukee. Virginia and I attended this meeting and met Smith again. The political appeals of the 1930s lacked resonance and were already replaced by those of the Cold War. Smith's message had lost its appeal to his midwestern Christian constituents, and he was on his downward slide into oblivion. This political rally was attended by a handful of enthusiasts and may have been Smith's last attempt to test the water and revive his political career. His issues and appeals had been replaced by those that focused on the reconstruction of Europe and Soviet expansion in Eastern Europe, shifting the grounds from under his message.

At the instigation of Leo Lowenthal, whom Virginia had known while she worked at the Institute for Social Research on Morningside Heights, Virginia and I worked together on a study based on our Smith data. Lowenthal was seeking contributors to a book eventually published as *Prophets of Deceit*. Although Lowenthal chose not to include our report in his book, Virginia fashioned it into her master's thesis under Gerth, published as "Gerald L. K. Smith Speaks at 'Cross Roads': a Social Psychological Study in Public Opinion." The thesis carefully documents Smith's rhetorical appeals to rural audiences and the reactions of the regional press to the invitation to Smith to speak at Viroqua at an important moment in American political history. At that point, neither Virginia nor I were attuned to the relationship between the content of political rhetorics and their underlying religious appeals. I learned later that secular politics in the United States are infused with religious premises. In *American Sociology: Worldly Rejections of Religion and Their Directions*, Stan Lyman and I examined the transformation of religion into secular rhetorics, fascinating transvaluations of religious premises into mundane language.

My summer in Viroqua gave me my first intensive exposure to Lutheranism and its culture as practiced by Norwegians. What I learned was consistent with the experience I mentioned earlier when I went to the Lutheran church and was presented with a catechism and advised to study it, learning that its severe dogma was relentless in its demands. In Viroqua, I saw some of the consequences of this dogmatic rigidity in the rebelliousness of young people; drinking and carousing was a common pattern among them that seemed to signify a rejection of the stern requirements of the faith. Either God was to be taken seriously on his own terms or ignored altogether. The Lutheran faith made heavy demands on Lutheran youth. This encounter with Lutheranism gave me another angle of refraction on the varieties of Christian faith. My next encounter with still other mundane implications of that faith in both Lutheran and Catholic versions was in Palau, an island in Micronesia that the US had recently acquired from the Japanese as part of its booty for the defeat of Japan in World War II, where I saw it expressed in the form of Christian missions.

An Expedition to Palau

In the fall semester of 1947, even before I had finished writing my MA thesis, John Useem received a grant from the National Science Foundation to do a study in Palau. George Peter Murdock was overall director of that Foundation's project called "The Coordinated Investigation of Micronesian Anthropology" (CIMA) and had selected Useem, whom he had known for his wartime work with native populations, to form a Palauan research group. Though I had been on Guam and Saipan during the war, I had never met a native, but I had taken Howells's course on Oceania; this was apparently enough to qualify me to be a member of this team. I joined Useem's group. The other members were Robert Ritzenthaler, staff anthropologist at the Milwaukee Public Museum; Francis Mahoney, University of Chicago graduate student; and Harry Uyehara, a linguist from Okinawa and speaker of Japanese and English whom Useem had signed up to act as our translator and who went on to study the Palauan language. Each of us was to formulate our own research problem. And, according to our contracts, we were responsible for submitting a final report to the National Science Foundation within a year of completing the field work; on submission of an acceptable report the Foundation paid participants five hundred dollars. The Palau expedition was an opportunity I could not turn down, despite the fact that my wife was pregnant with our first son who was, in fact, born while I was in Palau. I had already applied for admission to Harvard's Department of Social Relations and needed material for a dissertation wherever I studied.

Choosing a research problem on the strength of what I then knew about anthropology was a hit or miss proposition, but it was one that required immediate decision: Murdock wanted commitments. In my readings, I had come across an essay on nativist movements written by Philleo Nash, "The Place of Religious Revivalism in the Formation of the Intercultural Community on the Klamath Reservation," that appeared in a book edited by Fred Eggan on *The Social Anthropology of North American Indian Tribes*. I had also read about the Cargo Cults of New Guinea that were reported in the popular press; the cults were natives' reactions during the war to the vast military supplies, huge naval vessels, and spectacular airplanes. The faith of cult members was premised on the expectation of future shipments of cargo that would bring Nirvana to its believers. I decided to study what I thought was a similar Palauan movement called Modekngei, a term meaning "to bring them together," that was a response to and reaction against the colonial penetration of Palau. Useem was to study the Palauan clan structure as a form of social system. Mahoney was to administer thematic projective tests to a sample of Palauans for the purpose of deciphering Palauan character structure. Ritzen-thaler was to enumerate and classify Palauan "money" and study material culture, and Uyehara was to study the language. The expedition was to last six months.

Finishing my third semester of graduate studies did not allow time to learn much about Palau. Our main source of information on the islands was handbooks prepared by Murdock for the Smithsonian Institution during the war. The pamphlet on Micronesia was assembled from materials housed in the archive of the Yale University Human Relations Area Files. Murdock's Area Files were a vast collection of field data excerpted from past ethnographic reports and classified under a system of cross-referenced categories. Even without computers, Murdock's archive and its filing system lent themselves to distilling an ethnographic portrait of Palau's economy, political system, religion, physical geography, and so forth. The synopsis on Palau followed the same pattern Murdock had invented and reported in his book *Our Primitive Contemporaries*, and was included in a pamphlet devoted to the Western Caroline Islands. In addition to this report that stressed the dual structure of Palauan clans, Murdock supplied us with a few pages of translations on religion from the work of the German ethnographer Frobenius who had done his work during the German occupation of Palau and that of a Japanese ethnographer who had done his work during the Japanese occupation. One could not expect to gain a coherent image of Palau or even a foundation for conceptualizing a problem from this information. Murdock's handbook presented a composite portrait of Palau without regard to the fact that the ethnographic data were collected at different times by ethnographers whose orientations were formed within their own national traditions. Nonetheless, sketchy as it was,

Murdock's pamphlet was all the advance information we had, and it supplied us with our initial image of Palau and Palauans. Only a combination of innocence, self-confidence, and career imperatives concealed my lack of advance preparation for this project from me.

Useem, Ritzenthaler, Mahoney, and I met at Stanford University in the office of Felix Keesing, the Australian specialist on the Pacific Islands, with whom we discussed our projects. This was called a briefing, but in reality, our visit was more like a courtesy call on a gentleman who had proprietary anthropological rights on the territory. A few hours after meeting with Keesing, we boarded an eight-engine seaplane in San Francisco Harbor for an eighteen-hour flight at 120 miles per hour to Honolulu, Hawaii, where Uyehara joined the group.

CIMA had its headquarters in Hawaii. Its staff officer, Ernestine Akers, who later committed suicide, met us when we landed. She had arranged our itinerary to Palau, prepared our equipment, and arranged our financial matters. In Hawaii and beyond to Palau, we were serviced by the United States Navy; we were equipped by it, flew in its carriers, and shared the same privileges as naval officers. Convenient as it was for us to have this quasi-official relationship with the Navy, it also meant that if one wished, the entire CIMA project could be thought of as an aspect of naval intelligence to enhance the Navy's administration of the Trust Territory, an area that included all of the Micronesian Islands.

The Bernice P. Bishop Museum was an important center for anthropological studies in Hawaii. It was then under the direction of Te Rangi Hiroa, a New Zealand anthropologist who was also known as Peter Buck. Ms. Akers had scheduled a meeting for us with Buck. I was eager to meet him because I had read some of his vast work on the Maori in Howells's course on Oceania. Meeting this courtly, erudite Maori left a deep impression on me. The formal work I had done in Howells's course could now be attached to a live person who did not fall into conventional anthropological categories. Here was a Maori who was a student of the Maori, an anthropologist of his own culture who had written an essay with the ironic title "The Passing of the Maori" in which he presents demographic evidence to refute several authors who had predicted that the Maori were on their way to extinction. I never investigated where Buck had been educated or how he came to be the Director of the Bernice P. Bishop Museum. But he was a first-class intellectual who straddled two cultures, with one foot in each and no longer at home in either, an example of the true loneliness of homelessness in the modern world. Buck was an anthropological product of the Western conquest and commercialization of the Pacific Islands at a time when there was no hope for leading an independence movement in New Zealand. Instead, he had made his career within the profession for which he was also an anthropological object of study. Becoming the director of the Bernice P. Bishop Museum allowed him to promote Polynesian Studies within the framework of Western institutions. One could almost touch the discomfort that straddling the contradictions in his life caused him.

Travel to Palau, again in an eight-engine seaplane, was via Guam where we changed to a smaller plane for the last 600-mile leg of the flight to the lagoon that is Korror's harbor. Disembarking onto a barge anchored offshore, the group decided that Useem and I would act as its emissaries for a preliminary reconnaissance of the field. Trust Territory naval officials, some of whom knew Useem from his wartime service in the Pacific, were expecting us. Anticipating our arrival, these officers had secured an appointment for us to meet the

Aibedul, Chief of the Southern Palauan Confederation and resident in the city of Korror; diplomatic protocol required that we be received by the Aibedul before entering his territory to do our work. This ceremony amounted to a recognition by the naval officers and the researchers of the Aibedul's legitimacy as a traditional chief, and it meant that the Aibedul recognized and sanctioned the research team and authorized our work. Since we were identified with the Navy and the Aibedul, we could expect the cooperation of the Palauans.

At the outset of the American occupation of Palau, the recognition given by naval administrators to the Aibedul (and also to the Reklai, chief of the Northern Confederation) helped to legitimate his claim as a traditional chief. During the previous Japanese administration, the authority and legitimacy of the chiefs had been replaced by a policy of direct rule. This dramatic reversal in the chiefs' role was a result of an American policy designed to support the traditional ways of Palauan life. Murdock's pamphlet provided the image of tradition upon which colonial policy was to be guided by American administrators. That image was based on a composite of ethnographic reports collected by a variety of investigators in different time periods. It did not account for changes in Palauan society that had taken place over a period of seventy-five years of colonial rule. This meant that the chiefs and any other group whose status was based on tradition were privileged under the American occupation; the rights they had previously lost were returned to them. They could thank Murdock and the Human Relations Area Files for the new opportunities granted to them. By the same token, those who had committed themselves to changes in the social and economic relations over the years of colonial rule were denied privileges by the administrative application of Murdock's description of Palauan institutions. This was an applied anthropology that amounted to a restoration administered by Trust Territory officials.

During our session with the Aibedul, I confronted for the first time the full implications of the fact that I knew only one word of Palauan, Modekngie, that I could not learn the language in six months, and that the research group was wholly dependent on a translator to talk to Palauans. I was traumatized by this problem. Nothing in my previous experience had prepared me for it, and I was depressed by the expectation that our project might fail. I should have understood the importance of language from my wartime experience in Japan where I had learned only a few street phrases of Japanese and was largely isolated from the civilian population. All of the Japanese officials I dealt with as a procurement officer during the occupation spoke English. Palau was different: without translation the research could not proceed. Uyehara, fluent in English and Japanese, but not Palauan, who had expected to spend only part of his time translating, was to become the translator for all of us, a full-time job about which he never complained. Even so, the translation problem was formidable because, not knowing Palauan, Uyehara needed a Japanese-speaking Palauan to translate from Palauan into Japanese that he then rendered into English. Since after thirty years of Japanese colonization many Palauans spoke Japanese, we were provided with Japanese-speaking Palauan translators whenever we could not translate directly from the Japanese into English. The process of translations through two languages was cumbersome but unavoidable—and incidentally provided Uyehara with a means of learning Palauan. This total dependency on Uyehara meant that the research group was tied to Uyehara like dogs to a chain. As a consequence, throughout the six months of our fieldwork we lived, ate, and worked together as a collective.

Learning the native language and being able to communicate in it intelligently is a decisive requirement in anthropological research. Yet it is common knowledge that learning a second language is a time-consuming process. How this technical problem has influenced the substantive content of ethnographic reports and monographs remains a largely unexamined problem in the literature. For example, one can ask why so much of early anthropological reporting focused on "material" culture—essentially inanimate artifacts of the kind one finds in anthropological museums. When I saw Ritzenthaler collecting material culture, I could see that he could do it with a minimum of communication and yet produce results—that is, he could take pictures of an old man making fishnets in a traditional mode or photograph pieces of Palauan money, and both provided tangible, reportable data. However, without fairly refined communication between investigator and subject, interpretation of the social values and institutions of a society cannot be realized. Margaret Mead, in her books *Coming of Age in Samoa* and *Growing up in New Guinea*, claimed she could learn the native language in two months, but Paul Radin, who studied the Winnebago Indians for an entire lifetime and acquired fluency in their language, disputes Mead's claim in his book *The Method and Theory of Ethnology*. Historian and chronicler of Winnebago myths, tales, poetry, and social life, Radin was the rare anthropologist who could enter the world of the Winnebago on its linguistic terms, an achievement made possible only by a lifetime of extended exposure to their ways of life and language.

When anthropology became an academic discipline, field trips were usually for six months or a year because academics could not leave their teaching posts for greater lengths of time. By contrast, missionaries assigned to their missions for long periods of time, usually learned the native language and, in many cases, as illustrated by ethnographies written in the nineteenth and early twentieth centuries, produced invaluable descriptions of native life. An apt case is that of Lorimer Fison, a Wesleyan missionary, who with the anthropologist, explorer, and geologist A.W. Howitt, published *Kamilaroi and Kunai* in 1880. But also before the professionalization of the discipline, amateurs such as F. J. Gillen, a postmaster in the Australian bush, and Baldwin Spencer, an anthropologist and professor, collaborated to produce the great ethnographies *The Native Tribes of Central Australia* (1899) and *The Northern Tribes of Central Australia* (1904), studies that were still on Howells's reading list for his course on Oceania. These works left no doubt that their authors knew the native languages. In Palau, the German Lutheran minister, Father Fey, who had already begun his mission during the Japanese administration of the island, was a fluent speaker of Palauan, Japanese, German, and English. However, he was neither a good informant nor ethnographer because, in the older Lutheran German missionary tradition, he thought of the Palauans as children, yet to be saved from their paganism and their culture not worthy of study for its own sake.

However, for twentieth-century professional anthropologists, the English language had become a *lingua franca*, and the anthropologist might expect to find an English speaker almost anywhere except in the remotest areas of the world. To the extent that anthropologists have relied on English speakers as translators and informants, one may ask how such a practice has influenced the substantive contents of ethnographic reports and monographs. In extreme cases, such as studies on the Navajo Indians where almost all Navajo speak English, hundreds of reports, monographs, and books have been written by authors whose field work was accomplished in three summer months, or in a semester or a year. Unavoidable as this might be, it raises the possibility that anthropology may mirror the anthropologist and the religious assumptions underlying his or her own values as much as that of the world view of the natives.

Because Palauans were colonized successively by the Spanish, Germans, Japanese, and Americans, they came to understand the importance of learning their colonizers' languages: administrative power inhered in colonial authority. The authority of Palauan chiefs was dependent on that granted to them by whatever colonial administration was in power at a particular time. However, since as a matter of honor a Chief could not demean himself by speaking to foreigners in a language other than his own, the art of the translator and interpreter became a highly valued and rewarded skill. To be a native and an English speaker in Palau accorded not only high status, but also political influence when acting as intermediary between the native and the foreign authorities. For us, in practical research terms this meant that high status Palauan youths were eager to become our voluntary aides and assistants, hoping both to learn English and to discover what our research was about and, perhaps, to influence the formation of our images of Palau. One of our assistants was an unprepossessing youth named Ngoriakle. I learned much later when reading a news story on Palau in the press that he had become one of the dominant Palauan chiefs. The choice of those who became our aides and assistants was not a matter of chance: they were chosen because of their status rankings in Palauan society and because their association with us gave them exposure to the

English language. Understanding that the American administration was there to stay for awhile, those who learned English first could expect to gain the advantage of mobility within the new order dominated by Americans.

The American administration had chosen Sakuma (a.k.a. Takeo Yano)—a half-Japanese, half-Palauan scholar—to be its superintendent of the native school system. Under the Japanese administration, he had studied at the University of Tokyo and was already fluent in English. Being partly Japanese he was as marginal to Palauan society as he would have been in Japan. Having elected to remain in Palau rather than be evacuated with his father, the American administration had chosen him to set up a curriculum of studies that included training in the English language. On the one occasion I met him, he wanted to engage me in a discussion about the relevance of Immanuel Kant for an educational philosophy for Palau. I had neither read Kant nor wished to become his advisor on matters of practical educational policy.[2]

Our linguistic deficiencies, except for those of Uyehara, and our need under pressure of time to begin our research immediately made us wholly dependent on Palauans for scheduling interviews with informants and for acting as translators. That dependency was managed by Jose Tellei, a Palauan leader-politician who had been one of the first to make contact with American forces when in 1944

---

[2]   I did, however, include as appendices to my report to the National Science Foundation three papers written by Sakuma in English that addressed the subject of an educational policy for Palau. One called "Hope and the Obstacle of [sic] Development" was submitted to the foreign administration. The other two, both titled "Our Hopes," were delivered at the Korror school and pleaded for rejecting all Palauan traditions, including that of the system of chieftainship.

they had captured Palau from the Japanese, and by Meltel, a rank-ing person from Korror. Understanding the crucial significance of the intermediary's role, Tellei, though middle aged, was already conversant in English and had established himself as a key figure in Palauan-American affairs. Meltel did not know English but served as a counterweight to Tellei's influence and probably was a relative of the Aibedul. Their counterpart for us was Uyehara, who could talk with them in Japanese and who was the bridge between them and Useem. Useem, who knew more about Palau than the rest of us, chose our respondents in consultation with Tellei and Meltel who scheduled our interviews like clockwork and, if needed, provided translators on technical subjects such as Palauan money, the history of clan relationships, and the consequences for Palau of Japanese co-lonial policy. The Palauans cooperated with us to the full extent of their capacity. As hardheaded realists, they understood that resis-tance to the Americans was hopeless, but we could never know how their choices of informants and their translations of interviews from Palauan to Japanese affected our research.

Initially, it had been Useem's plan to concentrate our research in the district of Melekiok, where the Areklai, the tribe of the other paramount chief, lived. Provisioning ourselves with supplies bought from the US Navy and with other essentials—including liquor—secured at the Naval Post Exchange, we boarded a vessel for a half-day's travel up the east coast of Palau to Melekiok, located on the is-land of Babeldaub. From a local resident, we rented a small thatched hut with a corrugated tin roof, just big enough to accommodate five canvas cots on which we slept, ate, and wrote. The back of the hut had a thatched overhang under which we set up a two-burner Cole-man stove and a kitchen where we cooked three meals a day for four months.

The hut was located a short distance from the district schoolhouse originally constructed by the Japanese. There, seated around a table, we conducted all of our interviews. Between the hut and the schoolhouse was a magnificent mango tree, an unexpected bonus for our cuisine. Ritzenthaler knew and appreciated what a mango was, and we quickly learned from him the value of this tree and its fruit; mangoes became part of our daily diet. To supplement our diet of staples, essentially rice packaged in 100-pound sacks, we bought fish, turtle meat, fruit, taro, vegetables, and eggs from Palauans in exchange for dollars, then in short supply in the outer districts of Palau. Though food preparation was under field conditions, no one complained about the cuisine, but allocation of kitchen and dish-washing duties raised the problem of who cooked and who did the dishes.

Useem, as leader of the group, delegated household chores and duties to the rest of us. Ritzenthaler, the most sophisticated among us in the art of making martinis and other mixed drinks utilizing tropical fruits, quickly took charge of the bar; we enjoyed cocktails before dinner. Mahoney knew nothing of cooking, but he learned to wash dishes. Uyehara was our expert rice cooker, an art that he taught me so he could fulfill his important duties as the group's translator. By a process of elimination, I was put in charge of the kitchen and the commissary, the latter requiring trips to Korror to replenish our supplies and to make food purchases in the local market. This division of labor was inequitable and led to a conflict between Useem and me because my kitchen duties prevented me from participating fully in our collective interviewing sessions.

Our research routine included scheduled interviews in the schoolhouse during mornings, afternoons, and early evenings. Since Useem was researching the clan structure as a social system and I

Modekngei, an indigenous resistance movement that cut across clan loyalties and was a result of the revolutionary economic and social changes introduced by earlier colonizers, each of us could get the information we needed in the same interview. A problem arose because Useem dominated the interviews, but this was not insurmountable because answers to Useem's questions were usually as important for me as for him, and I could also throw in my own questions. In fact, I had a more sharply defined problem than did Useem and knew what I needed answers to while Useem frequently asked abstract questions that did not resonate with our informants. But the real problem arose because of my duties as the group's cook, especially the preparation of lunch and dinner. In order to have these meals ready and on time for the group as a whole, Useem directed me to leave the interviewing session while it was still in progress so that a meal was ready at the right time. On some occasions, I resisted Useem's instructions and this action not only irritated him but led him to take punitive measures against me such as sending me on unnecessary errands during interview sessions and, at times, excluding me from them altogether. Our relationship, though not openly abrasive, became a source of tension for the group as a whole, but despite this, our mutual dependencies restrained each of us from any action that might lead to an open break. While in the field, we maintained a civilized veneer and only later upon return to the United States were my accumulated grievances cause for bitterness.

The final two months of our expedition were spent in Korror. By the end of this period, we had interviewed dozens of Palauan clan leaders, the chiefs Areklai and Aibedul, leaders of Modekngie, women, Palauan historians, specialists in Palauan money, Trust Territory administrators, naval personnel, Palauan Christians, Lutheran and

Catholic missionaries, and our aides and assistants. These interviews were recorded in long hand, each of us recording his own notes. While we did not share field notes—for no other reason than that we were fully preoccupied reviewing and editing our own—we discussed each others' data and our interpretations of them every day. In fact, for six months we talked of nothing but Palau, for this was the common ground that had brought us together in the first place. I learned about Palauan money from Ritzenthaler. Uyehara gave us recaps of our interview sessions and contextualized them for us, giving us a clearer picture of the status and attitude of our informants. I did not participate in Mahoney's Thematic Apperception Testing (TAT) because it was designed to evoke a response from the informant to an abstract picture. Mahoney had chosen the most difficult problem and research method. The TAT had been designed to be applied to Westerners, and the interpretation of responses to it could only be made in terms of Western values. Without an independent standard based on Palauan values, it was difficult to interpret Palauans' responses though we engaged in many speculative discussions of what their meaning might be in light of Palauan values we were learning about. Useem's project was concerned with the formal structure of clans and the dual structure of the Palauan confederations. He was not interested in the substance of social change as I was; his research domain tended to go in the direction of kinship relations and was least compatible with that of the rest of us. Because he had already been familiar with Palau and had been attracted to the complexities of inter- and intra-clan relations, he had hoped to explain the fundamental character of the Palauan social order. He thought that the specifics of history and the substance of social changes were of less importance than finding a theory for the Palauan social system as a whole.

My original idea of studying Modekngie was gradually expanded into an investigation of the effects of colonial administration and its economic policies on Palauan institutions. Early in the research, I discovered that Modekngie was only one possible response to the presence of colonizers. Others included collaboration in the system of indirect rule, acquiescence to colonial domination, and opportunistic exploitation of the new values and rewards offered by colonial policy and economy. Each of the successive colonial administrations left their mark on Palauan traditions, causing transformations in them by the introduction of a money economy, wage labor, and new kinds of consumer goods. In a society in which matrilineal descent had determined status and wealth, the introduction of a money economy and wage labor favored men over women, leading to a weakening of the status claims of women. Since Modekngie was a movement that appealed to women, it became clear that their loss of status was related to a gain in men's status by virtue of their access to foreign currency. Access to foreign currency challenged a system of traditional gift exchanges on which women's claim to status and authority within the clan had been premised, resulting in clan and gender conflicts that spread throughout Palauan society. Each of the policies of the successive colonial administrations favored new and different status claimants, usually penalizing those who had been associated with the previous administration.

Each change in administration had been a consequence of defeat in war by a major world power. The defeat of Spain in the Spanish-American War of 1898 provided Germany with its opportunity to take Palau, Germany's entry into World War I provided Japan with the opportunity to take over its Pacific colonies, and the defeat of Japan by the United States in World War II led to the occupation of Palau by the American Navy. Palau, a small parcel of land in a vast oceanic territory, found itself on the world stage in a drama directed by others. As I learned more about Palau in the course of my research, I reformulated my research problem to focus on the relationship between foreign administration and changes in Palauan institutions. I also learned that any research problem formulated in advance of actual data collection is provisional and that discovery of the problem occurs in the course of the investigation, necessarily so because the original expectations of what might be discovered cannot foretell the reality encountered in the field.

At the conclusion of our fieldwork we returned to Hawaii—each of us carrying our precious field notes in canvas waterproof medical bags supplied by the Navy—where we reported on our work to local CIMA officials. On our return to San Francisco, Mahoney discovered that his wife had left him for a woman. This crushing blow led him to abandon his graduate studies and to take a job as a Trust Territory officer in Palau where he married a Palauan and fathered five children. Ritzenthaler returned to his position as curator at the Milwaukee Public Museum; he and I maintained a close relationship for many years until his death. Uyehara remained in Hawaii, returned to Palau on other occasions, and resided in Okinawa for many years until he died in 1974. Useem and I returned to Madison where we were interviewed about our research on the local radio station and where the strains in our relationship erupted into the open. After that, we never talked to each other. When I finished writing and defending my MA thesis, I left for Harvard University to study social anthropology. I reported my findings to the National Science Foundation under the title "Political Factionalism in Palau: Its Rise and Development" and in my PhD Dissertation, "The Political Impact of Colonial Administration," submitted in 1953 to Harvard's Department of Social Relations.

In 1980, my dissertation was published by Arno Press in a series devoted to the publication of Harvard, Columbia, and Chicago dissertations. I had never considered trying to publish the dissertation because I thought of it simply as fulfilling one of my requirements for my degree; the dissertation was a training exercise, and the real work was to come later. The managers of the Arno Press project selected dissertations for publication using as their standard the frequency rate of library withdrawals of the work. I had no idea who my readers were, but I assumed they were students of anthropology or researchers who were interested in Palau. Having thought that the Palauan part of my life was over, I did not systematically read about what was happening to Palau. At best, I read about it in the popular press, and in 1977, on a trip overseas that included a stopover on Guam, I visited Palau's representative in Trust Territory headquarters—he was not interested in talking with me and probably did not know I had authored a study of Palau. However, beginning in the 1980s, I learned that a new generation of activist anthropologists had identified with the anti-nuclear movement in the Pacific area. Following the American defeat in the Vietnam War, the US Navy had hoped to transfer its nuclear submarine base to the protected deep-water port of Korror. This led to a series of nasty episodes that included the murder of some Palauan political leaders who opposed the nuclearization of Palau, whereupon some American anthropologists joined the anti-nuke movement in Palau.

Among them, in 1987, was Lynn Wilson, a student at the University of Massachusetts, Amherst, whose book *Speaking to Power: Gender and Politics in the Western Pacific* was published in 1995, and Glenn Alcalay, a student in the Anthropology Department at The New School for Social Research, both of whom had read my dissertation and consulted with me on their work. Given to understand by

Wilson and Alcalay that there was a small Palauan anthropological industry, I sent a copy of the Arno Press edition of my dissertation to Ms. Olympia Morei for deposit in the Belau National Museum.

I had thought my field notes, photographs, and other research documents had been lost, but in the early 1990s, I accidentally discovered these materials in a trunk in my garage in Southampton. Because I had no further use for my primary source data, including a census and Kodachrome slides, I returned them to Palau, again to Ms. Morei for deposit in the Belau National Museum.

In 1997, I received a letter from Ms. Kazumi Nishihara, who was writing an MA thesis at the Center for Pacific Island Studies at the University of Hawaii at Manoa. The subject of her thesis was Modekngei. Hers is a study in the construction of anthropological knowledge in which she views the same project from the perspective of authors of different national origin writing over an extended period of time. In her thesis, she cites some thirty scholars, journalists, and officials who have published dissertations, journal articles, and official reports on Modekngei. One of these scholars was a self-taught anthropologist, Hisakatsu Hijikata, who, writing between 1929 and 1931, interviewed the leaders of Modekngei and provided a detailed description of Modekngei's tenets and practices. In 1941, Kenichi Sugiura published, among other works, an article, "Ethnology and Native Administration in Micronesia," in which Modekngei is treated as an administrative problem for the Japanese. In 1944, Otoji Ishikawa, a retired chief judge of the South Sea Government Supreme Court, reported Modekngei to be an occult religion that was an expression of the islanders' ill will against the Japanese. None of these sources was available to me when I did my study nor, since these were studies conducted during the Japanese occupation, had they been translated and filed in Murdock's Human Relations Area Files.

Between 1973 and 1984, Machiko Aoyagi made several visits of varying length to Palau and reported her research in four articles.[3] Her work takes issue with my interpretation of Modekngei. Ms. Nishihara's MA thesis, "Politics of Faith: Investigating Ethnographies About Modekngei," is devoted to a critical comparison of my work with Aoyagi's.[4] I learned from her thesis that my dissertation had become a standard reference work on Palau.[5]

Ms. Nishihara's purpose in contacting me was to ask for further information on the work of our CIMA group, and, specifically, my sources of information on Modekngei. My answers to her questions led to an exchange of half a dozen letters (now deposited at the University of Hawaii, Manoa, the Belau National Museum, and in my archive in the Fogelman Library of The New School for Social Research). Her questions were pointed and helped to evoke memories I had long since put aside. With little effort, however, I discovered that

---

[3] Editor's note: Aoyagi's work on Modekngei may be found in her book *Modekngei: A New Religion in Belau* (Tokyo: Shinsensha Press, 2002). A Japanese edition had appeared in 1985.

[4] The University of Hawaii, 1998.

[5] At least three PhD dissertations have had Palau and Modekngei as their subject: Donald Shuster, "Islands of Change in Palau: Church, School, and Elected Government, 1891-1981"; Karen Louise Nero, "A Cherechar a Lokelii: Beads of History of Koror, Palau 1783-1983"; and Richard J. Parmentier, "The Sacred Remains: Historical Anthropology of Ngeremlengui, Palau." None of these researchers, now respectively professors at the University of Guam, Auckland University in New Zealand, and Brandeis University in Waltham, Massachusetts, was known to me until I read Ms. Nishihara's thesis. Unbeknownst to me, my CIMA report and my dissertation have had lively lives in Micronesia and in Japan.

the essential elements of my Palau experience could be brought back to the surface in considerable detail—the more so as Ms. Nishihara persisted. When I began research for the book *Small Town in Mass Society*, I left Palau behind me and never looked back, least of all to acquaint myself with ongoing research in Micronesia. From then on, my attention was drawn to studies of American society. Ms. Nishihara taught me that six months of life devoted exclusively and single-mindedly, day in and day out, to a single objective leaves an indelible imprint on the mind, recoverable in great detail, even to the point of recovering pictorial images of informants, houses, boats, faces, and places, regardless of the passage of time. It is the personal, the idiosyncratic uniqueness, of this experience not shared by any other that compels me to try to share it.

6

An Education at Harvard
1948-1950

From Madison to Harvard

In Madison, where I studied from 1946 to 1948, MA students thought of the Department of Sociology and Anthropology as a take-off point for bigger and better things elsewhere. Harvard and Columbia were believed to be the places where one could find all the answers and the fundamental truths about the social sciences. Talcott Parsons had established a new Department of Social Relations at Harvard. Students wishing to study with Robert Lynd, Robert MacIver, Robert Merton, and C. Wright Mills (who was already known at Wisconsin as Hans Gerth's student) went to Columbia. The center of gravity in the social sciences was no longer in the Middle West. The once-prominent Chicago School had lost its luster. Edward Shils, who had just published a pamphlet entitled *The Present State of American Sociology*, was still a graduate student. Berkeley was an unknown entity; it did not become a magnet until 1952 when Herbert Blumer left Chicago to head its new Department of Sociology. Madison looked like a way station. The real thing was in the East.

W. W. Howells gave me the idea of going to Harvard. He knew little about the Department of Social Relations, but he introduced his students to Clyde Kluckhohn when he came to Madison to lecture. Kluckhohn had been a 1928 graduate of the University of Wisconsin and was now regarded as a major figure in the field; he had also collaborated with Parsons in the creation of the Department of Social Relations. The point was not to hear Kluckhohn's lecture, but to be introduced to him. Kluckhohn's visit had more than one purpose. He was recruiting applicants for the Department of Social Relations, and Howells served as a link in the recruitment network. Howells thought that three anthropology students—Robert Endelman, James Silverberg, and me—were prospective candidates. Endelman and I applied and were accepted. Silverberg remained in Madison, but confided to me after Kluckhohn had left that he had had an intimate relationship with Kluckhohn in a Madison hotel room. This bit of information later caused me considerable difficulties in my own relationship with Kluckhohn.

Gerth and Howells knew faculty members at Harvard and asked me to extend greetings to them: Gerth's to Talcott Parsons and Howells's to Ernest Hooton, his former professor of physical anthropology. Gerth had met Parsons when he first arrived in the United States in 1937. Carl Friedrich had given him his first academic appointment. This included tutoring some of Parsons's graduate students in the German language, including Robert K. Merton, Logan Wilson, and others. I knew none of this at the time, but discovering it later helped clarify my relationship with Parsons. In his work as a tutor, Gerth used as his texts some of Weber's essays on "The Methodology of the Social Sciences." Gerth was a student of Weber even before he had arrived in the United States. As he once recounted in an interview, he had read "Politics as a Vocation" when he was a gymnasium student in Kassel and determined then and there to study with Weber, only to discover when he arrived in Heidelberg in 1927 that Weber had already been dead for seven years. Parsons regarded Gerth as a competitor in what later became the "Weber industry" in the United States. When we left Madison, we made a point to say farewell to

Gerth and his wife Hedwig. Gerth was disappointed when students whom he had taught and to whom he was generous with time and advice did not complete their studies with him. Joseph and Marilyn Bensman had departed for Columbia a year earlier, and now Virginia and I were leaving.

Driving a fully-packed Henry Kaiser automobile (a gift from my parents, a sign of the importance they attached to my forthcoming Harvard education, and, to my regret, a constant problem because Kaiser was no better at making cars than ships), we stopped at Gerth's home. Gerth inspected the contents of the car loaded with a crib, baby bottles, diapers, household equipment, camping gear, and the trailer carrying books and furniture. Always a perceptive student of American culture, Gerth was impressed by the affluence of postwar graduate students in the United States. He was a lowly paid junior professor living on the margins of American affluence. After ten years in this country, he had managed to secure a mortgage to finance the construction of a modest home in Madison. The lifestyle of returned veterans was not much below that of his family, an academic disparity then incomprehensible in Germany. Gerth had adapted to the informality of American academic culture, making him even more accessible to students than his professorial American counterparts. He gained his recognition and status from students who appreciated his exceptional erudition and his willingness to share it in the informal setting of his home. His professional style elicited respect without the intimidation that his erudition and worldliness might otherwise have evoked. Like me, many of his students were sons and daughters of immigrants. For some reason that I am still unable to fathom, I had once brought my uneducated father to meet Gerth at his home. They had nothing in common, but Gerth rose to the occasion by interviewing my father about his life as a youth in Kropa. His sophistication compared to my father's simplicity made no difference to Gerth. He treated my father with the respect due his age. Leaving Gerth for the trek to Harvard was like leaving a surrogate parent.

Harvard's postwar graduate students were either veterans of the war, émigré victims of the war, or international students from countries everywhere in the world. Most of them were between twenty-five and thirty years of age. Married first-year students were provided with housing in the former army base known as Harvardevens, at Fort Devens, Massachusetts, located about thirty miles west of Cambridge. When the 1948 contingent of graduate students arrived during the first week of September, we began to form groups according to our fields of study. In the case of the Department of Social Relations, there were four people in addition to myself—Kaspar Naegele, Ralph Patrick, Robert N. Wilson, and Evon Z. Vogt. All of us were students except Vogt, who had already completed his doctorate at the University of Chicago and was an assistant in the Anthropology Program. Vogt had personal ties to Clyde Kluckhohn, who sponsored him for his appointment. This group formed a carpool for the purpose of sharing the cost of transportation for our daily commute, leaving Fort Devens early in the morning and returning at the end of the day. We also shared the academic pressures, career anxieties, worries about our futures, and domestic tensions that resulted from long absences from our wives and children.

That year in the carpool with the same mates sharing the same academic problems and personal anxieties was akin to a yearlong collective *rite de passage*, like a transition from boyhood to manhood in one of those so-called primitive societies described by anthropologists, say, for example, the Arunta of western Australia. The carpool irrevocably bonded us to each other, instilling in each an indelible memory of the other. Despite careers that eventually went in different directions, the intimacy we shared at a decisive turning point in our lives stayed with us. I am still unable to put from my mind Kaspar Naegele's inexplicable suicide in 1965. Ralph Patrick's premature death at age sixty does not prevent me to this day from evoking a sharply defined image of his face, physical frame, and gentle southern speech. Because of my later troubles with Kluckhohn, I lost touch with Vogt, but not with the memories of him and his subsequent career. Over the past fifty years, Wilson and I, despite differences in our sociological outlooks, remain in correspondence, sustaining the bond while still grieving and unable to explain Kaspar's suicide and Ralph's early death. Wilson has written poems in homage to both as if to consecrate the memory of the carpool.

When I first arrived in Cambridge, I made it a point to see Ernest Hooton, Talcott Parsons, and Clyde Kluckhohn. Getting appointments with these famous professors was much easier than I had anticipated. This was 1948 when there was still some social distance between professors and students, sustained by a degree of formality and a reluctance on the students' part to go immediately on a first-name basis. The easy accessibility of professors surprised me. Given the large number of new students wanting appointments, our professors must have given all of their time during the first few weeks of the semester to student interviews. I had not yet learned that, even at Harvard, professors needed their students as much as students needed them.

Hooton, who had his office in the Peabody Museum and was not associated with Social Relations, sensed that I had no interest in physical anthropology and treated me accordingly, accepting my greetings from Howells and sending me on my way. The museum was full of skeletons, precious stones, and artifacts. The latter represented the plunder of years and years of Harvardian expeditions. My reaction to the Peabody Museum was that it did not fit my image of the kind of anthropologist I wanted to be, and I never saw Hooton again. Nevertheless, the Museum became part of my life at Harvard because my anthropology course on Oceania taught by Douglas Oliver (required because of my Palau study) met in the Museum. I remember the presence of John Otis Brew, the Museum's director and author of *The Archaeology of Alkali Ridge*, my later reading of which gave me an appreciation for archaeology, and Hallam Movius, who was pointed out to me as an icon in studies of Asian archaeology. Clearly, the old Anthropology Department did not mix easily with that portion of anthropology affiliated with the Department of Social Relations. It was apparent even then that the split of anthropology into two programs was an administrative recognition that physical and social anthropology had almost nothing in common.

Clyde Kluckhohn's office was located in the newly created Russian Research Center of which he was director. His receptionist-secretary was Helen Parsons, Talcott Parsons's wife. Though the Center was located only a short distance from the Peabody, in spirit it was worlds apart. Its concerns were the Cold War and Sovietology, and it housed specialists in Eastern Europe and Russian and Soviet affairs. Its *raison d'être* was the application of the knowledge of the social sciences to the formation of social and political policy in the new Cold War nuclear age; it owed its existence to former members of the Office of Strategic Services (OSS). Its personnel consisted in part of academics who had moved from wartime service to academia. Many anthropologists, including Kluckhohn, had seen service in wartime intelligence activities, and it was on the strength of these services that Kluckhohn, as an anthropologist, was made director of the Center. Unlike the Peabody, the Center exuded an air of crisp, business-like efficiency; self-important visitors came and went to consult a staff of specialists. This is where I met Kluckhohn for the second time.

Though tense and high strung, as he usually was, and overburdened with administrative work, Kluckhohn was prepared for my appointment. He grilled me about my long-term plans and wanted to know what kind of anthropologist I wanted to be. At that time, my concerns were to learn all that I could about the social sciences and take the required courses needed to prepare for the qualifying examination. Kluckhohn knew from George Murdock that I had been in Palau. This was understandable inasmuch as Kluckhohn had sponsored David Schneider's study on Yap and was familiar with Murdock's CIMA project. We both understood that I owed the National Science Foundation a report within the year and that the Palau research was to become a dissertation. This was a business-like conference that left me with the feeling that my career was not entirely in my own hands.

Kluckhohn had not only passed on my admission to Harvard, he had also secured for me the Thayer Fellowship, providing me with several thousand dollars of support in addition to the funding I received from the GI Bill; he supported his students generously. Despite his intense work schedule and the excessive demands being made on him, he was solicitous of his students and regarded anthropology as his central professional concern. Among other things, he directed the Navaho Values Study and fielded a corps of the graduate researchers among the Indian tribes of the Southwest. He attempted to be knowledgeable in what were then considered to be the four subfields of the profession—physical, archeological, linguistic, and social/cultural—and attempted to write articles in each of them. He had hoped to inherit the status in anthropology that Franz Boas and Alfred Kroeber had held previously; as part of his plan, he hoped to inherit Kroeber's mantle by editing the book *Definitions of Culture* with him. Even then, viewing him from the limited perspective of a student, his ambitions appeared to be excessive, if only because the field of anthropology was already becoming fragmented into various specializations. That he chose to write on subjects for the purpose of establishing a reputation rather than the other way around—that is, writing on subjects he regarded important and basing his reputation on them—left me with the impression that he was less interested in the pursuit of truth than with the management of his career and the pursuit of fame.

Talcott Parsons and the Department of Social Relations

Parsons's office was located in Harvard Yard on the second floor of Emerson Hall, the former headquarters of Harvard's "social gospelers" and now the hub of the Department of Social Relations. On arriving for my appointment, I was received with an unhurried graciousness, as if Parsons had nothing to do but see me. Inasmuch as I was to study anthropology, my excuse for requesting the interview was to extend Gerth's greetings. I started by saying, "I studied with Gerth at Wisconsin, and he asked me to send you his regards." Parsons responded abruptly, "Gerth should learn how to write English." I had not expected this sharp retort and pursued the matter no further. This was my first encounter with the stiff competition among Weberians in the United States. I learned from the incident and from many subsequent occasions as well of the intense competition to claim priority in the translation of Weber's works. In 1946, Gerth and Mills published *From Max Weber: Essays in Sociology*, the first English edition of Weber's sociological writings, an event that had apparently annoyed Parsons.[1] In 1930, Parsons had translated *The Protestant Ethic and the Spirit of Capitalism*, and in 1937, he had published *The Structure of Social Action*, a book that he claimed superseded Weber's sociology.

Despite Parsons's irritation at the mention of Gerth's name, he did not hold my association with Gerth against me. On the contrary, he invited my wife and me to Sunday afternoon tea in his home and remembered me by name whenever we met in or out of the classroom. Making it a point to know his students, Parsons brought them into his intellectual fold with an indulgent, paternal embrace that was difficult to resist. Yet graduate students found it easy to criticize his book. Most first-year students found *The Structure of Social Action* not only ponderous in style, but excessive in its pretensions. Parsons showed no animus toward students who criticized his writing style or rejected *The Structure of Social Action*, but instead he tolerated them and engaged them in discussions in order to convince them of their errors. The best example that comes to mind is Jesse Pitts's performance at the first student-faculty party. Pitts took the occasion to spoof *The Structure of Social Action*. Providing the entertainment for the evening, he came onstage with an elaborately constructed tinker toy, announcing in a tone of mock solemnity, "This is *The Structure of Social Action*." The most critical among us, Pitts walked directly to Parsons and presented him with his creation.

---

[1] *See also* Guy Oakes and Arthur J. Vidich, *Collaboration, Reputation, and Ethics in American Academic Life: Hans Gerth and C. Wright Mills*, 19-20, 36, for evidence indicating this.

Though Pitts's irreverence was excessive, Parsons treated the performance as a joke and laughed, relieving what otherwise might have been a tense moment and allowing the rest of us to laugh too. Beginning as Parsons's severest critic, Pitts later became a disciple and one of Parsons's coeditors of the multi-volume collection of sociological essays, *Theories of Society*. I've digressed on this point because, as I shall show later, Pitts's case helps to explain why so many of Parsons's students, despite their initial negative reactions, eventually became Parsonians.

The Social Relations Department was created in 1946 as an administrative mechanism to support Parsons's main intellectual project—framing a theory for a democratic social system. Its curriculum included courses in sociology, anthropology, social psychology, and clinical psychology, but not courses in political science or economics, the latter a peculiar omission in light of Parsons's original education as an economist. The range of courses, spread over all these disciplines, distinguished the Social Relations Department from Harvard's sociology department of the late 1930s and early 1940s. Before and during the war, Parsons shared the stage with Pitirim Sorokin. Students during that period included Kingsley Davis, Robert Merton, Wilbert Moore, Arthur Davis, Nicholas Demerath, Robin Williams, Edward Devereaux, and Logan Wilson. Their readings included Parsons's economic essays, *The Structure of Social Action*, and also the works of Sorokin and Carl Zimmerman. In the 1930s, Parsons was still a disciple of Joseph Schumpeter, Thomas Nixon Carver, and Frank William Taussig. He wrote articles on capitalism while working on *The Structure of Social Action*.[2] He had not yet formulated his theoretical conception of the social system. During the war, Parsons submitted proposals to the Research and Analysis branch of the OSS and concerned himself with the problems posed by German fascism. His work on fascism reinforced his fears for the future of democracy and civil order in the United States. Later, he developed the idea of formulating a social relations curriculum and framed a comprehensive theory of the social system. During the years that the class of 1948 was in residence, the social relations curriculum was still not sharply focused.

Later, the theory of the social system provided a liberal image of what a social order should be. When Parsons wrote about substantive issues such as racial equality, the family, responsibility and obligations, the power structure (his critique of C. Wright Mills's *The Power Elite*), the functions of the executive, and the other dimensions of American society, he spoke from his soul, almost as an Emersonian and certainly as a Christian ethicist concerned about the moral order of society. At the time I was at Harvard, he was not the full-fledged *formal* social theorist he became later when fourfold tables and harmonics of the system almost became ends in themselves, more like a sociological metaphysics.

---

[2]   For a more complete discussion of Parsons's work at this time, see Stephen Turner, "The Origins of Mainstream Sociology and Other Issues in the History of American Sociology"; my book with Stanford M. Lyman, *American Sociology: Worldly Rejections of Religion and Their Directions*; and Charles Camic, editor, *The Early Essays* by Talcott Parsons.

In 1948, the social relations curriculum floated ideas in all directions. It was full of intellectual confusions and contradictions and attracted a remarkable collection of professors, instructors, and graduate students, whom Parsons organized into a loosely knit administrative unit. It included parts of the older prewar department of sociology in the professorships of Sorokin and Zimmerman. Parsons did not have the dominance that he achieved later. Moreover, he was striving to revive interest in *The Structure of Social Action*, the reception of which had been delayed by the war. Some ten years after its 1937 publication, Parsons rehabilitated the book by making it the focus of the department's proseminar.

In 1948, however, students could respond to professors of their choice, not only Parsons, Sorokin, and Zimmerman, but George Homans, Freed Bales, Kluckhohn, Henry Murray, Richard Solomon, Gordon Allport, and Samuel Stouffer. Moreover, these professors were housed in a number of separate buildings: some anthropologists were in the Peabody; Kluckhohn, Alex Inkeles, and Barrington Moore, Jr., were in the Russian Research Center; and Stouffer, Homans, and Parsons were in Emerson Hall. The psychologists Gordon Allport, Richard Solomon, and Jerome Bruner were in Emerson Hall, while the psychoanalysts were in still other buildings. E. G. Boring, B. F. Skinner, and George Miller were in the basement of Memorial Hall, and though they had no affiliations with the Social Relations program, they were a meaningful presence for psychology students. Henry Murray had his own headquarters, made famous in the book by Forrest G. Robinson, *Love's Story Told: A Life of Henry A. Murray*, which details Murray's tumultuous 40-year love affair with Christiana Morgan, a protégé of Carl Jung. Murray's great passion, even though I only learned about it decades later, adds a dramatic touch to my Harvard education. The dispersion of faculty offices lent a sense of freedom and lightness to academic life; one didn't feel under surveillance. The Department was composed of too many divisive elements to be brought under anything like systems of culture, personality, economics, and society.

In this hybrid department, the mix of students included aspiring sociologists, anthropologists, psychologists, and clinicians. Each subset oriented itself to a different group of faculty. Because of this multiplicity of intellectual orientations, every first-year student was required to enroll in the Department's proseminar, a kind of collective baptismal ceremony designed to certify us as members of a common congregation. The proseminar consisted of weekly lectures given by senior professors on the staff. Parsons, Kluckhohn, Murray, Allport, Sorokin, and Robert White are the names I remember as lecturers. I don't remember Stouffer lecturing, but if he was not included it was because he was then running IBM cards for the multi-volume study, *The American Soldier*. The seminar served as a display case for senior professors. Junior professors not included were Alex Inkeles, Barrington Moore, Jr., Freed Bales, Florence Kluckhohn, Frederick Mosteller, L. Postman, M. B. Smith, Benjamin Paul, Jerome Bruner, E. Hanfmann, not to mention the then lesser lights, David Aberle, Evon Vogt, John Roberts, and Gardner Lindzey. Noticeably missing from the seminar roster of lecturers were the traditional anthropologists located in Peabody Museum.

The seminar left one with a lopsided image of the total Social Relations faculty. It was heavily weighted on the side of Parsons, Kluckhohn, and Murray. However, Murray used some of his time to ridicule the idea of a systematic sociology; he said things like, "Speech is healthier than silence, even though one knows that what one says is vague and inconclusive." Or, as quoted on the jacket of *Love's Tale Told*: "Every man knows something about himself which he's willing to tell, and something about himself which he's not willing to tell. There's also something about himself that he doesn't know and can't tell." Murray inhabited the world of Herman Melville and Jungian psychology and provided an antidote to any claims for a rational, objective interpretation of the social world, not to mention the idea of a social system. His view of the social sciences was quixotic and gave courage to those of us who rejected the idea of closed systems.

Parsons dominated the seminar, giving Kluckhohn a supporting role and allowing Sorokin a single appearance. To the students, it was clear that Parsons was the leading figure; he held the key that could open the door to a future career. To underscore this point, Parsons distributed his paper, "Towards a Common Language for the Area of the Social Sciences," that proposed the development of a common vocabulary designed to transcend disciplinary differences and provide mutual understanding among them. This paper left a deep impression on me not only because it claimed that there could be such a thing as a common language through which social analysis might be reported, but also because George Orwell had just published *1984* in which he described the processes of thought control by linguistic means. This is not to say that Parsons had any such intention. His common language was that of a convinced believer in social science, more like that of a founder of a secular sect. The purpose of the proseminar was to lay out the distinctive intellectual line that Parsons was then formulating for his version of sociology.

Because the Social Relations curriculum included four disciplines, the proseminar was the means of their cross-fertilization. Each lecturer introduced us to the vocabulary of his (there were no women lecturers) discipline and its subject matter as he saw it. There could even be cross-fertilization within disciplines, for example, when there were two or more lecturers from the same discipline as was the case for sociology (Parsons and Sorokin) and psychology (Murray, White, and Allport). Exposure to a multiplicity of vocabularies did not lead inevitably to cross-fertilization or to an interdisciplinary perspective. Adding to the centrifugality of disciplinary vocabularies, each of the lecturers recommended the works of authors whom they regarded as significant figures in their fields. The names of Max and Alfred Weber, Emile Durkheim, Sigmund Freud, Alfred Kroeber, Franz Boas, Gregory Bateson, Susanne Langer, G. H. Mead, Leslie White, McDougall, Watson, Jung, and many others were added as crucial authors. Notably absent from the lists were the works of Karl Marx, Thorstein Veblen, and Weber's *The Protestant Ethic and the Spirit of Capitalism*. It soon became evident to us that no one could grasp the substance or the vocabularies of all the disciplines or read all the books in a semester or even a year. Yet we confronted an examination that included questions involving interdisciplinary knowledge. The prospect of this examination led us to our own solution to this graduate student problem.

Approaching our anxieties rationally, we formed interdisciplinary study groups. Each member of a group consisting of four or five students was assigned responsibility to provide digests of books and summaries of lecture notes. For example, one of us reported on Durkheim's *The Rules of Sociological Method*, another on *Suicide*, and a third on *The Division of Labor in Society*. Reports were duplicated, distributed, and discussed with members of the group, and in some cases, exchanged with other groups. In our graduate student argot, these digests were known as "hamburgers." We had put into practice a division of labor.

By this method, it was possible to acquire secondhand knowledge of dozens of major works prior to the examination. One could appear knowledgeable about books one had never read and courses one had never taken. For me, it led to a certain vagueness regarding which courses I actually took at Harvard and which books I actually read. A further consequence of this approach to scholarship was that it was not until years later that I had occasion to read some of the classic texts, although my secondhand knowledge of them enabled me to pass the examination. The class of 1948 was resourceful and gave its own pragmatic meaning to cross-fertilization and interdisciplinary studies. The classmates I remember are Jesse Pitts, Kaspar Naegele, Ralph Patrick, Robert N. Wilson, John White, Tom O'Dea, Robert Endleman, Kim Romney, Jack Fischer, Irving Rosow, Joseph Kahl, John Money, James Olds, Norman Jacobs, Donald Michael, John Gullahorn, T. M. Mills, Nathan Kogan, Monro Edmundson, Otto Von-Mering, Edward Winter, Iwao Ishino, Edward Wellin, Charles Lang, Robert Rappaport, Nahum Medalia, Michael Olmsted, Robert Feldmesser, and Norman Birnbaum.

Kluckhohn, the Navajo, and Me

Kluckhohn's study of Navajo values had been underway even before the creation of the Department of Social Relations. The Rockefeller Foundation sponsored it and supported the field research of a multitude of investigators, so many, in fact, that the joking answer to the question, "What is the composition of a Navajo family?" was "a husband, a wife, two children, and one anthropologist." The Indians of America's Southwest had long been a subject of intensive study for anthropologists and archeologists, and many monographs had been written about them. Kluckhohn's study was to be distinguished from earlier studies because of its focus on Navajo values,[3] a topic that was

---

[3]   See his essay "Values and Value-Orientations in the Theory of Action: An Exploration in Definition and Classification."

then also of central interest to Talcott Parsons, both in his work on his social system, action frame of reference, and in his research on suburban middle-class families. Parsons and Kluckhohn were collaborating in their research on values at the same time that Edward Shils was in residence in the Department of Social Relations working with Parsons on what later became their jointly edited book, *Toward a General Theory of Action*. The association of Kluckhohn's values studies with Parsons's works is indicated both by his contribution to this book and his claim, in his report to the Rockefeller Foundation on the first three years of his project, that *Toward a General Theory of Action* was a major publication resulting from his studies.[4]

Appointed by Kluckhohn as a data analyst on the values study, I read through the entries in the Navajo research files that contained cross-filed entries excerpted from field researchers' notes, reports, and monographs. Each excerpt from such sources was a paragraph in length and classified under a category pertaining to a given subject. The categories were, in part, the same as those originally formulated by George P. Murdock for his Human Relations Area Files at Yale University. A category such as "economics" contained numerous subcategories classified according to type of work, uses of money, trading, welfare, construction of houses, and others. Subcategories such as uses of money were sub-subcategorized into entries such as lending, stealing, and so on. Most paragraph-length entries

---

[4] I learned of this report, numbered HUG 4490.5 (7-19-4), from Willow Powers, who included a reference to it in a copy of her 1995 interview with me about my participation in the Ramah project. Dr. Powers interviewed me for several hours as part of her research for her PhD dissertation, which reassessed the data on the Indians in the Southwest produced under Kluckhohn's sponsorship. See Willow Roberts Powers, "The Harvard Five Cultures Values Study and Postwar Anthropology on the Indians in the Southwest." I have drawn on the protocol of this interview for parts of the discussion here.

contained references to more than one subject and were cross-filed under another sub- or sub-subcategory; a paragraph on stealing, for example, was also cross-filed under crime, interpersonal conflict, morals, and so forth. As more data were gathered and cross-referenced, the number of categories was expanded to meet the differences in nuances of data produced by different researchers. Even at this relatively early stage of the research, the subcategorized data and the cross-referencing of them had produced a substantial file.

I read through all of the entries under each major category and provided a summary of its contents. Since the data were already too extensive for a single individual to absorb, the method of producing summaries had the purpose of regaining some control over it. Kluckhohn needed a shorthand version of the contents of the files because he did not have the time to read them himself. My job was to describe the general content of a category and give an estimate of those areas in which the data were deficient. I then attempted to point out the relation of the data to the problem of values and suggest some lines of analysis in relation to values. For example, one set of categories I examined was "Inheritance," "Afterlife," and "Attitude toward Death." Although death and the dead are important areas of Navajo life and are areas surrounded by many fears, anxieties, prohibitions, and sanctions, no one had made systematic observations on this aspect of Navajo culture. I made my summary of the content of the categories under five points: description of burials for infants and adults, the relationship between death and witchcraft, death statistics, problems that occur when a Navajo dies in a hospital, and the Navajo fear of the dead. This summary, like others I did, didn't go anywhere. Although one can talk about death, architecture, women, and children, and summarize the contents of categories as I did, the result is the same data in a different form. Despite the fact that the field data were rich in content and covered vast areas of Navajo life, they could be made meaningful only if they were focused on a specific problem that provided an organizing principle for interpreting the data.

Nowhere in the data I encountered was there a reference to the central institutional fact of Navajo tribal life, namely, that the Navajo were a legally dependent tribal group under the jurisdiction of the United States government and the Bureau of Indian Affairs. They could not rightfully be called colonized, but they were subject to a system of indirect rule. Not that all researchable problems could be explained in terms of this relationship, but from the beginning, the institution of the "reservation" had transformed the internal order of indigenous Navajo institutions and values. The Navajo had been deeply penetrated by the dominant society for more than one hundred years, and the residues of this penetration remain to the present.[5]

Kluckhohn approached the study of values from the point of view of their definition and classification, but not from their historical setting or institutional context. While the terms "value" or "values" are basic concepts in the field of the social sciences, to give a precise definition to either of them can only lead to an empirically unworkable definition. If, however, one sets up a problem for investigation— for example, asking "What are the fundamental conflicts in values among the Navajo people, and what are their institutional causes?"— then one could ask who holds which values and how conflicts arise when the values are expressed in action. Some of the values held by youth are distinct from those held by their elders, but even the

---

[5]   This and related issues are discussed in Arthur J. Vidich and Stanford M. Lyman, "Qualitative Methods: Their History in Sociology and Anthropology."

values held by youth are not necessarily held by all youth; some of these youths might have been veterans returned from World War II, whose slant on life may have been influenced by their activities as Marine Corps communication specialists, a group recruited for their service because the Japanese were unable to crack the code of the Navajo language. If individuals, status groups, classes, or descent groups are specified, it is possible to examine the ideas, beliefs, and values that they hold. One can then ask how these conflicts in values affect the organization of Navajo society. One then has an intellectual problem. But the attempt to study values in the abstract led to the accumulation of data housed in files at the Peabody Museum, but not to the definition of a problem that could be examined empirically.

Ironically, anthropological investigators are themselves agents of penetration. By their presence and the questions they ask, they alter the social milieu in which they work and contribute to changing the character of the society they study. At the time of the values study, anthropological investigators did not acknowledge this fact because they failed to recognize the implications and consequences of their roles as members of the dominant society. In fact, research on the Navajo—as well as other Southwest Indian tribes—had become an academic industry whose products were dissertations and advanced academic degrees. It cannot be said that this industry was simply a matter of the exploitation of a dependent people. The investigators also added to the local economy by paying for interviews and consuming native goods and services. In exchange for data given them by the Navajo, the anthropologists became a part of their social world and helped connect them with the larger external world.

Because anthropology had become an academic profession, researchers' field trips were frequently of short duration carried out during summer breaks, academic intercessions, sabbaticals, or leaves of a semester or an academic year. Since research in the Southwest required no foreign travel, researchers could make repeated trips to the same sites, visiting and revisiting the same informants. Anthropologists not only had an economic presence in Navajo life, but also a social one, forming lasting friendships and emotional bonds with Navajo informants. I do not know if any Harvard anthropologists "went native" and married into the tribe, but this cannot be discounted as a possibility. From a social point of view, anthropologists were integrated into Navajo tribal networks, status systems, economies, and authoritative relations. As a result, the data in the files had been collected by many different investigators at different times, by different methods, from different angles of perception, and for different purposes, leaving an analyst without clues to researchers' biases.

When I was analyzing these data in the summer of 1949, in an office shared with Ann Parsons, a coworker, the data had not been identified by reference to who had obtained it, when it was gathered, and where it had been collected. It had the same disembodied quality as the data that Murdock had deposited in his Human Relations Area Files that he had used to write *Our Primitive Contemporaries*. Murdock had not collected his own data, and Kluckhohn had not collected the data I was analyzing. However, Murdock, who cast his data in an evolutionary framework, was able to present images (stories) of imaginary societies as if they existed at a particular moment in time; his book served a useful pedagogical purpose for instructors who taught college courses in introductory anthropology from the perspective of cultural evolution. The Ramah Navajo files could not be used for such purposes because there was not a mass market for a synthetic ethnography of the Navajo. The purpose of the Navajo values project had a higher aim: to make a contribution to a theory of values.

Earlier in his career, Kluckhohn had researched and written two monographs on the Navajo: *Navajo Witchcraft* and *Children of the People* (with Dorothea Leighton). He was an experienced field worker and probably knew more than anyone in his time about the Navajo, but he did not produce a final volume for the values study. It is worth speculating on why this was the case. I offer two explanations: he had lost a "feel" for the data, and he had become an academic administrator at both the Russian Research Center and the Values Project. The organizational apparatus of the Center and the Project required fundraising, periodic reports to sponsors, and management of a large bureaucratic machine; the apparatus of research became an end in itself and took its own course. As a result, Kluckhohn had little time to devote to understanding the data collected for the values study.

Large-scale interdisciplinary projects generate more data than can be digested by a single individual or, for that matter, by any collection of researchers. Despite this problem, a report must be written if only to satisfy sponsors and hopefully produce a book that leaves a mark on the field. In short, the project needed a writer, who should have been Kluckhohn. But Kluckhohn was too far removed from the spirit of the project and the research of his subordinates to be able to immerse himself in the specifics of empirical data. Digests and syntheses of data such as I was supposed to do were no substitute for firsthand knowledge of the field data. As a result, the Navajo values study produced innumerable reports, monographs, and special studies, but not a single report on its primary goal. It did not have a writer who could pick and choose data and find a perspective from which a report could be written. This was and remains the fundamental deficiency of organized group research. When the person who frames the research problem becomes an administrator, the project can only be completed with the help of a ghost.

The Effects of Social Relations on Some Students

In 1948-1950, the Social Relations Department meant different things to different professors and students. Our professors attempted to create an interdisciplinary milieu, but we students experienced an interdisciplinary schizophrenia. Parsons's formal sociology conflicted with that of Kluckhohn's empirical research. Henry Murray represented psychoanalysis and a faith in Jung such that his work could not be tied to any system of thought. Samuel Stouffer, with his faith in statistics, and Frederick Mosteller, with his faith in the harmonics of mathematics, represented yet other extreme positions. Sorokin, George Homans, Freed Bales (small groups studied through one-way viewing screens), Benjamin Paul, Alex Inkeles, Barrington Moore, Jr., Gordon Allport, and Jerome Bruner all held other viewpoints. Standing in the middle of this variety of perspectives was Talcott Parsons thinking he could integrate such disparities into the architectonic of Basic Social Science. No one can deny that there was enough interdisciplinarity in our hamburgers to fill anyone's stomach beyond capacity. But the interdisciplinary cross-fertilization that Social Relations hoped to achieve remained an abstraction that gave no leads to concrete research. Still the curriculum was open at most of its edges, leading students to respond to it as they wished, a possibility illustrated by the research lines taken by social relations graduates with whose careers I am familiar.

Some followed careers and did research that had no relationship to Parsons's systems and action theories. They oriented themselves to Parsons's substantive work in race, medicine, the middle classes, or values. Henry Murray influenced Robert N. Nelson and sponsored his dissertation on the sociology of poets. When it came to landing a job, however, he accepted a position as a field worker for a study in the organization of a hospital. Nevertheless, his research on poets gave him a worldview, and for the rest of his life, he remained a writer of poetry. Ralph Patrick, a southerner who struggled with the problems of race and equality, found no means for coping with this personal demon in his academic studies. He held positions at Washington University in St. Louis and at the University of North Carolina, but did not find a perspective from which he could analyze the racial inequalities he encountered as a youth in North Carolina.

Irving Rosow entered the sociology of medicine and became a gerontologist. Joseph Kahl wrote a book on the class system and held positions at Cornell University and at the University of North Carolina. Kim Romney was attracted to the architectonics of mathematics and followed Mosteller's god. Parsons encouraged Tom O'Dea, a Boston Irish Thomist, to study the Mormons; that turned out to be good advice because it made him a sociologist, a subject he taught at the University of Utah until his untimely death. I remember deep discussions O'Dea and I had about faith and non-faith when we were still taking life awfully seriously and thought we could find its meaning by studying social relations. Norman Jacobs became an Asian specialist and wrote books about the Far East. John White, an Englishman studying psychology, returned to England where he became a practicing psychologist. Robert Endleman became a psychoanalytically oriented anthropologist-sociologist and wrote books that probed the human psyche. Fred Stodtbeck, a student of Freed Bales, studied small-group processes in juries while a professor at the University of Chicago. Kluckhohn's students—Jack Fischer, Monro Edmundson, and Charles Lang—had careers as anthropologists.

Otto von Mering became an anthropologist of education. Robert Rappaport wrote about the family at the Tavistock Clinic in England. Nathan Kogan took a job in a gerontology institute in Boston, then moved to the Educational Testing Institute in Princeton as a research psychologist, and later came to the Graduate Faculty of The New School for Social Research as chair of the psychology department. Robert Feldmaster became a specialist in Soviet studies and took a position at Brandeis University. Norman Birnbaum, a self-conscious anti-Parsonian, had his first teaching positions in Great Britain and France, returning to the US in 1966 to take a position in social theory at the Graduate Faculty at The New School for Social Research. Later, he became a public intellectual and wrote in such journals as *The Nation*. In my own case, failing to find an intellectual focus, I fell back on the writings of Max Weber as presented in Gerth and Mills's *From Max Weber* and in Gerth's interpretation of them in his book with Mills, *Character and Social Structure: The Psychology of Social Institutions*. Parsons was no help in my effort. Ignoring the substantive problems Weber dealt with, Parsons eliminated the historical dimension of his work and left it an empty shell. Even *The Protestant Ethic and the Spirit of Capitalism* and Weber's essay "The Protestant Sects in America" were not points of orientation for Parsons in his course on American society. I could not accept the claim that Parsons's work had superseded Weber's and that the theory of action was a new beginning for sociology. Such extreme differences in theoretical dispositions and substantive areas of research suggest that my social relations classmates did not follow lines derived from their education in Basic Social Science.

Kaspar Naegele, whom we regarded as the outstanding member of our class, was a poet in the mode of Simmel and identified with Simmel's writings, but he agonized over his inability to live up to them.

Simmel did not appear as one of Parsons's authors in *The Structure of Social Action*, though he was included in Parsons's *Theories of Society*, jointly edited with Naegele. Naegele's exposure to Simmel and his undergraduate studies in Canada were not conducive to an "unpoetic" sociology. Stanford M. Lyman, who co-taught a seminar in social theory with Naegele at the University of British Columbia, told me that the course was organized around Parsons's systems theory; Naegele presented and defended it with Lyman criticizing it. Apparently Naegele was unable to find a way to integrate Simmel with systems theory and, under pressure to have a theory he could teach, he chose Parsons's. It cannot be said what Naegele might have done had he not committed suicide before he could synthesize the ideas that came to guide his thought.[6]

Harold Garfinkel was a special case. He had already matriculated for several years when I met him in my second year. As teaching assistants, we occupied adjacent offices and on many evenings after office hours walked together to our Gibson Street apartments. Garfinkel also studied with Alfred Schutz at the Graduate Faculty of The New School for Social Research. It was through Schutz that he had first become acquainted with phenomenology and a problem that continued to occupy him subsequently: Under what conditions might the structure of social action break down? This question seemed to be the obverse of Parsons's problem, which was to locate the norms that maintain social order. Garfinkel hoped to discover what happened in human interaction when the norms were violated. In 1948-49, he was doing his dissertation research on medical students, interviewing them about their hopes and prospects for careers. At one

---

[6] Philipp O. Naegele wrote a thoughtful appreciation of Naegele's life and work in his "Foreword" to Kaspar D. Naegele, *Health and Healing.*

point in the research, having established the students' confidence, he informed his subjects that they had little prospect of a successful career in medicine. Garfinkel's aim was to measure their reactions to this crisis in their lifeworlds. Only after breaking them down did he cool them off by informing them that they were merely part of an experiment. Parsons was not convinced of the value of Garfinkel's problem. He did not see it as the other side of the problem of social order, that is, the orderly performance of role functions. However, Garfinkel thought his work was consistent with Parsons's. What he had hoped to discover were the rules that exist below the level of consciousness. Garfinkel attempted to find what he called "recipes for living" that are the rules of everyday life. His was less a theory than a methodology, not a study of the social structure, but of persons and how they live their lives in relation to others. The difference between the Garfinkel-Schutz-phenomenological approach and that of Parsons was that Garfinkel was trying to get at the "taken-for-granted," whereas Parsons was more concerned with the social management of roles. In 1957, Parsons invited Garfinkel to spend a year at Harvard for the purpose of trying to integrate his work with that of systems theory. Garfinkel maintains that he was investigating some of the conditions for the production of social structure. However, Parsons did not seem to appreciate this despite the fact that his system theory could absorb almost anything—except Garfinkel.[7]

Neither Naegele nor Garfinkel can be said to have become Parsonians. Before coming to Harvard, both had had a formative intellectual exposure to another thinker—Naegele to Simmel and Garfinkel

---

[7] Stanford M. Lyman, in a personal communication, informed me that he was told that Garfinkel has authored a monograph entitled *A Parsons Primer*, which has circulated unpublished among Garfinkel's ethnomethodological colleagues and disciples.

to Schutz. Despite their attraction to Parsons, neither can be said to have become formal theorists. Moreover, they, like many of us in the class of 1948, when first confronting *The Structure of Social Action* and systems theory, thought them to be too far removed from the realities of everyday life. Each, however, was drawn to Parsons and was influenced by Parsons's thought.

A question that has intrigued me over the past fifty years is how it came about that Parsons's system theory became, for a time, the dominant and almost overwhelming theoretical orientation in the social sciences. His influence was not confined to the United States, but extended to Europe, South America, and other parts of the world. It is a question that arises for me because those of us who were exposed to *The Structure of Social Action* and *Toward a General Theory of Action* responded to them with a skeptical curiosity. The variance of this reaction from the subsequent dominance of Parsons's work requires explanation. The case of Jesse Pitts serves as a concrete example of a convert and a starting point for a more general explanation.

Jesse Pitts, who spoofed *The Structure of Social Action* with his tinker-toy construction, provides an example of how a conversion could occur. In his first year, Pitts was a member of the proseminar team, "Strategic Areas of Research in Basic Social Science," and wrote the section of its report titled "Some Structural Strains in the Relation of the Social Scientist to Society: Need for Significant Field Research in Sociology." Pitts argued that the field of sociology should be politically relevant. Emphasizing the priority of research over theory and the relevance of research for solving social problems, Pitts set out his research agenda:

> Beginning with the United States in which we live,
> if we wanted to test our knowledge of strategic

variables in the determination of human behavior
by making some predictions as to the outcome of
concrete situations we first request ... preliminary
data ... for the following structures: 1. the business
corporation, 2. the medium and small size enterprise, 3. the labor union, 4. the institutions of the
government, 5. the FBI and other police forces (state
and local), 6. the armed forces, 7. the professions (legal, teaching, medical), 8. the political parties, 9. the
churches, 10. the underworld, [and] the institutions
devoted to communication, training and entertainment such as: 11. the universities, 12. the movie industry, 13. the radio industry, 14. the great middle-
class magazines (Time, Life, The New Yorker, etc.),
15. the newspapers and pulp magazines.[8]

Pitts's strategic variables include the central institutions and organizations of American society, including the various bureaucratic
structures under which they are administered. Except for the omis-
sions of the class system, kinship, and family institutions, his research program covers the better part of social relations in the country as a whole. He continues his statement with an assessment of
"scientifically hallowed versions of ... official mythology." He wishes
to conduct research that contradicts such myths as

"Democracy is better"; "we have a mobile society with practical equality of opportunity for all";
"things will eventually get better and better"; "what

---

[8] This quotation and the one following are taken from Pitts's report to the
proseminar.

we need is more education"; "women should not have intercourse before marriage"; "people are really not different"; and "those who insist on being different are sick."

Despite these strictures designed to counter conservative and liberal myths, Pitts maintained that a task force to develop "all the aspects of a central conceptual scheme through disciplined research" was necessary. He went on to say that despite "their inherent dysfunctions … the integrative powers of schools," such as that of the Harvard Department of Social Relations, constitute the kind of structural reform that will lead to the fulfillment of his goal. Later, he assisted Parsons in editing *Theories of Society* and apparently reclassified the specific substantive areas of research that had originally animated him under the heading of "structural strains" as conceived in Parsons's *The Social System*. On the one hand, Pitts wanted to address real problems using data gathered from the sources he enumerated in his numbered points; on the other, he hoped Harvard's Department of Social Relations was the place where this could be accomplished. But given the extreme diversity of the Social Relations faculty, a centrally integrated conceptual scheme had never been formulated. The only person who could and finally did construct such a scheme was Talcott Parsons. Without an alternative from which he could develop an independent perspective against formal sociology, Pitts was hoisted on his own petard: his eventual choice to become a Parsonian came at the expense of his commitment to what he called the real problems of the social sciences.

The Success and Atrophy of Parsons's Work

Pitts's case is paradigmatic for those who came to Harvard hoping to find a theoretical perspective from which they might formulate their own approaches to sociology. Although such a student may originally have thought in terms of concrete substantive issues and rejected Parsons's formalism as did Pitts and, to a lesser extent, Naegele and Garfinkel, the act of criticizing Parsons provided a student with no more than a negative point of view. Such critical negativism, the stock in trade of many graduate students, is functional only up to a point. In the academic career, it does not serve as a guide for one's own research. The code of professionalism requires work that makes a positive contribution, an advancement of some kind in a field of knowledge. Converting critical negativism into research productivity becomes a problem at two points in the aspirant's career: writing a dissertation and constructing a teaching program based on a consistent theoretical perspective. The dissertation is usually not the test case because, as proof of the point, almost all Harvard sociology dissertations written during Parsons's tenure focused on conventional sociological subjects: the family, community, marriage, leisure, migration, demography, land use, social stratification, adolescence, sex ratios, alcohol addiction, fertility, gerontology, the Catholic church, local government, juvenile delinquency, urbanization, medical care, and so on—the usual fare of dissertation topics.[9]

---

[9] The topics appear in a listing of "Doctorates in Sociology: 1932-1989," published by Harvard's Department of Sociology in 1989. I thank my former colleague, Mustafa Emirbayer, for supplying me with this document. Most of the dissertations accepted by Harvard's sociology program did not explicitly deal with social theory. The list does not include the names of psychologists or anthropologists—such as David Schneider, Clifford Geertz, or myself—who, after the dissolution of the Department of Social Relations, which had conferred our degrees, do not appear on this list. Presumably, we are on the lists of graduates from the reconstituted departments of anthropology and psychology. [Editor's note: the document to which Vidich refers here has been updated and is now titled "Sociology Dissertations 1932-2007." It is available on the web site of the Department of Sociology at Harvard University. Thanks to Joshua Wakeham for help in locating it.]

It is relatively easy to find a ready-made theoretical framework to encapsulate a body of substantive data. In any case, in the American system of doctoral studies, in contrast to the German habilitation, the candidate's dissertation is not expected to anticipate a forthcoming intellectual career.

To formulate one's own teaching perspective and construct a course in social theory is another matter. How does one do this? If one has not replaced the negative graduate-student attitude with a positive perspective of one's own, one is left with nothing but the original negative, the theory that one had made a student career of fighting. But contesting a theory requires one to learn it. Once learned, it is part of one's intellectual capital. To discard it leaves a void. Therefore, when the time comes for the academic aspirant to teach the first course in social theory, he or she discovers the value of the capital investment already made. At this stage in the academic career, the void is filled by transforming the negative into a positive. For lack of an alternative, the mentor's theory is embraced. Something like this seems to have happened to some of Parsons's students.

Parsons's career at Harvard spanned more than forty years. He taught new cohorts of students every year from the 1930s to the 1970s, beginning with Robert Merton, Logan Wilson, Wilbert Moore, Gordon Blackwell, Nicholas J. Demerath, Freed Bales, Marion Levy, Robin Williams, and followed by Bernard Barber, Harry Johnson, Eugene Schneider, Edward Devereux, Toby Jackson, Albert Cohen, Walter Wardwell, Theodore Mills, Sherwood Fox, Thomas O'Dea, Robert Bellah, Homer Kent Geiger, Morris Zelditch, Edward Tiryakian, Neil Smelser, Vyautas Kavolis, and more than four hundred others. I term this group Harvard's Emissaries to the World. Very few, if any, of more than four hundred sociology dissertation topics listed for the departmental publication "Doctorates in Sociology:

1932-1989" indicate or suggest that the dissertations elaborated systems theory as such. (This does not include perhaps more than five hundred doctorates granted to anthropologists, psychologists, and clinicians during the period of the existence of the Department of Social Relations.) Social Relations graduates of whatever discipline did not specialize in theory. Nevertheless, for more than thirty years, Parsons created and developed the theory by which Harvard came to be known. For this reason, if one had a doctorate in social relations or sociology, it *ipso facto* defined graduates as theoreticians in a Parsonian mode. When these graduates began teaching careers, they were usually expected to teach the course in social theory. During the 1950s and 1960s, social theory itself came to be equated with structural-functionalism, the theory of action, and systems theory. Harvard graduates in social relations or sociology were assumed to be competent to teach social theory.

Most of Parsons's emissaries were not theorists. They were teachers of theory only because their employers expected this of them. When they did their own research, they studied a variety of subjects that included race relations, American values, medicine, chiropractors, Durkheim, kinship, Japanese society, and other themes that they had developed in their dissertation topics. But as teachers of social theory, they taught Parsons's systems theory.

The placement of Harvard's social relations and sociology graduates in departments of sociology in universities offering doctorate and master's degrees continued for more than thirty years. These graduates were carriers and disseminators of systems theory that led to its deepening penetration across the country. Such emissaries, however, carried with them that version of Parsons to which they had been exposed while they were his students. For example, when I was at the University of Connecticut in the late 1950s, the Parsons being taught there was still that of *The Structure of Social Action*. His later works, *Toward a General Theory of Action* and *The Social System,* had not yet reached Storrs. While Parsons had moved through a series of theoretical stages in his own work, his epigoni taught the social theory to which they had been exposed when they were his students, mummifying as gospel what they had originally learned. I call this an archaeology of structural-functional and systems theory in the United States, each stratified layer corresponding to that phase of Parsons's development to which an emissary had been exposed at Harvard.

It is difficult to know what the generations of students once-removed from Parsons could make of his theory, but it is clear that over the years the number of students who were exposed to it increased exponentially. In some instances, students were exposed to carriers from Harvard's cohorts and thus received Parsons's theory secondhand. A Parsonian orthodoxy took hold and sustained structural functionalism, action theory, and systems theory long after they were dead at Harvard, providing us with an example of Veblen's and Ogburn's theory of cultural lag. Jeffrey C. Alexander, the student of Parson's students, Mark Gould and Neil J. Smelser, is a case in point.

The transmission of ideas by colonial emissaries is insufficient to explain the overwhelming influence of systems theory in the United States and its penetration into other parts of the world. Once the Parsonian perspective took hold in the United States, it became a point of view from which textbooks began to be written. The texts then in vogue included those of Harry Johnson, Harry Bredemier, Kingley Davis, Wilber Moore, and Eli Chinoy, along with the works of Merton, Smelser, and Parsons himself, so that for graduate students and frequently for undergraduates as well, the terminologies of systems theory came to be equated with social theory as such. Moreover, in what appeared to be at least tacit understandings between the sociology departments of Harvard and Columbia, the idea was propounded that systems theory and survey research were mutually consistent and formed a unified theory and methodology for sociology as a whole. Thus, sociology found a theory and empirical method that defined the field. Once solidified as a compact package, the net product became an item for export abroad in the form of foundation-supported visiting fellowships and professorships, cross-oceanic and intercontinental seminars, and the distribution of texts in American information and studies centers.[10] While there is here the suggestion of an organized promotional campaign, this in itself is an insufficient explanation for the overwhelming acceptance of a unified sociological perspective.

The fact that such a perspective took hold during the Cold War could not have happened by chance. By chance alone, one would have expected a much greater diversity of thought and level of contentiousness. The rarity of sociologists deviating from this norm has not been confronted. It is precisely the sociologists whom one might have expected to raise the question of how a single system of thought came to dominate a discipline, but instead they remained in docile normative conformity, or as Harold Rosenberg once put it, a herd of independent minds. This conformity is explained partly by the

---

[10]   See Frances Stonor Saunders, *Who Paid the Piper: The CIA and the Cultural Cold War*, for an example of how American culture was exported to Europe during the Cold War years. Saunders's study covers all aspects of culture including art, music, literature, painting, book distribution, conference organizing, and so forth. It offers a detailed examination of the extra-institutional networks by which ideas and political orientations were controlled and transmitted to other parts of the world.

commanding prestige of Harvard University and partly by the successful efforts of the professional organizers of the discipline.

While Parsons had addressed the problem of social order and the integration of society, the overarching perceptions and beliefs in the decade of the 1960s were the activation of the civil rights movement, the futility of the Vietnam War, the disaffection and confrontation in the universities, and what then appeared to be the excessive rationality, one-dimensionality, and impersonality of corporate capitalism. As experienced within the intellectual community, these factors contradicted the assumptions of systems theory, which could only account for these phenomena as malfunctions, deviance, or anomie. Events in the world demonstrated conflict, divisiveness, and the "malintegration" of society rather than its integration.

Positing the concept of a social system, Parsons assumed by definition that society was integrated and presumed that actual, empirical societies were as well. In his terms, the task of sociology is to identify the structural elements in the system and attribute to them the functions of these elements for the system as a whole. Since this approach conceives society in analytical rather than historical terms, the task of the system theorist is simply to document the original assumptions of the theory.

If one assumes that the central problem of sociology is to explain structure, continuity, and change in society in both its historical and contemporary forms, then its task begins with observation of the world. A general theory of modern society might begin with the assumption that individual and social ends, values, groups, and institutions are diverse and frequently in competition and conflict. The problem of the unity of society can be posed in the light of individuals, groups, and institutional leaders seeking different, conflicting, and competitive ends. Despite the fact that these ends and values may be opposed to other ends and values, they are nevertheless part of the institutions and structure of society. Parsons's view of the social order as a self-sustaining system accounts for dysfunction, anomie, and deviance as system malfunctions or strains, but can only account for changes in the system and its underlying values within the framework of the system itself. If conflicting values and diverse ends are regarded as secondary aspects of society, that is, assumed to be parts of an integrated system, then social integration and continuity are self-sustaining. For Parsons, the major structural units in the system reinforce each other and sustain the system as a whole, making it unnecessary to view the social order as an open rather than a closed system.

The Department of Social Relations at Harvard University occupied a unique place in American sociology. Creating and dominating it for twenty-five years, Talcott Parsons set its intellectual agenda and was its chief executive officer. He came to believe that his theory of social action and social systems provided an invariant theoretical model for all of the social sciences and that it vitiated the need for other theoretical strategies. His creation of a closed system relegated the task of empirical investigators to that of providing confirmation of the theory. He was enormously successful in propagating and diffusing his ideas to many adherents. It is still too early to assess the costs and benefits for the social sciences of Harvard's social relations program.[11]

---

[11] On my encounter with Harvard, see also Arthur J. Vidich, "The Department of Social Relations and 'Systems Theory' at Harvard: 1948-50."

Further Reflections on Harvard

There was more to the Social Relations Department than the Navajo, the proseminar, and Parsons's system theory. Despite the all-embracing scope of the proseminar—its use as a device to expose us to the literature of four fields—each student, in addition, was expected to become proficient in one subject. Since "Social Relations" was not recognized as a discipline let alone a profession for which a job market existed, I knew that when I finished my studies I had to find a job as an anthropologist.

At mid-century, anthropology was an established subject in many American universities. It claimed a body of literature and a distinctive field of study, the non-literate, pre-literate world of primitive cultures, as they were then known. It had also divided itself into the subfields of cultural and social anthropology, archaeology, physical anthropology, and linguistics. Though the boundaries among these were permeable, the anthropology curriculum in the Social Relations Department was limited to linguistics and social and cultural anthropology. The field had not yet been subdivided into endless subspecializations, so it was still expected that all anthropology graduates in Harvard's Department of Social Relations be familiar with the extant literature in her/his field. This meant that we read ethnographies of nomads, hunters and gatherers, tribal societies, and African kingdoms written mainly by Americans, Englishmen, and some Frenchmen, and studied kinship systems, legal systems (the Ifugao), linguistic structures (Whorf and Sapir), and variations in the cultural values of American Indian groups. And we learned that Culture, with a capital "C," was anthropology's master concept.

My files contain reading lists for three of the anthropology courses I took: a seminar, "Concepts in Social Anthropology"; a course, "Social Anthropology"; and a seminar, "The Evolution of Culture."

"Concepts in Anthropology" was taught by Clyde Kluckhohn. He organized the seminar by assigning a concept to each student and asked for a report on it to the seminar. The concepts were culture, social structure, function, pattern, integration, cultural change, acculturation, progress-evolution, universal cultural patterns, modal personality, focus, and world view. For each concept he provided a list of questions and an extensive bibliography. In the case of Culture, the names on the reading list are Montagu, Bidney, Boas, Gillin, Goldenweiser, Kroeber, Linton, Murdock, Malinowski, Redfield, Roheim, Sapir, White, Wissler, Osgood, Lynd, Blumenthal, Ford, Stern, Sumner, and Kluckhohn. Names listed under Social Structure are Brown and Barnett, Chapple, Eggan, Evans-Pritchard, Fortes, Lowie, Radcliffe-Brown, Steward, as well as some of those listed under Culture. The references listed under the headings of other concepts amounted to almost all of the authors writing in the fields of anthropology, a disparate group of thinkers who wrote from a variety of theoretical perspectives and even more scattered substantive data. When one finished a seminar like this, one had a take on all the major writers in the field without having read them, but one could not synthesize them into a perspective of one's own.

Social anthropology was centered on texts by M. J. Herskovits, C. S. Coon, Audrey Richards, and Robert Redfield, supplemented with books about tribes or primitive communities, such as Barton's *The Kalingas*, Benedict's *The Chrysanthemum and the Sword*, Embree's *Suye Mura*, Fortune's *Sorcerers of Dobu*, Landes's *The Ojibwa Woman*, Schapera's *Married Life in an African Tribe*, and so on. The research for most of these studies had been conducted before World War II, during the decade of the 1930s, and they were now the exemplars of anthropological field work conducted by the method anthropologists called "participant observation," that is, to enter the society under study as both a participant and observer. Participant observation distinguished anthropological field work from that of sociologists.

"The Evolution of Culture" began with Morgan, Spencer, and Tyler, who were labeled "early evolutionists" and included readings under the subcategories "Expressions of an Anti-Evolutionist's Point of View" and "Evolutionism Pro and Con," suggesting the lack of a settled professional attitude about evolution. We learned the names and points of view of recognized authors in the fields of physical, cultural, social, and economic evolution, and, overall, that the modern West was at the highest stage of evolution. That the evolution of the physical and biological world was the same as that of the cultural and social was disquieting but not a subject for critical examination.

Anthropology was the "Study of Man," an all-inclusive term we were told, that embraced everything having to do with the human species, women and American society included. If and when an anthropologist's name, such as Clark Wissler's, was associated with a study, as was the case of the Lynds' study of Middletown, that study could be absorbed into anthropology. Before going to Muncie, Indiana, the Lynds had consulted Wissler, an anthropologist at New York's Museum of Natural History, who provided them with the ethnographic categories they used to organize the presentation of their data. In practice, at the level of pedagogy this imperialistic inclusivity meant that my head was stuffed with theories and discreet items of ethnographic data, rich in description but impossible to integrate into a meaningful theory. Nor was theory at this stage in anthropology a necessity for such integration. It was enough that anthropologists should study primitive societies wherever they appeared on the face of the globe in order to capture their ways of life while they still existed. Thus could the anthropologist be idealized as someone giving his life to a noble cause even while enduring the hardships of the lone participant observer far from civilization and under conditions of primitive deprivation from the comforts of home. Field work was both a sacrifice and a heroic activity in the service of Science and Man.

In my innocence and enthusiasm for being selected to study at Harvard, I believed that if I read everything, I could discover what anthropology was. I had already done field work in Palau and had yet to write a report on it to the National Science Foundation, but after a year of graduate studies and extensive reading, I had no more of a focus on what anthropology was than I had had when I left Wisconsin. In addition to what I might have learned from reading bloated bibliographies, I also learned a few lessons in academic impression management.

My novice's faith that instructors' reading lists were carefully and rationally designed to cover the parameters of the subject was quickly disabused, and I learned a lesson in a pedagogical technique. It was not necessary to read all the citations. Reading lists had other purposes. One is intended to give the student an impression of the instructor's wide range of learning. Bibliographic overkill is a way of saying to the novice, "I have read these books, and you know nothing until you have too." By virtue of the disparity in authority between student and graduate professor, the former cannot challenge the instructor's implicit claim because it is a breach of etiquette to question a professor's knowledge of books on her/his own reading list. The hapless student cannot empirically determine the extent of the instructor's knowledge, hence the reading list remains a quasi-sacred document, presumably to be referenced more carefully later when it becomes necessary to make a reading list of one's own, perhaps for the same purpose: the intimidation of other novices. My Harvard reading never gave me a coherent understanding of the discipline, nor did I learn why Culture was its master concept. In *Culture: A Critical Review of Concepts and Definitions*, Alfred Kroeber and Clyde Kluckhohn define culture as "consisting of patterns, explicit and implicit, of and for behavior acquired and transmitted by symbols, constituting the distinctive achievements of human groups, including their embodiments in artifacts." They codify culture under six definitional categories—descriptive, historical, normative, psychological, structural, and genetic. To me this meant that culture was just another word like "society" or "social system," a word to be used in a sentence when you needed a term to refer to a totality such as "American culture," a meaningless expression unless given a specific and more limited content. That is, it might be possible to define culture only after it has been studied in all its empirical manifestations, but the result of such empirical work could include everything and amount to nothing. A concept that includes everything is of no help as an analytic tool when confronting a specific research problem. The term "culture" is anthropology's metaphysic.

During my time as a first-year graduate student, I was analyzing the data I had collected in Palau. The image of primitive society that I acquired from that experience was difficult to square with my formal studies. One of the first Palauans I had met was Sakuma, the superintendent of schools, whose father, a Japanese soldier, married a Palauan. Sakuma received his BA and MA degrees in philosophy from a Seventh Day Adventist university in Tokyo and spoke Palauan, Japanese, and conversational English. He was thirty, just a few years older than I, and sought to engage me in a discussion concerning the work of Kant and Hegel and how their ideas might be used to create a philosophy for Palau's educational system. In my fieldwork in Viroqua, in a region with a population greater than that of Palau, I never met a native, including the ministers of the local Lutheran churches, who was the intellectual equal of this informant. This experience disabused me of the notion that the Palauans were primitives. In fact, Palau already refracted international culture and the central trends and tendencies of the nineteenth and twentieth centuries, and I understood that it could not be comprehended outside this larger framework. I was impressed that wherever I traveled in these islands, there was a short-wave radio that the natives listened to eagerly to learn what disposition the superpowers, whom they already understood to be in a power struggle of global proportions, made of them. I could not understand why Homer Barnett, who was then leading another team in Palau, had chosen to study the remotest village in the expectation of finding a pure representation of aboriginal Palauan life in all its irrational and exotic manifestations. Palauans' beliefs and lifestyles were not derived from a mythic past. Nor, with the exception of a few anthropological reports, did they have a written history. The search for aboriginal values and beliefs was at best a quixotic endeavor that might capture some of the exotic premises of Palauan behavior, but even such a purpose could only add to the anthropological inventory of the strange ways of the natives. But, even so, accepting the natives' value presuppositions in order to highlight their peculiarity from a Western rationalistic point of view does not address a larger question, namely, given the value premises from which action ensues, the conduct of the natives is as rational as that of the natives in the West. Instead of searching for the aboriginal premises, the problem, it seemed to me, was to study changes in the premises, in this case as a result of colonial penetration.

I had hoped that my course work would provide me with a theoretical orientation for interpreting my data. When I found that it was of no help, I decided to audit William Yandell Elliot's and Carl J. Friedrich's courses in the political science department, hoping to fill the political gaps in the social relations curriculum. Unfortunately, Elliot's course was scheduled at the same time as Kluckhohn's course on linguistics. When Kluckhohn discovered I was not in attendance, he didn't tolerate this defection. I signed up for linguistics and thereafter never broke ranks with the department. Yet what I learned in Palau contradicted my training in anthropology.

During the fall 1948 term, I had been reading and rereading the stacks of interviews I had gathered in Palau earlier in the year. The Harvard housing authority assigned me a study room, detached from my living quarters, a former army barracks where, surrounded by four bare walls, I relived the immediacy of the Palauan world. It was there that I organized my field notes by spreading them over the floor according to categories that seemed to flow from their contents. I had begun my research as an investigation of a Palauan anti-Japanese resistance movement, but in the course of the field work had changed it to an examination of the effects of colonial administration on Palauan society. Since the latter part of the nineteenth century, Spain, Germany, Japan, and the United States had successively claimed dominion over Palau. Facing my data in its original form posed the problem of finding the problem in it. I needed a framework that both accounted for the data and provided a coherent explanation of it. At first I thought to use some of the language I was learning in the proseminar and in my anthropology classes—roles, cultural patterns, structures, systems, modal personalities—but I was unable to make linkages between the concepts and the changes that colonial policy had wrought on Palauan social organization. This experience was the beginning of my education in the meaning of research— or, rather, one might call it search—namely, that a research problem cannot be solved by deduction from *a priori* concepts. In my report to the National Science Foundation, I tried to use some of this conceptual terminology—mostly because I thought I needed footnote references to Kluckhohn's and Parsons's work—but my efforts amounted to window dressing that served no other purpose. Forced to confront the specifics of the interview data in relation to the questions I asked, I had no choice but to ignore the formal concepts that were so much a part of academic life. In the dissertation version of my study, I made reference to studies of colonialism and eliminated my citations of Parsons's and Kluckhohn's concepts.

The Second Year at Harvard

Harvard's Housing Bureau assigned second-year graduate students to housing in Cambridge. I was assigned to apartment 1-A at Gibson Terrace off Mount Auburn Avenue, where I first met Harold Garfinkel and where I later learned from Talcott Parsons, in a rare moment of interpersonal intimacy, that he had lived in the same place while writing *The Structure of Social Action*. Living in Cambridge opened up new possibilities for life in the university, Harvard Square, and the city. This was my first experience with living in a cosmopolitan city. West Allis, Madison, Viroqua, Palau, and the towns I passed through while I was stationed in Kyushu had none of the cultivation of Boston. Nagasaki had been a great city, but by the time I arrived there, it no longer existed. Cambridge was full of bookstores, theaters, restaurants, and museums and was only a short distance from downtown Boston. Cambridge and Boston had the flavor of the East, unlike Madison that was still a provincial state capital in a rural region. Cambridge was unlike anything I had experienced before.

The Cold War was beginning to heat up. Truman had been elected president. The Soviet Union was producing its own atom bombs, and hydrogen bombs were designed to escalate the destructiveness of future wars. The political loyalty of intellectuals had come under scrutiny. If professors and students had been members in the 1930s of organizations listed by the FBI as subversive, their loyalty to the country was questioned. The FBI's regional headquarters in Boston was in direct contact with President Conant. Professors, including Parsons, who had been faculty advisor to the John Reed Society, were being investigated for possible disloyalty to the United States. President Conant and Dean McGeorge Bundy provided at least one sacrificial lamb (Sigmund Diamond) to the FBI, going along with the emerging anticommunist hysteria. In this tense situation, the famous humanities professor F. O. Matthiessen, an eminent scholar of American letters, a man of the left, and an open homosexual, committed suicide by jumping from a window of a Boston hotel. In conjunction with the activities of the FBI, Senator Joseph McCarthy of Wisconsin was already beginning to attack the State Department for allegedly employing homosexuals and communists. The irony here is that despite the wartime work of the Social Relations faculty who had proved their loyalty to the country—no one could fault Parsons, Kluckhohn, or Murray on that score—the FBI could make unfounded accusations that might require innocent people to defend themselves. The anticipation of potential intimidation could poison academic openness among faculty and graduate students who had been youthful radicals or were homosexuals.

It was in this inquisitorial atmosphere that I met Richard Hobson, a new first-year anthropology student and former employee of the State Department whom Kluckhohn had recruited into the anthropology program. On our first meeting, Hobson confided to me that he had left the State Department because of his homosexuality and was worried that it might interfere with his career as an anthropologist. I tried to assure him that his sexual orientation made no difference to his future prospects. Remembering James Silverberg's confession to me of his passing homosexual affair with Kluckhohn, I cited Kluckhohn as a case in point of someone who was both a homosexual and an eminent anthropologist. Silverberg's tale of intimacy with Kluckhohn had been amply confirmed over the years. Even Kluckhohn's wife openly alluded to her husband's homosexuality. And Kluckhohn's behavior at the parties he gave at his apartment for graduate students openly proclaimed his inclinations. When Kluckhohn kissed me as I was leaving one of his parties, I learned something new about eroticism in academia. Still, although homosexuality was not a big secret in New England preparatory schools and Ivy League colleges, most homosexuals had not left the closet. My intention in mentioning Kluckhohn's case to Hobson was to bolster Hobson's self-confidence in the face of the assault on homosexuals by the FBI and critics of the State Department. Yet my conversation with Hobson later came back to haunt me.

Kluckhohn was generous in the care and support he gave to the furtherance of my education. During my second year of residence he assigned me as teaching assistant to courses taught by Alex Inkeles and Barrington Moore, Jr., both of whom were attached to the Russian Research Center and taught courses in the Social Relations Department. Inkeles taught a course on the Soviet Union and Moore on the sociology of power. Inkeles's course was on a subject entirely new to me, Moore's less so, but in both cases, acting as an assistant meant that I took the courses just as if I were a student, listening to the lectures and reading student assignments. Of the course work I did at Harvard, I learned most from these and remember them the best.

Inkeles had been recruited to the department from the OSS and was a member of a new generation of "Sovietologists" created to meet the challenges of the Cold War. The Soviet Union had been designated one of a new class of "area studies" then being formed at American universities. Originally, the anthropological areas of the world had as their focus the study of "primitives" or "ancient civilizations." Any anthropologist who had a PhD was expected to be a specialist in an area. My area, for example, was Oceania, designated as such because of America's commercial and military interests that coincided with Admiral Perry's visit to Japan in 1854 and the colonization of Hawaii by Bostonians. There was already a hint in the anthropologist's concept of area studies that the interests of the United States were global. The decolonization of many parts of the world after World War II, however, led to the establishment of new national states and a re-mapping of the world that did not coincide with the older anthropological areas. By a logical extension of the original concept, the world could now be reclassified into new geographical entities, each of which could become the object of specialized study. Because the concept of area studies was borrowed from anthropology, an anthropologist was the logical choice to be the director of the Russian Research Center. Area studies now included not only Oceania, but also Africa, the Middle East, Asia, Eastern Europe, Finland, the USSR, Japan, China, India, Vietnam, Nigeria, South Africa, and any other place in the world thought to be of strategic interest to the US. In response to Cold War national policy interests, area studies programs were parceled out country by country and area by area to various universities and had become a growth industry in departments of anthropology, sociology, and political science. Harvard and Columbia were centers for Soviet Studies. Inkeles had been educated at Columbia and had been given a joint appointment in the Department of Social Relations and the Russian Research Center where he had his office.

Inkeles's course on the Soviet Union consisted of three lectures a week given to about 100 students. As his apprentice, in addition to attending his lectures, I advised students, corrected examinations, and reported to him on a weekly basis. Inkeles was an excellent lecturer and a fast talker who delivered masses of material in tightly packed sequences. He prepared his material in advance and had full command of the literature. No other professor I knew at Harvard possessed his skills as a lecturer, pouring it on with unbelievable speed. He did this for a full semester—forty-three lectures—never pausing in mid-sentence or taking an obvious breath, like an opera singer. Out of the mass of material he delivered, it was my duty to make a mock-up of the mid-term and final exams and to grade the examination papers—my first lesson in grading a mass of 100 responses to the same questions and the stupefaction that this exercise can induce even in a conscientious reader.

Inkeles's course was designed to confront and contradict any Soviet ideological claim that might have an appeal to his students. The Soviet claim that it was a classless society of workers was answered by a careful analysis of the inequitable income distribution of the Soviet class system, ranging from the poorest peasants to the nomenclatura. The classical peasant described by Sir John Maynard in *The Russian Peasant and Other Studies* was used as a foil to statistically support the disasters of Stalin's forced collectivization of agriculture in the 1930s. Soviet elections showing ninety-eight percent of the population voting for party-appointed candidates were a sham—window dressing for purposes of propaganda. The image of the Stakhanovite known as the "New Soviet Man" was a mass media propaganda campaign to boost the morale and productivity of industrial workers. Everything that Inkeles said was both true and selected for doctrinaire ideological purposes and was comparable to the Soviets' anti-American propaganda campaign that stressed the image of the bloated capitalist, destitute black Americans, and exploited American workers. At that time, when postwar idealism—as symbolized in the United Nations—was still alive, it was a disappointment to learn that sociological analysis could be embedded in a propaganda framework. Inkeles's commitment to foreign policy objectives vitiated Weber's strictures on the meaning of objectivity in the social sciences and the scholarly idealism of the Department of Social Relations.

After leaving Harvard, I met Inkeles only once again. In the 1960s, at the time of the beginning of the Kruschev "thaw," I went to Cambridge to attend a lecture in Emerson Hall given by a Russian sociologist, Yuri Zamoskin, whom I had met and befriended in New York. When I saw Inkeles after an interval of more than ten years, he asked me where I was teaching. His response to my reply that I was in the Sociology Department of the Graduate Faculty was, "Oh, you're way out," suggesting that the status of The New School did not meet his standards of respectability, a reaction that seemed to me to be consistent with the earlier careerist implications of his teaching about the Soviet Union.

Barrington Moore, Jr., had arrived at Harvard's Russian Research Center along much the same route as Inkeles's—service in World War II and the OSS—but other than that they came from different worlds. Inkeles, a Jew and an aspiring academic, had been co-opted into the establishment while Moore was already a part of it by virtue of birth. Moore, a scion of New England's upper class, graduated from Williams College in 1936 and received his doctorate from Yale

University when its sociology department was still oriented to the sociology of William Graham Sumner.[12] Working in the OSS was a career choice made by many other Ivy League graduates of his age. While in the OSS, his colleagues were Henry Murray and H. Stuart Hughes, also members of the New England establishment, but his associates also included German émigré scholars such as Franz Neumann, Otto Kirchheimer, and Herbert Marcuse, all older and cosmopolitan, who supplemented his Sumnerian education. These biographical details help to explain Moore's later research into the problems of revolution, totalitarianism, democracy, authority, and political power.

Political power was a subject not otherwise treated in the Social Relations Department's curriculum. Moore used as texts Gerth and Mills's translation *From Max Weber* and A. M. Henderson's and Talcott Parsons's translation of Max Weber's *The Theory of Social and Economic Organization*, Wilfredo Pareto's *The Mind and Society*, Gaetano Mosca's *The Ruling Class*, Robert Michel's *Political Parties*, and George Sorel's *Reflections on Violence*. His lectures were formal and systematic summaries of the ideas in these books. He contrasted, compared, and interpreted them, but he did not introduce new material. His lectures were an exercise in close reading of texts, and it seemed as if he were working through this literature for the first time. These titles could not have been part of his education at Yale, and I assume that he must have been introduced to them

---

[12] *See also* Robert Jackall, "The Education of Barrington Moore, Jr."

by Neumann, Kirchheimer, and Marcuse at his post-doctorate education in the college of OSS. The course had an enrollment of ten
students. Despite the small number, Moore lectured from behind a
podium, and there was never a hint that the class might turn into
an informal discussion group. Moore's style was uncompromisingly
serious, humorless, and impersonal. I cannot remember him ever
telling a joke, though he often accented his discussions of the irrationalities and ironies of social life with wry smiles. My conferences
with him took place at his home on Larchmont Drive in Cambridge,
where his wife met me at the door and escorted me to his study. Our
meetings were always to the point, never included small talk, and
when concluded, I was escorted to the door. As a teaching assistant,
there was no way to break through the stiffness that I associated with
Weber's inner-directed Puritan, a trait that when given expression
as scholarly work, resulted in unmatched, prodigious research, all
bearing the mark of a scholar who posed his own problems, without
reference to current academic fashion.

Moore and Inkeles were historians as well as sociologists, and
neither thought in terms of closed systems. They taught me that I
need not concern myself with the abstract concepts of basic social
science and that one could do work without reference to formulating
the functional prerequisites of a social system.

The subjects of the Soviet Union and the sociology of power were
not outside the purview of the anthropology curriculum, but my main
concern in my second year was to prepare for the PhD oral examination in social anthropology. The department's requirements then
included tests in statistics, a foreign language, and an oral examination before a committee of professors. I passed the French exam by
translating a passage from Durkheim's *Division of Labor* and failed
Moesteller's statistics exam. The oral exam was a unique experience.

During the spring of 1950, the department decided, under a new ruling, that the oral exam had become a *pro forma* meeting between
committed advisors and their favorite students. Under new, stiffer
rules, exams were to be attended by at least one representative from
each of the social relations fields. When called into the room, I faced
eight professors, including Parsons, Inkeles, Postman, Aberle, Paul,
and Roberts, and two others whose names I can no longer remember, but not Kluckhohn (who was out town). Most of the questions
came from Inkeles and Aberle. In answer to one of Inkeles's questions, I used the word "elites," a term I had picked up from Moore,
offering Palauan chiefs as my example. Inkeles objected to this use
to describe the Palauan political system and took me to task for my
misuse of it. What followed was a murky discussion of definitions
of the word and its appropriateness to describe power relations in a
small-scale society. Aberle quizzed me about double-descent kinship
systems. In those days, George Peter Murdock and Radcliffe-Brown
were engaged in acrimonious debates about types of kinship systems,
even debating the evolutionary trajectory of systems as if systems
had teleologies of their own. Murdock, for example, classified 250
societies into eleven types on the basis of two features—descent and
cousin terminology. In the English tradition as exemplified by Radcliffe-Brown, emphasis was placed on forms of relationships, such as
joking, avoidance, and respect in the functional context of society.
Common to both approaches is an emphasis on standardized terminology. In this arcane area of anthropology, logical analysis took
precedence over empirical reality. I remembered but did not mention
the stories I had heard in the Pacific, where it was rumored about
Murdock's kinship studies on the island of Truk that he brought his
informants to his cabana on the beach to interview them about the
Trukese system and corrected his informants if their descriptions of

kinship relations did not conform to the logic of his theory. I drew a diagram of the double-descent system on the blackboard and argued against its theoretical logic on the basis of the *ad hoc* and arbitrary adjustments in reckoning kinship relations in Palau where multiple marriages were common and descent lines could become extremely complicated in the intermixing of matrilineal and patrilineal reckoning. The double-descent system I drew on the blackboard became the focus for a discussion of kinship systems' permutations, a subject I had not studied in detail, but still argued (against theorists of kinship systems) that differences in meanings of kinship terms among members of a society are probably typical of all but unchanging, dead societies, and that any society undergoing intensive contact or economic and political change necessarily experiences changes in kinship relationships. Ranges of the meanings of a term among individuals can represent differences in the acceptance or rejection of rights and claims of those individuals who are defined in the relationship: usage differences are language representations of conflicts of interest. In short, if a distinction is made between empirically observable societies and theoretical models, it is possible to substitute theoretical models with their logical completeness and harmonic interrelations for the chaotic, illogical, and often changing configurations of behavior as empirically observed. After two hours of a frustrating experience, I was asked to leave, feeling that I had performed badly and did not deserve to pass. Instead, I was told that I had indeed passed and was politely congratulated by the members of the committee, who were no doubt as relieved as I to have it over with. Since that time, I have sat as a committeeman on many oral examinations and understand that decisions to pass or fail are not based solely on the quality of a student's oral performance. In my case, I had already accepted a Fulbright grant to study at the University College of the

University of London, thanks to Kluckhohn's sponsorship of me. The department was compromised. Because Kluckhohn had supported me for the appointment, the department could hardly send me to England as a lame duck.

7

European Odyssey

Earlier in American history, America's rich regarded a European tour as a kind of finishing school for its youth who, upon completion of studies at an Ivy League college, took a mandatory year abroad—a rite of passage into adulthood—before entering the family business or a profession. Now here I was, the son of immigrant parents, being given the same opportunity by the Department of Social Relations. I was not the only Harvardian given this opportunity. Having the best of connections with foundations and government agencies, Harvard sponsored cadres of students for research and study abroad. For example, Francis F. Sutton had done research in Karelia, Finland; Harry Basehart went to South Africa; and David Schneider, who had gone to London as a Fulbrighter the year before I did, took a position as an instructor at the London School in his second year. Other Harvard students whose years abroad coincided with mine were Norman Birnbaum, Harry Eckstein, and Charles Tilly. Grants for research and study in Europe provided money, leisure, and freedom to a new generation of aspiring middle-class youth, democratizing what had been the prerogative of the upper classes.

For my generation, the opportunity to go abroad was, in part, another reward for having fought and survived World War II. I still qualified for two more years of monthly stipends under the GI Bill of Rights, including supplements for wife and children. In addition, the Fulbright grant paid a similar amount, including transportation costs for a family of four to England on the Queen Mary and return trip on the Mauritania. My income in England was greater than any I had ever had before and exceeded the salary I eventually earned when I took my first academic job at Cornell University. I accepted this largesse as compensation for having been sent to the Pacific Islands and not to Europe during the war, where, according to my friends, military duty included the pleasures of cities like London, Paris, Rome, Oxford, or Innsbruck. Although I did not realize it at the time, this career opportunity was a consequence of World War II. My Fulbright income was paid in English pounds by the English in recompense for America's wartime loans and was only one of many programs designed to export and support the carriers of American values to Europe. With the Cold War well under way, I was a participant in the spread of American influence throughout the world and was happy to have a chance to be part of it.

I found an apartment at 10 Highgate West Hill diagonally across the street from the tombstone that marked Karl Marx's grave and a short bus ride to the British Museum, Piccadilly Square, and the center of London. Occupying half the first floor of an old mansion, now subdivided into apartments by a real estate speculator named Appleby, the space included two bedrooms, a kitchen, a parlor again as large as the whole unit, and three coal-burning fireplaces. Hot water poured forth when a shilling was dropped into the coin slot of an electrical unit. Coal and many foods, except Brussels sprouts, were rationed. Children were favored with special rations for milk, bananas, and medical care while England was still reeling from shortages caused by wartime deprivations. A mood of national solidarity carried over from the unity of wartime psychology. The systems of rationing were policies of the Labor Party then in power under Clement Atlee's and Anuoran Bevin's leadership. The English bore their austerity with pride, knowing that they had carried the burdens of the cost of war. Their claim to dignity was not consumption, but pride in cultivation.

English culture included scrounging for coal and the bits of starter wood needed to get up the fire in an elegant, old English parlor room. No fire of any size, however, could warm it. At best, given enough coal, warmth penetrated to an area only a few feet from the fireplace. Luckily, our neighbors used electric heat and gave us their coal ration coupons, enabling me to keep a small area of the parlor warm during the evening hours. It was almost like camping out on a cold night, sitting before a fire, first warming one side and then the other, moving closer and closer to the source of heat as the evening wore on. Despite the housing shortage, no Englishman would have rented 10 Highgate West Hill.

When our neighbors offered us their coal rations, their gesture broke the barriers between English reserve and American informality. Peter Carey, an Oxford graduate, worked in the British Foreign Office and lived adjacent to us on the ground floor with his wife and a child about the same age as our younger son Paul. Start Walters was an advertising executive and lived in an apartment above ours. Before long, we exchanged tea with each other and shared weekend parties in our flat with other Americans. I remember the Christmas party of 1950 because my parents, who were experienced senders of care packages to our Slovenian relatives, added me to their list of recipients. They knew that meat was scarce in London—horse and whale meat were the only non-rationed products on the market—and sent me a smoked ham, rings of *kranjski kilbasi* made by a Slovenian butcher on 62nd Street in West Allis, a sack of rice, and rolls of *potica*, the pastry traditionally found in Slovenia's Alpine region. Adding gin to the mixture, we created a version of the American university-style cocktail party, our small contribution to the Americanization of English culture.

Our flat was located at the edge of Parliament Hills Fields, a grassy park larger than New York City's Central Park. In the fall and spring, in good weather, this was the place to visit to see and meet the English. On a Saturday or Sunday afternoon, one could observe strollers representing every stratum of the English middle and lower classes. Week after week, one could see them pursuing hobbies such as kiting, miniature sailboat racing, hiking, chess, and reading. I also learned, but much later, that it was a favorite place for Soviet handlers to meet their English spies, among others Kim Philby. Parliament Hills Fields was a microcosm of a segment of the English social order and a place where all sorts of mischief could take place. It was there that I met Toby Hancock, a lowly paid clerk in a London business office and a chess master. He was an example of a person whose intelligence far exceeded the demands of his occupation but for whom, in the closed world of the English class system, opportunities for mobility did not exist. His solution to restrictions on occupational mobility was to invest his energies and ego in chess. Largely because there were no status barriers between Hancock and an American foreigner, as there might be between two Englishmen, we could become friends. White-collar workers whose income levels and work hours were fixed were left with leisure time and the problem of what to do with it. There was also the larger question, in Kim Philby's case, of how to make an otherwise potentially dull life more interesting. My encounter with Hancock's lifestyle, and those of the other middle strata I saw, was a harbinger of what I was later to see when I did fieldwork in Springdale, New York, where Joseph Bensman and I made our first observations of the emergent middle classes in the United States.

Peter Carey, a ballet buff, took me to my first Royal Ballet performance at Covent Garden, and I was hooked from the beginning. I liked dancing from the time I was a child and taught myself tap-dancing well enough to enter an amateurs' contest at the Paradise Theater. I learned my rudimentary steps from the Nicholas Brothers, Ruby Keeler, Fred Astair, and Shirley Temple, and I thought that Charlie Chaplin had the movements of a dancer. I had also seen performances of modern dance at the University of Wisconsin Student Union. Except for its more studied discipline and specified choreography, I equated the rhythm and movements of dancing with that of baseball, football, and tennis, but from the movement I saw at the Royal Ballet, I knew there was more to ballet than anything I had seen before. Tap-dancing was a conversation between feet and a solid base; ballet was elevation, suspension, and the illusion of the ethereal. The physical part of ballet had attracted me, but ballet combined dance with music and a story, like an opera without the singing; it was nothing like Busby Berkeley's choreography that I had seen in American movies. Just after the war, Ninette de Valois and Frederick Ashton revived English ballet at Covent Garden and Saddlers-Wells featured Margot Fonteyn, Alicia Markova, and Anton Dolin in performances of *Sleeping Beauty, The Nutcracker, Petrouchka,* and Ravell's *Bolero,* danced solo by Dolin in Spanish flamenco. This was an education in high culture guided by an experienced teacher.

Before arriving in England, I had read George Orwell's *1984,* but once there I discovered Victor Gollancz's New Left Book Club and its editions of *Keep the Aspidistra Flying, The Road to Wigan Pier,* and *Down and Out in Paris and London.* I picked up anything of Orwell's

I could find in bookstores. When I read *Homage to Catalonia*, my eyes were opened to the political complexities of the Spanish Civil War and its larger implications; when I was in high school, my social studies report on that war saw it as a struggle for military dominance between Franco and the Republicans. Orwell had been there and saw it in its full Machiavellian dimensions. When I read *A Clergyman's Daughter*, I learned more about my wife, also a clergyman's daughter, than I cared to know. Thinking I should learn English history, I read Elie Halevy's *A History of the English People* but found, despite Professor Reynold's history course at the University of Wisconsin, that Halevy's and Trevelyan's histories of England were something that could not be mastered by a casual student. In bookstores, I came across Parliamentary White Papers on dozens of current political topics and read them to try to ground myself in English politics, but even an understanding of English socialism was hard to grasp. Nevertheless, the cultural mark London left on me far exceeded that left by my anthropological studies.

A short walk from 10 Highgate to the bottom of a small hill took me to the double-decker bus that carried me to University College via Tottenham Square to Gower Street in the vicinity of Soho and the British Museum. When I took this trip on a damp foggy morning, coal-burning fireplaces produced a smog so thick that visibility on the street (and in our flat as well, where one could not see from one end of the parlor floor to the other) was only a few yards. The bus's conductor, walking ahead of the double-decker, guided it through the murky fog at a slow pace, as if leading a horse. The bus took me within a few meters of Gower Street in a neighborhood of London's antique district where the English shopkeepers were liquidating silver, ceramics, furniture, and tapestries to American antique dealers, evidence of the war's cultural costs for England. Although Karl Marx had done much of the writing of *Das Kapital* in the British Museum, his name was never mentioned by anthropologists in London.

My Fulbright sponsor at University College was Daryll Forde, who supplied me with an office and required only that I attend his staff seminar along with John Barnes, Lucy Mair, and several other students. Lucy Mair deferentially catered to Forde. John Barnes had a quixotic demeanor that he expressed with diffidence in order, I thought, to conceal an underlying skeptical attitude about Forde's ideas. Forde's specialty was the relationship between ecology and tribal organization. He argued what I thought was an untenable position, namely that forms of social organization among tribal groupings were the result of an adaptation to ecology and natural habitat, a kind of materialist theory that overlooked the reciprocal relationship between ideas and the material conditions of human existence. Though he did not challenge Forde, I knew that Barnes disagreed with him. When I learned that Barnes had published a book in 1994 entitled *A Pack of Lies*, I read it and found that it examined processes of dissimulation and concealment, confirming the impression I had of the attitude he had expressed years before; he shared the same sensibility about truth as that found in Nietzsche's essay "On Truth and Lying in an Extra-Moral Sense." Forde's seminar was not memorable, but this may be because, given the English academic calendar of long fall and spring breaks, it met on few occasions. Forde recommended me as a reviewer to the English anthropology journal *Man* for which I wrote a half dozen reviews, including a negative one of George Homans's book *The Human Group*—an audacious thing to do inasmuch as Homans was a faculty member of the Harvard Social Relations Department. During most of the time I was at University College, I sat in my office with my Smith-Corona portable and wrote my Palau research into a dissertation, barely talking about anthropology with anyone and having no desire to learn more about English anthropology than I had learned at the University of Wisconsin two years earlier in C. W. M. Hart's course in anthropology theory. Hart, a Canadian, had given us synopses of books by A. R. Radcliffe-Brown, E. E. Evans Pritchard, Meyer Fortes, Raymond Firth, Bronislaw Malinowski, Audrey Richards, and Phyllis Kaybarry. I had read most of them in Madison and thought I knew what English anthropology was. Holing up in my office and writing, I might just as well have been anywhere. University College was a convenient and comfortable place to be, but it left no traces on my education.

Like other anthropologists visiting in London, I was invited to attend the London School of Economics Empire Seminar, the membership of which was composed of researchers returned from the colonies for a leave or sabbatical in London. Now after the war, it also included, besides me, the American visitors William Schwab, Paula Brown, and David Schneider, even though the United States was no longer part of the Empire and, in fact, was in the process of colonizing England. The year I was there, the faculty participants included, among others, Raymond Firth (*We, the Tikopia*), Max Gluckman (*The Zulu*), Funer-Heimendorff (returned from India), Audrey Richards, F. S. Nadel, and an Igbo scholar, Okokon Ndem, as well as other visitors from the West Indies, Canada, and Australia. The seminar's program consisted of presentations by faculty and students who came to London with newly minted field data. Over the years, its graduates had included Jomo Kenyata and most of the luminaries of British anthropology. Cosmopolitan and well educated, the Brits were far more internationally minded and sophisticated than the Americans. At least, that was the impression I had in the course of the six or seven sessions of the seminar I attended. When it came to my turn, I presented my interpretation of the social and political consequences of colonial policy on Palauan society, a subject that English field workers knew at firsthand from the point of view of administration, not that of George Orwell as portrayed in his essay "Shooting an Elephant." The Brits still thought in terms of empire even though theirs was being liquidated and converted into a commonwealth. Nonetheless, one had to be impressed by their worldly range, rhetorical eloquence, and razor-sharp wittiness in the give and take of a seminar. Comparing their style to mine could put one on the defensive. The English could speak with ease in their debates about literature from all parts of the world. By contrast, I felt decidedly unworldly. Add to that the flatness and directness of my American English usage. In short, I was intimidated.

My purpose for being in England was to finish my dissertation on Palau. Concentrating on writing it put me in a Palauan mindset more than an English one. I planned to defend the dissertation as soon as I returned. Since Kluckhohn was my supervisor, he was the person to whom I was psychologically tied. I wrote to him regularly explaining what I was doing and frequently asked him for possible leads on job openings for the following September. Thinking that he might possibly have something in mind for me, it did not disturb me that he did not respond to my inquiries. On one occasion, I asked David Schneider why Kluckhohn was not writing back to me, and David assured me that he had received only one letter—the letter I later learned must have been for his appointment as an instructor in the Department of Social Relations. I eventually returned to Cambridge with a dissertation, a wife, and two children, but no job.

Flush with money and not pressured by academic responsibilities, my year abroad provided ample opportunity for travel. I was interested in seeing the Continent and did not think to explore England. I never visited Oxford, Cambridge, Scotland, Northern Ireland, or the

Midlands. On a weekend trip to Liverpool with my family, we visited John and Ursula White, friends I had met the previous year when we were students in the Social Relations Department and neighbors at Fort Devens. We took a train both ways and explored nothing in between. I preferred the lights of London, its civility, Big Ben, Picca-dilly Circus, and the ballet, although not the food. If I were to leave London at all, it would be to tour the Continent.

The Continent and Encounters with Slovenia

Harry Eckstein, a Harvard political scientist, and I met at an ori-entation gathering for Fulbrighters, became friends, and discovered that both of us hoped to visit the Continent. Harry had relatives in Frankfurt who had survived the war. He had emigrated from Frank-furt before the war and settled in Indiana where he married Irenne, an American. He hoped to return to Frankfurt for a visit with his rel-atives. Harry's plan gave me the idea that I might visit Slovenia—if he had relatives, so did I—and so my first visit to Slovenia was inciden-tal to the larger plan of a European tour. Given the negative descrip-tions of it that my parents had supplied throughout my youth, I saw no special reason to visit there, except perhaps to confirm the fact that I actually had some relatives. I remembered my father's stories of his miserable life as an orderly to an officer in the Austro-Hungarian Army where he was ill-fed and ill-paid, and the hopelessness of his future as a blacksmith's apprentice in Kropa. My mother's accounts were even more bleak and critical and were supported by the fact that she had been sending remittances to relatives from the time she worked as a governess in New York and throughout the years after World War II. I had no idea what kind of people these relatives were, nor had my parents ever mentioned them to me. My parents' lives in Kropa were in a world that stood apart from mine.

I had followed news reports on the war in the Balkans and was sympathetic to Tito's socialism, in part because Louis Adamic, whom I had met on one of his speaking engagements at the University of Wisconsin, spoke in favor of it and because of his mysterious death in a house-fire in Quakertown, Pennsylvania, in 1948—a fire some attributed to the nefarious designs of his political enemies. Tito had fought Draža Mihailovic, the royalist general who was Hitler's puppet, and Adamic was Tito's outspoken supporter in the United States. I had also read, on Peter Carey's recommendation, Stephen Clissold's *Whirlwind*, a detailed account of FitzRoy MacLean's tour of duty in Tito's military headquarters to which Clissold was attached. Clissold romanticized the fearlessness and ingenuity of a ragtag, victorious, decentralized military campaign that had forced Hitler to overextend his military resources in the Balkans. Despite my parents' negative views about their country of origin, a trip to Slovenia would not only allow me to assuage my curiosity about my ethnicity, but would also give me a chance to see Tito's communism in practice.

Harry and I joined together with our wives for a European tour that was to include Ljubljana and Frankfurt. This meant I had to write to my parents for the names and addresses of some relatives whom I could contact in anticipation of my visit. At that point, all I knew was that one of my mother's brothers, France, had returned to Kropa before World War I. In response to my request, my mother sent me the name of her sister Lojzka's son, Marjan Sadar, a textile factory manager in Ljubljana, who had been wounded in the leg while fighting as a Partisan. Without knowing the language, I thought a visit to Slovenia might be awkward. Considering that Yugoslav-American relations were strained after the war, I was uncertain of the reception we might receive. Tito had aligned with the Soviet Union, and his break with Stalin only occurred in 1948. His relations with the

West were still troubled over the issue of "Trst" (Trieste). Nevertheless, I wrote to Sadar in Ljubljana and announced my intention to visit with my wife and friends.

Leaving our two children in the care of English nannies, Virginia and I traveled in a rented Austin sedan through France and Italy. We saw Paris for a few days, where I tried out, not very successfully, the French I had studied in order to pass my language exam. I had my first taste of an artichoke (this reminded me of my sisters who called me "artichoke") in a provincial restaurant in central France, and we stopped in Monte Carlo, which we thought of as tasting a bit of "sinful Europe," for an evening of small-scale gambling. We eventually arrived at the Yugoslav checkpoint bordering on Trieste where we were given clearance to enter Yugoslavia. We were among the first Americans to enter Slovenia by this route since the end of the war. The road from Trieste to Ljubljana, unlike the roads in France and Italy, was unpaved, narrow, and ungraded, a sign that the Italians who had invaded Yugoslavia during the war were not welcome, and a sign that Trieste, which both Yugoslavia and Italy wanted, was still an unresolved issue between the two countries. Customs officials enthusiastically stamped us through with their personal good wishes and made us feel like long-lost brothers and sisters from the West, another indication of Tito's break with Stalin (who, after all, had tried to have him killed in 1948) and his new, independent-minded diplomacy.

Doubts I had had about the reception we might receive dissipated the moment we arrived at Marjan's apartment in Ljubljana. Marjan was already learning English and was eager to use it—since the break with Stalin, English quickly replaced Russian as Slovenia's preferred second language. Considering that all I had known of Marjan and his wife Boza were their names until the moment we met, the four of us were greeted with unqualified acceptance, like long-lost members of a family. It surprised me that Marjan was able to question me about details of members of my family. Only later did I learn that over the years my mother had kept her family in Kropa up to date about her life and that of her children in America, a discovery that led me to reopen my curiosity about my ethnic past, an issue that I thought I had closed and put behind me.

From the time I left West Allis to go to the University of Wisconsin, ethnic names and ethnic heritages were no longer an issue for me. I was successfully Americanized and could believe in the melting pot because I never felt prejudice or rejection for reasons of ethnicity. In high school and college, I had no trouble dating girls with the names West, Fidler, Keech, Richardson, and Wicks. And though I dated Scandinavian girls, with the names of Jensen and Carlson, I considered myself so completely Americanized that I never went out with the Slovenian girls in my high school class, a reverse prejudice consistent with my Americanization. My idea of going to Slovenia was to make a connection with someone we could visit on route to Austria and Germany in order to complete a circular tour of the Continent before returning to England via Calais. I thought that to visit remote relatives might be an imposition on their hospitality and, therefore, did not include a visit to Kropa in our itinerary.

Marjan was shocked when we told him that our travel plans called for a stay of a day or two in Ljubljana, and he heard none of it, not only insisting but demanding that we visit Kropa: "You must go, people in Kropa know you are here, they expect you." His was one of the most insistent and enticing invitations I had ever had and, according to him, could not be refused. We went to Kropa and stayed four days on a visit that included side trips to visit relatives in Kranj and Radov-ljica. This change in our itinerary had lifelong consequences.

I met dozens of relatives spanning three generations. My mother's two brothers and two sisters were still alive as were my father's two sisters. I met aunts, uncles, cousins, and their children, but I had no living grandparents. Instead, I visited their grave markers that are crafted of Kropa's wrought iron. I saw the houses where my parents once lived and that their siblings now occupied, and in the basement of my mother's home, the historic copper still my grandfather had used to make his own slivovica. Kropa was a village of large, beautiful stone dwellings, nestled in the mountains and bisected by a fast-moving stream that provided the power for the smithies. During our four-day visit, I ate, drank, talked endlessly about family relationships (genealogical charts) and politics, danced, and sang wartime partisan songs. For the first time in my life, I met people whose physical appearance closely resembled that of my sisters and me: it was an eerie and unforgettable experience to discover that I had a doppelgänger in my Cousin Vlad. And, in fact, I was mistaken for him on several occasions. This congregation of relatives was as much a curiosity to me as I was to them. It was a fast and intensive encounter that gave me reason to reflect on myself and my past. Four days was a short time to sort out and exchange biographical details.

My relatives were not happy with Tito and his relations with Moscow. Even apart from ideological differences, most of them were oriented to the West: Tito's policies isolated them from the culture with which they were familiar, and they identified with the United States when the Cold War began to heat up. For them, I was not only a relative but a novelty as well, standing as a concrete sign of the new opening to the West. My newfound family pleaded with us to extend our stay. Had I been alone I would have stayed, but our tour included a visit to Eckstein's relatives in Frankfurt. To make amends, I promised to make a return trip later in the summer.

When we arrived in Frankfurt via Graz and Köln (a city whose magnificent cathedral had been bombed and not yet restored), the aftereffects of the war were much more visible than in Slovenia. Frankfurt suffered from bombings, but Eckstein's relatives were alive. It did not seem strange to us that they had survived despite the aerial bombardments and that they were Jews. At that time, the Holocaust was not the public issue later made into an organized campaign against the Germans as a whole. Because I had met these Jewish survivors, I have never accepted the argument put forth by some Jewish organizations that all Germans were accomplices in the Nazi campaign of extermination. I also learned that American bombings and sorties were selective in their choice of targets. For example, not targeted was the headquarters of a major pharmaceutical manufacturer—Bayer, as I recall—jointly owned by German and American investors, among whom, it was rumored, were members of the Dulles family. Ethical constraints in the exercise of modern warfare take forms consistent with the interests of those who conduct it.

Back in England, I wrote to my parents describing in detail what I had seen and whom I had met in Slovenia and proposed that they join me on a return trip the following summer. Even after I conveyed the lavish welcome they could expect, they were not interested in a "native's return." Failing to convince them, I planned to return to Kropa in the summer for a few weeks with my wife, and this time with our children too.

I mentioned this plan to my friend Joseph Bensman, to whom I had described my earlier visit and who was working as a propaganda analyst under Leo Lowenthal's supervision at the Voice of America (VOA) in New York City. Bensman wrote back to ask if, while in Slovenia, I could undertake an informal study of Yugoslav reactions to BBC, Radio Moscow, and VOA broadcasts. The VOA promised to pay me $500 for the fieldwork summarized in a written report. However, when Lowenthal asked Washington for clearance to sponsor the study, the request was rejected by the American Ambassador to Belgrade. In light of the fragile relations between Washington and Belgrade, official sponsorship was too risky, let alone for a study to be conducted by an independent researcher. Bensman told me that there could be no formal agreement, but that if I did the study on my own, without a contract, the VOA promised to buy it when submitted. I accepted this proposal and cavalierly agreed to do the study on my own time and at my own risk. It did not occur to me that this might be regarded as a form of spying or that I was an accomplice in Cold War propaganda operations. I was interested in the $500, all the more so because it offered me the chance to extend my stay for another month. And, because I had no immediate job prospects upon my return to the US, I needed money to tide myself over until I found a job.

My return to Slovenia had two mutually reinforcing purposes: to meet relatives and do the study. Having learned from Marjan on our first visit that there were acute shortages of toothbrushes, razor blades, thread, sewing needles, and safety pins, we bought as much of them as we could, stretching our resources to the limit. At the last minute, we added our bicycle to our list. We were prepared to come bearing useful gifts. In preparation for the research, I consulted Peter Carey, who worked in the Foreign Office on the Yugoslav desk. He gave me the names of Zinka Milanov and her brother in Zagreb,

Lawrence Durrell, British Attaché in Belgrade, and a Professor Filipovic, a Shakespearean scholar also in Belgrade, and wrote in advance announcing my impending visit. Readied for the expedition with wife, two babies, and a bicycle, we boarded a train at Waterloo Station headed for Paris for a connection on the Simplon Orient Express to take us to Ljubljana. Even in third class, the accommodations on the Express were comfortable until we reached the Yugoslav border at Trieste where we were required to change from French to Yugoslav cars. The Yugoslav train was more like a cattle car outfitted with wooden benches, like the train I had traveled in from the east to the west coast on my way to San Diego Harbor, the embarkation point for the Pacific front in 1944. It was already loaded with passengers in a festive mood, headed for local shops on the way to Ljubljana. Offered bread, wine, and slivovica, we were incorporated into the group; old Slovenian peasant women insisted on caring for the children, and old and young alike wanted to engage us in sign-language and broken-English conversations. This was only the first sign of the hospitality we received for the rest of our journey, and it was the beginning of my understanding of the Slovenes. Despite all this, the Simplon Orient Express was not the romantic and mysterious version I had seen in the 1930s movies.

Marjan was again our host in Ljubljana, but this time preparations for our arrival included the use of a state-owned car (one of the few cars then in existence in all of Slovenia) with a driver provided by another cousin's husband who was now Communist party chief in Slovenia. We were delivered directly to what was to be our base residence at my aunt Lojzka's apartment in Rodovljica, where she lived with her unwed daughter to whom we gave the bicycle, a gift that was appreciated far beyond its monetary value in a country where a functioning bicycle was a rare commodity. It was a gesture that created a lifelong bond between me and Cousin Stana, who has never since failed to send me Yuletide greetings containing an annual report on births, deaths, and marriages of family members. Aunt Lojzka, my mother's youngest sister, was only six years old when my mother left Slovenia. It was from her that I learned that my mother left Kropa to follow my father to New York against the wishes of her parents who objected to both her departure and her plans, at the age of 18, for marriage; apparently, it was a union that involved too large a status difference between the partners. Lojzka was a perfect informant for my purposes. She spoke Slovene with a Kropa accent that I could understand because it was the same language my parents spoke to each other. I discovered I could understand the Kropa dialect and even respond to it. Widowed and living with her daughter, she was willing to talk and told it like it was.

Mixing Family Matters with Research

The subject of radio propaganda was of intrinsic interest to Yugoslavs at precisely the moment of my visit. Since Yugoslavia was in a pivotal position in the conflict between the US and USSR, Yugoslavs were being bombarded with messages from the VOA, BBC, Radio Moscow, and domestic wavelengths, the latter usually distrusted. Since propaganda agencies were working overtime to influence opinion and Yugoslavia's fate had not yet been sealed, almost anyone whom I met was a radio listener, eager, like the Palauan listeners, to learn what disposition the superpowers planned for them. I learned quickly that it was easy to talk to people about propaganda.

In the course of casual conversations, I asked the person if they listened to VOA. Whatever the response, I then asked about BBC and Radio Moscow. My questions could be nonchalantly introduced as part of a conversation with an American who was naturally interested in VOA broadcasts. I discovered this method in my first interview, which was with Lojzka and Stana in their home in Radovljica. From that beginning, I put the same series of questions to all the relatives I met in Slovenia. Since my hosts included the chief of the Communist party of Slovenia, I was provided with an interpreter for my visits to Kropa, Ljubljana, Bled, and other scenic sites of the country. This part of my research for an agency of the American government was subsidized by the Communist government of Slovenia.

I used the same method in interviews conducted in Zagreb and Belgrade. I mentioned to Marjan that I wished to go to those cities to see other parts of the country and had contacts there given me by Peter Carey. Paying for an airline ticket was not a problem. All the relatives had jobs and plenty of dinars on which there were few consumer goods to spend them. I was handed the tickets and prepaid hotel reservations for a tour of Zagreb and Belgrade. In Zagreb, I talked with Zinca Milanov, the opera singer, and a group of her pianist brother's friends. That group was comprised of disaffected old bourgeoisie who distrusted the regime that likewise distrusted them. They survived because they had international reputations, and they welcomed a visit from an American student because it gave them an opportunity to tell their side of the story. In Belgrade, I went directly to the apartment of Professor Filipovic where we talked for an afternoon. My other contact, Durrell, was unavailable. This missed opportunity meant little to me until later when I learned he was the author of *The Alexandria Quartet* that he was then writing while acting as England's cultural attaché. In addition, I spoke to people wherever I met them—on park benches and in airport lounges. This gave me a sample of responses from a mixed bag of strangers. This part of the study for the VOA was supported by the British Foreign Office and financed by my relatives.

Altogether I conducted about fifty interviews, only a small portion of each directly related to radio listening. When doing my interviews, I was unable to take notes for the obvious reason that the study did not officially exist. Keeping a record of the interviews was a problem. Though I had plenty of experience interviewing from my field study in Viroqua, and had even conducted interviews through a translator in Palau, this project presented additional problems that I had not encountered before. Since I could make no notes, I had to remember as much of an interview as possible until I could record it. I kept a visual image of an interview's setting and memorized key words and phrases in order to be able to reconstruct the conversation. Since the questions were the same for each interview, they provided a structure onto which I could reconstruct the account. I recorded my notes whenever I could, usually late at night in the privacy of my bedroom. Once recorded, I hid the notes in my baggage, always fearing that it might be examined and my notes discovered. My worst fear was that they might be confiscated when I left the country, but with US-Yugoslav relations on the mend, customs officials at the border waved us through. For me, thinking of myself as an amateur spy, a lot was at stake, but no one in Yugoslavia could have cared less. I continued my interviews until the day I left, and despite my worries, no one bothered to probe into the personal affairs of a father traveling with a wife and two children. The fact is that, if I had been discovered, it would have been US officials with whom I would have had trouble, not the Yugoslavs.

Acting as the organizer of my Yugoslav itinerary, Marjan scheduled visits to the homes of uncles, aunts, and cousins on both the maternal and paternal sides of my family; in sheer numbers, they made a considerable group. It had not occurred to me that my mother's and father's relatives might not be joined to each as I was to my parents. That Marjan, my mother's nephew, included my father's relatives in my itinerary led me to assume that the two sets of relatives were also bonded by the marriage of my parents, a fiction that was maintained throughout my visit and supported by a festive dinner at the local *gastilno*. Relatives on both sides attended. Despite these appearances, this show was a fiction designed to shield me from the bitter animosities that had originated in the war.

Kropa, sitting at the foothills of the mountains, had been a redoubt for the Partisans and a place from which they could harass the German occupiers and retreat to the mountains for safety. The Partisans, the Slovenian Liberation Front (SLF), however, included both socialists and communists, so that within its ranks the war was being fought for different postwar futures.

Kropa was a strong center of resistance to the German occupation. The local population protected the SLF and retreated from the town into the mountains whenever they were the objects of German search-and-destroy missions. A small force, harbored and sustained by Kropa, engaged Nazi forces far in excess of its numbers. Local citizens became participants and victims of the war. My Aunt Rezika's husband was blinded by a German mortar explosion. Marjan's knee was shattered by a bullet. Lojzka, a slight woman just five feet tall, was deported to Germany as a slave laborer at Dachau where she cleaned huge cooking containers larger than herself. Her daughter Stanka was forced into a sexual relationship with a German officer and bore that scar as a single woman for the rest of her life. When Vinko Hafner was the object of a Nazi search-and-destroy mission, my father's sister Paula Azman hid him in the attic of her home at great risk. He later married my Aunt Paula's daughter Lucija. It was war stories like these, including those of the deaths of many others, that became the prism through which I learned about the lives of my relations. As a reward for its role in defense of Yugoslavia, the new national government modernized the iron works.

My visits in 1950 led me to revise the attitude toward Kropa that I had inherited from my parents. These visits were also the beginning of many more excursions made over the next forty-plus years. I returned to Kropa whenever I had occasion to be in Europe for sociology meetings or those of the sociology seminar of which I was a director along with colleagues at the University of Zagreb at Dubrovnik's Interuniversity Center. I was awarded a Fulbright Grant for 1974-75 to lecture in Zagreb and took the occasion to live in Kropa in a rented house with my second wife, Mary, and our children for the summer months. There we entertained a stream of visiting American friends. During these visits, I gradually pieced together additional biographical data on the history of the family.

As the war in Slovenia progressed, Vinko Hafner distinguished himself as a leading communist partisan. Self-taught and self-confident, opposed to both the bourgeoisie and the socialists, he was committed to a future under communism. That commitment entailed a purge of the socialists, not to mention the bourgeoisie who had, in any case, already fled to Austria. When the communist partisans consolidated their hold on Slovenia, they pressured the socialists to join their ranks. My mother's brother Stanko Pesjak, owner of a scale-making shop in Kranj, had two daughters and two sons. The sons, who were raised in the socialist tradition of the Pesjak family, were shot dead by a firing squad in the street facing the family residence, in full view of parents and siblings. Vinko Hafner had ordered the executions: two of my cousins were killed by the husband of a third.

On my first visit, I only learned that my Uncle Stanko's sons had "died in the war," and that, of the surviving daughters, Zorka had been bedridden for years with arthritis so pernicious that she felt pain throughout her entire body; it was too painful even to cut her fingernails, which were inches long. Her retreat to her bed was her reaction to witnessing her brothers' executions. Zorka died before I made another visit to Kranj. Of Stanko's four children, Branka was the only one who survived.

As the story unfolded, I learned that Istok, now Branka's husband, had been taken prisoner and deported to Germany as a slave laborer. When he returned to Kropa after the war, he came under suspicion and was refused his prewar position as a railway engineer. He suffered unemployment for years, but was eventually reinstated. The animus between the Pesjak family and Vinko Hafner, whose career included various positions in Belgrade and finally the presidency of the Slovene Republic, remained alive and unresolved for most of the lives of the survivors. I met Hafner and his wife Lucija, my cousin, on several occasions. In the mid-1980s, Branka, her parents and sister now dead, asked to join me in a visit to the Hafners in their apartment in Ljubljana. We met with Vinko and Lucija in what was a reconciliation between the two sets of cousins. As Branka put it, "It is now time to forget the past." This was forty years after the execution of her two brothers.

In the course of those forty years, my sisters and their children, and my children and their children, have visited Slovenia. Cousins and their children in Slovenia have likewise visited us in the United States. As the number of descendants has multiplied, visits to and from Slovenia have become annual pilgrimages. In time, the third and fourth generations created their own networks with each other. There are now Slovene relatives who visit Wisconsin, Arizona,

California, Nevada, and Utah. Likewise, American relatives visit Kropa, Kranj, Radovliyca, Ljubljana, and Portoroz. A niece with the name Green still makes policä and has a son who honeymooned in the Julian Alps. None of this could I have imagined in 1950 when I thought of my first trip to Ljubljana as a casual visit to a place selected for the convenience it offered when planning a tour of Europe.

After my second visit to Kropa, I wrote my parents an eight-page, single-spaced letter detailing my experiences and describing the conditions of each of the members of the family. I urged them to visit Kropa and offered to travel with them. Without explaining why, they did not accept my invitation nor others that I extended later. I could not understand their refusal and was determined to learn why. Lojzka finally told me enough to enable me to construct an explanation. According to her, my mother's family neither approved of the marriage to my father nor her departure to America. My father, though handsome and ambitious, was from a cottager family and had not achieved my mother's level of education: the marriage violated local standards of class endogamy. Why, then, after they had determined to make the break, did they send remittances and care packages to both sets of relatives for more than forty years, and why had they kept their families in Kropa informed in detail of the activities of their children? Both of my parents, each in their own way, still had parts of themselves in Kropa. The gifts, in addition to helping parents and siblings, were also a status claim that affirmed their economic success in America and, by the same token, vindicated their defiance of parents and community norms and their decision to leave Kropa. Immigrants gain psychic satisfaction from being admired in their community of origin for their economic success, although they seldom recognize this need in themselves. The community of origin remains a primary reference group throughout the years of diaspora.

Then why not return to the community of origin where economic success was rewarded with status and recognition? The explanation lies elsewhere in my parents' case.

That my handsome, enterprising father never as a youth or as an adult achieved his wife's level of education and cultivation, was, during my youth, a point of contention and dissatisfaction for my mother: he remained the immigrant Slovene while she strove to Americanize herself and children. My mother revealed her dissatisfaction with my father to me in a telling moment when I was a boy of sixteen. She took me aside and asked my advice on whether she should leave my father. Stunned by this question and shocked by its confidentiality, my instant response was, "Where would he go, what would he do?" Not another word was said, and she never broached the subject again. I understood from this incident that she felt trapped and had no means of escape from a partner who did not share her ambitions, but who was also indispensable to achieving them for herself and her children. A return visit to Kropa, I assume, might have revealed what she wished to conceal. The remittances underscored her economic success in America and established her status among those she had left behind, but matrimonially, her decision to leave Kropa had not been vindicated; in the long run, she had been proven wrong in her choice of a mate, and her parents and community proved to have been right. The disparities in my parents' orientations to the past remained with them until death. In her last letter to me, written at age seventy-eight, when she was willingly dying from a stroke from which she could have recovered, she said, "If I had known it was going to turn out this way I would have done it differently." I took this to mean that she expected my father to die first and that since he had not, she should have left him while she was still physically able to. When, at age eighty-six, my father lay dying a slow death with tubes attached to his lungs and nose, he thought of Kropa: "In Kropa they wouldn't do this to you, they would let you die." Only one person from Kropa, my mother's sister's daughter's son, Peter Smitek, met my parents in Milwaukee before they died. Peter's was only the first of many familial, cultural interchanges between Kropa and the United States. The marriage between Paulina Pesjak and Josef Vidic made them all possible.

Return to the United States

In August 1951, I boarded the Mauritania in Southampton bound for the US with a wife, two children, no job, and not even a lead on a possible interview for one. Joe Bensman met us when we arrived in New York Harbor and took us to Marilyn Bensman's family home on Eastern Parkway in Brooklyn, where I retrieved the car I had loaned to Ralph Patrick for the year. My plan was to drive my family to Quakertown and deposit Virginia and the children at Louie and Markoosha Fischer's summer home—the parents of my university friends, George and Victor (Vite) Fischer. We had visited this place on other occasions and were friends of the family. We went to Quakertown because we had nowhere else to go and needed a place to stay while I wrote my report on radio listening. As soon as I settled my family in Quakertown, I set off for Cambridge with the purpose of paying a visit to Kluckhohn at the Russian Research Center, now located in new and expanded headquarters. I stayed in Bob and Arlene Wilson's apartment.

I walked unannounced into the Russian Research Center and asked Mrs. Parsons, the Center's receptionist, for an appointment to see Kluckhohn. Mrs. Parsons knew me well enough that such informality was acceptable, and she ushered me in. My memories of the interview are still vividly impressed on my mind. Kluckhohn stood up when I entered his office. I said, "Hello, Professor Kluckhohn." (I never went on a first-name basis with professors), and offered to shake his hand. He rejected the gesture with the comment, "You have been spreading vicious rumors about me. I have nothing to say to you." I was stunned by this response and could not immediately fathom what he meant. Nevertheless, since I had come prepared to ask for some leads on jobs, I asked him if he knew of any openings. He knew of one job at the Johns Hopkins Operations Research Office and gave me the name of the person to contact. That ended the interview, and I left, never to see him again. I followed the lead and had an interview at Johns Hopkins only to discover that it was an overseas position to study two-man firing groups on the Korean front. It was a research position on a US Army-sponsored study of the morale of infantrymen paired in a foxhole. I rejected this opportunity though I was never offered the job.

Depressed, I left Kluckhohn and went to talk to Wilson, my closest friend in Cambridge. Reflecting on what Kluckhohn might have been referring to, I was carried back to my conversation with Richard Hobson shortly before I left for England. I began to understand the source of my problem. I surmised that Hobson must have reported our conversation to Kluckhohn and that explained why Kluckhohn had not responded to my letters from abroad, an apt example of the unintended consequences of what was meant as a sympathetic gesture. Not only did I face the prospect of no job, I was also left without a dissertation supervisor. It was Wilson who advised me on a course of action.

He suggested that I talk to Peter Rossi, who was visiting Harvard as Paul Lazarsfeld's assistant in the Department of Social Relations. I met Peter and Alice Rossi at lunch and told them my story, explaining that I was dumbfounded by Kluckhohn's reaction. The

Rossis had heard of a field director's position at Cornell University and told me that Talcott Parsons was the person to see about it. Even though it was the beginning of a new school year, Parsons saw me the next day and gave me the job description and the name of Urie Bronfenbrenner, director of the project, Studies in Social Growth in the Department of Child Development and Family Relations in the Cornell School of Agriculture. With the help of Irving Rosow—who gave me the correct spelling of Ithaca (not "Ithica" as I had it)—and Harold Garfinkel who advised me not to drop the letter into "just any old mailbox," but to take it to the main post office—I sent off my *curriculum vitae* and application. At the same time, I made preparations to salvage my academic standing in the Department of Social Relations.

I went to Gordon Allport's office, who was then managing the department. I spoke to the secretary and explained that Kluckhohn had recused himself as my dissertation chair. She paved my way into Allport's office. No questions were asked, nor do I believe that Allport consulted Kluckhohn. I was given a committee with Barrington Moore, Jr., as chair, Jack Roberts, and, to my surprise, David Schneider, who was now Assistant Professor of Anthropology in the department. I made an appointment to see Moore and handed him a copy of my dissertation. Mine was the first he supervised at Harvard. He was a close and critical reader and demanded revisions and additions, including an additional chapter, which, as it transpired, required another year of work before it could be distributed to the committee. To anticipate the ending of this episode, I was never called to Harvard to sit for a defense of the work. Each committee member signed off on it, and Moore informed me that it had been accepted. I graduated from Harvard in 1953 and did not attend the commencement ceremony.

My only job prospect was the position at Cornell University. The letter was sent and, back in Quakertown, I anxiously awaited a reply. Meanwhile, Virginia and I finished the VOA report on Yugoslav radio listening and contemplated my chances for a career in a field other than anthropology. My only other option, as I saw it, was to return to West Allis to take up the political career I had abandoned when I went to graduate school. Virginia, who knew she could not fit into life with my parents, let alone the ethnic life of West Allis, was depressed by the thought of life as a politician's wife. During the weeks of waiting for a call from Cornell, having completed the VOA report, we submitted it to Joe Bensman in New York City. To my surprise, within a week I had a call summoning me to Washington for an interview and debriefing with a State Department functionary on the Yugoslav desk—all expenses paid, but no honorarium. From this experience, I learned that the propaganda divisions of governmental operations were efficiently integrated. My participation in America's Cold War propaganda efforts have always left me with a feeling of discomfort, not so much because it may have helped the VOA, but because I had done the research surreptitiously among relatives and friends. That the VOA paid me five hundred badly needed dollars helped me justify the moral compromise, but not until forty years later did I list the study on my *curriculum vitae*. Nor did I ever mention it to anyone in Yugoslavia.

The five hundred dollars was our sole source of income while I waited for a reply from Ithaca. The invitation for an interview came just as I was preparing for a trip to the Midwest to visit my parents and explore my prospects in West Allis. While there, I received word that I could begin work immediately as the project's director in residence in Candor, New York.

8

Cornell and Springdale

I never expected to be a field director for the Cornell College of Agriculture or thought I would study an upstate New York rural community called Candor for three years. But my qualifications for the job certainly matched its requirements. I had had previous fieldwork experience and had written research reports. One of my responsibilities was to analyze the social structure of Candor. In addition, I was married to a sociologist and had two children. This gave the appearance of a solid, respectable family to the community, and thus promised to blend us into its social life easily. The decision to hire me was not, however, without its problems. My *curriculum vitae* necessarily listed the names of Kluckhohn and Useem, both of whom, I learned later from Alan Holmberg, an anthropologist at Cornell, had been consulted and raised questions about me. Apparently the questions they raised were not decisive factors in my appointment. I never found out what they said, nor did I ever again have occasion to use them as references. My chief sponsor had been Robert Dalton, a former Protestant minister and chair of the department in which the project was housed. For its irony, I have always liked to believe that I got the job because my wife's father was also a Protestant minister, a connection that allowed me to ride in on his coattails.

My worries about being banished from an academic career and looking for another in politics were put aside. This job was good for three years at \$4,800 per year and a month off each summer. It also connected me to the Cornell anthropology department where, at Lauristan Sharp's behest, I taught a course on Oceania and participated in departmental colloquia. It also provided me with an opportunity to closely examine the inner workings of an American community and to discuss its structure and social psychology with Joseph Bensman over the three years that I was in residence in the town that we called Springdale. Eventually Bensman and I wrote *Small Town in Mass Society: Class, Politics and Religion in a Rural Community,* the result of our mutual effort to explain some facts of American values and their institutional consequences. The book has appeared in three editions, the last in 2000. In retrospect, Kluckhohn's rejection ended up giving me the chance of a lifetime.

I had already studied a variety of communities and learned something of how they functioned. In my study of the success aspirations of young men in Viroqua, I learned that they held aspirations about their futures far in excess of any reality principle. They believed in success and continued to believe in it even when it was not achieved: the belief that they lived in the best of all possible worlds sustained illusions of success. In Palau, I discovered that its social structure had been radically transformed several times as a result of bureaucratic decisions made elsewhere. Kropa's status and class systems were determined by the existence of its factory even though there was no rational economic reason to build such a factory since all of its raw production materials and presses had to be imported. The factory existed as a reward for the wartime patriotism of Kropa's inhabitants. Moreover, although accessible only by a dirt road, there was nothing isolated about Kropa. In the early years of the Cold War, local residents could listen to broadcasts from Moscow, England, and the Voice of America (just as Palauans had in 1948).

Having grown up in West Allis, the ethnic industrial suburb of Milwaukee, I knew that Allis Chalmers—a major producer of tractors and turbines—and several other machine tool industries not only dominated the life of the community but also held its repeatedly reelected and incompetent mayor a virtual hostage to the requirements of industry. To be aware of this sociological datum did not require research in the usual sense; everyone in town knew that the political life of the community was dominated by major economic interests. Before I arrived in Ithaca, I had lost any illusions I might have had about life in small towns.

The directors of the project, Urie Bronfenbrenner, a psychologist, and Edward Devereaux, a Harvard-trained sociologist, had chosen Springdale as a research site for a study of social growth and creativity. They had established relations with the community leaders before I was hired. In addition to being a field director, I was also a member of the Department of Child Development and Family Relationships. Before moving into the field, I was to be integrated into the culture of both the project and the department, and for that purpose, I initially established residence with my family in Ithaca; as it happened, our accommodations were World War II barracks exactly like those at Fort Devens when I was a Harvard graduate student. I was also assigned an office in a similar barracks that housed other members of the project's staff that included psychologists, a sociologist, graduate student trainees, interviewers, and technical administrators. This was my first experience in a large-scale research project affiliated with a department composed of more than thirty professors. My socialization into it was never successfully completed.

My first departmental meeting struck me as surreal. The department sponsored a nursery school. The agenda for this meeting was to decide on a new design for the toddlers' toilet facilities: Where should the toilets be, how high, how segregated, how private, age-graded or not? Granted, this was a research institution and any model established by Cornell University for the design of nursery school toilets might become a standard for an entire region; nevertheless, it seemed to me that this was a technical problem that might be better analyzed by interior design specialists in collaboration with nursery school teachers. Yet, here we were, three dozen professors, all of whom wished to make their presence felt, expressing opinions on the subject almost as if talking were a professional requirement demanded by the occupation. Since the meeting was conducted on the democratic principle that all participants had a right to comment, not speaking might also be construed as harboring unacceptable private opinions or, worse, disdaining the pettiness of the subject. Making a contribution to the discussion confirmed the seriousness of the subject and reinforced the department as a unified collectivity sharing a common purpose. I sat there listening but could not believe what I was hearing. Luckily, since I was the new member of the group, I was not expected to voice an opinion on the subject. To have said what I really thought—that the discussion was a collective waste of time—would have been a violation of academic protocol. I might have been labeled a troublemaker, a risky identity at that stage of my life. Nursery school toilets were the agenda of the first faculty meeting of my career and the beginning of my education in the ways of academia.

The Springdale project was well underway before I arrived. Project directors had surveyed several communities in the Ithaca region as possible research sites. Having selected Candor, they had already made contact with community residents. Preparing the town for a Cornell study of it was accomplished by using the Community Club as the point of entry for gaining acceptance of the field researchers. In order to gain this acceptance, the project promised members of the Club that its results were to be reported exclusively in statistical terms.

I was introduced to the community at a club meeting where I met the county agent and community leaders, including the newspaper's editor, the mortician, village clerk, legal advisor to the village board, pastors of the local churches, and leading farmers. It was these contacts that enabled me to make inquiries about the housing facilities for my forthcoming move into the town. Before entering the field in the winter of 1952, however, I remained at project headquarters where, in addition to finishing the additional chapter of my dissertation written at Barrington Moore's behest, I began the work of field director.

Essentially, this involved mapping the town and preparing a survey instrument to be applied to each of the community's 750 households. All senior members of the project played a part in constructing the survey instrument. Its purpose was to acquire basic, census-type data on each household: number of persons, ages, education, incomes, occupations, years of residence in the town, home ownership, place of employment, and a series of questions related to knowledge of public affairs. For example, we asked whether a respondent could identify United States Senator Joe McCarthy, who was then a very publicly visible person. Once in the field, however, we discovered that respondents were more familiar with another Joe McCarthy, the manager of the New York Yankees baseball team. Committees worked out the design of this instrument. Completing it to the satisfaction of the project directors was an arduous and time-consuming task that required endless revisions to accommodate the different images of the community that various project personnel held, not to mention the already existing differences in expectations about the conclusions to be reached at the end of three years. From the beginning, it was apparent to me that the directors' conceptions of small-town life were not the same as mine. They thought of Springdale as a harmonious community in which social equality and a harmonious democratic spirit prevailed. They romanticized the independent-minded, self-confident farmer and the ethically upright small businessman. For them, Springdale represented, and indeed was, the antithesis of urban sophistication—a genuinely wholesome way of life. Bronfenbrenner's and Devereaux's image did not correspond to the image of small-town life that I had formed from my earlier studies.

An opportunity to rent a farmhouse arose when its owner sold it to a neighboring farmer, who, wishing to expand his operation, bought it on the strength of the rental income I could pay him for the duration of my Cornell contract. A dairy farmer, Mr. Ramann, rented me a house without central heat but with a large garden plot, a non-functioning outhouse, and a chicken coop. My one-on-one rental transaction with Mr. Ramann authenticated me: I had become a community resident who paid his way independently of Cornell University. Hence, my status in the town was comparable to that of a local extension agent on the payroll of the New York State Agricultural College at Cornell University, but, in my case, I was studying the town and could not separate the personal from the professional and theoretical.

When my wife and I moved into town, our two sons, aged three and one, became participant residents of the town, if not participant observers. In 1953, the arrival of another son created something of a nursery atmosphere in the household and helped to reinforce my identity as a responsible family man. Of course, while everyone seemed to pretend that I was just another Cornell employee, the reality was quite different.

My wife, a trained sociologist and interviewer, worked part-time for the project. She made her own research observations but shared them with me. She also attended the Congregational Church and enrolled the children in its nursery school. In an effort to patronize local commerce, we bought our groceries at the local store and often ate at the restaurant. We regularly attended Community Club meetings where we met other members of the community, some of whom became friends with whom we socialized, visiting their homes. However, our pattern of sociability did not include visits by our local friends to the field headquarters; the only villager who regularly entered the field headquarters was a housekeeper who cared for the children and cleaned the house. Student fieldworkers and interviewers also became part of the household. When senior staff visited the town to attend Community Club functions, they did not come to the field headquarters, that is, our home, and generally kept their distance from its day-to-day operations. The field headquarters was a mixture of family and business activities and the place where information about the town was exchanged: fieldworkers neither entered nor left the town without my knowing it.

I approached Springdale with the same attitude I had used to examine Palau—that of acceptance of the town on its own terms, observing its rules of etiquette, while objectifying myself in relation to them whenever I was not acting in the field. Performing the social acrobatics to maintain this dual consciousness was made easier for me by the requirement that I make regular reports about what I was seeing in Springdale to project directors in Ithaca; when making such reports, I had to be objective about my life in the town using the same split consciousness obtained in my discussions with fieldworkers at field headquarters. Splitting myself into two halves was an occupational requirement and became a habit. As a matter of practice in fieldwork, this kind of intellectual acrobatics can only be described in terms of George Herbert Mead's distinction between the "me" and the "I," where the "me" is the unselfconscious actor in the act of acting, and the "I" is the self in the act of reflecting on the me.

My first fieldwork assignment was to supervise, from my home, a staff of graduate student interviewers in applying the census-like survey instrument to the 750 households in Springdale. The interview schedule was short, six or eight pages. I did many of the interviews myself and read and edited all the others. All this information went into my head before it was machine processed at project headquarters. By the time the survey had been completed, I had memorized the names, places of residence, and the occupations of most of the households in the community. Over the three-year period, I helped to construct and supervise a half-dozen other surveys and interviewed, both formally and informally, hundreds of community residents. Living in a town for two and a half years for the sole purpose of studying it—that is, living night and day almost exclusively in this circumscribed universe—filled my head with indelible images of people, places, and events.

Memories that are still vivid include our unheated parlor room where we slept; endless theoretical speculations about how the town functioned; hundreds of trips on Route 17 to project headquarters in Ithaca; a solitary midnight winter's ride carrying an oxygen-deprived infant to an oxygen tent in Ithaca Hospital; sharp images of roads, byways, the swimming hole, Oswego and the Susquehanna River; the Finnish community in Spencer; the firehouse; the abandoned railway depot; the banker's mansion and the squat, unpretentious cement bank building, legacy of a distant past; the feed mill; the post office where social security beneficiaries gathered the first of each month; the front office of the *Candor Courier*; traveling the dirt roads to the four corners of the town; conducting joint interviews with husbands and wives hoping to discover some unfathomable truth about spousal relationships; raising chickens and learning the value of chicken manure as a fertilizer; inventing and telling "Lonesome Pete" bedtime stories to children who nudged me to keep me awake as I dozed off before I finished the story; preparing Sunday school lessons for high school students at the Congregational Church; preparing lectures to teach for Lauriston Sharp's seminar on Oceania in Cornell's anthropology department; devising policies about who could and could not enter the town's public space. (For instance: Could an Egyptian be an interviewer: yes. Could the black spouse of an interracial marriage enter the town with his wife: no.) There were also endless public relations decisions to protect the town from what we thought it needed to be protected from. Once embarked on this train of thought, I am flooded with scattered, endless images—of townspeople's faces, merchants, houses, streets, the school and its community room, railroad tracks—that have cluttered my mind for fifty years.

My reminiscences of specific experiences focus on colorful incidents. Farmer Ramann's barn, fifty yards from the house, burned to the ground one late-October evening. The school's guidance counselor and I entered into a joint venture to raise a pig that lived in the unused privy stall on my garden plot. When the pig escaped and ran down the highway, the housekeeper and I gave chase. Luckily she knew that the way to immobilize a running pig is to grab one of its hind legs. Pig farming detracted from my respectability and endeared me to no one. Another season, I granted our postman's request to graze his geese on my plot. This effort at communal cooperation ended tragically when my dog broke loose and killed all the geese. On a similar rampage, he killed one of Jones's sheep. Although the dog was unaware of the gravity of his actions, the owners of his victims regarded him as a menace and a criminal. According to local mores, there was only one solution for this problem, namely, to have the dog "put down," a service provided for me by Cornell University's Department of Animal Husbandry. Thus my image as a responsible citizen was upheld, but, in the eyes of my family, I was the criminal. The owners of the dead livestock made no claims against me, nor did the members of the community ever mention the incidents. My status as field director and my affiliation with Cornell University gave me a form of protection not available to an ordinary citizen of the town. On another occasion, my landlord complained to the project headquarters because he was unhappy with what he regarded to be the unkempt condition of the part of my lawn facing the highway. One of the project directors visited the landlord and intervened on his behalf, advising me that I was not maintaining respectable appearances, an action that struck me as violating my rights in my relationship with my landlord, confirming again the ambiguities of my role as a resident of Springdale.

All the while I lived in a glass house, watching and in turn being watched by the community and by my university supervisors. There was no escape other than in the company of friends from other times and places. One was Warren Paley, a bridge-playing friend from my undergraduate years at the University of Wisconsin. He had settled near Ithaca as a mink farmer. During pelting season, I worked as a pelter, accompanying him with his load of pelts to auction houses in New York City. Paley's hillside farmhouse overlooked Ithaca. It became our retreat during holidays when Springdalers withdrew into their established social circles, a further indication that our acceptance in the town was qualified and did not include acceptance into intimate social settings. Another friend, also from the University of Wisconsin, was Joseph Bensman. The Paley and Bensman families were our "psychic economy," making endurable an otherwise unbearable occupational and public life in the community and in the project.

As I noted earlier, Bensman and I had originally met while we were undergraduate students at the University of Wisconsin. He had grown up in Two Rivers, Wisconsin, a farming region where his father was an immigrant shoemaker. After the war, we both returned to Madison to continue graduate studies in the Department of Sociology and Anthropology where we collaborated on a report in John Useem's seminar on social systems. Bensman was then Hans H. Gerth's student helping Gerth to edit some of his Max Weber translations, and I was studying anthropology and listening to Gerth's lectures. It was the exposure that Gerth gave us to Weber and to his own unique synthesis of Marx and Weber that provided a common ground for Bensman's and my approach to the problems posed for us by Springdale. For this reason, we dedicated *Small Town in Mass Society* to Gerth.

Bensman did graduate studies at Columbia University. After finishing his course work at Columbia, he initially found a job at the Voice of America (VOA) that led to the survey I did in Slovenia. Senator McCarthy mounted an attack on the VOA and succeeded in closing down the New York office, whereupon Bensman lost his job. He found work as an aircraft wing-assembler in the Grumman aircraft factory on Long Island. Both of us felt professionally isolated. So when Bensman and his family visited, we talked about the only sociological data we had at hand—Springdale. Our discussions of the town raised questions and problems we thought were worthy of investigation.

Viewing the town from a sociological perspective, we initially turned to the question of isolating and differentiating the groups and classes into which the residents of the town could be sorted. Attempting to grasp the contours of Springdale's class structure, we had to find categories that allowed us to place every family in a typology of classes. In the Weberian sense, certain common features among individuals, but not necessarily all features, make up a type. To classify each household, I impressionistically sorted the 750 interviews into different piles on the floor of my office, each pile differentiated from the others by its social and economic characteristics. The first sorting produced twenty or thirty discrete piles. I then asked myself why I had included the given schedules in the same pile: What did they share in common? After completing this exercise with all the schedules, I began a process of regrouping and combining until each pile was distinguished from the others in terms of categories of income, occupation, consumption patterns, lifestyles, social status in the community, and orientations to savings, investment, and consumption. This formulation of the class system made it possible for us to examine how the social-psychological orientation of each class was played out in the daily life of Springdale. Our chapters on classes and politics—including the politics of school, religion, and leadership—analyze the functioning of community institutions in relation to the town's class system. While still grappling with the class structure, and after more than a year in the field, I began to formulate my ideas about the processes by which external agencies penetrated the town.

I then wrote a paper, "Introduction to Springdale's Social Structure." From the beginning, it was the project's expectation that I was to analyze the town's social structure and that somehow my observations were to be integrated into the project's focus on community creativity and social growth. When I wrote this paper, my mind was on Palauan colonialism; this fix led me to look for all conceivable external influences on the town. The paper was an attempt to find a theoretical framework for linking the local community and its social processes to larger economic, political, and cultural institutions. To this end, I itemized all these interconnections and their significance for the functioning of the town. The paper, titled "The Colonial Position of Springdale in Relation to the Larger Society and its Consequences for the Microcosmic Social Structure," argues: "In the recent past—20 to 50 years—the structural relationships between Springdale and the larger society have been drastically altered. These changes are largely a consequence of changes that have occurred in the major institutional complexes of the larger society. A description of these latter changes and their psychological correlates is necessary for an understanding of the microcosmic social structure."

The paper goes on to identify the forms of institutional penetration and specifies their carriers. The paper never elicited a response from my project supervisors, but Bensman, with whom I shared it, thought it was a good statement. He said in a letter to me that it was "one of the best things I have seen on the analysis of rural society." However, he had a number of reservations:

> [T]he criticisms I ... make are based upon the fact
> that you are presenting so much material in so small
> a space that you give the reader constipation. You
> have an element of mixed empiricism and theoreti-
> cal analysis which in a small space does not do jus-
> tice to either. A great many problems would disap-
> pear, if the form for this were a large book and your
> paper was a conclusion.... You presented a picture of
> the causes and dynamics of the community without
> presenting the community behavior itself.... One of
> the problems that interests me is that in terms of the
> daily fabric of life the appearances are completely
> different from your analysis.

His response assured me that I was on the right track. This was our
conscious beginning of a book about Springdale.

In the first instance, the term colonialism was inappropriate for
the case of Springdale inasmuch as there were neither colonial administrators nor a system of indirect rule. The institutional means of
penetration were largely invisible, and external cultural influences
were simply regarded as the American way of life. However, if one
participated in the life of the community, the invisible became visible and cultural penetration transparent. For example, during the
early hysterical stages of the Cold War and after the Soviet Union
had successfully produced an atomic bomb in 1949, military planners initiated policies of civil defense designed to prepare the population for a possible nuclear attack. These plans included a network
of aircraft warning sites throughout the East operated by a volunteer
civilian Ground Observer Corps. Springdale, chosen as one of the
sites, responded by constructing a hut with a telephone on a hill and
had it manned twenty-four hours a day. I volunteered my services,

and during the midnight watch to which I was assigned, I was to look out for enemy planes. From a military standpoint, the entire project was meaningless—even if a plane were spotted, the untrained observer could not identify it—but from the point of view of civil defense policy, it was a propaganda campaign designed to assure Springdalers that we were participating in the defense of the nation. Somewhere in Washington, DC, in the office of a civil defense planner, Springdale existed and had been selected to play a role in a national propaganda campaign. Springdale responded on cue to this propaganda campaign, just as it did to the policies and programs created by central educational, agricultural, religious, and political party bureaucracies.

One of the ironies of Springdale's cultural penetration was that the project's focus on the Community Club as an example of creative community action had been originally instigated by Cornell's extension agent, Jack Grainger, who became its first president. Nonetheless, the project research problem seemed to assume that this had been an autonomous community creation. Other forms of cultural penetration included state-mandated educational requirements for the consolidated school and the introduction of the new medium of television. Also, in the Sunday school classes that I taught in the Congregational Church, at the invitation of the local pastor and with the approval of project headquarters, all instructional materials were imported from church headquarters.

A perspective that focused on external penetration of the town posed a theoretical problem not treated in the existing literature. The traditional sociological dichotomies of rural and urban and secular and sacred societies, then in fashion, inevitably narrowed and distorted an observer's perception of the local reality. By connecting the class and leadership systems with the forms of penetration, Bensman and I had found a way to bridge the space between the "isolated" community and the larger society.

Without an analysis of the systems of class and penetration, the dynamics of the social processes could not have been explored. As Bensman had noted in his critique of my paper, the problem this analysis presented was that our portrait was completely different from the appearances of the daily fabric of life in Springdale. This discrepancy raised the question of how to reconcile phenomenological appearances and sociological analysis, that is, how the daily fabric of community life and its surface illusions conceal the underlying dynamics of social processes. We resolved this issue by introducing social-psychological variables to reconcile appearances and institutional realities.

From the beginning, my dual roles as a participating member of the community and as a sociological analyst of it presented me with a paradox. The project expected me to analyze the social structure of the town; that was why they hired me, an anthropologist, as a field director to live in the town and make direct observations of it. This position contradicted the project's promise to the community that the report was to be presented exclusively in statistical terms, a method of reporting that in the end the project could not fulfill. All protocols collected in the field were machine-processed and cross-run for correlations between different variables. As the data from surveys began to accumulate, the number of variables increased and the cross-runs for correlations multiplied. It had been hoped that the machine process might provide leads to significant variables from which community creativity and leadership could be understood. But the pile of printouts from this procedure became unmanageable, leaving the project analysts with a loss of focus on a specific theme or problem. As a result of this style of investigation, the project was never able to produce a full-length monograph, that is, a study reporting the findings of its three years of research. The reports I submitted to the project were written as chapters that later became part of the book *Small Town in Mass Society*. Because of its commitment to the community to report only statistical data, the chapters I wrote were, by definition, of no use to the project. When Bensman and I published them, the paradox of my dual role in the town became a public issue. Many in the town—including friends who were later my house guests in Puerto Rico, where I had taken a position after leaving Cornell—were shocked and felt betrayed when they read the book. I knew this would be the case; the publication of other community studies had produced similar results. I did not allow this knowledge to act as an anticipatory form of censorship of our analysis of the data. Our findings pleased neither the project directors nor some members of the community. To have satisfied them, however, would have required a different study, written with a view to anticipating and mollifying their potential reactions. The paradox of my situation presented the problem of doing justice to the data or an obligation to please the "objects" of the research. One either serves a "scientific ethic" or a "social-contractual ethic." One can't serve both.

No erasure can wipe out the consequences of my residence and work in Springdale. My children, knowing that Bensman and I had written *Small Town*, were curious to know where they had been during that portion of their lives. I was never able to fully clarify for them their sojourn in Springdale until my fourth son, born in Puerto Rico and raised in Connecticut, decided to study in The School of Arts and Science at Cornell University. His choice led me to take several trips to Ithaca via Springdale, and, upon his graduation, the

entire family revisited the farmhouse and its environs, finally completing a circle in the family history. For me, the name of the town
is still Springdale because, by agreement with the ethical rules of the
project, the use of its real name violated the project's understanding with the town. Even some of the pseudonyms I invented to refer to public figures in the town seem more real to me than their
real names. The three years of my life with my wife and children
in Springdale are bracketed apart from my life before and after the
research. Yet despite the bracketing and the necessity of engaging in
such linguistic juggling acts, my family and I have been tied to the
town throughout these years as if by an umbilical cord that refuses to
be cut. For example, when I first moved to Greenwich Village in New
York, my second wife, Mary Gregoric, went to pick up a prescrip-
tion for me at McKay's drugstore on Sixth Avenue and Fourth Street.
The pharmacist asked her if she was related to the same Vidich who
had written the book, and she acknowledged that she was. He then
informed her: "I saw your husband hung in effigy." According to the
local Springdale newspaper, something of the sort had indeed occurred and on top of a pile of manure during Springdale's Fourth of
July parade the summer following the publication of the book. In an
article entitled "Candor Calls It Even," the *Candor Courier* of July
4, 1958, describes the scene: "The people of the Village of Candor
waited quite a while to get even with Art Vidich who wrote a 'Peyton
Place' type book about their town recently. The featured float of the
annual Fourth of July parade followed an authentic copy of the jacket
of the book *Small Town in Mass Society*, done large scale by Mrs.
Beverly Robinson. According to a thirty-year anniversary retrospec-
tive on the book written by Michael Gulachok in the *Tioga County
Courier*, residents of Candor followed the float with the book cover,
riding masked in cars labeled with the fictitious names given them

in the book. But the pay-off, Gulachok reports, was the final scene, a manure-spreader filled with very rich barnyard fertilizer, over which was bending an effigy of 'The Author.'"

Golachok's articles reviewed the initial reactions of the town and Cornell to the book and repeated comments about Bensman and me that appeared in the local press. Golachok also visited the town and interviewed Jack Grainger, the county agent: Kinserna, a Polish farmer: Henry Hanks, the Tioga County legislative chairman: and several other Springdale figures. Golachok's articles repeated much of the content and tone of the press reports published just after the first edition of *Small Town* appeared. They reject the book's major conclusions and once again vindicate the authenticity of small-town life. A more recent journalistic comment appeared in the July 14, 1999, issue of Springdale's newspaper. Reporting on the winning floats in the town's Fourth of July parade, it mentions that under the category of "prettiest," the Springdale Historical Society received first place for its entry, "Small Town in Mass Society." In this rendition, the float carries an eight-foot-high mock-up of the cover of the book and a sign declaring, "The Hysterical Press: Cornell's Candor Study Pirated: project leader steals data, flees to Puerto Rico with partner and PUBLISHES! Citizens Outraged." A banner attached to the base of the float reads: "1958: THE YEAR CANDOR [SPRING-DALE] BECAME – in – FAMOUS!" suggesting that the town has not only digested the book, but that it also takes some pride in the recognition it has received.

I have had telephone calls from friends in different parts of the country who told me they met someone who knew me in Springdale. My children tell me that, at least while they were still in college, their names identified them with *Small Town*. In 1982, I was invited by Jones's son, Howard, to spend a summer restudying Springdale. He had returned to the community when I first met him in 1953, after he had a successful career as an engineer. His letter of invitation read in part is follows:

> Art, we became friends in 1953 when we came back to [Springdale] and you were completing your notes and observations on life in 'Springdale' ... Though the community reaction to your book ... was violently adverse, I knew you had assessed the community ... accurately except for one thing—motive. Here you were wrong. You assigned selfishness as a motive for most actions when community welfare was the actual motive. I think you owe it to yourself and to the community to correct that mistake. Why don't you spend the summer here ... and reassess the situation.

In my letter replying to this invitation, I demurred and told Howard I could not accept. I had thought that the analysis of the Community Club might, in part, be an indirect answer to his criticism that we stressed selfishness as a motive, but in sociological analysis, interpretations of motives are notoriously difficult to substantiate, actors themselves frequently being unaware of their own motives or unwilling to reveal them. This invitation was received thirty years after the fact; by this time, I was thinking about other things and lacked the inclination and emotional stamina to face my friends in Springdale.

A few years ago, I received a telephone call from a Vietnam War veteran who had chosen Springdale as a place to live and to open a restaurant. When the restaurant failed and he lost his investment, he bitterly condemned all of Springdale for its hypocrisy but actually was expressing resentment against Springdalers for not patronizing his establishment. He wanted me to support his gripes against the town by agreeing with me that the book's description was accurate, putting me in the odd position of defending the mores of Springdale.

The Book and the Profession

The book was finished in Puerto Rico, where I took a job after completing my three-year contract with the project. Bensman and I exchanged revisions of chapters by mail and made visits to each other on a number of occasions. Several chapters were presented at meetings of the American Anthropological Association and the American Sociological Association. The manuscript was completed in 1956, but getting it into print and assimilated into the mainstream of social science literature illustrate the many vagaries of publication and reception in the public domain.

Finding a publisher proved to be difficult. Four commercial presses to which we submitted the manuscript seriatim rejected it for reasons such as "already having recently published a community study," "lack of a market for such a specialized work," and "its excessively technical language." Discouraged because we had not been able to find a publisher for more than a year but still persistent, we decided that each of us should submit the book independently in the hope that one of us found a publisher. We simultaneously submitted it to two university presses, Bensman to Princeton and I to Harvard. In light of our earlier failures, we learned with surprise that both presses accepted the book: Princeton at the urging of Melvin Tumin, whom Bensman had contacted, and Harvard under the sponsorship of Barrington Moore, Jr. However, readers at both presses were critical and requested revisions, extensive ones in the case of Harvard. Princeton's primary reader savaged the manuscript, seeing nothing whatsoever worthy in it:

> The style of this manuscript is painfully inadequate. There are two styles … one is the plodding style of simple declarative sentence, jacked up with the offensive jargon of the Sociologist; the other style, which has more changes of pace, is souped up with offensive jargon of the Psychologist. The clumsy structure of the sentences might serve as a microcosm of the clumsy structure of the entire manuscript…. These collaborators brought to their task certain standards of measurement which made it inevitable that they should arrive at their findings, such as they are, before they began their measurements.

Princeton's acquisition editor also expressed doubts:

> The authors' methodology, focus, and on the whole their presentation seemed good as I went along, but I was bothered by what might be excess of detail in certain spots (discussion of the political structure, for example), by some repetition, and, in particular, by the lack of reference to the findings of comparable studies.

Despite these assessments, Bensman and I were convinced that we had written a good book. Moreover, despite its primary reader's dismissive treatment of the manuscript, Princeton published the book. The review process seemed to matter less than the intervention of Melvin Tumin, whose informal defense led to its publication.

Harvard's primary reviewer, an anthropologist who had also published an American community study, offered a qualified endorsement of the manuscript but insisted that publication depended on substantial revisions:

> I recommend the publication of [the] book, but with a certain lack of enthusiasm. I believe that there is value in the manuscript but that it would be much improved by careful re-examination and some perhaps rather far-reaching changes.... There are two major flaws in the manuscript. The first and most important is conceptual and stems from the particular nature of the community and the particular emphasis of their self-imposed problem.... The second major objection is the failure of the authors to adduce adequate evidence to support many of their statements ... no chapter is entirely free of this fault.... I am not so much asking for proof as for specific illustrations ... I want to see the evidence. If the authors spent as much time in the field as they indicated, they must have far more data than they can possibly encompass within a single volume.... The third objection is perhaps of a lessor [sic] order, but still seems significant to me. The book purports to be a case study, presumably offering insight into an aspect of American society—at least broader than the immediate community of Springdale. Nevertheless, the authors frequently resolve problems on a purely local basis, and fail to draw the sociological generalizations that might have usefulness for understanding social processes in the US.

This reviewer's assessment required additions of considerable material that was in the possession of the project and entailed a much longer and unwieldy book, bordering on ethnography and diluting the theoretical framework. Barrington Moore, Jr., came to the book's defense, rejecting the need for more illustration, but making some criticisms of his own:

> The manuscript has more than its share of annoying typographical errors.... I am dubious about its thesis that village gossip seldom poisons friendly relations. Finally, I think the book would be greatly strengthened by a concluding chapter that would tie the findings into a broader intellectual stream interpreting the processes of change in American society.... [The] manuscript is after all, a careful sociological study of the impact of modern industrial society on the rural scene.... The authors should make clear the broad implications of their findings.

Moore's comment about the typographical errors is correct. The manuscript had been typed at the University of Puerto Rico in its College of Social Sciences typing pool by Spanish-speaking typists; that it needed editing was indisputable. In retrospect, I believe Moore was right in his criticism of our treatment of gossip, but because I was an outsider to the town, I was rarely admitted into this relatively private sphere of social relations; in fact, I was also protected from whatever gossip there was about me. Moore's request that we write an additional chapter required generalizations about American society from a specific case study. We preferred to leave the study of Springdale as a self-contained case from which any reader might draw his or her own conclusions.

Though neither press expressed unqualified enthusiasm about publishing our manuscript, both accepted it for publication. Harvard's acquisition editor "definitely wanted to publish our manuscript, provided that it is seriously and quite drastically revised," adding that it "needs a good deal more work than we can cover in our budget." This editor continued: "I think it is clear that you and Mr. Bensman have produced an important book about the social attitudes of a certain large group of people. Thus, we are very anxious to have it put into shape so that we can publish it. At the same time it has the faults of many books of this sort. It falls apart, and it is not nearly as well written as it ought to be. What do you and Mr. Bensman think you can do about it?"

This editor seemed to think that the book was mainly about social attitudes and did not respond to what we thought was its institutional framework. He groped for a way to accept it but, unsure of the ground he was on, told us that the book "falls apart," leaving us equally unsure of what ground we stood on.

Princeton's editor expressed more enthusiasm and noted, "Our acceptance of your work does not depend … on your revising your manuscript.… However, we have asked you to forego royalties on sales up to 1,700 copies … because we shall be investing funds in publication at some risk and will break even only when sales have reached 1,700 copies. When I say that there will be a risk, it is because of the fairly technical nature of the work; we feel sure it is high *quality*, or we should not be willing to publish it."

With this assurance, we accepted Princeton's offer. However, this was not the end of the affair. Harvard regarded our withdrawal of the book from their consideration and our acceptance of a contract from Princeton as an insult and a breach of publishing ethics: we had not informed either press of the double submission. Harvard's editor took umbrage at our withdrawal of the manuscript because it had been accepted by Princeton without a request for revisions. In his view, we had set his press in an unseemly competition with

Princeton. However, instead of complaining to us, he complained to Princeton. Informed of this by Princeton, we accepted an ever-so-slight slap on the wrist from Princeton for our misdeed.

The birth of *Small Town in Mass Society* was difficult and protracted. Finding a publisher and cleaning up the manuscript took more than two years and taught us a few things about the practices of the publishing business. A reviewer, we discovered, can write with personal pique and ignore the substance of a work or, as in one case, can respond competitively and negatively when he himself had written a book in the same general area. Yet despite reviewers' reports, editors who receive the most negative reviews may still decide in favor of publication; there seemed to be no logic to the process. We also learned that with perseverance a book can get published despite rejections and negative reviews.

In its first run, Princeton printed 2,500 hard-cover copies. Many of the books in that run were lost in a warehouse fire, and there were no royalties on that edition. When positive reviews by Dennis Wrong and Harold Rosenberg appeared in New York magazines, Princeton subcontracted the book to Doubleday Anchor. During the ten years it held the rights to the book, Doubleday sold 137,672 copies. Princeton regained its rights in 1968, and in seven printings of a second edition, sold 86,296 copies, taking it out of print in 1997 as *Small Town* reached its fortieth birthday. When Herbert Gans published his 1997 essay, "Best Sellers by Sociologists: An Exploratory Study," he did not mention *Small Town in Mass Society*. His research for the study also failed to produce data for C. Wright Mills's *White Collar* and Gerth and Mills's *From Max Weber: Essays in Sociology* and *Character and Social Structure*, all of which are still in print and have been best sellers for fifty years. Gans based his study on his belief "that the discipline must increase its usefulness to the general public." He must have judged that these books served no useful purpose. The University of Illinois Press published a new and revised third edition of *Small Town* in 2000.

The readership of the earlier editions consisted largely of graduate students and undergraduates in departments of sociology, political science, and American studies; Protestant ministers and administrators; and, of course, residents of Springdale and the region surrounding Cornell University. It also included students who read chapters that were excerpted in scores of anthologies. Judging from the number of inquiries I have had from sociologists writing from abroad, the book has had an active life in Scandinavia, Western and Eastern Europe, and Russia. In 1991, Thomas Luckmann, who used *Small Town* as a text in his course, Soziologische Theorie II: Empirische Wissensoziologie, at the University of Konstanz, sent me a copy of a student paper devoted to an analysis of the book's theoretical perspective, saying "you might be pleased to see that your book with Joe Bensman is still being intensively studied." Many of these inquiries focused on the methodological essays and the conflict over ethics reported in the second edition, but others responded to its theoretical implications. In the original edition of *Small Town*, Bensman and I said nothing about the source of theory that guided our analysis. In the second edition, we published an essay, "Social Theory and Field Research," that describes how we heuristically employed the theories of others to arrive at the interpretation of our data. Before the second edition went to press, we had not completed an essay called "Social Theory and the Substantive Problems of Sociology." Until 1991, this remained "Some Notes on Social Theory." Bensman had originally drafted the essay, and I expanded and completed it. It makes explicit the sources of our intellectual orientations and how they influenced our choices of problems.

Our readership did not, however, include anthropologists. This surprised and bewildered me because I thought that *Small Town* was written with the attitude of an anthropologist, that is, the study of Man (as it was then known) without regard to place. I thought we had done an anthropological study comparable to my work on Palau, with the difference that Springdale had a written history that went back to the westward expansion of New England. Moreover, there was an ethnographic literature of community studies, not only that of Thorstein Veblen's chapter on the country town in his book *Absentee Ownership*, but also such sociological case studies as the Lynds' Middletown and the Yankee City series, the latter conducted by the anthropologist W. Lloyd Warner. Such materials gave an anthropologist studying his own society access to cases and theories from which to draw an orientation of his own.

Yet when the book was published, it did not penetrate the field of professional anthropology in the United States. Stanley Diamond, my colleague for many years at the Graduate Faculty of The New School for Social Research, treated the book as a study in rural sociology. His view was representative of anthropologists in general. Its failure to make an impact on anthropology led me to reassess my relationship to that field. Palau had already taught me to give up some of the sacred beliefs of that profession: for example, that by studying natives we could learn about ourselves, or that there was some urgency to complete the task of studying primitive societies before they disappeared, or that the natives were incapable of rational action. As I saw it, there was no difference between studying Palau as an anthropologist from the United States and studying Springdale as if I were an anthropologist from Palau. For me, the barriers between sociology and anthropology had broken down, and I decided that I no longer knew what made anthropology a distinctive discipline. This led me to drift back to the comparative and historical sociology of Max Weber. However, because I needed to have a professional label, I decided to call myself a sociologist-anthropologist, not knowing that I had chosen a designation that placed me in an academic no-man's land, too general to fit into any of the increasingly specialized branches of either field.

Some readers were also unable to deal with the economic foundations of our sociological analysis. So far as I know, economists did not read the book, perhaps because econometrics dominated, and still dominates, that field. Sociologists had largely abandoned an economic conception of class structure and were mainly concerned with prestige and status, omitting an inquiry into its economic foundations. Among sociologists, Marxism later focused on cultural phenomena that did not include the analysis of class as central to an understanding of culture. When the book was published, it was fashionable in the social sciences to talk about interdisciplinary studies, but despite *Small Town*'s economic, political, social-psychological, and sociological orientations it was never dubbed an interdisciplinary study.

The fate of the book in the hands of American sociology's arbiters of respectability deserves more extensive comments. Even occasions of honor for *Small Town* can reveal an effort to dispute its lasting value to the mainstream of sociological work. In 1987, Ruth Horowitz, the chairperson of the Helen and Robert Lynd Award Committee—an award given for contributions to sociological research on communities by the American Sociological Association's Community Section—presented the Lynd award to *Small Town in Mass Society* (shared with Maurice Stein for his book *The Eclipse of Community*). At that same gathering, Dennis Wrong, speaking on behalf of Jonathan Reider's *Canarsie: The Jews and Italians of Brooklyn Against*

Liberalism, took the occasion in his remarks to observe that Reider's book had displaced or superseded the relevance of *Small Town,* as if to make this commemoration a burial ceremony. Wrong's remarks surprised me because, as noted earlier, his review of *Small Town* in the *New Leader* shortly after it was published lauded the book and helped to make it a success. Wrong's estimate seemed gratuitous and disturbed me—in part, perhaps, because his reviews of some of my later books were also negative—but I believe that in this case Wrong was wrong.

Of course, it is understandable that our essay "The Springdale Case: Academic Bureaucrats and Sensitive Townspeople," published in the second edition, endeared us neither to university officials concerned with their relations to constituencies in academia nor to leaders of the organized academic professions. As far as I know, the book has no standing in the American Sociological Association's Citation Index; perhaps it is difficult to cite, but there may be other reasons as well. For example, a working paper summarizing community studies published by the Committee on Historical Studies at The New School refers to *Small Town* as a "C. Wright Mills type study" and lets it go at that. Apparently, the book is both difficult to fit into conventional categories and caused some embarrassment to the upholders of academic respectability. After the first edition of the book came out in 1958, controversy erupted with Cornell University over its publication.

It focused on the ethics of publishing *Small Town* and the use of data I had collected while I was a Cornell employee. It cast a shadow over our careers in American academia because it implied a disloyalty to university employers. As a consequence of this controversy, fully reported in the second edition, questions of ethical norms in community and ethnographic research are now widely discussed.

The November 1997 issue of *Lingua Franca* contains an article by Charlotte Allen reviewing a number of sociological reports that have raised ethical questions. Titled "Spies Like Us: When Sociologists Deceive Their Subjects," it notes that "the ethics of deceptive research did not become a controversial topic in the profession until 1958. The occasion was a massive Cornell University study of participatory democracy in a local community and its unanticipated spin-off book *Small Town in Mass Society*." The article continues:

> For many years afterward, sociologists who feared that Vidich's conduct had jeopardized the field's newfound respectability, argued over whether he had done anything wrong. On one hand, everyone in [Springdale] knew he was the director of a Cornell research project. On the other hand, many [Springdale] residents might have thought (and been encouraged by Cornell to think) that the project consisted of the fieldworker's ethnographic survey. In the end, sociologists failed to resolve the ethical questions that Vidich's course of actions raised.

At a time when many sociologists are employees of organizations attempting to project a positive public image, issues of ethics become muddled with those of public relations. In consequence, the sociologist is left with several options. Either accept the censorship of the organization, engage in self-censorship, or disregard all forms of anticipatory censorship and take the consequences for reputation, career, and professional stigmatization. I was in the fortunate position of having been given my freedom by Kluckhohn when he severed my tether to Harvard. Although that left me without a sponsor, it also meant that I was no longer accountable to him. Leaving Cornell at the end of my three-year contract meant that I was no longer bound by editorial interference from project directors. Having no other options, I took a job at the University of Puerto Rico where I was distanced from the town, detached from my personal relations with members of it, and immune to the town's potential reactions to the book's publication. Not only was I freed of organizational pressures to censor the book, but also I was now in a position to make my claims in the academic marketplace on the strength of the worthiness of the book itself.

An entirely new dimension of my tether to Springdale appeared a few years ago when Paul Piccone, whom I knew for many years, bought one of Springdale's stately houses, took up residence in the town, and became one of its new immigrants. Piccone was also editor of the journal *Telos*, located on East 12th Street in New York. Learning, apparently for the first time, that I had co-authored *Small Town*, he wished to read the book. I supplied him with a copy. What he read did not conform to his image of the town, and this displeased him. In an essay entitled "Postmodern Populism," he took the occasion to defend Springdale against our interpretation of it: "Contrary to the dark forebodings of New Class Sociologists, modernization has not overwhelmed whatever 'organic communities' there ever were in the US. Rather their survival and continued viability is a function of their ability to resist or otherwise avoid modernizing procedures." Selectively quoting from our essay "A Theory of the Contemporary American Community" that appeared in the second edition and was intended not as an analysis of Springdale, but as a sketch of some possibilities for the future of the United States, Piccone wrote:

> In their mid-1950s study of a paradigmatic rural (organic) community, Vidich and Bensman not only projected the imminent obliteration of such communities, but, in typical "end of ideology" style,

warned about the potential fascist implications of what they saw as "fundamental and perhaps irreversible trends" in the very structure of American society.... Four decades after the study was completed, "Springdale" has yet to succumb to these "fundamental ... irreversible trends." The village has still no fast food facilities or other obvious signs of irreversible "modernization," and it still runs pretty much as it did in the 1950s by the direct descendants of those very people Vidich and Bensman ridicule in their "scientific" treatise and, more importantly, by scores of new villagers who have moved in since and who, contrary to dark foreboding of "populist" intolerance,... have become integral members of an ever changing dynamic organic community.

In Piccone's view, Springdale is one of the last organic communities in the United States, one that he found and moved into. However, his is an effort, like that of Howard Jones, to affirm the authenticity of public appearances against unappealing realities. Actually, there are many communities like Springdale. The fact that they are not dissimilar in external appearances from what they were fifty years ago indicates that small-scale farming is still a viable business, that opportunities exist to commute to work at white-collar and industrial jobs in the surrounding region, and that fast-food chains do not see a mass market for their products in towns like Springdale. Despite Piccone's assertion of the community's organicism, it would surprise me if the culture wars and their political implications have not penetrated Springdale. In fact, Bensman and I made no predictions that the town would be obliterated, but only suggested that its dilemmas and contradictions were solved by complicated patterns of social and personal self-deception that permitted Springdalers to retain their systems of beliefs while at the same time acting within the framework of social realities that denied these beliefs. Perhaps these same mechanisms are available to and utilized by intellectuals. If one considers the history of the treatment of the Springdale study by the American sociological establishment, this seems to be the case.

In our introduction to Princeton's second edition of *Small Town*, Bensman and I referred to our forthcoming book, *The Third American Revolution*. In fact, the book was published in 1971 as *The New American Society: The Revolution of the Middle Classes*. When writing this book, we had in mind Barrington Moore's suggestion that we add a chapter to the original edition to locate Springdale in a macroscopic framework. As we conceived of *The New American Society*, the connecting link between it and *Small Town* was our conception of Springdale's new middle classes, whose ideas, cultural forms, and lifestyles ran counter to most of the town's traditional values. Although we began with this idea, we treated *The New American Society* as an independent macro-analysis of changes in American society from the postbellum period to the 1960s. Recognizing that we had not directly addressed Moore's suggestion, we wrote a new chapter, "A Theory of the Contemporary American Community," for the 1968 edition of *Small Town*. This chapter extrapolates our Springdale findings to the then newly emerged middle-class suburbs, university towns, and urban middle-class enclaves. We stressed the potential for a clash between traditional American values and the new lifestyles that had gained currency among the upcoming generations in the 1960s. In our conclusion, we wrote:

> [T]he new life styles are not based on un-American ideas, but rather have evolved out of fundamental, organizational, economic, educational,

and demographic changes in American society.... Whether one likes the direction of these trends or not, they cannot be wished away, abolished by law or reversed by going back to the past without doing violence to the emergent society.... A direct confrontation based on these opposing orientations will have to be avoided if the United States hopes to cope with its other problems.

We could not then know how that confrontation might work itself out, but it is apparent that now, in the year 2002, it is taking place. On one side are those who uphold the sanctity of the family and of the nation as a community requiring reverence for quasi-sacred traditions and support for the moral sentiments of kinship, fidelity, and patriotism. On the other are the realities of racial and ethnic tensions, new family norms, sexual styles that do not conform to older standards, novel forms of entertainment, and varying consumption patterns.

Commitments to these competing values and moralities are expressed in legal struggles, propaganda campaigns, and the direct use of violence. Moral and lifestyle issues are also played out in national politics and legislative confrontations in Congress and among a multitude of think tanks on the Washington Beltway. What is at stake is no less than the soul of American society. Our original discoveries in Springdale revealed incipient cultural tendencies that later became paradigmatic for the society at large.

9

Exiled in Paradise:
Puerto Rico

My contract with the Cornell project was for a period of three years. I had neither a desire to extend it nor an invitation to stay. That put me back on the job market. It helped that in the meantime I had completed the dissertation and had the degree from Harvard and, though I had every intention of using these credentials in my search for a new position, I took it as a point of personal pride not to ask for help from any of my former professors in the Department of Social Relations. Nor did I need to. Quite unexpectedly I received a letter from Pedro Muñoz Amato, Dean of the College of Social Sciences at the University of Puerto Rico. Without so much as an interview, he offered me a position as an assistant professor of anthropology. Reuben Hill, I learned, recommended me to Muñoz Amato. Hill had been one of my undergraduate professors at the University of Wisconsin. I had been President of the Student Union when he was its Assistant Director. Since then, Hill had become an authority on the family largely as a result of publishing a successful book of collected essays with Howard Becker that he had parlayed into a consultancy at the University of Puerto Rico's research center. He knew that I had returned to the University of Wisconsin after the war, but how he knew that I was at Cornell mystified me; we had never corresponded. I surmise that Muñoz Amato, who was then hiring social scientists, had probably asked Hill for recommendations of possible candidates.

In academia, if you are a consultant you are also expected to be familiar with names in the field who might be eligible candidates. If you cannot name names, your status as a consultant loses some of its luster. So somewhere in a conversation with Muñoz Amato, Hill must have mentioned my name and presumably took a chance in promoting me. That, I believe, is how I got the job in Puerto Rico. I went as a greenhorn who had everything to learn about one of America's well-known former colonies.

This was in August 1954. After dismantling a household and storing its contents, my wife and I, with three children aged six, four, and one, left Candor, our farmhouse, and Cornell University. We headed for New York City and a flight to San Juan. Upon landing, a university representative received us at the airport and took us directly to our new residence in a university housing project known as La Finca. La Finca sat on the edge of a dairy farm. The spacious area surrounding the apartments was still used as a pasture, and a group of cows greeted us on our arrival. We had moved from a residence on one farm to another, but in this case, the farm was surrounded by Rio Piedras.

Living in La Finca and being from the mainland with a degree from Harvard endowed me with a status superior to any I could have had on the mainland. My neighbors included distinguished South American and exiled Spanish intellectuals, artists, poets, and social scientists, as well as a new generation of internationally educated Puerto Rican scholars. I found myself a member of an expatriate and cosmopolitan community far exceeding my expectations of what life in Puerto Rico might be like. La Finca was an enclave of privileged foreigners welcomed and accepted by equally privileged Puerto Rican academics among whom I was accepted simply on the strength of being there.

The lifestyle at La Finca included maids, cooks, gardeners, servicemen, nursery schools, and university-affiliated grade schools for the children. These were the colonial-style benefits accorded university personnel. I had no domestic chores. Domestic help was affordable on an assistant professor's salary supplemented by income from an occasional contract for a market research study for an American businessman. The one I remember was a study of potential uses for bagasse, an otherwise unused byproduct of sugar cane. My wife was free to take commercial and university research jobs. On our joint income, we were able to travel to what for us were the exotic Caribbean Islands and to explore the outer reaches of Puerto Rico.

Our apartment was large enough to entertain frequent visitors from the mainland. Joe Bensman and his family visited on occasion while he and I were working on the final stages of *Small Town*. When Warren and Clair Paley and their five children visited for two weeks, we sublet an apartment for them in La Finca. Other visitors included my Harvard friend Bob Wilson when he came to the island in connection with a research project sponsored by Hollingshead at Yale University. In addition to in-laws, a couple from Candor—the storekeeper and his wife with whom we had become friends—also visited us. Frequent contacts with mainlanders dispelled any sense of isolation from our past.

When our fourth son, Joseph, was born in 1956 (all costs covered by university medical insurance) he had his own nanny who arrived in the morning before he awoke and cared for him until his bed time, relieving his parents of all the onerous tasks of child care. Virginia Betancourt lived in Puerto Rico with her exiled father, Romulo Betancourt, a former president of Venuzuela. She was a student in my class and took over the household and managed it while my wife Virginia was recuperating from childbirth. Never had I been so superfluous as a father and husband. Puerto Rico was the place to have children if you were a college professor. As it later transpired, it was also convenient for Joseph to have a Puerto Rican birth certificate. When he became eighteen and applied for admission to Cornell University while we were living in Storrs, Connecticut, he received a letter from Cornell offering him a full scholarship to attend that school's College of Engineering. Cornell was recruiting minority students and had classified Joseph as a Puerto Rican because he was born there, a kind of latter-day manifestation of a colonial attitude in the days of an emergent multiculturalism.

I knew next to nothing about Puerto Rico, but this did not deter my enthusiasm for being in the tropics to which I had become addicted in Guam, Saipan, and Palau. I was confident that my undergraduate courses in beginning Spanish gave me a base for learning the language and looked forward to studying it and lecturing in it. This was my first full-time teaching appointment, and it required me to develop my own repertoire of courses. The teaching load was three courses, but research was also encouraged, and a pool of secretaries was available to serve the needs of the faculty. It was apparent from the beginning that the university administration provided the faculty with the best of facilities. The Faculty Club included a lounge and a restaurant that served a Puerto Rican cuisine that included *arroz y habichuelas rosadas*, a dish I've appreciated ever since I first tasted it. The university had its own journal called *La Torre* that published essays written by the faculty, and it sponsored visiting speakers from Spain, South America, and the mainland. Academic life in Puerto Rico was sharply different from being a project field director and participant observer in a small, rural New York community. President Jaime Benitez hoped to make an international reputation for the university.

Life in Puerto Rico was full of promise. Within a few weeks of my arrival, I had a family membership in the Condado Beach Club located in San Juan on the sandy shores of the Caribbean. On Sunday afternoons, the children could entertain themselves in the pool or on the beach. Waiters in white jackets served drinks poolside or on the beach. Other exotic weekend diversions included visits to El Yunke, Puerto Rico's tropical rainforest. In the interior, Luquillo Beach was an idyllic expanse of shoreline and coconut trees. On a Sunday afternoon, young boys climbed a tree to fetch a coconut and opened it with a machete to make it ready to add one's own rum to its juice. Drinking the combination on a hot Sunday afternoon was a rare experience. Later, the boys returned to split the husk in half exposing the rum-drenched soft coconut meat, making a dessert of it. There was also Loizà Aldea, a quaint town of Afro-Puerto Ricans that was a historical reminder of slavery on the island. The town took pride in its artists, especially the mask makers who used the husks of coconuts as the raw material for making an endless variety of facial expressions. Mata de la Gata, a small island retreat on the south shore of the island, was tended by a caretaker who held his job as a political concession from the governor. He often provided evenings of quiet isolation surrounded by the waters of the Caribbean shelter and lobster dinners prepared to perfection. These were the days before Puerto Rico became a haven for middle-class tourists from the mainland and before the tourist industry left its mark on the spontaneous hospitality of the islanders.

My knowledge of Puerto Rico was that of the average reader of the *New York Times*. Julian Steward, a Columbia University anthropologist, in collaboration with a group of his students, had completed a large-scale study called *The People of Puerto Rico*, but I had not read it. A few years earlier, a group of Puerto Ricans who opposed the mainland's influence on their island made the headlines of the *Times* when they entered a US congressional session and shot several congressmen; I had yet to learn about the complexity of the island's politics. I knew that the United States acquired Puerto Rico from Spain in 1898 as part of a peace agreement that also included the acquisition of the Philippines and Guam. I was also aware of Puerto Rico's strategic military importance to the naval defense of the western hemisphere during World War II and that German U-boats had dominated the Caribbean shipping lanes, isolating Puerto Rico from the mainland for the better part of the war. I also knew that Puerto Ricans had been granted citizenship status in 1918 and that in 1948, the island had been granted the status of a "Free Associated State," at which time Muñoz Marin, a popularly elected Puerto Rican governor and leader of the *Partido Popular*, replaced the last US colonial governor, Rexford Tugwell. Tugwell was a former professor at the University of Chicago, a university originally endowed by John D. Rockefeller to bring the raucous Midwest the civilizing influence of the eastern seaboard. And it was through Tugwell that the University of Puerto Rico was partially colonized by the University of Chicago. I noticed, of course, that the consequences of Puerto Rico's past colonization might be comparable to those I had studied in Palau and that I was willy-nilly a representative of the dominant colossus to the North.

After World War II, colonialism was not fashionable and ran against the tide of anti-colonial movements around the world; former colonies demanded self-determination and independence. For the United States, competing for world domination in a cold war with the Soviet Union, it was a patent ideological contradiction to proclaim itself a democracy and be a colonial overlord. In order to resolve this contradiction, Puerto Rico was redefined as a Free Associated State.

Later, borrowing from England's post-colonial history, it was called a Commonwealth, an arrangement that fell short of complete independence. To compensate for this political equivocation inspired by strategic military considerations, the United States hoped to make its "former" colony an exemplar to the world by inaugurating a policy to make Puerto Rico a showcase to the world of democratization and enlightened economic development.

Tugwell had joined Roosevelt's "Brain Trust" as Secretary of the Interior in the 1930s, and from that position, he was later assigned the task of designing the formula for decolonizing the island. Muñoz Marin, already a spokesman for Puerto Rican interests in Washington, became his collaborator in defining the conditions of Puerto Rico's "independence." The conditions included the freedom to form political parties and to elect governors in a popular election. That was how Puerto Rico achieved its independence and became a democracy.

Puerto Rico was not a state like the other forty-eight mainland states. Under the terms set by its new status as a Free Associated State, Puerto Ricans retained their rights as citizens free to move between the island and the mainland. This right was to be facilitated by a Puerto Rican Labor Office set up in New York City for the purpose of managing the importation and exportation of seasonal workers from the island and to guide the settlement of islanders into towns and cities other than New York. The new status also included participation in the armed forces, access to certain educational and welfare benefits, and freedom from payment of federal income taxes. In addition, trade between the island and mainland was tax free, and taxes collected in the United States from the sale of Puerto Rican rum were reimbursed to Puerto Rico. Such policies were designed to stimulate economic activity, provide jobs, reduce levels of poverty in rural areas and urban slums, shift part of the island's population to the mainland, and encourage capital investment by mainland businessmen in local industrial enterprises. The terms of the relationship between the two entities were enacted by the Congress of the United States, which retained legislative authority over the island. Not being a state like the other forty-eight, Puerto Ricans were not represented in Congress. However, since Puerto Ricans paid no taxes to the mainland, they could not claim taxation without representation.

Congress enacted a series of tax abatements and tax incentives designed to encourage American businessmen to invest in the island. Businessmen were offered the opportunity to take advantage of a low-cost labor pool and tax-free export of products to the mainland. Low costs and high prices enticed investors and producers to enter the market and, hence, stimulate the growth of the economy. This formula worked. By 1954, Puerto Rico was well on its way to a new economic prosperity. Mainland businessmen set up shops for the production of textiles and pharmaceuticals. These businesses transferred fully amortized machinery from the mainland to island factories. The low price of labor compensated for the low productive efficiency of obsolete equipment. Other businessmen practiced the ancient putting-out system, paying rural seamstresses by the gross for hand-sewn gloves, brassieres, and undergarments. In addition to low labor costs, cheap air freight rates made it possible to transport the finished products to the mainland. Tax incentives for the housing industry attracted investors to build prefabricated low-cost housing. Roads and transportation facilities supported by federal subsidies provided access to the four corners of the island and put in place the infrastructure required for the tourist industry. In a short period of time, between the end of the war and the time I arrived, Puerto Rico had been transformed into a model of economic development for a former colony. Muñoz Marin, in collaboration with the mainland government, was the architect of this economic development plan and made it the lynchpin of his career and his administration. In his popular appeal to the rural masses and displaced urban dwellers, he portrayed himself as a man of the people who extolled the rustic countryman, the wholesome, hardworking *jibaro*, who was the carrier of Puerto Rico's authentic values. He called his program "Operation Bootstrap," a slogan suggesting that Puerto Rico could pull itself up on its own and thereby create its own radiant future.

From the point of view of American foreign policy, Puerto Rico was to be a showcase to the world of enlightened post-colonial policy. By 1954, when both decolonization and the Cold War were well under way, Puerto Rico had acquired a positive public relations value for America's struggle against the Soviet Union. It was promoted by the State Department as both an example of a successful transition to democracy and the effectiveness of capitalism for the economic development of the world's former colonies. This little island, seventy miles long and forty miles wide and with a population of two million, was given a role to play on the world stage. Like the hub on a wheel whose spokes point in all directions, it drew visiting observers from all directions—Asia, Africa, South America, wherever former colonies hoped to become independent states with viable economies. Puerto Rico was inundated with State Department and United Nations sponsored visitors who came to witness Puerto Rico's success and to apply its methods to their own countries. America's formerly neglected colony now basked in the glory of this new form of colonial exploitation, a *quid pro quo* designed to serve both the *Partido Popular* and American foreign policy.

Operation Bootstrap, in fact and in psychological effect, instilled a sense of economic vibrancy and optimism in the island's population.

It left no part of the island or its political, social, and cultural institutions untouched. Among those affected was the university.

The University

The University of Puerto Rico's (UPR) president was Jaime Benitez, friend and close political ally of Muñoz Marin. While Muñoz portrayed himself as a man of the people who extolled the *jibaro* as opposed to the urban sophisticate, Benitez was the elegant, worldly man of culture. The two were collaborators in a project to remake the image and the reality of Puerto Rico. Muñoz provided the university with the money it needed to grow and to take on new functions, and Benitez was to give respectability to the university as an institution of higher learning and to make it the scientific and cultural focus of the island.

In the overall scheme of Operation Bootstrap, the university was to serve both economic development goals and the cultural aspirations of its leaders. It was to be a pragmatically oriented university designed to train generations of students for participation in the new economy, to support research in and for social planning, and to sustain the island's Hispanic heritage. This was a mission that followed more in the image of pragmatic American rather than Latin American or Spanish universities. It was to be integrated into society and to serve the public good rather than exist as an entity apart from the state.

The university's Social Science Research Center was directed by Millard Hansen, a mainlander and graduate of the University of Chicago. The research center sponsored projects to further knowledge about the social and economic state of Puerto Rican society and the practical means for its improvement. Muñoz Marin was its supporter and took a personal interest in the research that it conducted.

In addition to Julian Steward's study, the center had also sponsored a study by Melvin Tumin (assisted by Arnold Feldman) that was published as a comprehensive survey of Puerto Rico's class system. John Kenneth Galbraith, before he became famous, and his assistant, Peter Gregory, assembled a team of local researchers to examine the characteristics of the Puerto Rican labor force. August Hollingshead, a social psychologist affiliated with Yale University, directed a study of the Puerto Rican character with the assistance of Robert N. Wilson and Lloyd Rogler. These were a few of the dozens of studies that the center sponsored in the 1950s. In addition to providing useful information for planners, these also provided research training for advanced students at UPR. Those were the days in the post-World War II period when faith in research aimed to support the rational planning and administration of society could still command the kinds of resources made available to social scientists during the war. The center also hired a variety of consultants who were brought in for a week or two: Robert Redfield, Herbert Blumer (whom I met for the first time, and whose essay on economic development, presented at UPR, I published forty years later in an anthology of his work), and Daniel Boorstin (who later became the Librarian of Congress), all from the University of Chicago. Reuben Hill and Porter Butts came from the University of Wisconsin. Butts, the creator and long-time director of the Student Union at Wisconsin, of which I had been president, was brought over to evaluate UPR's Student Union and its place in the culture of campus life. Butts, of course, had invented the very idea of student unions. So he was an authority and consultant on this unique campus institution to universities throughout the United States. When Butts learned that I was on the campus, he contacted me and offered me the directorship of UPR's union, a job that would have reconnected me to a part of my past I wished to forget. UPR was a crossroad where social scientists, many of whom later became eminent, began their careers. Had I not been in Puerto Rico, I would never have met them. With so many Americans consulting and doing research—many of them living in La Finca—I had no need to feel like an exile; the mainland had come to me. From the point of view of some Puerto Rican social scientists, however, these mainland researchers and consultants were viewed as another form of colonial penetration.

In practice, Benitez distanced the University of Puerto Rico from American influence by making it international and cosmopolitan. He appointed a diverse faculty that included such republican Spanish exiles as Francesco Ayala (humanist, writer, and social theorist, and later a professor of sociology at New York University); Eugenio Granell (author and surrealist painter whose paintings now occupy a museum of their own in Santiago, Spain); Garcia Palayo (political scientist and legal theorist); and Federico O'Nis (Spanish literature and language, formerly the head of Columbia University's Spanish Department). These Spaniards were a remnant of the "Generation of 1936" who opposed Franco and Stalin and lived in exile in the Caribbean and Latin America. Other members of the faculty were the Mexican painter Rufino Tamayo; the Chilean philosopher José Echeverria; an Argentine social philosopher and specialist on George Herbert Mead and American pragmatism; Franz von Lichtenberg, a world-renowned expert in the study of shistosomiasis, later appointed a professor at Harvard Medical School; Belagi Moncur, an Indian specialist in electronic microscopes, later hired by the University of Connecticut; Kurt Bach, an MIT-trained psychologist; Leopold Kohr, an Austrian economist and proponent of small-size states; Gordon Lewis, English specialist on the Caribbean region; Beate Salz, an anthropologist trained at The New School for Social Research and the daughter of the émigré economist, Arthur Salz; and other poets, philosophers, and scientists whose names I no longer remember. This illustrious collection of professors recruited from around the world gave UPR an international luster unmatched elsewhere in Latin America.

Knowing these people opened my eyes to other worlds. For example, the Spaniards gave me their interpretation of the Spanish Civil War and opinion of George Orwell's *Homage to Catalonia*. But also their presence added to the impression held by some in the university that jobs that rightfully belonged to Puerto Ricans were being given to outsiders. Academic colonialism seemed to pervade the university.

In fact, a strong residue of colonialism in the form of language policy was still a reality as it had been when Puerto Rico was a colony. Though English was no longer mandated as the official language of instruction, the island in practice was now bilingual. Many students, however, were not fully bilingual. Some were disadvantaged when they took courses with English-speaking professors; the burden of accommodation was on them. By the same token, a linguistic divide existed between Spanish-speaking and English-speaking professors. Though almost all Spanish-speaking professors (except for a few Spaniards) spoke English, many English speakers could not speak Spanish. If independence had been achieved, the island's official language would have been Spanish, and non-Spanish speaking visitors would have borne the burden of accommodating to its usage. In fact, however, Puerto Ricans were expected to speak English to mainlanders, that is, to accommodate to the linguistic deficiencies of the outsider, the visitor, and the stranger. Since both languages were acceptable in any situation, the first to speak English determined by default the language of choice. Moreover, an American, even when in a Spanish-language conversation, had the privilege of reverting to English at any time, whereas the reverse was not acceptable. The burden to participate fully in the English-speaking community was placed on the Spanish speakers rather than the other way around. For Puerto Ricans, such linguistic etiquette could be a constant source of irritation. By the same token, in order to avoid the discomfort of bilingualism, the intruder could be selectively excluded from intimate gatherings of Puerto Ricans. A sublimated cultural divide that separated the Puerto Ricans from the Americans pervaded the public life of the island.

This, however, was only one dimension of the language problem. Spanish as it is spoken by Puerto Ricans has its own inflections, elisions, pronunciation, and tempo. It bore almost no relationship to the academic Spanish I had studied as an undergraduate. I was confounded all the more when my private tutor thought I should learn a pure Castillian Spanish and emphasized its diction—the rolled "r" as in *perro* and the aspirated "c" as in *gracias*—rather than grammar, vocabulary, and syntax. As a result, even after three years in Puerto Rico, I never learned the language well enough to lecture in it. Failing to achieve fluency was a disadvantage that limited my participation in the public affairs of the university. I was lucky that my colleagues in the social science faculty generously accepted me along with my limitations. Some of them, including sociologist Hector Estades, political scientist Milton Pablon, anthropologist Eugenio Fernadez Mendez, and psychologist Carlos Albizo, had studied at the University of Chicago (the old Rexford Tugwell connection), and others— economists and philosophers—had studied at mainland universities. They generously conducted their conversations and group discussions in English when I was present. This was not just a matter of etiquette but an effort to make me part of their community, despite the linguistic concession it required them to make. I was, after all, still a quasi-representative of the older colonialism that persisted into the era of the Free Associated State.

The College of Social Sciences

It made no difference to Muñoz Amato that I had little teaching experience. It was also of no concern that I could not lecture in Spanish; it was enough that I had a Harvard degree and an affiliation with Cornell. That my prior teaching experience consisted of a seminar in Oceania in Cornell's anthropology department, and before that, while still a graduate student, a summer school course in social problems I had taught at the University of Rochester was hardly worth mentioning. Everything I knew about Oceania was irrelevant to Puerto Rican students whose intellectual horizons were the Caribbean and South America. Muñoz Amato advised me that I could define my own curriculum and that my courses were intended for advanced students. Some of the courses I remember teaching are American Society, The Sociology of Community, and Social Structure and Personality. The latter was my variant of the then trendy subject in anthropology called Culture and Personality. Gerth and Mills's *Character and Social Structure: The Psychology of Social Institutions* was published in 1953, and I used it as my text in this course. It provided me with a comprehensive introduction to Max Weber's sociology. I had previously only read his essays in *From Max Weber*, edited by Gerth and Mills. I read the book like a bible and wrote a review of it for *American Anthropologist*. Teaching this course was a major learning experience for me. I have no idea what my students may have learned, but two of them at least, Manuel Maldonado and Anna Basso Bruno, grasped it and understood its framework and historical perspective. They taught me some fundamental lessons about the teaching racket, namely, never to underestimate the intellectual capacity of undergraduates and to make my teaching a learning process for both my students and myself. That I was lecturing in English to some students who were not proficient in English required extra effort on my part to ensure that I was being understood. When I used a technical term that I thought might be new to some students, I took to asking the class for its Spanish equivalent. I could tell the extent of comprehension by the number of students who volunteered a word. That was a measure for me that I had contact with the class. The need for this practice also taught me a fundamental lesson about lecturing—to encourage students to respond and question as a part of the process of lecturing.

Teaching a full load of courses was a new experience for me and conflicted with the time I needed to finish the *Small Town* book with Bensman. Bensman and I sent chapters back and forth for more than a year before we had a rough draft of the book, not including the first chapter, which we wrote last. I usually did my writing in the evening after the children were put to bed. I wrote until two or three in the morning, staying awake by smoking packs of cigarettes and drinking Baranquilla rum until I could no longer stay awake at the typewriter. As we finished chapters, I submitted them for presentation at sociology and anthropology meetings. Hans Speier accepted the chapter on Springdale's class system for the sociology meetings held in Detroit in November of 1954 and, in 1955, the anthropologists accepted a paper on social structure and the psychology of adjustment that I presented at meetings in Philadelphia. Had we not had the help of Muñoz Amato's secretarial office at the College of Social Sciences, we could not have prepared the manuscript copies we needed for submissions. I handed drafts to Ernestine Ferrer de Ballester, who assigned them to one or two of the ten typists in the pool and, presto, within a few days, she supplied me with the work. That typing pool was an academic luxury I've never encountered in any other university. When we thought we had a book, we sent copies to commercial publishers, five of whom rejected it before both Harvard and Princeton reluctantly accepted it in early 1957, as I described earlier. With the book and the complex negotiations with publishers out of the way, I had time to do other things.

I wrote an essay, "The Social Role of the Anthropological Advisor." This was a subject that first caught my attention in Palau where I had observed anthropologists giving advice to naval officers under the pretense that they did so as objective scientists. In the immediate postwar period, anthropologists seemed to be completely unaware of the implications and subtleties of playing this role. I noticed similar attitudes on the part of American advisors to social policy-makers in Puerto Rico and wrote the article as a critique of the practice on the grounds that it was a form of political influence. It was published as a brief communication in the *American Anthropologist*, the only article I published in that journal. I was already on my way to distancing myself from anthropology.

Despite Benitez's efforts to make UPR a pragmatically oriented place, many academicians were, if not obsessive, at least preoccupied with the island's political status. The island's dependence on the United States rankled Puerto Ricans. Theirs was an anti-colonial mentality that could not be directly expressed as colonialism because that status had been ended. Surrounded by colleagues who expressed dissatisfaction with America's influence on the island (Gordon Lewis, the English political scientist and historian, was vociferous and incisive in his critique of the excessive presence of the United States), and especially the use of Puerto Rico and the university as a dumping ground for incompetent Americans who could not succeed on the mainland, I decided to do a study in order to discover how the island's political status was refracted in the countryside. I began a study on a small town, Trujillo Alto, located a short distance from Rio Piedras. With the help of Anna Basso Bruno and Gilberto Valcarcel, an older student and a member of a respected family in the town, I began this study after finishing the *Small Town* project. I investigated two questions: 1) Who commanded the loyalties of traditional *caciques* who were pivotal gatekeepers in the electoral process; and 2) What kind of political influence did Catholic, Evangelical, Spiritualist, and Scientologist religious leaders exercise? I interviewed local leaders and gathered some historical data, but never finished this study, despite putting a substantial amount of work into it and, after leaving the island, returning twice to gather more material. The work remains a manuscript called *Trujillo Bajo*. I didn't try to publish it because I never had confidence in either my framework or my data, and I had not solved a problem. Nevertheless, I learned a few things about the political psychology of the islanders. At least it gave me some background for talking about the island's politics.

That knowledge was useful in the long-winded discussions I had with Gordon Lewis while we drank coffee in a local *cafetin* across the street from the social science building. In one of these discussions, we decided to organize a small group for the purpose of discussing what we termed Puerto Rico's political problems.

The intellectual community in Puerto Rico was small but conspicous. Like gossip in a small town, the word spread with remarkable rapidity about any event on the island that might have the slightest politcal implications. Our purpose was to analyze the changes taking place in Puerto Rico under Muñoz's administration and their consequences for its future. We named the group the Country Circle and decided to meet off campus at Gordon and Sybil Lewis's house, located on the road to Trujillo Alto. Our format was to be that of a seminar limited to ten members with one member presenting a paper each month, followed by an open discussion. Hector Estades, Carlos Rosario, Carlos Albiso, Eugenio Fernandez Mendez, Milton Pabon, Beate Salz, Sybil Lewis, and Delia Pabon agreed to join. We had not thought of this as an exclusive group, but rather as a group of compatible friends (I was godfather to Lewis's son). Occasionally, we invited visitors assigned to the research center.

Though nothing exceptional had transpired at any of our first three or four meetings, the group's existence became known. In short order, we received requests from others who wished to join. Among those was Muñoz Marin himself. Why, we asked, and what should we do? We all understood that the governor could not be refused, but we also understood that the group was now too conspicuous to survive in its original form. When we met with him, Muñoz made no special claims for deference and seemed to enjoy an open discussion among a group of younger professors, something that was perhaps a reminder to him of his days as a free-floating radical intellectual in New York's Greenwich Village. Our discussion focused on the hottest issue of the island, the status question. Muñoz used the occasion to measure the range of academic opinions concerning his political creation. What he discovered was, no doubt, what he already knew—that, under the ethos of Cold War psychology, Puerto Rico had no other alternative. He also discovered this group had no intention of becoming a political movement and could conclude that we were both harmless and posed no threat. We assumed that like any other master politician he was simply checking us out as he did with any other new group that might talk about the island's politics. We had been discovered, and after that it was impossible to keep the Country Circle small. Too many others, whose requests to join we could not refuse lest we appear to be exclusionary and elitist in this recently created democracy, meant we could no longer meet in the Lewises' living room. When we scheduled a meeting with Robert Redfield, who was visiting from the University of Chicago, we changed our format to an open meeting held on university property, and the public was invited. Like the others who attended, I became another member of the audience, and that was the end of the Country Circle.

The Political Status Question

The question of the political status of Puerto Rico dominated all discussion of the island's political parties. After fifty years of American colonial rule, the quasi-independence granted under the arrangement of the Free Associated State was a relationship that was neither independence, nor colonialism, nor indirect rule. Muñoz had staked his political career on this arrangement, but it was not universally accepted. On the far left, there was Albizo Campos, a communist doing time in jail and a powerful symbol of anti-Americanism. Another outspoken enemy was Vito Marcantonio, a Puerto Rican living in New York and organizer of disaffected Puerto Ricans living in the city. He was taken seriously as a political opponent, so much so that he was killed in what appeared to be a politically inspired assassination. The murderer was never apprehended. Albizo Campos and Marcantonio were the last of the 1930s and 1940s radicals who were categorically opposed to capitalism and American colonialism.

Muñoz's formula for mediating the relationships between Puerto Rico and the United States subverted the issue of colonialism. Under the Free Associated State, the issues became political autonomy and economic development aided and abetted by the United States.

Muñoz and the *Partido Popular* could take pride in their economic consequences. New factories, roadways, luxury hotels, and construction projects resulted in jobs, higher income levels, greater opportunities for education and health care, and higher standards of living. Mainland economic penetration was accepted along with an admiration for American consumption styles in the form of cars, clothing, and industrial production and efficiency. While the American way was accepted and admired, its acceptance was tempered by the effect that this new penetration was having on traditional Puerto Rican institutions. Traditional festivals were disappearing, and even the *jibaro* was becoming a slum dweller in the larger cities or an industrial worker in regional cities.

Spanish, the mother tongue, was being vulgarized with words borrowed from English. Americans as governmental advisors, factory managers, researchers, and university professors appeared like carpetbaggers from the North. Traditional cultural practices were changing under the overwhelming weight of mainland influence and technology. A social psychology of ambivalence developed as a result of the tension between admiration for and resentment against the United States.

However, the resentments could not be expressed directly. US-owned factories could be seen as exploiting the local labor force for profits that were returned to the mainland, but the same factories provided jobs and stood as symbols of economic reconstruction. Some saw the US military bases—Vieques in particular—as foreign sovereign domains within the society, but because they were partly staffed by Puerto Ricans and provided employment to local civilians, they could be both resented and appreciated as a source of employment. Individual Americans in the midst of the Puerto Ricans were almost as inaccessible as targets of resentment as that of the abstract, symbolic Navy. Americans could be regarded as "crypto-carpetbaggers," interested only in short-term, selfish gains—good jobs—at the expense of the indigenous population; they did not commit themselves to Puerto Rico, but lived off it. The same Americans, however, brought the industrial, bureaucratic, and commercial skills through which Puerto Rico's economic development was taking place, so that the Americans, even the incompetent ones, were surrounded by the halo of prestige that adhered to almost anything that represented the mainland way. What might otherwise remain free-floating, diffuse resentments were given focus by the diverse ideologies of the political parties.

The Statehood party stood for absorption into the United States. The party ignored the issues of traditional culture and American penetration. It identified with industrialism, American lifestyles, and the English language. In fact, it eschewed traditional culture, believing that statehood would make Puerto Ricans full citizens of the United States.

The Independence party identified with an image of Puerto Rican society free of external domination. Stressing the negative features of the relationship with the "Goliath of the North," it promised the creation of a sense of identification with Puerto Rican cultural traditions—the Spanish language, traditional songs and dances, the preservation of the past, and full autonomy: Puerto Rico for the Puerto Ricans.

Muñoz's *Partido Popular* stood for partnership between unequals, and thus both expressed and gave legitimacy to the prevailing ambivalence that was intrinsic to the society at almost all levels of institutions. It provided a dual structure of identification, affirmation of selected elements from the past, and the promise of a future based on acceptance of US penetration.

The status ideologies that the parties invoked mobilized and organized the emotions of the population by providing points of focus for forming a political identity. In each case, however, the identity was defined by a reaction to the penetration by mainland institutions. To the extent that the various status ideologies organized the social psychology of the population, they provided focal points around which the identification of individuals could be organized, but it appears that in the case of each of the available alternatives, the character of the identity was negative.

Independence allowed for a potential re-creation of a sense of identification with the past along with an expression of a sense of hostility toward foreigners. Cultural items such as music, dance, traditional places, linguistic usage, and social types were selected and emphasized as points of identification. The selection itself was shaped by the hostility to the penetration of island society and culture by American institutions. Even the idea of *independentista* nationalism is an imported product learned from the study of American, rather than Spanish, history. But irrespective of the source and content of the ideology, it provided a basis for identification that rested upon *ad hoc* selections from a myriad of possibilities. The symbols were selected self-consciously and did not comprise an integral pattern of identification that reflected immediate experience.

Statehood emphasized specifically American elements and deemphasized both tradition and Spanish history. In identifying with an image of the United States, specifically Puerto Rican experiences were denied and ignored. This meant a denial of one's own past and an organization of the self around a set of self-imposed expectations of what it meant to be an "American." The identification with the elements of penetration made the proponent of statehood a carpetbagger in his own society. This identification rested upon an equally *ad hoc* selection of elements of Americanism combined with hostility to one's own society and resulted in a similarly negative and artificial identity.

The ideology of the Free Associated State was an attempt to provide a dual structure of identification; the Spanish past was affirmed, and the American penetration was acknowledged and accepted. This resolution was not easy to absorb since all of the consequences of penetration resulted in deeper modernization and greater dissolution of the past. At times, the penetration appeared to be so great as to create anxieties concerning the loss of all links to the past. On such occasions, the Spanish heritage and Puerto Rico's past were reaffirmed. This reaction could temporarily result in changes in educational policy—renewed efforts to teach Spanish, attacks on the cosmopolitan university—or legislation designed to favor local agricultural producers over imported products. At other times, if for example, rates of emigration fell off or large federal housing or highway grants were announced that gave further stimulus to the economy, it could be asserted that Puerto Ricans were American citizens with equal rights. Such shifts in referents left few stable reference points. In this case, the identity was less negative than artificial and was a dynamic that skirted the existence of dependence, but did so by providing an ever-shifting set of identity referents.

At the same time, however, the entire society continued to respond to the events, decisions, price fluctuations, legislative acts, and so on that occurred in the United States. When there was a recession in the US, emigrants returned, business fell off, remittances declined, and the economy presented new problems. When technological, scientific, and educational changes took place in the US, these were brought to Puerto Rico irrespective of internal policies. There was no way for insular politics to determine the fate of the island, and so each of the political parties gained its focus by responding to evolving trends in the United States. It is in this sense that the ideologies of the parties were artificial rather than intrinsic to a uniquely Puerto Rican experience.

Paradise Lost

After three years in Puerto Rico, I too was drawn into its insularity and ambiguous relationship with the mainland. Now was the time to choose—either stay or return to the mainland. I calculated the implications of the decision. If I chose to remain with my family, neither my wife nor I could become Puerto Ricans and our children would have an ambiguous identity as American Puerto Ricans. Because our families and friends were on the mainland, most of my personal and intellectual past was linked to the United States. When I went to the island, I had not been forced into exile by events beyond my control. Instead, I had voluntarily elected to take the job I was offered rather than undertaking the more risky and sometimes lengthy process of conducting a job search. I had no education in Caribbean or Latin American history or culture and was not a fluent Spanish language speaker. After finishing the Springdale study, I realized that the subject of my research and study was American society. As the son of Slovenian immigrants who from the beginning felt marginal to American values, I did not want to repeat that marginality in Puerto Rico. Despite a pay raise, promotion to tenure, and an associate professorship, I decided to leave the island.

My academic marketability was not quite the same as it was when I left Cornell, though I had been very active professionally. I had read papers at conventions, published several articles, and had a book accepted for publication. I had Barrington Moore as a referee, and I learned indirectly that Moore had told Clyde Kluckhohn of my whereabouts. In 1956, without an accompanying letter, Kluckhohn sent me copies of two of his articles that he signed, "Regards, Clyde." It was an invitation for reconciliation, and I was expected to respond. It had been more than five years since Kluckhohn abruptly cut me out of his world. But I had survived the initial shock and had gained my independence from a mentor who, no matter how unceremoniously, had actually given it to me. It didn't take me long to decide what to do. I looked at the copies of the articles, tossed them in a wastebasket, and decided not to respond. I felt no need for reconciliation. I no longer wanted Kluckhohn's help. That was the final episode in my relationship with Clyde Kluckhohn.

Still I had no trouble finding another job. Through a concatenation of circumstances, I was offered a job at the University of Connecticut. I had met a visitor from that school, Denison Nash, at the faculty club while he was a tourist in Puerto Rico. This was a casual encounter that gained significance only later after Reuben Hill, again consulting at the University of Connecticut, recommended me to James Barnett, head of that school's Sociology and Anthropology Department. Nash could say that he knew me and seconded the recommendation. That is how I got the job as an assistant professor at the University of Connecticut.

In those days, James Barnett hired staff without formal consultation with the department, doing it, instead, on his own authority, and in my case, without letters of recommendation. The position became vacant when Melford Spiro, who had also been on the CIMA project studying Ifaluk Island with Edwin Burrows, resigned his position and Burrows died. This was the second time my fate was affected by

Reuben Hill's intervention. I had not seen him since 1943, but when I met him again in Moscow in 1966 at the International Sociology Association meetings, I had the occasion to thank him for his unsolicited help. Later, when he was a candidate for the presidency of the American Sociological Association, I voted for him in an election he lost. Although we were worlds apart in our attitudes toward religion (he was a Mormon) and our perspectives on sociology (he was a moral advocate for family values), none of this mattered when it came to remembrances of a fraternization that had its beginning at the University of Wisconsin.

It was a jolting experience to exchange the warm, vibrant Hispanic and Caribbean culture for the cold winters and Congregational culture of Connecticut. At this stage in my life, three years was a long time, and I had no desire to cut myself off—as I had from Cornell and Candor—from friends and my research in Trujillo Alto. The next two summers, I continued my research and, even later, I was invited to give a public lecture at UPR. Throughout the years, Puerto Rican colleagues funneled graduate students to me at the University of Connecticut and The New School for Social Research. Virginia Betancourt and her father, Romulo, who regained the presidency of Venezuela in 1958, became lifelong friends —we exchanged children for summer vacations. When Eugenio Grannel and Francesco Ayala came to New York City, we picked up where we had left off as neighbors in La Finca. I supervised the dissertation of Hector Estades's sister at The New School. I had a reunion with Eugenio Fernandez Mendez when we accidentally met in the *Museo Nacional de Antropología* in Mexico City and years later another reunion with Manuel Muldonada when we met in a hotel in Bogota. I maintained a lifelong correspondence with my colleague Beate Salz, who lived in retirement in Saskatoon where she wrote about her garden and read the *National Geographic*, and she regularly sent me her love. When I first arrived at the University of Puerto Rico, I was given a desk in her office. She had given me my orientation to Puerto Rico and later, at my suggestion when I was at The New School, made a bequest to the sociology department from which she had received her degree. Though it has been forty-five years since I left the island, my experience there left me with a lasting admiration for the vitality, passion, and spontaneity of its people.

10

First Years at The New School

I first learned about The New School from Hans Gerth when I was a graduate student at the University of Wisconsin. Gerth, who had joined Wisconsin's Department of Sociology in 1940, had grown up in Germany during the heyday of Germany's Weimar culture and had studied with Karl Mannheim in Heidelberg and Frankfurt during the 1920s and early 1930s. He had known Hans Speier, Carl Mayer, Adolph Lowe, Hannah Arendt, Günther Stern (Arendt's first husband), and other scholars, some of whom later became the faculty at the University in Exile, later called the Graduate Faculty of Political and Social Science. Gerth had published essays in *Social Research*, the Graduate Faculty's journal. After his death, his essay on Max Weber's reception in America was published in *Politics, Culture and Society*. Gerth had an easy familiarity with other German exiles—Max Horkheimer, Theodor Adorno, Herbert Marcuse, and Otto Kirchheimer, all from the Frankfurt school—who had set up the Institute for Social Research in Morningside Heights, near Columbia University. Gerth also introduced us to the work of Walter Benjamin and told us the story of how Benjamin had committed suicide at the French-Spanish border, believing he would be refused admission into Spain and concluding that the only alternative to suicide was death in a concentration camp. When Mannheim's *Ideology and Utopia* was translated, Gerth's students in the faraway Midwest learned that there was a sociology of knowledge.

Hannah Arendt's *The Origins of Totalitarianism* was published in 1951. I heard about it from Gerth when I returned to Madison from Harvard for a summer visit. Gerth had read her book carefully and disputed her claim about the imperialist and colonial origins of European totalitarianism. When Gerth and Mills published *From Max Weber*, I already knew enough to know that it was a book I should read, even though I could not square its contents with the anthropology curriculum I was reading in Harvard's Social Relations Department.

I was one of hundreds of students at Wisconsin who were introduced to the sociological and philosophical literature of Weimar Germany by Gerth. When in 1978, I called Susan Sontag to inform her of Gerth's death, her first words were, "I don't know what would have become of me if I had not known him." She had never been a student at the University of Wisconsin, yet in a more powerful way, Gerth had educated her. While she and her husband Philip Reiff were students at the University of Chicago, they visited Gerth on weekends at his home not far from Madison where, sitting at Gerth's feet, they listened to the monologues he was famous for delivering to any audience of worthy listeners. Their encounter with Gerth was a turning point in their lives. As he did for other parochial American students, Gerth opened my eyes to an intellectual world that I barely understood, one that I admired out of all proportion to my ignorance of it. For good reason, I thought of The New School as an exotic place. Taking a job there at a salary too low to support my family seemed a small sacrifice for an opportunity to join the Graduate Faculty. I was eager to learn more about it.

Founded by the leading editors of *The New Republic* and dissident Columbia University historians and philosophers (Charles Beard, James Harvey Robinson, and John Dewey) in 1917, The New School for Social Research has always occupied an ambiguous place in the culture of New York City and the higher learning in America. Committed to social reform, social criticism, cosmopolitan internationalism, and cultural modernism, it was generously supported by New York's uptown wealthy German Jews and the lower Fifth Avenue Protestant elite, mostly Presbyterians. In its earlier years, it held to a policy of refusing to accept endowments on the grounds that they interfered with the intellectual independence of its faculty. Nicolas Murray Butler, then Columbia's President, never relented in his efforts to denigrate and even eradicate The New School because he regarded it as subversive of American values. The New School lived most of its history in an academic no-man's-land, outcast because of its image as an unconventional and radical, if not revolutionary, non-degree-granting experimental adult educational institution operating out of the rebellious milieu of Greenwich Village. Throughout its history, it specialized in harboring iconoclastic, independent-minded, critical thinkers. Some of these were unwanted by other universities. For instance, The New School hired Thorstein Veblen and W. I. Thomas, both fired by President William Rainy Harper of the University of Chicago. Veblen's economic writings offended John D. Rockefeller, the school's major benefactor. Thomas had allegedly bedded another faculty member's wife. When he was accused of the impropriety by Harper, he is said to have responded: "Well, I've tried them all, and they're no good." The school also hired Horace Kallen, a Jew fired by the University of Wisconsin for opposing the ideology of assimilation, as well as Alexander Goldenweiser and Bernard J. Stern, both left-leaning anthropologists. But The New School also gave refuge to a whole coterie of remarkably talented and employable European intellectuals exiled by European fascist governments, including Hans Speier, Emil Lederer, Gerhard Colm, and Max Wertheimer. The New School was always in financial trouble and aroused the concern of its major patron, the Rockefeller Foundation, which thought The New School's faculty to be excessively foreign and Jewish.

The Graduate Faculty was only a small part of The New School for Social Research. While the school itself was founded as the first non-degree granting adult education center in the history of American education, the Graduate Faculty became certified in 1934 to grant advanced degrees (the MA and PhD degrees in anthropology, economics, political science, philosophy, psychology, and sociology). Later, the Graduate Faculty also offered a master's and doctoral degree in social science for candidates who had already achieved the doctorate. From its very beginnings, the Graduate Faculty elected its own officers, prepared its own budget, determined its own curriculum, and was solely responsible for hiring and firing faculty. The Board of Trustees of The New School for Social Research included a Graduate Faculty governing committee that guaranteed the autonomy of the Graduate Faculty within the larger structure of The New School. The Graduate Faculty's independence was established without objection from the New York State Board of Regents. Later, however, this arrangement was deemed illegal, and the Board's autonomous governing committee for the Graduate Faculty was abolished. But the original plan successfully instituted a relationship of simultaneous autonomy and cooperation between two entities with very different educational aims. Briefly, the Graduate Faculty could not survive without the financial backing of The New School for

Social Research, but it did not wish to be identified with The New School's adult education curriculum.

The adult division catered to thousands of non-degree students choosing courses from an academic cafeteria that contained offerings ranging from wine tasting to cooking, painting, ancient philosophy, and Shakespeare. Its professors were drawn from the vast array of talent in New York City. They were non-tenured faculty paid on a piece-work basis at the rate of fifty percent of each student's fee, whatever the tuition for a given lecture or course might be. The fee to attend a single lecture by a well-known public figure was usually ten dollars. Erich Fromm, in the 1950s, gave lectures attended by 500 paid subscribers and thus earned $2,500 per lecture. It was a system that attracted celebrities and specialists in almost any field who, in turn, gave the school its cachet and cash. There were no tenured professors, few administrators, no medical insurance, no retirement costs, and no property taxes. The adult division thus had low overhead and high profit margins on the sale of its products.

By contrast, the Graduate Faculty's economics were exactly the opposite: high overhead in the form of fixed salaries for tenured professors and low income from tuitions and student fees. Because the Graduate Faculty never paid its own way, it was always the pariah division in The New School apparatus in the eyes of the school's administrators.

From the early 1920s to the mid-1950s, The New School survived on the strength, determination, and conviction of its leading figure, Alvin Johnson, a scholar-administrator-editor, reared of Danish Protestant immigrant stock and educated in heartland Nebraska. He was a university president who governed less by consensus than by a sense that his educational mission was righteous, an academic entrepreneur who believed his creation of The New School provided its own vindication.

In one sense, The New School has always been cosmopolitan, the quintessential New York institution, especially in its rejection of cultural philistinism. But not even New York City, let alone the rest of the country, was prepared to receive the brand of European culture brought to it by political refugees escaping from fascism and Nazism in the 1930s. Alone among American universities, The New School under Alvin Johnson's direction had the foresight and courage to bring to the United States German, Italian, French, and Spanish intellectuals whose lives were endangered because they were unwilling to submit to the demands of totalitarian states. In 1924, in connection with his work on a projected seven-volume edition of the *Encyclopaedia of the Social Sciences*, Johnson had traveled to Europe seeking scholars to make contributions to this project. There he met Emil Lederer and many other top European social scientists. It was on the strength of his familiarity with continental social scientists that, in 1933, Johnson was able to recruit the scholars who became the first faculty of the University in Exile.

But starting a school requires money. And Johnson became legendary for his unorthodox money-raising methods. A famous story recounts how he got a grant from the Rockefeller Foundation for the purpose of rescuing Europe's social scientists. As he walked uptown from West 12th Street to Rockefeller Center to meet with Rockefeller executives, he contemplated the amount of money he needed, raising the ante with each block he traversed. By the time he reached midtown, he had settled on a sum of five million dollars. To his surprise, the Rockefeller boys gave him that amount without a blink. This began the myth of Johnson's money-raising legerdemain. But the reality was that Johnson knew how to cultivate the loyalty of people with money and influence. For example, he selected as the preliminary governing committee of the University in Exile Charles Burlingham of the New York Bar Association; Wilbur Cross, Governor of Connecticut; John Dewey, Professor of Philosophy, Emeritus, Columbia University; Felix Frankfurter, Professor of Law, Harvard University, later member of the United States Supreme Court; Ernest Gruening, Department of Insular Affairs, later Governor of Alaska and United States Senator from Alaska; Oliver Wendell Holmes, former justice of the United States Supreme Court; Robert M. Hutchins, President of the University of Chicago; Robert M. MacIver, Professor of Sociology, Columbia University; and Herbert Bayard Swope, a noted journalist and incomparable publicist who made and broke the careers of several New York luminaries in the early twentieth century. Among the Board of Trustees, headed by Ira A. Hirschmann, were Benjamin J. Buttenweiser, Elio Deming Pratt, Eustace Seligman, Hiram J. Halle, Howard M. Morse, and Francis T. P. Plimpton. Those were illustrious names and influential personages. Collectively, they made it possible for Alvin Johnson to make his claim on the Rockefellers for five million dollars.

The original University in Exile faculty included nine professors: Emil Lederer (its first dean who had been a Full Professor at Berlin University where he occupied the chair previously held by Werner Sombart), Frieda Wunderlich, Karl Brandt, Hans Speier (its first secretary), Max Wertheimer, Arthur Feiler, Eduard Heimann, Gerhard Colm, and Erich von Hornbostel. The University in Exile faculty members' conception of sociology, for instance, included philosophical schools, political theory, politics, and political economy.

Karl Mannheim had been invited to join the original faculty, but he disappointed Lederer by rejecting the invitation and choosing to stay in England. Mannheim already had a reputation in the United

States, and his presence would certainly have added luster to the new faculty. His refusal was considered a blow to this fledgling group.

Beginning in 1934 and continuing throughout the 1940s, faculty appointments were selected from among other émigré scholars, including Hans Staudinger, Jacob Marschak, Kurt Rietzler, Arnold Brecht, Leo Strauss, Max Ascoli (student of Benedetto Croce), Carl Mayer, Albert Salomon, Hans Neisser, Erich Hula, Kurt Goldstein, Salomon Asch, Julia Meyer, and Alfred Schutz. One American, Horace Kallen, a student of American pragmatism, was added as a gesture to the faculty's host country. With the addition of these and other new appointments, the faculty was constituted into five departments: sociology-anthropology, economics, psychology, philosophy, and political science.

A myth has since circulated that the Graduate Faculty was primarily or even entirely Jewish in its composition, but this was hardly the case. It was made up primarily of Germans and German Jews. The Jews among them—at least those I later met—were indistinguishable in their social character, cultural styles, or their secular attitude from the Germans. When I joined the Graduate Faculty in 1960, it still observed only two calendar holidays—Washington's and Lincoln's birthdays—signifying the faculty's acceptance of American political values. On principle, it observed no religious holidays, a standard established by the original faculty in 1933. The Graduate Faculty was meant to be an aggressively secular institution upholding Enlightenment ideals of scholarship and inquiry.

Indeed, the secular idealism of the Graduate Faculty was expressed in its original constitution ratified by the faculty and the Board of Trustees in 1935. Article I reads:

In order to assure the continued application, in the conduct of its affairs, of those principles of academic freedom and responsibility that have ever been the glory of The New School, it shall be a condition of the appointment of every member of the Board of Trustees, every regular member of the Faculty, the President, and every member of the administrative staff of The New School that he: (a) accept the obligation to follow the truth of scholarship wherever it may lead, regardless of personal consequences; (b) shall not be a member of any political party or group which asserts the right to dictate in matters of science or scientific opinion; (c) bind himself, both individually and when acting collectively with others in all official action, especially in recommendations and elections to the Faculty in promotion of members thereof, to be guided solely by considerations of scholarly achievement, competence and integrity, giving no weight whatsoever to scientifically irrelevant considerations such as race, sex, religion or such political beliefs as present no bar upon individual freedom of thought, inquiry, teaching and publication.

The ideas in this statement had their origins in experiences that Graduate Faculty members had had in Germany, especially on the issues of race and political affiliation. The Nazis routinely dismissed anyone they thought politically unreliable or anyone who didn't accept the Nazi party's political philosophy or its versions of academic standards. The refugees' idealism was rooted in the pre-Nazi German University and perhaps in their adherence to the values articulated in Max Weber's essay, "Science as a Vocation." But the statement also revealed some misconceptions about how university presidents and deans in American universities think about and use their authority.

I certainly agreed then, and still agree now, with the high-minded ideals in this statement, though they are regularly violated in practice. As The New School rationalized and professionalized its administration, the clarity of its originating principles, including those governing research and scholarship, often got blurred under the pressures of organizational exigencies, administrative demands, the multiplicity of competing truths, and ideologies.

The University in Exile had set itself up as a self-governing, democratic institute for graduate studies in the social sciences. This operating conception was an extension of The New School's original *modus operandi*, but it was also a child of circumstance as much as it was Alvin Johnson's creation. Its members' experiences with fascism committed the faculty to the political defense of freedom. Their European training had inculcated in them an interdisciplinary attitude toward the social sciences. In the 1930s, its faculty taught and wrote passionately about issues that had directly touched their lives.

From the beginning, the faculty's intellectual orientation was focused on social theory in the traditions of Kant, Hegel, Marx, Weber, Durkheim, and Simmel, with attention to phenomenology, Gestalt psychology, and classical political theory in the Straussian tradition and on political economy that addressed problems of unemployment, labor, the work force, state finance, and monetary and fiscal policies that had their origins in Weimar economic planning right after the First World War. The integrating theme that gave a common intellectual ground to these diverse approaches was German fascism, the rise of Hitler, and the social psychological and political consequences of his regime.

The forum for the faculty's debates was the General Seminar, a weekly meeting of the entire faculty given over to a member's presentation of a paper and a discussion of it. In the years 1934-1939, the faculty's concerns and problems were theoretical and practical, scientific and political, European and American. Coming from a European intellectual milieu in which debate can be personally antagonistic, the faculty focused on divisive topics: fascism, democracy, freedom, public opinion and propaganda, economic policy, mass psychology, and social-political psychology. Most faculty writings of this period may be found in the early issues of *Social Research*, a journal created by Johnson to provide the faculty with an outlet for the expression of ideas and to force them to begin writing in the English language.

In their seminar discussions, faculty brought to bear theoretical and firsthand political experience earned in universities, ministries, union halls, and the streets of Germany, Spain, and Italy. Emil Lederer, an economist and social theorist (and author of *The New Middle Class*; *State of the Masses: The Threat of the Classless Society*; and *The Problem of the Modern Salaried Employee*, among many other works); political scientists Frieda Wunderlich (author of *British Labor and the War*, *Labor under German Democracy*, and *Farm Labor in Germany*); Max Ascoli (author of *Intelligence in Politics* and *The Power of Freedom*); Hans Staudinger, a civil servant (author of *The Inner Nazi: A Critical Analysis of Mein Kampf*); Hans Speier, a sociologist (author of *German White Collar Workers and the Rise of Hitler*); and Kurt Riezler (author of *Man, Mutable and Immutable*) were representative authors in that faculty. As socialists and liberals, theoreticians and empiricists, economists, sociologists, and political scientists, they brought to America a worldly intelligence and confronted each other in the small enclave that was the Graduate Faculty. They attempted to understand, define, and defeat the political forces that had forced them into exile.

The Graduate Faculty came to define fascism in terms of its democratic opposite. In shaping their image of totalitarianism that anticipated Hannah Arendt's work on the subject by two decades, faculty members working on the subject gradually had to abandon ideas and ideals intrinsic to European social thought, that is, intellectuals' almost instinctive affinity for socialism instead of capitalism. But it's a mistake to understand the Graduate Faculty's consensus about the nature of totalitarianism and democracy as a consequence of its members' cultural Americanization. In fact, these scholars' work in America continued investigations already well begun in Europe, and some faculty members stressed the continuities in European social and political life both before and after the fascist takeovers in 1922 (Italy) and 1933 (Germany). To be sure, their ideas changed in the context of their experiences in the American diaspora. Certainly exposure to America's raucous political life shaped their images of the nature of modern political democracy. It was this mix of life experiences that provided the source of the University in Exile's creativity, a creativity fostered by social and intellectual marginality.

From its beginnings, the émigré generation suffered a slow process of attrition. Erich von Hornbostel, the psychologist and eminent ethnomusicologist, died in 1935, and Dean of Faculty Emil Lederer died in 1939. Age differences among the faculty at the time of emigration accounted for a steady succession of retirements. The end of the war in 1945 made it possible for some émigrés to return to their homelands. Despite the length of their American sojourn, the impulse to return to Europe was common among most of the Germans, including among those who were Jews.

Arnold Brecht, as late as 1938 and at the risk of his life, returned to Germany for visits. While in America, he always lived in two rooms in a hotel with a rented piano, never doubting his final return to his homeland. Alfred Schutz, in his essay, "The Homecomer" wrote: "What belongs to the past can never be reinstated in another present exactly as it was ... the perspectives have changed." Benita Luckmann's essay "The New School: Variations on the Return from Exile and Emigration" recounts the experiences of some of those who returned. When the war was over in 1945 so was the necessity of exile. Hans Speier returned to Germany in 1945 in an American military uniform. In his book *From the Ashes of Disgrace*, he says he went back as an American, yet his impulse was to return to the streets of Berlin searching for the house that had been his parents' home and his birthplace. He could not forget or put aside his past or, as he put it, "that damned Hitler [who] has taken Germany away from me." Hannah Arendt has since become the most famous case because of her relationship with Heidegger. When she returned to Germany in 1949 as a representative of an organization for Saving Jewish Culture, her experience of hearing German spoken on the street "made me incredibly happy," and this was despite her observation that the turning point in her memory was not the year 1933, but the day when she heard about Auschwitz. Karl Löwith went back to Heidelberg in 1952, choosing to return at the first opportunity that came to him. Werner Marx, who had been Löwith's student at the Graduate Faculty, left for Freiburg in 1962. The moment Carl Mayer retired in 1965, he left for Switzerland. Adolph Lowe returned to Germany to live in retirement with a daughter. Those who did not return to Europe felt homeless except for their ties to the Graduate Faculty, the only community they had in America. Most continued their associations with the Graduate Faculty, regularly attending seminars, even after they achieved mandatory emeritus status at the age of 75 and were not permitted to lecture. Benita Luckmann reports in the words of Arnold Brecht: "They wandered around the school looking a little lost." In this country and in Europe, the generation of émigrés found different ways to come to terms with ambivalent feelings about their countries of origin and adoption. Matthias Greffrath in his book, *Die Zerstörung einer Zukunft: Gespräche mit emigrierten Sozialwissenschlaftlern*—a collection of interviews with Hans Gerth, Günther Anders, Marie Jahoda, Adolph Lowe, Leo Lowenthal, Karl August Wittfogel, Toni Oelsner, and Alfred Sohn-Rethel—gives poignant examples of the double marginality felt by his subjects. Germany was no longer what it was when they left, and America, now in the midst of a Cold War conflict with the Soviet Union, left them without space in either world. They had become artifacts of a lost past. Gerth had returned to Germany in 1971 to take a Professorship at Frankfurt University only to be confronted by radical students who disrupted his lectures, invaded his office, removed his library, and left his office in a shambles. He remained a professor, but he never taught another course. For the upcoming generations of students, the émigrés had become part of a past to be celebrated or excoriated in books about them. In reports like H. Stuart Hughes's *The Sea Change*, Anthony Heilbut's *Exiled in Paradise*, Tom Wolfe's *From Bauhaus to Our House*, Peter Rutkoff's and William Scott's *New School*, Dagmar Barnouw's *Weimar Intellectuals and the Threat of Modernity*, Claus-Dieter Krohn's *Intellectuals in Exile*, and Lewis Coser's *Refugee Scholars in America*, a mythology about them was created. Refracted back onto the Graduate Faculty, the mythology became mythic history after the refugee faculty had exhausted itself or expired; its reputation in academia acquired a halo that distinguished it from the dominant American tradition of positivism and pragmatism. Its social-scientific orientation was thought to be European in the tradition of Weber, Marx, and Durkheim: humanistic, critical, historically oriented, and sympathetic to the integration of political theory, psychology, and philosophy. Aided and abetted by its association with the origins of The New School for Social Research and its early faculty including John Dewey, Thorstein Veblen, Horace Kallen, and Bernard J. Stern, it could also be thought to be a hotbed of Greenwich Village radicalism and critically oriented social sciences. The truth was that the problems that had energized the Graduate Faculty in the 1930s and 1940s—fascism, constitutionalism, political economy, Gestalt psychology, and the puzzles of ancient and European philosophy—had either disappeared from its agenda or no longer had salience in the curriculum.

When I arrived in 1960, many of the distinctive features of the original faculty had long since withered away. The General Seminar used to be organized around thematic topics each semester of the academic year: for example, "Methods and Objectives of the Social Sciences" (1935), "Public Opinion in the United States," and "Liberalism Today" (1939-1940). On some occasions, the seminar was open to the public. It had been used as an instrument both to forge the group into a faculty and to serve as a meeting place for other expatriate intellectuals. The early seminars attracted academics from other schools in the city. Kurt von Fritz, a classical scholar, and Paul Tillich, then at the Union Theological Seminary, were frequent visitors. The seminars were often jointly given by scholars from different disciplines, say, a sociologist, philosopher, and psychoanalyst as in a seminar given one year by Hans Speier, Max Wertheimer, Kurt Riezler and Karen Horney. The seminar's distinctive feature was its stress on addressing specific problems from a variety of points of view. In that sense, it was unselfconsciously interdisciplinary. To be sure, departmental and academic specialization had not yet stifled broad learning in American universities. That came later. But the organizational forms developed by the Graduate Faculty were still singularly idiosyncratic. Departments were loosely formed groups headed by a "spokesman," not a chairman. Papers presented at seminar symposia were published in *Social Research*, and thus the journal reflected the lines of inquiry addressed by the faculty. However, in the long run, this synergy between the journal and an interdisciplinary faculty was not sustained. The seminar lost its function as an interdisciplinary faculty forum and as a source of material for publication in *Social Research*. Under pressure from the American academic marketplace, departmentalization of the faculty became more rigid. Departmental spokesmen became chairmen in a more formally organized administrative hierarchy. As the members of the original faculty expired, so too did many of the institutions they created.

But despite its transformations and its adaptations to American academic norms, the Graduate Faculty survived its past. I was a member of this new faculty for forty years. This is the story of that part of my life and career in and around 66 West 12th Street.

The Graduate Faculty in 1960: Some Realities

In 1960, The New School and the Graduate Faculty were housed in two buildings spanning a space between 12th and 11th Streets between Fifth and Sixth Avenues. Its main entrance was at 66 West 12th Street.

Between the two buildings at ground level was an open courtyard approximately 200 by 200 feet in size referred to in jest as the campus; it contained several stone benches and sculptures. Hanging over the courtyard at the third-floor levels of the buildings was an enclosed passageway that linked the six-story buildings to each other. The president's office was on the sixth floor of 66 West 12th where he presided over both The New School's adult education divisions and the Graduate Faculty.

The Graduate Faculty offices were on the second floor of the 11th Street building. Its windows faced the courtyard below, and the office's occupants were visible to passersby crossing the third floor walkway. The entire faculty of some forty professors were housed in six offices—one for the dean and one for each of the departments of economics, philosophy, political science, psychology, and sociology-anthropology. The dean's secretary, Henny Greenberg, was shared by the entire faculty of about thirty full-time members. A conference room located at the end of the hall was capable of seating the entire faculty. A registrar's office not much larger than the conference room faced 11th Street: its staff consisted of Mary Lynn, who was the registrar, and two assistants. Between the conference room and the registrar were an elevator shaft and a stairway, both of which led to the third-floor cafeteria. A small library administered by Ester Levine was in the basement of the 11th Street brownstone. I never visited that library. The layout of the Graduate Faculty suggested intimacy and bore no resemblance to the architectural arrangements of any other university I had known.

The office of each department was furnished with two metal desks, each with six drawers, and four chairs, two on wheels with cushioned chairs for faculty and two straight-backed chairs for students when consulting with professors. Six or seven faculty members and part-time appointees shared the desks and drawers. These offices could not be used for writing or research. Professors had their own offices and libraries in their homes, a sign that the university had not yet separated the professor from the tools of his trade. The space was small, but, in practice, it was adequate for the purposes at hand. Professors taught their courses on different days and at different hours, but only between 4 p.m. and 8 p.m. Enrollments were low. My own course enrollments averaged about ten students. If ever three professors wished to consult with students at the same time, one of us repaired to the cafeteria and used it as a temporary office. The simplicity, the total lack of pretentiousness, of these accommodations was accepted as matter of fact by both professors and students. What mattered was the lingering mystique of the European intellectual émigrés who courageously opposed fascism and left to us, their successors, an enduring social science legacy. That the faculty was small and housed in compact quarters was not only unimportant, but suggested a positive absence of a bureaucratic hierarchy.

In the academic year 1960-61, Abbot Kaplan acted as the school's interim president. Hans Simons, the president when I was hired, had died. A search was underway for a new president. It came as a great surprise and disappointment to me to learn that Alfred Schutz had also died in 1959. I didn't know much of his work, but I had heard of him from Harold Garfinkel while I was at Harvard. Garfinkel used to travel to New York to listen to Schutz's lectures on phenomenology. In the late 1950s, Schutz was the department's most publicly visible member for precisely the reason that fascism was no longer his concern or his problem. These deaths, I found, coincided with a university-wide fiscal crisis in the order of budgetary deficits of several hundred thousand dollars. Deficits, I learned, were common occurrences, almost a tradition, covered annually by Clara Meyer, the adult education division's dean and vice-president of the school and a wealthy uptown German Jew who had been in the habit of playing this role for many years. Clara Meyer was not the only such benefactor, although she was an exceptionally important one among a group of downtown and upper West Side liberals who thought of The New School as their major charity. Some of these benefactors were trustees, but others were not. I met some of the latter at Johnson's ninetieth birthday party in 1964. Frail, but still robust of voice, surrounded by a bevy of older women well into their later years, he gave a speech recounting the past of The New School. When he finished, this cluster of women cheered and screamed in a style reminiscent of the screams of a group of bobbysoxers. Could this group have been the economic foundation of the school? It seemed so, for they all appeared to love Alvin with a passion far exceeding anything evoked by formal institutional loyalties. The significance of this scene was clear to me. It marked the end of The New School's epoch of charismatic leadership and patrimonial administration. I had joined a faculty whose economic future was dubious.

Henry David, an American who affected an English accent, had been appointed to succeed Hans Staudinger as the Graduate Faculty's dean in 1959-60. Carrying out a charge to rebuild the faculty, it was David who had hired me and, unbeknownst to me until the day I arrived, Thomas Luckmann as well. Luckmann was to replace Schutz and I was to replace May Edel, an adjunct anthropologist. Luckmann commuted from Geneva, New York, where his family lived and where he had been teaching at William and Hobart College. I commuted from Storrs, Connecticut. Neither of us could afford to live with our families in the metropolitan region, so we shared an apartment on Jane Street in Greenwich Village.

Luckmann and I both descended from Slovenian parents. He had grown up in Jeseniča, a steel mill town to the north of Kropa where my parents were born and from which they emigrated. His grandfather and father had been the prewar owners of Jesceniča's steel mill while my own ancestors had been smiths. His father had sided with the Germans and was killed by the partisans. As a child, Luckmann was sent to Germany for schooling. He was too young to participate in the war and came to the United States as an émigré at war's end. As different as were the trajectories of our lives—one the son of an industrialist knighted by Franz Josef and the other the son of an industrial worker who was a foot soldier in Franz Josef's army—we were now the Slovenian future of the Graduate Faculty's sociology-anthropology program. Brought together entirely by chance, our fates were now tied to that of Henry David.

David moved very fast. After one year as a dean, he was appointed president of The New School. He made Howard White, son-in-law of Kurt Riezler, acting dean of the Graduate Faculty, and late in his first year, he fired Clara Meyer as Dean of the Adult Education Division, presumably because her influence with trustees was greater than his and because she opposed his plans. He received a grant from the Heckscher family's Twentieth Century Fund for a conference designed to plan a study of poverty, a theme that John F. Kennedy had taken up in his 1960 campaign for the presidency, later reinforced by Michael Harrington's *The Other America*, published in 1962. David had also entered into negotiations with the United States space program with the idea of securing grants from the federal government. He made me a member of the poverty conference and recruited an old friend of mine from the University of Wisconsin, Robert J. Lampman, who had made a career as an economist studying inequalities in income distribution. Even while he was president, he taught a joint class in American political thought with Saul Padover and me. David had a plan for remaking the Graduate Faculty in his own image and made me one of his accomplices in this project.

Having learned of the school's economic precariousness, I considered my prospects. Judging that recruiting outsiders to join the staff posed problems, I realized that I was an administrator's asset. To safeguard my position, I applied to be considered for tenure during my second year. I qualified as an applicant because I had an appointment as an associate professor and had presented a paper to the faculty's general seminar—a prerequisite before applying for tenure. After the department supported my application, I was called by David, who informed me that Adolph Lowe of the economics department requested a postponement of consideration until the following year. I rejected Lowe's suggestion. When I mentioned this to Carl Mayer, my chairman and the person who submitted my application to the president, Mayer was not surprised. Indeed, he advised that I had done the right thing. And Lowe acquiesced and did not push his point to the faculty at large. This was my first indication of a tradition of friction between the Graduate Faculty departments, a conflict whose origins lay in what was already a murky past. But, within just two years, I had become tenured, learned more about the inner-workings of the school, and had served under two deans and two presidents.

Firing Clara Meyer was David's fatal mistake. At the end of his second presidential year, the board fired David. The board's action was meant as a gesture of reconciliation to Meyer. Meyer, who felt she had not been adequately defended by the board when David forced her out, did not accept the gesture and from that point on dissociated herself from the school and ceased providing the subventions needed to meet the school's annual deficits. So began the urgency to put the school's finances on a more rational foundation.

To replace David as president, the Trustees chose as acting president Robert MacIver, who was himself a trustee and the vice-chair of the trustees' executive committee and formerly a distinguished professor of sociology at Columbia University. He was also the father-in-law of Robert Bierstedt who was then a sociology professor at New York University. The trustees expected MacIver to conduct a search for candidates to replace himself, but this was not to be the case. He wanted to be the president of a university, took the job seriously, and tried to generate money-making research projects. At the time, I was invited by Venezuela's *Centre de Estudios del Desarrollo* to design a study of Venezuelan leaders. I designed the study, but backed out of the project when it was taken over by MIT's study on third-world leaders headed by Max Millikan. I did not belong with that group, but still MacIver urged me to stay with it fearing the loss of overhead funds for The New School. He liked his new job enough to pressure me not to leave the MIT connection. At age eighty, the job gave him a new lease on life, leading him to drag his heels on conducting the search for his replacement. It was only under pressure from the trustees that he resigned and then only after his second year (1964-65) on the condition that he be appointed the director of a newly created Center for New York City Affairs, an entity created and financed by Jacob M. Kaplan explicitly to move MacIver out of the presidency. In his place, the trustees appointed John (Jack) R. Everett, the recently resigned president of the City University of

New York. Everett later hired as his Chancellor Harry D. Gideonse, a former president of Brooklyn College known for his pacification of radicalism at that school. Everett served as president of The New School from 1965-1983, a period during which The New School made a series of corporate acquisitions and rationalized its administration and accounting.

The virtues of intellectual independence accruing to The New School from its policy of rejecting endowments from vested interests made it a cash-and-carry institution. In practical terms, the school's lack of an endowment meant that its budget was regularly balanced by *ad hoc* bailouts. Students' tuition and fees had never been sufficient to meet its operating budget.

Let me illustrate the deficit-driven economy of the Graduate Faculty by the case of the sociology-anthropology department. The department had five full-time professors and four adjunct or visiting professors. As an associate professor, I was paid $9,500 and Luckmann about the same. So our combined costs came to about $20,000. The New School did not then have a retirement plan; most of the émigré professors eventually received retirement benefits from German sources. The three full professors received salaries of $20,000 each, so the salary budget for the full-time faculty came to about $80,000. The four part-timers were paid $2,000 to $4,000 each, depending on the number of courses each taught. So the total departmental budget for salaries was less than $100,000. Each of the five departments was staffed at about the same rate, making the total faculty salary budget for the entire Graduate Faculty roughly a half million dollars annually. Even if there had been a cost-accounting system for allocating to departments charges for support services—office space, classroom use, telephones, and other charges such as heat and electricity on a prorated basis—such charges did not add excessive amounts to departmental budgets. Incomes produced by departments were far below their costs.

In the academic year 1958-1959, tuition fees were $25 per credit or $75 per course. A full-time student enrolled in four courses paid a maximum of $300.00. There was a registration fee of $6, a library fee of $1, and maintenance-of-status fee of $20 per year. A charge of $30 was imposed on a student at the completion of the degree. The Graduate Faculty also sponsored a student organization called the Cosmopolitan Club for which students paid $1 for membership. The cost per year to a student for an education and a degree at the Graduate Faculty was about $700.00. At this rate, the department of sociology-anthropology needed the equivalent of about 150 full time students to meet its own payroll apart from its overhead costs. In practice, full-time equivalent enrollments were far less than this number, probably in the range of 50 to 75 at most, if one considered that average enrollments per class were in the range of 8 to 12. In budgetary terms, the Graduate Faculty was a financial burden.

But while the Graduate Faculty could not support itself, its value to The New School was out of all proportion to its economic fragility. It provided the institution with a halo of prestige not given by adult education. Its original faculty of émigré Europeans had bequeathed The New School a lasting and illustrious reputation. It shared this reputation with the Frankfurt School's Institute for Social Research on Morningside Heights, and vice versa. Taken together, these entities represented the elite of post-Marxian and post-Weberian European scholarship. Whatever the economic reality, the Graduate Faculty gave The New School its panache. Every president knew the panache that the Graduate Faculty gave to the New School, and none of them had the temerity to tamper with it, even under pressure from cost-accounting treasurers. As the jewel in the crown, the Graduate Faculty was sacrosanct even in the face of its deficits.

The jewel was in much worse financial shape than I had imagined. From its beginnings, it had been generously supported by uptown German Jewish philanthropists whose wealth was firmly secured in banking and natural resources. Their identification with the University in Exile affirmed their sense of themselves as representatives of Germany's great cultural and intellectual traditions. These men and women had Max Weber's books in their libraries. They were fully Americanized, though, and by the 1930s, they had not been accepted socially at a level commensurate with their wealth by New York Society. The University in Exile gave them a philanthropic opportunity to share their wealth with an American cultural institution. But by 1960, these philanthropic sources no longer existed. They were the last of a generation. Their descendents sought their status in other more prestigious New York philanthropic endeavors. When The New School needed the descendent generation's money, the new generation was giving to Lincoln Center, The Metropolitan Museum of Art, and Harvard University. The death of President Hans Simons in 1959, and Henry David's sacking of Clara Meyer, ended that source of revenue, and it had not been replaced with another. A natural revenue replacement source could and should have been the recently arrived waves of Eastern European Jews who had begun to make their fortunes on New York's Seventh Avenue in the rag trade. But Upper West Side Jews regarded this cohort as vulgar, uncultivated, and socially inferior. The New School, still chasing its past, lost an opportunity to tap into and socially legitimize a new source of philanthropy.

This certainly was not the case for Brandeis University, where I was moon-lighting on Mondays as a member of a graduate seminar on philanthropy at the Florence Heller School for Advanced Studies in Social Welfare. The Heller School's dean was Charles Schottland, a former director of the nation's Social Security system and a master fund raiser himself. One member of the seminar was Charles Francis Adams, scion of Boston's Adams family. Brandeis had been established in 1948 on the campus of a defunct medical school in Waltham, Massachusetts. Abram Sacher, its president, needing money, saw his future on New York's Seventh Avenue textile district. Brandeis University was named after United States Supreme Court Justice Louis Brandeis (from whose daughter I had taken a course on "The Economic History of New England" while I attended the University of Wisconsin). Sacher was an entrepreneur who had no inhibitions about the sources of money for his school. The joke was that Sacher had rooms, brooms, and chairs, as well as buildings named after donors. When a broom wore out, a new donor was found to buy another one. Here was a school that needed money and knew how to get it without concern for the social status of its sources. While the Graduate Faculty paid me a salary of $9,500 for a full-time load, Schottland paid me $5,000 for one seminar, plus additional stipends for supervising dissertations. The money I earned from Brandeis was what The New School failed to tap. Several years were lost before The New School began to compete with Brandeis on the same philanthropic field. The event that signified The New School's shift in orientation to the acceptance of Jewish textile money was the mid-1960s gift to the school of a new Graduate Faculty Center of Lane's Department Store on Fifth Avenue and 14th Street. This new generation of donors remembered that Alvin Johnson had rescued anti-Nazi and anti-fascist intellectuals, and they identified with the Graduate Faculty. They saw it as the bearer of European social, economic, and political thought, a reputation that demarcated it sharply from other

American social science graduate schools. That intellectual legacy was the invaluable bequest of the University in Exile to succeeding generations of faculty at The New School.

The Graduate Faculty in the 1960s

In the 1960s, émigrés in residence and still writing books were philosophers Hans Jonas, Aron Gurwitsch, and Werner Marx; political scientists Arnold Brecht, Otto Kirchheimer, and Erich Hula; economists Hans Neisser, Alfred Kahler, Adolph Lowe, and Hans Staudinger; psychologists Rudoph Arnheim, Solomon Asche, Hans Wallach, and Kurt Goldstein; and sociologists Carl Mayer, Albert Salomon, Julia Meyer, and Arvid Broderson. Their writings included Hans Jonas's *The Imperative of Responsibility*; Arnold Brecht's *Political Theory and The Political Education of Arnold Brecht: An Autobiography*; Otto Kirchheimer's *Political Justice: The Use of Legal Procedure for Political Ends*; Albert Salomon's *The Tyranny of Progress*; and Adolph Lowe's *On Economic Knowledge*. Still, despite their vitality, their days were numbered.

Over the years, in their efforts to preserve their intellectual identity, the émigrés did not hire many scholars who focused on American society and thought. The significant exceptions were Saul Padover, a political scientist who was a specialist in Thomas Jefferson and James Madison; Horace Kallen, foremost student of American Pragmatism and multiculturalism; and Dorian Cairns, a student of Charles S. Peirce and American philosophy. These appointments signified some commitment to American democratic and philosophical thought, but not an end to the faculty's émigré traditions.

In an effort to preserve the past, the émigrés appointed their own graduates: Howard White in political science (Kurt Riezler's son-in-law); Mary Henle in Gestalt psychology (Max Wertheimer's student);

Thomas Luckmann (a student of Alfred Schutz); Felicia Deyrup (Alvin Johnson's daughter); Bernard Rosenberg in sociology (a student of Albert Salomon); Oscar Ornati in economics (a Triestian Jew who once asked me what a Slovene was doing amongst so many Jews and answering his own question said, "I know some of your best friends are Jews," to which stereotype I replied with annoyance, "All of my best friends are Jews."); and Werner Marx and Murray Green in philosophy (students of Karl Lowith and Hans Jonas, respectively). Meant to preserve the Graduate Faculty's European intellectual orientation, such in-house appointments also suggested that the faculty lacked network connections into its host country's graduate schools. Inevitably, such efforts to replenish itself with its own graduates or Europeans could not be sustained. That they were not is symbolized by the appointment in 1958 of Joseph Greenbaum, an American-trained experimental psychologist, as the chair of the psychology department, and, in 1960, of David Schwartzman, a University of California economist, and me, with a degree in Social Relations from Harvard. Thus began the reconfiguration of the Graduate Faculty and its transformation into a hybrid European-American institution.

Carl Mayer and Albert Salomon presided over the reconstruction of the sociology department. I take this case as the paradigmatic example of what happened at the Graduate Faculty. The core of the departmental curriculum was oriented to European thinkers. Still, Mayer included some features of American sociology in the department's course offerings. Courses in statistics were taught each semester by adjunct professors Paul Neurath and Columbia-trained Henry Lennard. David Abrahamson and Bernard Rosenberg, both adjuncts, taught courses in criminology. Edward Saveth's course on "The American Aristocracy: History, Structure, and Ideology" represented a gesture to the faculty's professed commitment to the culture, politics, and origins of democratic institutions in early New England. However, Mayer's and Salomon's orientation to European thinkers gave the curriculum its profile.

Mayer taught courses in "Pareto's Sociology," "Religion and the Rise of Capitalism," "The Rise of Modern Anti-Semitism," and "Max Weber." His reputation was as a Weber scholar. But after many years of teaching, his rendition of Weber had become lifeless, almost like a Lutheran catechism. Undoubtedly, he had read and reread all of Weber's writings, but in his lectures, he reduced Weber's sociology to neatly categorized classifications of concepts. I learned this when I heard students mentioning phrases like "value neutrality," "types of political legitimacy," "religious rejections of the world," or the "Protestant Ethic and the Spirit of Capitalism," as if these represented invariant truths. Literally reading his lectures from a folder, he taught from canned notes. Since he taught from the same notes year after year, students constructed their own copies of these notes. Duplicates of them were transmitted from generation to generation of graduate students who used them in preparation for examinations, leading students to believe they could understand Weber without actually reading Weber's books. Forty years later, Cyrus Yegameh, one of Mayer's students, visited me. He remembered Mayer's Weber course and noted that he still had his course notes in outline form, organized point by point, in a bound folder. Given Mayer's pedagogical style, Weber's investigative spirit and his unique ability to frame intellectual problems were not communicated. It seemed that Mayer, mainly out of a sense of duty, felt motivated to introduce American students to Germany's greatest sociologist. Originally in the 1930s, Salomon taught this subject. But after publishing in *Social Research* three succinct essays evaluating the Weber oeuvre, he abandoned this subject, leaving Mayer to cover Weber. There is no evidence that any of Mayer's students carried forward the spirit of Weber's scholarship, although it is also true that Mayer contributed to the advancement and propagation of Weber as an icon in the sociological pantheon.

For his own part, Salomon taught an astonishing range of courses in the history of sociological ideas. In a single course, "Foundations of Sociology and Social Psychology," the authors he listed in his course description were Erasmus, Loyola, Pascal, Montaigne, Descartes, Fontenelle, Saint Simon, La Rochefoucauld, La Brugere, Machiavelli, Montesqueiu, Jean Bodin, Pierre Bayle, and Hobbes. He did not include Weber or other Germans in that list. Though he had published the Weber essays, he cut himself off from German thinkers when he learned of the Holocaust. For him, the Holocaust betrayed his intellectual heritage. (In a department meeting devoted to constructing the next year's course offerings, Mayer asked Salomon to teach a course on anti-Semitism. Salomon demurred, saying, "No, thank you, that's your problem, not mine.") After abandoning Weber, he started a love affair with French authors. He not only refused invitations to return to Germany, but came to terms with his American sojourn. In 1941-1942, he added American sociologists to his teaching curriculum. He taught a course called "The History of Sociology," in which he included Florian Znanieki, Robert MacIver, Talcott Parsons, Robert Merton, Robert Lynd, Howard S. Becker, Pitirim Sorokin, Georg Simmel, Max Weber (who appears as just another sociologist), and Thorstein Veblen. In 1945, he taught "Main Trends in the History of American Ideas" that focused on F. O. Mathiessen's *American Renaissance: Art and Expression in the Age of Emerson and Whitman*. Even as he adapted to his American milieu, his central concern was with the French, teaching its thinkers individually and collectively in such courses as "Balzac as a Sociologist." He wrote his lectures on cards that are preserved in abundance in his archives at the University of Konstanz and the Leo Baeck Institute in New York City. Salomon found his refuge in a Talmudic-like examination of sociological and philosophical texts, endlessly discovering, re-examining, and teaching the works of familiar and newly discovered thinkers, always finding in them their sociological relevance. To his students, he was an inexplicable phenomenon, a professor whose intellectual scope fascinated, intimidated, and overwhelmed them. His scholarship was formidable, but it lacked the audience it deserved at a time when the sociological profession was undergoing rampant academic professionalization and specialization.

Mayer and Salomon lived within the circumscribed world of the Graduate Faculty. While Salomon initiated correspondence with American sociologists, there is no evidence that either he or Mayer attended meetings of the American Sociological Association. When faced with the problem of reconstructing the department, they relied on the advice of their own graduates. In the first instance, these students were Thomas Luckmann and Bernard Rosenberg. Luckmann had studied with Alfred Schutz and was hired to replace Schutz, who had died the year before. On the strength of a recommendation from Joe Bensman, and a favorable review of *Small Town in Mass Society* in *Social Research*, Rosenberg promoted my candidacy as the department's first full-time anthropologist. These jobs were not advertised, nor was a search conducted for other candidates. I owed my job to Bernard Rosenberg, who was Albert Salomon's favorite student and who had written, under Salomon's supervision, a dissertation published as *The Values of Veblen*. Considering that Mayer and Salomon were reaching the ages of retirement, Luckman and I were in effect designated the future caretakers of the department. Two years later, Dennis Wrong and Peter Berger were hired. Again, neither of these positions was advertised and no other candidates were considered.

Wrong had written a dissertation on demography at Columbia under Kingsley Davis ("It was the easiest way to get through.") and earlier had been an assistant to George F. Kennan at the Princeton Institute for Advanced Studies. Teaching at the time at Brown University, he was a political sociologist associated with the magazines *Dissent* and *The New Leader*, New York's left-leaning anti-Stalinist journals. He had also favorably reviewed *Small Town in Mass Society* in *The New Leader*, a further indication of intra-familial incest. In Berger's case, the hand-in-glove relationship within the department was like a marriage of first cousins because he, like Luckmann, was one of its graduates. At the time, Berger was teaching at the Hartford Theological Seminary. He had not yet published any of the books that made him famous, but he became slated to be Carl Mayer's successor in the sociology of religion. In hindsight, these were impressive appointments of scholars whose later careers vindicated the department's, that is, Mayer's, choices.

My role in approving these appointments was only that of a rubber stamp. I was the outsider in this group, a minority of one who willingly acquiesced to these appointments, not only on the grounds of their intrinsic worth, but also because I hoped that the department and the Graduate Faculty remained in business. Thinking that I might influence the composition and academic direction of the department—actually, to retain its Weberian orientation—I nominated Hans Gerth as a candidate for a professorship. This was not just a mistake, but a blunder. My nomination was instantly vetoed by Mayer. Unbeknownst to me, Mayer had known Gerth in Germany and, in 1928, the two had had a run-in in a debate about Max Weber at a sociology meeting in Davos, Switzerland. Mayer, a man with a long memory, reacted to Gerth's name as if that encounter had occurred the previous week. I had inadvertently stumbled into one of the internecine Weber wars that were then flourishing on both sides of the Atlantic and had walked into a quicksand of a history whose source lay in the contrast between Gerth's Weberian-Marxism as opposed to Mayer's formal, religiously oriented Lutheran interpretation of Weber. Mayer's instant put-down of my recommendation should have taught me a lesson to stay away from this terrain, but I did not learn this lesson well enough. A year later, when Wrong left the department to take a position at New York University, I took the opportunity to push Joe Bensman as his replacement and nominated him for the position. The others knew that Joe and I were friends and collaborators. That I should have the effrontery to nominate my best friend did not seem to matter. After all, Berger and Luckmann were also co-authors and friends, so what might be called a practice of insider trading was a departmental norm. The department agreed to invite Joe to give a talk to the faculty as a whole, the usual procedure when presenting a departmental candidate. Following Joe's presentation, the department met to take a formal vote on the appointment. Mayer polled each member. Each voted yes until it came to Mayer, who said, "I must oppose," giving no reason. Despite Mayer's objection, I considered the vote favorable and asked that the approved nomination be forwarded to the faculty as a whole. At that general faculty meeting, I reported an affirmative vote of five in favor of Joe's appointment with one dissent, and the floor was opened for discussion. Much to my surprise, Berger and Luckmann, who had not informed me in advance, announced that they had changed their votes to no. This left the department without a positive recommendation. To my embarrassment, I learned that a commitment to a vote was malleable.

Up to that moment, I had kept Bensman informed in detail of the progress of his candidacy, leading him to believe it was a certainty.

Joe and I were shocked and disappointed. We had expected to be in the same department, an arrangement that would have made our collaboration much more efficient. When we assessed why this happened, we concluded that it was because Joe had been Gerth's foremost student. And Mayer's authority prevailed over the students of his enemy. From this experience, I learned two things. The first was that democratic procedure in academic affairs counted for little. The second was that I was the outsider in the departmental club.

I should mention that this was, in part, a language problem. While English was, of course, The New School's official language, Mayer, Salomon, Luckmann, and Berger usually spoke German with each other, switching to English in my presence. But when Mayer held department meetings at nearby Village restaurants, colloquial German was the language of choice among my four colleagues as we walked to and from meals. I didn't speak German, and my language deficiency reminded me of my marginal status. Because Henry David, who had co-opted me to further his own plans, had been sacked and Robert MacIver was being pushed out, I began to reconsider my future in a department that seemed increasingly inhospitable.

As the outsider and the only native-born American, my influence on departmental affairs was negligible. I had no administrative responsibilities. My duties in the department were minimal, limited to teaching three classes of two hours each per week that I could do on Wednesdays and Thursdays. I taught one course and attended department and general faculty meetings on Wednesday. I taught the other two courses on Thursday. Teaching six courses a year, I could accumulate a one-semester sabbatical after every third year of teaching or a full-year sabbatical after every sixth year. The sabbatical was an earned right that did not require the dean's approval. My two-day-a-week teaching schedule left me five free days. Breaks during intercessions and the summer months added more time to that freedom. Despite the low pay, I gained a lot of advantages by being affiliated with the Graduate Faculty. The most important advantage, of course, was that the prestige and intellectual status of the Graduate Faculty's old illustrious faculty was transferred to me simply because I was now a member of the Faculty. Unexpectedly, I gained an unearned enhancement of my reputation. I hadn't anticipated this, but I certainly accepted its consequences in both monetary and psychic rewards. I found I could both distance myself from the Graduate Faculty and enjoy the benefits of the status membership that it conferred.

My new found freedom and reputation gave me time to supplement my income and to carve out a way of life that was equal to that of a professor at a research university. I had a low-paying, high-prestige job that for four years enabled me to do other teaching and consulting and my own research on both America's new middle classes and politics in both Venezuela and Colombia.

I was offered and took jobs at Brandeis University and Clark University. I needed the money. It was easy work because I taught the same material I was teaching at The New School. For Clark and Brandeis, this did not matter. From their point of view, they could advertise me as a visiting professor from the Graduate Faculty. I gladly participated in being marketed in exchange for the money, but it was at considerable cost to my energy. Moonlighting at this pace was a form of self-exploitation and was not intellectually productive.

However, accepting Charles Schottland's offer to join the philanthropy seminar at Brandeis proved to be a genuine research opportunity. This seminar not only paid well, but concerned itself with the meaning of philanthropy as an American institution. American philanthropy had its origins in Calvinist conceptions of stewardship, wherein wealth holders, under an injunction from God, were obliged to give back their wealth to the community. Steward-ship became philanthropy. That this religious motivation had long since been transformed did not diminish philanthropic endeavors. Instead, philanthropy had become a big business in its own right, administered by philantropoids and development officers trained in university degree programs for the express purpose of cultivating and nursing potential donors to universities, foundations, and other charitable organizations. Its motivations were transvalued to gain-ing political advantages, tax exemptions, favorable public relations, and secular immortality. What had originally been a religious call-ing had become an exercise in rational calculation. Economically, philanthropy became a redistributive mechanism that alleviated class polarization and countered the Marxian prediction of mass immiseration and revolution. As it happened, that work dovetailed nicely with the research that Joe Bensman and I were doing for our book *The New American Society* that contains a chapter called "Phi-lanthropy and the Service Economy."

Our work on that book included data secured from several oth-er unorthodox sources. At the time, Joe was director of research at William Esty and Company. He was designing studies on various consumer products, and I did his field research. We drew our own conclusions from these studies and incorporated them into our con-ception of the emerging new middle classes. One of Joe's studies was sponsored by Milwaukee's Miller Brewing Company. The company's marketing division speculated that taste preferences for beer were moving to lighter varieties and that middle-class women, a highly desirable consumer target, might more readily drink a light beer if beer could be made a respectable drink for such women. Up to that point, beer was a drink for working-class men and women. The test of the hypothesis was to be conducted on a Boston area sample of heavy ale-drinking Irish working men who consumed a case or more of ale a day on weekends. These were men who cared little for social respectability despite earning good wages, but whose wives' social status was incommensurate with the family income. It was easy for an agency in Boston to find the sample.

The interviews focused on changes in taste from heavy as opposed to lighter beers: for example, Ballantine Ale as opposed to Rheingold beer. The results indicated that respondents' wives objected to the strength and inebriating effect of ale. Ale was the chosen beverage for heavy drinkers, but it carried with it the connotation of beer bellies, a slight high, and an incapacity for sex after drinking. Ale connoted low social status. On the strength of this study, the Miller Brewing Company introduced the slogan, "Miller High Life: the Champagne of Bottled Beers," a product addressed to women in the middle classes. It was meant to evoke champagne's elegance and to open the beer market to status-conscious women in the new suburbs. Unfortunately, the advertising campaign was ahead of its time. It failed and resulted in an economic crisis for the company. But the trend was validated. The middle-class women's beer market was opened up. "Light beers" later became a respectable drink for men and women. Specialists in the beer-marketing business taught us something about middle-class status symbols.

The beer study was one of four that focused on changing middle-class taste preferences. The other products were cigarettes, gasoline additives, and paper products. Almost all cigarette advertising in the 1960s stressed cigarettes' taste. Smooth, cool, refreshing, and menthol were the words then in use, the adjectives differentiating one brand from other. The Parliament brand, for example, in an effort to capture the women's market, came out with a longer cigarette with a recessed filter (designed to distance the tongue from contact with the filter). Despite advertising's emphasis on taste-smoking for the smoker, smoking was associated with bad breath, a need for nicotine, coughing, hacking, and personal discomfort. Nevertheless, among cigarette producers, appeals to taste defined the arena of competition, and so one of the objectives of the study was to find new vocabularies to describe taste. Interviewing smokers for this purpose proved to be a daunting task. As it happened, words used by informants to describe taste were the same as those used in Madison Avenue's advertising. Smokers entirely lacked vocabularies of their own to describe the "taste" of cigarettes. Based on this evidence, the sponsor of the study, Winston, concluded that it was pointless to search for new vocabularies. Instead, marketers invented the slogan, "Winston Tastes Good Like a Cigarette Should." A few years later, taste advertising disappeared from cigarette advertising. When the health hazards of smoking became a national issue, it was replaced by claims about the percentage of tar content in a cigarette. But the theoretical point remained the same. The power to impose a vocabulary is the power to define experience. For purposes of our research, we had rediscovered Orwell. We gained an empirical insight into the relationship between marketing and linguistic usage.

The claim of a gasoline additive manufacturer was that its product cleaned an automobile's engine by removing impurities like "sludge" produced by imperfect combustion of gasoline. Respondents were asked what they thought the additive accomplished. They believed that it purged the motor and the exhaust system of unwanted residues. When asked to describe the process of purging, our respondents evoked images of a digestive system; gasoline, from ingestion to elimination, passed through filters, pistons, and the exhaust system. In the consumer's usage, keeping motor parts clean was compared to that of a healthy diet. Analogical thinking allowed respondents to sustain their faith in the product despite their inability to conduct a reality check. Where there is a will to believe, reasons based on faith will be found. One can also note that comparing the complex nature of an internal combustion engine with that of the functioning of modern-state bureaucracies suggests that individuals in both instances lack the resources to comprehend political processes in a rational way.

The paper products study was sponsored by Kimberly-Clark, a major manufacturer of products such as toilet paper, hand towels, tissue paper (Kleenex), writing paper, envelopes, school pads, and typing paper. The study was designed to discover the distinctive product taste preferences of various family members. Our sample was drawn from my neighbors in Storrs. Housewives wanted envelopes the size of the checks with which they paid their bills. The adolescent daughter wanted thank-you-sized scented matching envelopes and stationery. The toilet paper shouldn't be too thin. Paper napkins should be serviceable for dinner parties. Such finely discriminated consumer taste preferences indicated that the middle classes were well on their way to becoming artful consumers, each according to his or her needs and preferences. Finely discriminated consumption standards ordinarily associated with the upper and upper-middle classes had descended to the new middle classes.

The Keynesian revolution and postwar prosperity—the beginnings of the short-lived Golden Age of American Capitalism—created a stratum of new middle classes whose lifestyles emulated those of the older middle and upper classes. Limited by fixed levels of income, their emulation was incomplete, and the choices of styles they pursued were largely shaped by the media and consumer magazines. Their political psychology was now linked as much to the influence exercised by media propaganda as by the rational evaluation of direct experience. C. Wright Mills's *White Collar* had relied for its perspective on Lederer's and Marschak's and Speier's studies of the German middle classes. Our fieldwork suggested that the American new middle classes, relative to other classes, had become much larger than Mills anticipated and more dependent on significant expansion in new service occupations. From a practical point of view, the advertising industry had its own formulas for understanding the changes occurring in the characteristics of the new middle classes. However, it saw these changes from the standpoint of the increasing segmentation by region, income, and lifestyles of consumer markets. The industry knew what to sell to whom, but it didn't draw the sociological or political implications of the trends to which it responded. Bensman and I extrapolated the industry's unanalyzed assumptions about the class structure and reported these and their political implications in *The New American Society*. Later, I continued this investigation in my edited volume *The New Middle Classes: Life-Styles, Status Claims, and Political Orientations*.

11

Excursus: Research in South America

Venezuela

I never anticipated doing research in South America, so it came as a surprise when Venezuela's Centro de Estudios del Desarrollo (CENDES), a research organization affiliated with Universidad Central de Venezuela, called on me for advice. As I mentioned earlier, I had known Romulo Betancourt while he was living in exile in Puerto Rico, and his daughter was one of my students. By 1960, Betancourt was again the president of Venezuela. I was now the former teacher and friend of a South American president's daughter. When the Venezuelan Sociological Association hosted a South American Sociological conference in 1961, I was an invited guest. During the conference, I was also invited to a reception at the president's mansion where I met Fernando Henrique Cardoso, a future president of Brazil, and William Faulkner, whose books I had read at the University of Wisconsin. Meeting Faulkner was something of a disappointment because he was already drunk and had no interest in talking about his books with still another reader of his works. But my association with Betancourt left the right impression on the people at CENDES. As a result, Jorge Ahumada, the director of CENDES, and his assistants, Jose Silva Michelena and Julio Cotler, asked me to visit CENDES headquarters where I was asked to design a plan for a study of Venezuela's leaders.

John F. Kennedy had by then declared a new South American policy called the Alliance for Progress. Fidel Castro's Cuban revolution had been successful and the Bay of Pigs Invasion had not only failed, but was an embarrassment to Kennedy's new administration. Beginning as not much more than a speech, the Alliance was premised on duplicating in the rest of Latin America what the United States had done in Puerto Rico in the years after World War II. The idea of the Alliance was attractive to the Organization of American States (OAS). The OAS affirmed that South American governments saw opportunities for economic aid and other forms of support to counter Cuban-inspired insurrectionary movements. Within a short period of time, dollars were flowing into Venezuela, Colombia, and other South American countries. The beneficiaries of some of these dollars were American social scientists, including myself.

Having only a layman's knowledge of the history and sociology of Venezuela, I was briefed in these matters by Jose Silva Michelena and Julio Cutter. My first lesson was given while dining in Caracas's elegant restaurants that also catered to the local elite. As expected, tables were chaired by politicians and likeminded businessmen. One table was frequently shared by CIA agents. Though the agents were supposed to be incognito, their distinctive attire distinguished them and, indeed, they were pointed out to me. Agents seemed to make no effort to conceal their identities, mingling freely with Caracans, as if their presence was an accepted condition of inter-American relations. I had not seen anything like this in Puerto Rico. My Latin American political education had begun.

The big issue was Venezuelan oil, especially that lying under Lake Maracaibo. No one could contest the importance of this oil to the United States, nor the holdings in it by the Rockefellers. Nelson

Rockefeller maintained a four-thousand-acre estate in that country. It wasn't possible to study Venezuela's leadership structure without considering absentee owners.

After a month sitting at a desk at CENDES, I came up with a research proposal titled *Research Project on Leadership and Power Relationships in Venezuela.* The following was my statement for the research's rationales:

> The study of leadership and power relations prepared below forms one part of a three-part study design aimed at examining the salient problems of Venezuelan social change. The other parts of this study's design are a study of class structure and a study of social integration. The dominant focus of the *Centro de Estudios del Desarrollo* centers on economic and social planning, particularly the statement of economic and social alternatives for the future development of Venezuelan society. It is a basic assumption of CENDES that it must rest its planning proposals on an awareness of existing economic and social realities of which the understanding of leadership, the distribution of power, and the interconnections between power groups constitute a fundamental precondition for all future planning.

Such organized and systematic planning as may take place depends on knowledge and assessment of:

1. Who are the major leaders in the country?

2. What are the leadership jurisdictions of the different leaders?

3. What are the interconnections between leaders whose jurisdictions differ?

> 4. What conflicts of interest and purpose exist between leaders?
>
> 5. From what perspective and on what levels of information do the leaders make their political judgments?
>
> 6. What, if any, are the historically stylized social, political, and economic patterns which lie beneath the emergence of types of leaders?
>
> We feel that answers to these questions will throw considerable light on how decisions are made, why decisions are made or not made and the probable direction of decisions under given political and economic circumstances.

The study called for in-depth interviews with 300 political leaders distributed over all institutions, including foreign investors and directors of foreign enterprises. Briefly, it meant interviewing such personages as Betancourt and Nelson Rockefeller. Lurking behind this design was both C. Wright Mills's book *The Power Elite*, published a few years earlier, and the leadership analysis that Bensman and I had done in our book *Small Town in Mass Society*. Mills had simply postulated the existence of the power elite. He had not conducted any empirical studies to verify it. In *Small Town in Mass Society*, we had the empirical data and analyzed the relationships between leaders and processes of decision-making. Venezuela, I thought, could be sociologically analogous to the microcosm of a small town, but in this case the study was that of a small country in a big world.

In retrospect, I can't imagine how this study could have succeeded even with its projected budget of a half-million dollars. I doubt that the information collected could be distilled into the mosaic of inter-institutional networks and *in camera* decision-making on which its conclusions would have to rest. It would have required the development of a unique theoretical framework for the governance of Venezuela—or any other small country in a dependency relationship with a super power. Nevertheless, its perspective was on target. This was confirmed for me a few years later when I was no longer a member of the project. I learned from a visit Betancourt made to see his grandson visiting at my home in Connecticut that he had made a private visit by train from New York City to Albany to confer with Nelson Rockefeller, who was then the Governor of New York. Nelson Rockefeller appeared to be Venezuela's absentee viceroy. No formal study of leadership or decision-making, whatever its methodology, could evoke this type of data.

For better or worse, my study was not carried out. Nor from the beginning did CENDES have any intention that I should do it. From CENDES's point of view, I was recruited for quite another purpose.

Jorge Ahumada, CENDES's director, knowing that the MIT Center for International Research was conducting a series of researches on leadership in third-world countries, submitted my proposal to MIT with a request for funding. MIT Director Max Millikan agreed to sponsor it, but on the condition that its staff join the project. As a consequence, I was invited to visit the MIT Center and met some members of its staff, including Shmuel Noah Eisenstadt, Daniel Lerner, and Frank Bonilla. MIT had its own formula for conducting such studies that it was then sponsoring in various parts of the world. MIT housed one of the major international centers then conducting counter-insurgency research.

Despite MIT's participation, I was to be included in the project. But, in Caracas, at a planning meeting between Lerner and Bonilla, both MIT representatives, and me, whom they called The New School group, it became clear to me that I did not belong to the MIT team. Consulting no one, I withdrew from the project with relief that a heavy weight had been lifted from my back. I remember that day vividly. It was the same day that the Cuban Missile Crisis reached its crisis point. Kennedy and Kruschev were having their showdown about the evacuation of Soviet missiles from Cuba. Soviet ships were steaming towards Cuba while Kennedy threatened to use atom bombs to deter them from reaching their destination. During those same hours, I was on a flight from Caracas to New York, unaware of what was taking place below the airplane on which I was sleeping. Eighteen years after Hiroshima and Nagasaki, the atom bomb had become a conventional instrument of diplomacy.

Extricating myself from this project was not without problems. It meant that I had to inform President Robert MacIver of The New School of my withdrawal and, as I mentioned earlier, he was eager to have me continue. It also meant disappointing my family. The children had already begun making plans for a year abroad and had advertised this exciting possibility to their friends. As my son Andrew put it: "What will I tell my friends?" But CENDES and MIT went ahead without me.

After five years of study, MIT Press published *The Politics of Change in Venezuela* in three volumes: *Strategy for Research on Social Policy*; *The Failure of Elites*; and *The Illusion of Democracy in Dependent Nations*. The last was published in 1971, ten years after the beginning of the project. Imagine the length of time The New School could have had a retainer! I read the first volume, but not the others. In the first volume, I found in the foreword that "Under Dr. Ahumada's leadership, and with the invaluable assistance of Dr. Arthur Vidich.... [t]he basic hypotheses on which the research rests were identified, and a preliminary study plan was developed."[1] The author's efforts to develop a methodological apparatus appeared to be a daunting task. A list of 1,088 leaders was compiled. The list was submitted to a panel of ten judges who were asked in a complicated procedure to scale the listed individuals "in terms of their power to propose, intervene in or influence decisions of national import."[2] This procedure reduced the list to 375 names. The list did not include "the activities of foreign investors and firms [that] had from the start been considered a separate subproject."[3] Not studying the firms and agencies with extra Venezuelan influence removed significant actors from the study. I can only conclude from the titles of the second and third volumes that these reports were critical of Venezuela's elites and pointed to their responsibility for the illusions of Venezuela's democracy. The study's assumption of Venezuela's autonomy in the world led the authors to place the blame for Venezuela's failures on the 375 local elites in their sample. It seemed to me that a strategy for research in social policy necessarily required including a consideration of the effect on social policy of external actors, interests, and agencies.

Colombia

A few months after I severed my ties with the Venezuelan project, I received a letter from a Ford Foundation representative inviting me to be an advisor to a new graduate program in sociology that

---

[1]   Bonilla and Michelena, v.

[2]   Bonilla and Michelena, xvii.

[3]   Bonilla and Michelena, xvi.

the Foundation was supporting in Bogota, Colombia. I took this invitation as a booby prize for detaching myself from the MIT project. My name may have reached the Ford Foundation via a network connection at MIT. The only thing I knew about the Ford Foundation I had learned from Dwight MacDonald's *The Ford Foundation: The Men and the Millions*, originally published in *The New Yorker*, where he called the Foundation a "large body of money completely surrounded by people who want some." In a few short years since Kennedy announced the Alliance for Progress, the organized apparatus of aid programs had fallen in place with remarkable rapidity. Americans appeared everywhere as missionaries, social science researchers, intelligence agents, foundation representatives, and economic advisors. There was even a place in this apparatus for me, and I was available.

I had earned my sabbatical from The New School and didn't need a dean's permission to accept the offer for the fall semester of 1964. The contract stipulated that I teach two courses and evaluate the new sociology program directed by Orlando Fals Borda at Colombia's National University. Financially, it was plush: all expenses paid, housing (for a family of seven, including a niece), an automobile, and a generous salary. I had wanted to drive in my own car to Bogota on the Pan American highway, but on the grounds of risk, the Foundation advised against it. Yet I wanted to make this a family excursion, so the Foundation and I compromised. I drove to Mexico City, exploring the Mexican Coast on the way, and parked the car in Mexico City for the duration, flying the rest of the way to Bogota. In Bogota, we moved into a fully furnished suburban home, complete with two domestic servants, located in a *cul de sac*. Its previous occupant had been Ivan Illich, later recognized for his radical theories of education and other social institutions. I also inherited his jeep. Never before or since on an overseas appointment have I felt more like an honored guest.

The Foundation was investing heavily in the sociology program. It had subsidized the construction of a new building as well as appointments of domestic and foreign professors. It supported a local office staff managed by a full-time representative who conspicuously drove a red convertible Thunderbird. It sponsored a steady stream of occasional consultants, such as the sociologist David Riesman and executives from the New York office. One of the latter was Champion Ward who, before becoming a Ford Foundation Philantropoid, had been a dean at the University of Chicago. Later, when the Graduate Faculty came under a New York State Review, an episode that I describe in detail later, I met him again as my provisional dean. For such visitors, we sponsored either an academic seminar or a game of tennis. As it happened, I played tennis with Champion Ward. Distinguished visitors were treated with deference and were left with the appearances of a successfully administered program.

The chair of the sociology program was Professor Orlando Fals Borda. His American credentials were impeccable. He had his BA degree from Dubuque College in Iowa, an MA in sociology from the University of Minnesota, and a PhD in rural sociology with T. Lynn Smith at the University of Florida at Gainesville. He professed the Presbyterian faith. He sat astride both cultures and had an unerring understanding of both. The Foundation could not have found a better person as its point man.

The resources available to him were formidable. In addition to those provided by the Ford Foundation, they included grants from UNESCO, the Land Tenure Center of the University of Wisconsin, the Social Science Research Council, and the Banco de la Republica, among others. It was such external financing that left him open to criticism from leftist students who distrusted the motives of Fals Borda's benefactors even while being recipients of their money. To counter such domestic adversaries, he had to prove that his actions were in the best interests of students and country. Facing an unimaginably delicate combination of diplomatic pressures with conflicting interests impinging on him from all sides, he played his role with alacrity, fearlessness, determination, and a measure of success that, in an overall perspective, proved he was no one's errand boy.

Claims by radical students that Fals Borda had sold out to American money could not easily be sustained. He distributed his resources without regard to ideology to Colombians, South Americans, Americans, and Europeans. His sociology staff included outstanding independent-minded Colombian scholars like Virginia Gutierrez de Peñeda (author of a classic study on the Colombian family comparable in scope to Arthur W. Calhoun's three-volume study, *A Social History of the American Family)*, Miguel Fornaguerra, and Camilo Torres. Lauchlin Currie, a Canadian-born economist who had been attacked by Senator Joseph McCarthy in the latter's witch-hunt after World War II against the Old China Hands, had gone into exile in Colombia (as did John Service in Peru for the same reason). He became an economic advisor to the Colombian government and taught political economy as a member of the faculty. Camilo Torres, who had a doctorate in sociology from The University of Louvain, Belgium, was an ordained priest and a member of the faculty. He also had a Ford Foundation grant to study public administration. In recognition of a long tradition of Colombian-German relations, Hans Krysmanski, a young radical German scholar, had an appointment as an exchange student. Luis Ratinoff, an Argentinean, was Fals Borda's administrative assistant. I was appointed to teach two courses and to evaluate and submit a report on the program. In the course called "American

Society," I included the works of C. Wright Mills, Paul Goodman's *Growing Up Absurd*, as well as Herbert Marcuse's *One Dimensional Man*. The other course, "The Community," started with the Lynds' *Middletown* and ended with *Small Town*. I said in those classes what I have said anywhere. It was difficult for radical students to accuse Fals Borda of being a front for nefarious American intentions. He was committed to his own vision. Nevertheless, radical students did exactly that, not because of any larger understanding of the implications of American policies, but because their psychology was guided by an inexhaustible sense of youthful resentment.

Still, despite Fals Borda's efforts, the American presence in Bogota could not be concealed. American social scientists such as David McClellan, Eugene Havens, Everett Rogers, William Flinn, and others conducted studies on rural life, land tenure, motivational psychology, and *La Violencia*. My wife, Virginia, began a demographic study on infant mortality that later became her dissertation at the University of Connecticut. A Princeton seminary student, Larry Carney, was sent to Bogota by the International Studies Program, an anti-missionary group that sponsored theology students for study in countries where, without appearing to have a mission, they could become students in national universities.

In August 1965, Fals Borda organized a sociological conference to inaugurate the University's new Social Science building. The conference theme was "Sociology and Society in Latin America." Several hundred sociologists from throughout the hemisphere, Europe, and Asia (but not the Soviet Union or China) were invited. American delegates included Talcott Parsons, Seymour Martin Lipset, Wilbert Moore, William Goode, Juan Linz, Rex Hopper, Manning Nash, and twenty-five others. (I later encountered many of these same people at international meetings in Germany and Italy; apparently, they were regulars.) In size, the American contingent was exceeded in numbers only by the Colombians, but the Americans presented a disproportionate number of the conference's papers. Radical students understandably saw the overwhelmingly American presence as intellectual colonialism. And, taken together, the presence of such eminent American scholars combined with American missionaries, consultants, foundation representatives, CIA agents, and steady streams of visiting dignitaries certainly did give the appearances of an American style of colonialism.

That the Foundation chose the field of sociology as the instrument through which to extend its influence is understandable. Focusing on the social sciences, the model applied to Colombia by the Foundation under the Alliance for Progress was similar to the one devised for Puerto Rico in the 1950s. There, a Social Science Research Center had carried out the function of importing American social science and social scientists to train Puerto Ricans in sociology, political science, and economics. Puerto Rico's Operation Bootstrap, under the administration of Governor Muñoz Marin, sought to integrate Puerto Rico with the mainland. In intervening years, however, a more complex machinery of political and cultural penetration had been put into place. The machinery had become much larger and included the integration of the policies of the State Department and the Foundation with professional social science associations. Subsidization of the sociology program at the National University was designed to serve two purposes. On the one hand, it was meant to transmit American social science perspectives and theories to South American students and, on the other, to recruit indigenous students for training in American universities. In addition to exporting our theories—of economic development, the social system, the necessary pre-conditions for democracy—we wished the

South Americans themselves to be carriers of our ideas. I carried a variant of American social science values, and I played my part just like the others. I established lifelong friendships with students and professors whom I met during my stay and contributed to an enduring nexus between the two countries. The benefits to those co-opted by these policies were academic and career opportunities unavailable to them otherwise. In exchange, they became our cultural emissaries. The cost to the United States of such cultural imperialism was insignificant relative to the benefits received from acculturating to our values third-world intellectuals, some of whom might otherwise become revolutionaries. Yet, despite the successes of the program, such processes of co-optation were not always accepted.

In the turbulent 1960s, sociology departments in the United States and elsewhere had become a major breeding ground for new left ideologues and some radicals and revolutionaries in the third world refused to be co-opted. Camilo Torres, sociologist and priest, accepted Ford Foundation money, but gave it as alms to his impoverished parishioners, making the Foundation an accomplice in his own project. Operating under a moral calculus of his own, he refused co-optation. Torres descended from the Restrepos, an old oligarchic family, but he shunned the military career of his father. Religiously rejecting things of the world, he was regarded by many as a saint. I knew him as a faculty member and friend. One weekend on an excursion with my family, along with Hans and Renata Krysmanski, to Villavicencillo on Colombia's Eastern frontier, I unexpectedly met Torres riding into town on horseback with a corps of cavalry men. He had joined the National Liberation Army and was participating that weekend in one of its exercises. On weekdays, he continued to teach his courses and tend his flock. His dual roles were apparently common knowledge among the *cognoscenti*. On another visit to Colombia a year or two later, I sought him out in Bogota. Chauffeured in a 1950s green Chevrolet sedan, he picked me up at my hotel. By this time, he was fully committed to the National Liberation Army, but he still continued to show up in public in Bogota. He seemed to believe, with almost childlike innocence, that he was invulnerable. But I sensed danger even riding with him in his Chevrolet to an obscure restaurant. Two months later, I learned that he had been ambushed and killed by forces of the Colombian National Army. He had become the Leader of the National Liberation Front. His disregard for concealing himself made it easy to pick the time and place for his demise. His fate was a powerful reminder that cultural policies by themselves were not sufficient to counter the lures of insurrectionary movements or to prevent the reaction that revolution inevitably prompts.

In 1959, Fidel Castro succeeded in toppling the deeply corrupted Batista regime in Cuba. After John F. Kennedy's inauguration to the Presidency of the United States, Castro defeated, to Kennedy's great embarrassment, the CIA-led Bay of Pigs invasion. Che Guevara, Castro's collaborator and advocate of permanent revolution, appealed to romantically idealistic youth and revolutionaries throughout South America. From the point of view of America's historical Monroe Doctrine, South American revolutionary movements could not be tolerated. The Alliance for Progress was the Kennedy administration's response to socialistic and communistic movements in South America. The stakes were high, no less than the protection of American business investments (some already lost in Cuba) and oil resources in Central and South America. Exacerbating the already existing Cold War tension between the Soviet Union and the United States, the Cuban Missile Crisis in 1962 led to a showdown between the two superpowers, bringing the world to the brink of nuclear war.

My visits to South America allowed me to see some new dimensions of American Cold War practice. First of all, I realized that, by accepting appointments in Caracas and Bogota, I was part of that practice. That I designed a study of Venezuela's leaders that hoped to analyze how the power structure functioned did not matter. The point for conducting such a study was to accomplish the intellectual and institutional co-optation of the Venezuelans. My role was to be one of the co-opting agents.

While I was not commissioned to do research in Colombia, the implication of my appointment was the same. In my role as a teacher and advisor to students, I established enduring relationships with Colombians. And I was only one of hundreds of researchers, missionaries, intelligence agents, businessmen, and economic advisors playing similar roles. The two societies inevitably achieved a measure of integration. Thinking in sociological terms, my personal experience was part of a much larger social phenomenon. Realizing that to be the case, I sought to objectify myself in relation to the social and political processes of which I was a part. I aided and abetted Cold War South American policies and accepted the opportunities they offered me, but was never able to become a spokesman for them.

Private Life in Latin America

I could hardly speak of a private life in Bogota. The fact was that the Foundation provided my family with all the amenities needed to make an instantaneous accommodation to the life in the city. The house assigned to me came furnished with four bedrooms, dining and living rooms, a kitchen, an enclosed interior garden, detached maids' quarters, and two maids. Prepared in advance for our arrival, the maids assigned us to our bedrooms. My wife, Virginia, and I were given the largest bedroom, my niece, Ann, had another, the two eldest sons, Charles and Paul, had another, and the two youngest, Andrew and Joseph, had the fourth. The maids who came with the house had serviced our Ford Foundation predecessors and were set in their expectations of how we should live in their domain. They knew when and how to do the family shopping, made the menus, automatically knew when and how to rid the mattresses of live creatures, and followed their own schedules for rest periods during the day and on their days off. They found a Spanish language teacher for the members of the family and knew where to find schools for the children. As the head of household, my own main domestic responsibility was to adjudicate frequent petty disputes that the maids had with each other. Their quarrels were over minor matters that stemmed from differences in their rank and pay. Having read Jean Genet's *The Maids*, where Genet describes the psychological relationships between a mistress and two maids and the mechanisms that operate to maintain peace in the household, I was prepared to handle my new duties as arbitrator. It was the better part of prudence to accept the already existing terms and conditions for living in this household in return for many advantages.

Of the many changes of jobs and residences I have made in my academic career, this was the first that freed me of the details of household management. In all other instances—London, Candor, Rio Piedras—I had had to find and train maids. I fell into this role by default. Virginia's virtues were not in the area of household management. She was young when her mother died and was a minister's daughter whose strongest identifications were with her father. She had completed a master's degree in sociology at the University of Wisconsin. She always worked as researcher on one project or another, helping to support the family. Her academic career was interrupted when I was accepted for admission to Harvard in 1948. When we settled in Storrs in 1957, she saw an opportunity to resume studies for a doctorate in sociology. She became a full-time student. That meant that the household was composed of five students, leaving me as its manager. I bridled in this role, but considered it a fair exchange. Virginia had postponed her career when we had children and supported me while finishing my degree at Harvard. In anticipation of our visit to Bogota, she made plans to collect data for a dissertation on Colombia's population demographics. Our lifestyle in Bogota not only gave her ample freedom to pursue her research, but also entailed no sacrifice on my part. The household almost managed itself. This was not the life of the new middle class as we lived it in Storrs, but was at the level of an established rentier family. In its academic version, we were able to simultaneously pursue each of our careers independently of the other. Never before in married life was I so free of domestic responsibilities.

Three weeks after our arrival in Bogota, Virginia, Paul, and Joseph were diagnosed with hepatitis A, one of Bogota's common afflictions transmitted by residues in drinking water. Its therapy of rest and diet was administered by the maids. When I had an opportunity to make an excursion to the Colombian Llanos, I felt free to take my eldest son, Charles, with me for a three-week expedition exploring the Meta River as far east as the border town of Uerto Caron and Puerto Ayacucha in Venezuela where the Meta and Orinoco rivers join. Hitchhiking rides on recycled National Army World War II DC 4 mail carriers, we visited remote Guahibo Indian villages and vast cattle ranches. Life on this frontier was a reminder of what the American West must have once been like. Rivers were unregulated. Their depth might vary by two hundred feet from season to season. In the dead of night, enormous cattle barges designed to transport livestock to Ciudad Bolivar in Venezuela crashed through the waterways making deafening noises. Colombia's eastern regions were like a self-regulated autonomous region. Its few settled villages and towns were self-sufficient and self-regulated. Yet, throughout this expedition, even at one point when the motor of our small boat gave out and we spent the night at river's edge, Charles and I had no sense that we were in danger. The frontier had its own civilization in no way comparable to that of Bogota, where the risks to life were greater.

Bogota and Colombia as a whole were in the midst of an armed struggle between the two dominant political parties. Each party claimed jurisdiction over various sectors of the region and unofficially supported their adherents against their competitors. This political struggle, called *La Violencia*, had been underway for a number of years. For the most part, a tacit agreement between the parties restricted inter-party murders to areas other than Bogota, which was defined as neutral territory. Nevertheless, many Bogotanos, for purposes of self-defense, were armed. As a matter of course, submachine guns were common sights in a vehicle chauffeuring important politicians or businessmen. My language instructor carried his pistol in a shoulder holster. Neighborhood policemen were armed with pistols and, when they witnessed a crime, were prepared to shoot on sight. Some of the victims were street children who were seen shoplifting from supermarkets in affluent neighborhoods. The city was geographically divided between the poor, the working classes, and the affluent. The latter were protected by guards in the equivalent of walled enclosures. All classes met and intermingled in the central city. It was there one met beggars, hustlers, and pickpockets. Among such entrepreneurs were the policemen themselves who were prepared not only to ticket jaywalkers who crossed streets against lights, but also on the spot to collect fines, making them part of their personal incomes. These were not the kind of entrepreneurs Ivy League social scientists were hoping to discover in their efforts to locate the enterprising spirit thought to be a prerequisite for the economic development of the country.

Social welfare was the responsibility of the Catholic Church and Protestant missionaries. On one occasion on a visit to central Bogota, Virginia encountered a begging mother with an emaciated baby. Virginia felt a personal responsibility stemming from her Congregational faith for this desperate mother and child. She brought them home to be cared for by our maids. A few hours after they arrived, much to the mother's anguish, the baby died in our living room. Ideally, one should have last rites performed by a priest before death. Nonetheless we sent for a priest, who administered the holy oils, and the mother was satisfied that her child was saved. This seemed to help alleviate her grief. An officer arrived to remove the body—no questions asked about its disposition—and the mother was sent away with a few pesos. One could hardly fault such therapeutic functions served by the Catholic Church to those in dire need.

Bullfighting in Bogota was a popular municipal sport that drew large, boisterous crowds. Matadors, picadors, and banderilleros were imported from Spain. They hoped to gain professional experience in the "provinces" performing before audiences whose aesthetic standards were below those of Spanish fans. None of this mattered to us. We too were amateurs. Yet even amateurs could distinguish between a ballet-like performance and one in which the matador lost control or the picador missed his mark. In point of fact, aesthetics were secondary to getting drunk on local red wine along with a few thousand other Bogotanos in the hot afternoon sun. Despite the second-rate pageantry, the side seats, and the locally produced bulls, an afternoon at the bullfight was exhilarating. One had the feeling of a genuine encounter with South American culture.

My last obligation to the Ford Foundation was to submit an evaluation of Fals Borda's sociology program. I dreaded this job. It meant getting all sorts of data on student enrollments, curriculum requirements, and so forth. Just as I began to make my first inquiries to secure the data I needed, I learned that Luis Ratioff had anticipated my request. He had already written my report, an elaborate statement of some twenty pages covering all the points a Foundation executive in New York both needed and wanted. It was a masterpiece of bureaucratic reporting designed to assure the continuation of Foundation support. My responsibility was to take credit for this report. I assumed everyone, including local and New York officials, knew how such things were done, but still this was the first time I had signed my name to another's work. That I had assumed responsibility for the report left me with a queasy feeling that I might have to justify its contents. But it was accepted, and I never heard about it again.

I had arranged for my tour of duty to end in December of 1964. I had to return to Mexico to retrieve my car within six months from the time I had impounded it with the Mexican authorities. According to Mexican law, I stood to suffer severe penalties if I failed to take the car out of the country before the end of the six-month grace period.

Our departure from Bogota entailed the usual social affairs whose purpose is to soften the forthcoming separations between colleagues and friends. Such ceremonies involved parties and receptions, vows to stay in touch, and promises to return. The etiquette of such separations leaves its imprint on the memory of participants and serves to bind relationships at the very moment that their future is in doubt.

The family's attachments to Colombia were made tangible in a collection of objects thought to be representative of Colombian culture. I collected a small library of books by Colombian authors. When in the Llanos region, I bought Indian artifacts, including fishing and warrior spears. Virginia visited the museum in the national bank, where replicas of gold masks and other objects were sold to the tourist trade. She bought a sizeable collection of these. Each of the children accumulated trinkets according to their tastes. An abundance of photographs of family, friends, and scenes were included. All these objects, as well as the rest of my library, household objects, and clothing, were packed and shipped to Storrs by a cartage company supplied by the Foundation and duly insured by me. No part of this shipment ever reached Storrs. At first, this seemed like an unjust and unbearable exorcism of a six-month period in our lives. How were we to remember this past? The solution was simple. We quickly forgot the objects, even the books and the precious artifacts. We did not need a miniature Colombian museum to remember where we had been and what had happened to us in Colombia.

Before returning to Storrs, we made a stopover in Mexico City where we retrieved our car from the Mexican authorities. We had one week to leave the country with it. We drove it to Guatemala, crossed the border, and immediately re-entered at the border, thereby legalizing the car for another six months. This allowed us to carry out our plan to explore Mexico for another month before returning to Storrs.

Returning from the border, we tried to cross from Puebla in central Mexico to Veracruz on the east coast. We tried traversing a newly created dirt road, but after a few miles encountered another car returning from the direction in which we were headed, only to be informed that the road was not passable. Oddly enough, the driver of that car was another American and even more surprisingly his name was Norman Thomas, obviously named by socialist parents in honor of one of their political heroes. An encounter like that in a remote area of Mexico is a memory that sticks with you the rest of your life.

The only route to Veracruz was via Mexico City. It was there that we celebrated Christmas and the New Year before continuing to Veracruz and Mexico's east coast as far as Yucatan. The coast at that time had not been industrialized nor had the oil deposits been developed. There were neither modern hotels nor other tourist attractions. In Villa Hermosa, overnight accommodations for a family of seven could be had on hammocks for two dollars. In the coastal town of Ciudad del Carmen, we had similar accommodations on the beach in the Gulf of Mexico. Up the road was Isla del Carmen, crossed by ferry on the way to Campeche. That was a place to stay for a few days, swimming and eating fresh fish cooked on an open campfire. We could also explore a few miles inland ancient sites of Mayan civilization. Campeche and the Yucatan Peninsula were still regarded by anthropologists at the University of Chicago as their territory. Robert Redfield's studies in that area were part of standard reading lists in college anthropology curricula. These territories were still considered to be remote and different—even strange—to Americans for whom reports about them were exotic. Not realizing it at the time, we were part of a beginning wave of tourists to Mexico's beaches on the Gulf, finally culminating in Cancun and North American students' festivals on its beaches, complete with luxury hotels and bacchanals. Within a few short years, the tourist industry transformed the Yucatan Peninsula, not unlike a similar transformation of Palau, which has now become a resort area for scuba divers and Japanese businessmen golfers on Palau's exotic golf courses. Pemex, Mexico's state-owned oil corporation, has drilled the Gulf oil deposits and transformed the coastal areas into a major source of national wealth and corruption. I remember Isla del Carmen as it was then. Otherwise, that past can only be recaptured by reading the reports of anthropologists.

12

The Re-Making of the Graduate Faculty

The New Department of Sociology

I returned to The New School in fall 1965 to an institution on the verge of momentous changes. Things had begun to shift fundamentally in the very early 1960s. When I joined the Graduate Faculty in 1960, it still exhibited some of the characteristics of a German university. For example, in 1961-1962, a dissertation defense took place before the entire Graduate Faculty, or as many faculty members who wished to attend. In practice, anywhere from ten to twenty professors showed up. Some may have not read the dissertation, but that was no obstacle to the obligatory interrogation of the candidate. My first experience with this system was the candidacy of Norman Matlin, who had written a study on higher education (later published as *The Educational Enclave: Coercive Bargaining in Colleges and Universities*) even more irreverent than Thorstein Veblen's *The Higher Learning in America*. Matlin's independence of mind precluded mentorship of his dissertation by anyone. By default, I became his supervisor. At the open defense before the faculty, Howard White took umbrage at Matlin's work and for two hours refused to approve it. At four o'clock, when professors had to leave the meeting in order to attend classes, a rump committee adjourned to White's office where we continued the debate for two more hours. Meanwhile, Matlin sweated in the hallway, supported by his friends, including Ruth Westheimer, and contemplated the apparent end of his stillborn academic career. I argued the case until six o'clock, when White conceded because he had to meet a class. Surprisingly, my doggedness established my reputation for principled fearlessness in the face of authority and won the respect of White, who as a follower of Leo Strauss, respected those who took principled stands. This was my introduction to the idiosyncratic Greenwich Village conception of the German university that White hoped to uphold. By 1962-1963, faculty attendance at dissertation defenses had been reduced to four required members. Attendance by the faculty as a whole was merely encouraged, and standards dropped precipitously. That same year, I was asked to be an examiner of an economics dissertation entitled *The Great Ascent* by Robert L. Heilbroner that I discovered was a short monograph already published as a trade book. By prior arrangement, the economics department had already accepted the work, and I was the junior faculty member chosen to rubber stamp its decision. Since Heilbroner makes a great deal about the importance of elite leadership in driving African economic development, I couldn't help asking him about leaders in Africa. His response demonstrated that he was embarrassingly ignorant about Africa, its sorry post-colonial history, and the endemic corruption of its supposed leaders. This marked the beginning of a system in which departments, acting independent of the Graduate Faculty as a whole, set their own standards for the quality of dissertations. Too often, dissertation supervisors reached agreements with colleagues to compromise on marginal candidates in return for favors down the road.

Books written by the sociology faculty—Peter Berger, Thomas Luckmann, Dennis Wrong, and myself—set a tone for a distinctive Graduate Faculty sociological style. Berger bounded into prominence with the publication of *Invitation to Sociology*, an engaging and smoothly written tract that quickly became a bestseller and put his name on a huge sociological billboard across the country. The book was the antithesis of C. Wright Mills's *The Sociological Imagination*, not as an assault on disciplinary elites, but as an ode to sociology as a way of life. In "How to Acquire a Biography," Berger invited his readers to see his book as social science—the systematic analysis of society—and a way of living with a sociological attitude, all done in a beguiling, irreverent tone. It attracted students who were searching for careers as well as formulas for changing the world. His earlier book, *The Noise of Solemn Assemblies*, suggested that religion was irrelevant as a vehicle for social change. Paired with this earlier book, *Invitation to Sociology* made the sociology department a magnet for career-changing Protestant and Catholic seminarians turning to sociology as a substitute for Christian metaphysics and morals. A few years later, Berger and Luckmann published a small book called *The Social Construction of Reality: A Treatise in the Sociology of Knowledge*. Derived largely from Schutz, Husserl's later work, and Mannheim, it had a profound influence on students prepared to embrace the truism that social reality is socially constructed, and, by implication, that social reality can be changed. These books opened sociological interpretation to varieties of analysis and possibilities of seeing the mundane from new points of view. From all parts of the country, students came to study with Berger and Luckmann.

Wrong had abandoned his work on demography, the subject of his dissertation at Columbia under Kingsley Davis's supervision, and identified himself with Max Weber. He made a prescient choice. At that time, Max Weber's sociology had come into prominence, in no small measure because of Gerth's and Mills's *From Max Weber*.

My contribution to the advertisement of the sociology department was *Small Town* and *Sociology on Trial*, the latter co-edited with Maurice Stein. *Small Town* was misread by urban sophisticates as an attack on small town life and institutions. Its central theme, the penetration of rural society by centralized bureaucratic administration, was meant to show that small-town life was neither isolated nor culturally removed from the central tendencies of modern society. It was widely accepted for the wrong reasons. As Michael Hughey has noted, it might just as well have been entitled *Mass Society in Small Town*. *Sociology on Trial* was read as an incendiary attack on the establishment, an impression that was reinforced by its title and its dedication to the memory of C. Wright Mills. Some years later, when I gave a lecture at a western state university, the student who introduced me brought the book with him, hoisted it dramatically above his head, and declared, "This is the book that inspired us during the revolts." Stein and I had neither the right nor the intention to put sociology on trial, but the publisher liked the title as a marketing device. The authors we included in the collection—Karl Mannheim, Hans Gerth, Barrington Moore, Jr., Lewis Feuer, Robert A. Nisbet, and others—were hardly revolutionaries. However, two essays were frontal assaults. One by C. Wright Mills, "The Bureaucratic Ethos," taken from *The Sociological Imagination*, attacked Merton, Lazarsfeld, and Parsons. The other by Daniel Foss, "The World View of Talcott Parsons," deconstructed Parson's abstract systems theory, calling it a battleship at war with C. Wright Mills's PT boat. *Sociology on Trial* was seen as a display of irreverence against some of the official shibboleths of the profession, such as the idea that there is progressive accumulation of sociological truths. It also reminded the profession that sociological analysis should be placed within its appropriate historical context. Editors at Prentice Hall sensed the mood of a new generation of aspiring sociologists and rushed it into a paperback edition that they marketed successfully. Contracts were signed for Brazilian and Italian editions. *Sociology on Trial* became a brand name for Brandeis's and The New School's sociology. The book's success and its adoption by young radical sociologists became important in the crisis of the Graduate Faculty during the late 1970s.

The heterodoxy of the Graduate Faculty made it attractive for students intent on making their studies politically relevant. They had begun to define themselves as a messianic counterculture, and the Haight-Ashbury district in San Francisco was their Mecca. Timothy Leary was one of their heroes. They were anti-authoritarian antinomians. A distinctive group came from Brandeis University, where they had been students of Herbert Marcuse and Maurice Stein and classmates of Angela Y. Davis. They were self-confident, not other-directed, in Riesman's famous description of the type. They wanted to change the world and saw themselves as doing it within the university. Some regarded themselves as Marxists, Trotskyites, Leninists, or social democrats. They joined political parties such as the American Worker Party and the Independent Socialist League. They believed that members of the old left such as Sydney Hook, Irving Howe, and Daniel Bell had betrayed their radical ideals by supporting the anti-communist war in Vietnam. Many of them were supported by generous scholarships provided by the State of New York and the federal government under programs initiated after the Soviet Union successfully launched Sputnik in 1957. At that time, Washington politicians, traumatized by the fear that the United States was falling behind the Soviet Union in its scientific achievements, began to pour money into universities. As a proto-professional group, these students were a privileged group. University teaching positions in the social sciences were opening up rapidly with the creation of state university systems. In a market where demand exceeded supply, some of our ABDs (all but dissertation) were hired as assistant professors.

In some cases, they were granted tenure without completing the degree. They were careerists at a time when the civil rights movement and the anti-war movement intersected to give them their political orientation. Their organizational vehicle was Students for a Democratic Society (SDS). Their program was *The Port Huron Statement*, written by Tom Hayden in 1962. These circumstances set the stage for the radicalization of our sociology students and ultimately for the participation of some of them in the Weather Underground.

1965: The Turning Point

I demarcate 1965 as the end of the old and the beginning of the new New School. In that year, John R. Everett was appointed as president. Under his management, the older system of patrimonial administration and Graduate Faculty self-governance were replaced by a system of central administrative control. His previous presidency had been at the City University of New York, where he had attempted but failed to gain control over the autonomous colleges that were the backbone of the university and provided the university with its faculty. With the exception of Harvey Gideonse at Brooklyn College, city university college presidents opposed Everett's centralization program and forced his resignation. His failure at City University was a powerful lesson for Everett. In centralizing the administration of The New School, he paid special attention to bringing the Graduate Faculty under his control. In this initiative, he acted with the self-assurance and confidence derived from being a lineal descendant of the Everetts that founded the American colonies, the Virginia, not the Boston branch of the family, as he was pleased to point out.

Everett's first act was to sack Howard White, the last bearer of the old guard's conception of faculty governance, but an ineffectual fighter against presidential prerogative. In his place, Everett appointed Joseph Greenbaum as Dean of Faculty. Although this decision had already been made, Thomas Luckmann, who had experienced the older system of faculty governance, took the occasion to advise Greenbaum that "he was an inappropriate candidate for the position and should not accept it." Instead, he proposed the appointment of Peter Berger as Dean of Faculty and professor of sociology. When Luckmann gave me a report of his meeting with Greenbaum, he stressed the acrimony of the exchange. This incident left a permanent residue of tension between the dean and the sociology department, as if other members of the department had been part of a conspiracy organized by Luckmann. Greenbaum became dean in 1966 and remained in that office until 1979. The faculty responded to his appointment with murmurs but did not challenge presidential authority. Within a short time, the faculty statement on principles of academic freedom that had been printed in Graduate Faculty bulletins each year since 1934 was deleted. Heads of departments became chairs instead of spokespersons. Chairs represented their departmental members in a dean's committee called the Budget and Executive Committee that reviewed departmental recommendations for new appointments and any other items the dean wanted to discuss. Budgets, however, were off limits and were treated as closely guarded administrative secrets. The balance of power between faculty and higher administration had come full circle.

In 1965, Carl Meyer retired and Luckmann left to take a job at the University of Konstanz. I had just returned from my sojourn in South America and became the chairman of the department by default. Berger, who had joined the department in 1962, left in 1963 to take a distinguished professorship at Hunter College of the City University of New York. When he quickly became dissatisfied with that position and resigned, we reappointed him to a professorship in the department and gave him the editorship of *Social Research*, replacing Dennis Wrong, who had resigned to take a professorship at New York University. Salomon died in 1966. I was now the chairman of a department that I could recreate as I wished at a time when the school was flush with money and under the direction of an entrepreneurial president.

To reconstruct the department, I proposed the candidacies of Norman Birnbaum and Stanley Diamond. I had known Birnbaum when I was a graduate student at Harvard. He had since gone to England and Strasbourg where he gained a reputation as a political sociologist and social theorist. He accepted a non-tenured appointment with my personal assurance that I would propose and support his tenure after two years. I had met Stanley Diamond during my association with Brandeis University. He had studied at Columbia University and written an outstanding dissertation called *Dahomey: A Proto-state in West Africa*. He was also a careful student of Paul Radin, whose works I greatly admired. These positions were not advertised, and both were approved.

Everett's first initiative as president was to create a Liberal Studies program, the first of a plethora of such programs. It was designed to grant MA degrees earned by taking cross-listed courses in any of the then existing five departments of the Graduate Faculty. Piggy-backed on existing faculty resources, the program was a low-cost method of using existing resources to increase enrollments and revenues, on the premise that enrollments were the measure of a department's worth. Everett's first candidate to direct this program was Richard McKeon, the University of Chicago classicist and medievalist. Champion Ward, then a dean at the University of Chicago, was the broker in these negotiations. McKeon proposed to keep his position at Chicago while heading the Liberal Studies program at the Graduate

Faculty. However, the University of Chicago was unwilling to accept this moonlighting arrangement and forced McKeon to reject The New School appointment. As a substitute, McKeon and Ward suggested Benjamin Nelson, a medieval historian who had held a visiting appointment at the University of Chicago's Committee on Social Thought and was then teaching at the State University of New York at Stony Brook. Everett phoned me one afternoon. Did I know Nelson and would I accept him in the sociology department? Without hesitation, I answered yes to both questions. The members of the department were neither consulted nor did they object. Everyone knew and admired Nelson's work *The Idea of Usury: From Tribal Brotherhood to Universal Otherhood*. Nelson accepted what was essentially a presidential appointment, becoming the director of the Liberal Studies program and a member of the sociology department.

Entering the new age of student revolts, the senior members of the department that I chaired were Birnbaum, Diamond, Nelson, and Berger. Carl Mayer was emeritus, and Julie Meyer was near retirement. Deborah Offenbacher, a sociology department graduate, and John Williams, a statistician, were assistant professors. The visiting professors were a mixed group. Arvid Broderson, a former member of the faculty, was in his last year as a visitor. John Cowley was a self-styled moderate English radical. Joseph Bensman was my friend. George Fischer was in the process of becoming an ultra radical; a year later he joined the protesting students at Columbia University and was arrested for biting a policeman's finger. F. William Howton was a protégé of Joseph Bensman. This group proved to be unmanageable, and it later imploded. For example, Birnbaum and Nelson were locked in mortal combat, perhaps over Nelson's disapproval of Birnbaum's radical stance in the classroom. Birnbaum allowed students to grade themselves, a practice that Nelson and others found abhorrent. The two had a catastrophic fight, and Birnbaum lost his job at the Graduate Faculty. Because I had promised to support him for tenure, I opposed his firing, a battle that I lost. Through Benjamin DeMott, a member of The New School Board of Trustees, Birnbaum secured a job at Amherst College, where he remained for some decades. Years after his termination from The New School, Birnbaum approached me as if this had never happened, asking me to support his candidacy for Dean of Faculty of the Graduate Faculty.

Neither the sociology department nor The New School administration was prepared for the radicalization of its student body. Nor did anyone comprehend its implications. By 1965, course enrollments in all Graduate Faculty departments had escalated to unimaginable heights. Psychology enrollments numbered more than 1,400. However, the psychology students were apolitical, principally interested in obtaining certification to further their careers in education or business. The Department of Sociology was close behind with 1,200 student enrollments. In my course on Contemporary American Social Theory, I lectured to 400 students. In 1966, when Carl Mayer returned from Switzerland to teach Max Weber, his course enrolled 500 students. Following its traditional open admission policy, justified by Howard White as providing educational opportunities for "late bloomers," the Graduate Faculty became self-supporting even as the school lacked the classroom space to accommodate its burgeoning student body. For the first time in its history, the Graduate Faculty was a flourishing, money-making business. Ironically, the school had become a beneficiary of Lyndon Johnson's military draft. Students were exempt from the draft as long as they remained in school. Anti-war young men, vulnerable to the draft at the time of graduation from college, enrolled in graduate studies. "Draft dodgers," paying high tuitions, sought refuge in a curriculum that they thought supported their political views. A mythology at The New School, not entirely false in light of some of the appointments I had made, was the source of this appeal to a new generation of aspiring sociologists.

The European origins of the University in Exile were the key to its appeal for our students. In undergraduate courses, these students had heard the names Weber, Durkheim, Marx, and the rest of the litany of classical theorists. These names were conspicuously displayed in the sociology department's course listings. Moreover, Carl Mayer and Albert Salomon were still living presences of sociology's glorious past. Berger and Luckmann, also Europeans, were seen as bearers of European thinking in the United States, transvaluing and applying its meanings to the American scene. The perception of the faculty as European was reinforced by a steady stream of German visiting professors. In 1963, Helmuth Plessner of the University of Göttingen visited the philosophy department, followed a year later by Otto von der Goblentz from the Free University of Berlin. A few years later, Theodor Heuss, the President of West Germany and something of a Weber scholar himself, created a chair financed by West Germany for an annual appointment of a German scholar to the Graduate Faculty. This chair became known as the Heuss Professorship (subsequently financed by the Volkswagen Foundation). In 1966, it was held by Jürgen Habermas and in 1967 by Renate Mayntz. Given the terms of their selection by committees of a conservative German professoriate, it is not surprising that appointees to the Heuss Professorship generally did not embrace the leftist ideologies favored by our burgeoning student body. Habermas's sociological viewpoint was formed in 1952 when he attended Talcott Parsons's democracy seminar in Germany, a formative experience that led him to make democracy a central focus of his work. Renate Mayntz had completed her PhD at Columbia and was a committed survey sociologist. And, of course, the University in Exile in general and the sociology department in particular had rejected leftist ideologies and all forms of radicalism. Thus, the sociology faculty did not meet student political expectations. For a few years, this posed no problem. Only later, in 1968, when the student movement began to heat up and take a more organized radical turn, did it become clear that the curriculum was at odds with the temper of the students. By that point, students had begun to learn more from each other and the student movement than from their faculty.

Under Jack Everett's new administration, the school was given a new sense of hope. On the strength of expanding enrollments and philanthropic gifts, a mood of optimism prevailed. Following years of fiscal stringency, its future appeared radiant.

Sixty-Six West 12th Street no longer contained sufficient space to accommodate the growing number of scheduled classes. In 1966, another building located at 64 Fifth Avenue was acquired. The sociology department was moved from 12th Street into the fifth floor of that building, an open space partly partitioned into makeshift offices. When Jürgen Habermas saw the shabby facilities, he was shocked, though he always made the best of it. As I noted earlier, Albert List then gave Everett a building at 65 Fifth Avenue, the former Lane's Department Store, whose slogan had been "Fifth Avenue Value at 14th Street Prices." The entire Graduate Faculty was transferred to this new two-story building equipped with elevators and a library space in a basement the size of the square footage of the building's footprint. Each department was allocated its own quarters, and professors were assigned individual offices. The dean acquired a spacious office on the second floor with windows facing Fifth Avenue. Adjacent to it was the faculty's new conference room, complete with mahogany paneling and a king-size conference table capable of comfortably seating the entire faculty. Except for the elevators, all traces of the building's previous existence as a department store had been eliminated. As a whole and in its various parts, the building had the appearance of a corporate headquarters.

President Everett continued to manage the Graduate Faculty from his office on the top floor of the building at 66 West 12th Street. New administrative officers were added to his staff in rapid succession, including a vice-president for development and public relations, a director of public information, a director of development, and a chancellor. As his appointment for the chancellor position, Everett selected his friend from his City University days, Harry Gideonse, whom he also appointed as a professor of economics. In short order, administrative staffs throughout the university began to grow at prodigious rates. Deans appointed assistant deans, and assistant deans appointed assistants. The registrar's office, only a few years earlier staffed by two persons, now had more personnel than any of the academic departments.

President Everett and his Board of Trustees invested much of their energy and resources in the faculty. Among other things, they joined TIAA-CREF to provide the faculty with a retirement plan for the first time. They sought funds for the creation of distinguished professorships and subsidized the school's in-house journal, *Social Research*. The Graduate Faculty, it seemed, might truly become the jewel in the crown of The New School for Social Research.

Everett had a proprietary interest in the success of the faculty he had rebuilt. With the aid of his collaborator, Harry Gideonse, he exercised a close but covert scrutiny over the faculty. He had hand-picked its dean, who served at his pleasure and who had been provided with an apartment for his family in a brownstone owned by the school. The dean was the president's liaison to the faculty, his personal legate and source of information on its problems, controversies among professors, and trouble-making members of the faculty, especially those who took an interest in budgetary matters. Everett also made a point of entertaining faculty. An invitation to the president's home for a dinner or cocktail party was a new experience for me. The trustees had provided Everett with an ample apartment in the Butterfield House on West 12th Street. Invitations to parties in honor of distinguished lecturers and visiting professors became part of a new Graduate Faculty culture. Following the presidential lead, the dean emulated this new fashion in his apartment. The new administration's style not only gave the faculty a clubby flavor, but provided faculty members with opportunities to impress administrators.

To all appearances, the administration had resolved many of the traditional problems that had faced the Graduate Faculty. But this occurred precisely at the moment that the student movement in New York City began to gain momentum.

Radical Students

By the late 1960s, students at the Graduate Faculty demanded more courses that were "relevant" to their immediate interests, more Marx instead of Weber, more Gramsci instead of Simmel. They also demanded a complete transformation of the governing structure of the university as a matter of student rights, using the by-then familiar rhetoric of "participatory democracy." Several students who were battle-hardened veterans of the 1968 debacle at Columbia University called for an equal voice in departmental governance, including course offerings, new appointments and re-appointments of faculty, and in faculty tenure and promotion. Their list of demands included equal participation in the general faculty meeting and on the board of trustees and an end to executive all-faculty sessions. Their battle cry against The New School inverted the old Lane's Department Store slogan: "14th Street Education at Fifth Avenue Prices." At one point, students threatened to shut down the entire educational operation of the Graduate Faculty. The dean appointed Hans Jonas to chair a faculty-student committee to work with the students on behalf of the Graduate Faculty and administration. In addition to Jonas, the original committee included Leon Festinger, Robert Heilbroner, A. Neale Ronning, and myself. I served as secretary for a year and during that time wrote all the reports that went out in the committee's name. In later incarnations, the committee included Arien Mack, Hannah Arendt, Jacob Landynski, and Emil Oesterreicher. Briefly, the Jonas committee tried to forge a compromise with students. Its strategy was to grant them equal voice in curricular matters and in negotiating some degree specifications, such as foreign language requirements, but to retain decisions on appointments, promotion, and tenure as the exclusive preserve of the faculty. Nor did the faculty wish to give up its right to meet in private executive sessions. I committed a tremendous amount of time and energy to this work. When the matter finally came up for a faculty vote in spring 1970, I was on leave. I wrote Dean Joseph Greenbaum stating my own position on the issues. This letter read in part:

1. The [student] clubs by their methods of selection of representatives must be required to represent all strata of students in the university. In other words, candidates must be selected from the different strata.

2. It should be clearly understood (and was so understood by the committee last year) that student representatives do not attend all faculty

meetings (general and departmental) but attend only those meetings whose agendas contain items on which students have a vote.

3. The critical issue and the one which remained unresolved even after a year of deliberation centered on areas on which student representatives should have a vote. Since last year, my own ambivalence on this question has been resolved. My position now is that students should not vote on faculty appointments, degree requirements, or curricular questions.

4. Furthermore, in light of the present situation, I would vote to recommit the question of student representation and participation to a faculty committee which would work parallel to an all-university student committee on the following tasks: a) establishment of student organizations and systems of representation to serve in a consultative relationship to the faculty; b) re-examination of the entire question of areas in which student representatives would have the right to vote in faculty meetings.

The faculty voted to maintain its traditional prerogatives. The student revolt at The New School lost momentum and collapsed by the end of the spring semester 1970. Some of the radical students benefited from the knowledge of bureaucratic tactics they gained during these struggles and put them to good personal use when they later joined the once hated "establishment." Indeed, one of The New School student radicals went on to head the national bank of a Latin American country. However, another student, David Gilbert, became a Weatherman and chose to play out the role of unbending radical to the end. He participated in the ill-fated 1981 Brinks armored-car robbery in Nyack, New York, along other members of the Weather Underground and members of the Black Liberation Army. For his efforts to help finance black revolution in America, he was convicted of the murders of two Nyack police officers and a Brinks security guard.

In 1969-1970, I was on leave teaching at the New College in Sarasota, Florida. I had received the invitation to the New College from Lazlo Deme, who admired *Small Town* and other of my writings. I was happy to take the post there because of a crisis in my personal life. My wife, Virginia, and I had decided to divorce. I was involved with Mary Rudolph Gregoric, whom I had met in Storrs, Connecticut. Mary was also going through a divorce from her husband, Michael. Mary and I weren't married as yet because of legal delays in each of our divorce cases. When the final divorce papers came through, we planned to return to New York City to get married. As it happens, our marriage plans were facilitated by an invitation to lecture at Roger Williams College in Rhode Island, an opportunity that helped pay for our trip. We were married in City Hall by a civil servant; Joe and Marilyn Bensman were our best man and maid of honor. This trip north coincided with an important meeting in the sociology department that proved to be crucial.

The joint Department of Sociology and Anthropology was in turmoil. In my absence, Stanley Diamond had begun agitating for splitting anthropology from sociology, a move that I opposed on intellectual and curricular grounds. While I was away, Benjamin Nelson pushed for Stanley to be the chairman of the still joint department and the dean agreed. As chairman and with the support of the American Anthropological Association that was then urging anthropologists to become independent, Diamond was able to separate the two disciplines. Anthropology became an autonomous degree-awarding department with Diamond, of course, as chairman. He was committed to the notion of the "primitive." In his view, the critique of modern society through the lens of the primitive was anthropology's principal purpose. Diamond had already begun a career of advocacy against the British colonial legacy in Nigeria. By late 1967, he had emerged as a champion of the "possibility of Biafra" for the Ibo-speaking Nigerians. This was a role he embraced with prophetic fervor, writing a great many articles on Biafra for the *New York Review of Books* and trying to shape his new department into a beacon of "public anthropology." He continued to play this part with considerable enthusiasm until his death in 1991, long after the disastrous end of the Biafra venture.

Meanwhile, Peter Berger insisted that the new, now reduced-in-size sociology department hire Hansfried Kellner, his brother-in-law and sometime collaborator. Unless Kellner were hired, Berger threatened, he would leave the department. Because I was already in New York to get married, Dean Greenbaum asked me to participate in a department meeting to discuss Berger's demand. Berger curiously did not attend the meeting, but he was represented by Deborah Offenbacher, his former student and current colleague. Thinking that I had been summoned by the dean to come to New York in order to attend the meeting, Offenbacher asked me who had paid for my trip from Florida. After I explained the arrangements with Roger Williams, my personal business in New York, and Dean Greenbaum's request that I participate in the meeting since I happened to be in the city, Offenbacher fell silent. I opposed Berger's proposal, and Kellner was denied an appointment. Berger then decamped to Rutgers University.

In fall 1970, I returned to The New School to find that the split between anthropology and sociology was a *fait accompli*. The sociology department, depleted and demoralized, launched a search for a new senior sociologist. At that time, I was an editorial advisor for Appleton Century Crofts Publishers. They had received a fascinating manuscript from Stanford M. Lyman, then at the University of California, San Diego, and Marvin B. Scott, of Hunter College, entitled *A Sociology of the Absurd*. I met with both authors over lunch and recommended some changes to the manuscript. Although Scott demurred in a somewhat acrimonious way, Lyman and I quickly came to terms. I recommended that the department consider Lyman for the senior post. Lyman appeared for his interview wearing a flowered Hawaiian shirt. Hannah Arendt, one of the members of the appointment committee, was put off by what she considered Lyman's sartorial vulgarity. Moreover, Dean Greenbaum had heard rumors of Lyman's volatile personality, always a danger signal to deans and search committees. However, Lyman gave a smooth and seemingly effortless performance, even charming Arendt with his erudition. The department ended up hiring Stanford Lyman. He proved to be a larger-than-life figure of prodigious energy and learning, generously endowed with a capacity for passionate enthusiasms, both intellectual and emotional. Stanford and I began a fruitful collegial relationship that lasted for more than two decades.

The New York State Review of the Department of Sociology

In 1978, New York State evaluated all doctorate-granting programs in the state. All the professors in each of the Graduate Faculty's six departments devoted an inordinate amount of time to this review. We in sociology compiled two volumes of information about our department in response to standardized queries from the state office.

Most important, we provided extensive information about courses offered in the department, faculty scholarship and other profession-al achievements, and the post-degree careers of our students. Daria Cverna Martin, our extraordinary secretary, indeed the chair of the department in everything except rank and title, coordinated this en-tire effort.

The following sociologists were appointed to the "Rating Commit-tee" assigned to review our department: William Sewell, University of Wisconsin; E. Digby Baltzell, University of Pennsylvania; Ernest Q. Campbell, Vanderbilt University; William A. Gamson, University of Michigan; and Lee Rainwater, Harvard University. Sewell chaired the committee, a worrisome prospect. At the time, he embraced the positivist, quantitative, methodology-over-substance orientation to sociology still dominant in the profession. Indeed, in the decades since I had taken his class in rural sociology at Wisconsin, Sewell had become a born-again positivist who equated empiricism with num-ber crunching—"these numbers are real"—rejecting as unscientific any form of interpretive sociology. Only a year after his elevation to the Chancellorship of the University of Wisconsin, Madison, he was forced to resign due to his response to student protests and campus unrest. *Sociology on Trial*, which had enjoyed a certain cachet among student radicals and sharply critiqued exactly what Sewell stood for, certainly did not endear me to him.

Edward Tiryakian of Duke University, conducted an on-site visit to the department in advance of the Rating Committee's report. His visit gave the Graduate Faculty a useful if ominous preview of what conclusions the Rating Committee would reach. In his meeting with faculty, he berated us for the absence of minority professors. He then met with a group of graduate students. Michael Hughey, who was

finishing up his course work in the Graduate Faculty at the time, offered the following the report:

> The meeting with Tiryakian was odd. He clearly had
> an agenda and a negative view of The New School at
> the time he met with us. The issues and questions he
> raised were all framed in such a way as to try and so-
> licit material to be used against the school in his re-
> port. For example, he became somewhat fixated on
> the idea that The New School students were unlikely
> to ever publish in the *American Sociological Review*
> or the *American Journal of Sociology*, implying that
> not only were we not the equals of, say, Duke stu-
> dents, where he taught, but that we should feel badly
> about the comparison. It probably didn't help mat-
> ters with him that we suggested, quite undiplomati-
> cally, that The New School students were not intel-
> lectually inferior even to Duke students, but also
> that we didn't really care about publishing in those
> "mainstream" journals with their methodological
> obsessions. We told him, in fact, that there would
> be other outlets for our work and that we regarded
> ideas and analyses as more important than statisti-
> cal manipulations. From his point of view, I'm sure
> that all of this simply confirmed that we had been
> successfully brainwashed by our faculty and that
> we were being dismally prepared to join the broth-
> erhood of modern sociologists. I had read some of
> Tiryakian's work before this visit and, based on that,
> had felt he would be somewhat sympathetic to The

New School and its approach to sociology and scholarship in general. I remember leaving that meeting feeling completely disabused of that preconception. It became clear to all of us later that the thrust of the report had clearly already been decided by the Rating Committee. Tiryakian's site visit was nothing more than a search for ammunition. The target had already been selected.

The Rating Committee issued a seven-page report on the department. It began by praising its distinguished past as "an outpost of European sociology" and its role "in furthering the influence of phenomenological thought on American sociology." But it then entered an erroneous account of the relationship between the Graduate Faculty and the adult education division of The New School. Denigrating the Graduate Faculty's late-afternoon, early-evening class-time schedule that permitted its students to earn a living while earning a degree, it criticized in a casual fashion the notion of graduate students working at all. Noting that the department required a reading knowledge of two languages, a more stringent requirement than doctoral programs in sociology generally impose, the Committee attributed this rule to the department's strong emphasis on European sociology. But it sharply criticized the department precisely for that emphasis. The Committee argued that that tradition "contrasts with the systematic empirical research tradition that dominates most of American sociology." Indeed, the Committee's report argued, the Graduate Faculty's sociology department had a "relative neglect of American social theory" and almost no emphasis on methods of social research. The report included a confusing and misleading exposition of the department's consortium relationship with the sociology departments at New York University (NYU) and the City University of New York

(CUNY), arguing that these arrangements were not widely utilized and that the courses students took at NYU or CUNY were not recorded on their transcripts. Nor was the Committee impressed with the academic positions achieved by sociology graduates from The New School. For the most part, the report claimed, these were jobs at local community colleges in the New York area.

The sharpest criticisms were reserved for the sociology faculty. Noting the loss to the department caused by the death of Benjamin Nelson (1977), the Committee stated that the faculty had "little national visibility." It praised Stanford Lyman's productivity and name recognition "in his subfield" without, however, identifying that field. Arthur Vidich, on the other hand, was said to have been "less productive in recent years and his reputation rests largely on a co-authored work of 20 years ago." Neither Lyman nor Vidich had received "any major national honors, nor would either be regarded as a major figure in the field." The report said: "[t]he current sociology faculty of The New School lacks the range and stature necessary for an effective PhD program. The senior faculty are respectable, but the Department lacks the major scholars necessary to such a small program. We doubt that the program will be able to attract a person or persons of sufficient national or international stature to change this situation in making senior appointments." Indeed, the "mission" that the Committee ascribed to The New School department as a "purveyor of European thought is being better fulfilled elsewhere. In fact, it is being better fulfilled in other programs in New York State." The Committee's conclusion could hardly have been more dismal: "We see no advantage in the offering of a separate degree in sociology at The New School.... [W]e find the doctoral program in sociology at The New School for Social Research to be inadequate and recommend that it be discontinued. We suggest that the needs of its students might be better served by the further development of the PhD program in social science."

All of us were dismayed by the Rating Committee's assault on the department, the history and tradition of the Graduate Faculty, The New School itself, and Stanford Lyman and me personally, even as we recognized that the report's numerous errors considerably weakened its argument. Nonetheless, we obviously had to frame a careful, vigorous, and decisive response. This took the form of a "Statement of Factual Errors Contained in the Report of the Sociology Rating Committee." In that twenty-five-page document, Stanford Lyman and I pointed out all the numerous errors and mischaracterizations in the Committee's report. We stressed the following:

1. The Graduate Faculty is an autonomous unit composed of six departments and none of these participates in The New School's Continuing Education Program in Adult Education.

2. The program in sociology emphasizes the systematic and empirical tradition of sociology that is characterized by the Euro-American sociological tradition.

3. The program in sociology does not forge a dichotomy between European and American theory but rather stresses the interrelationships between these approaches.

4. The [faculty members of the sociology department] teach research courses or seminars in those methods of research central to his/her subfields. This provides a broad and deep coverage of methods focused on the specific research needs of each student and permits the widest

application of various research strategies to the solution of sociological problems.

5. The consortia arrangements with the Graduate Center of the City University of New York and New York University play an important part in expanding the offerings of the Department of Sociology.

6. The Graduate Faculty's sociology program ranks fifth of eleven programs in New York State in the number of PhDs awarded in the period between 1972-1976.

7. There is no evidence whatsoever to substantiate the Rating Committee's implication that the outside work of graduate students slowed their progress toward the doctoral degree.

8. The department as a whole, as well as its individual professors, are systematically engaged in seeing students outside of the classroom hours in individual meetings, special tutorials, conferences in preparation of oral examinations, conferences on dissertation proposals, and conferences on dissertation work in progress.

9. Graduates of The New School have been hired for positions in prestigious national academies and institutions of higher learning, including the University of California, Berkeley, the Graduate Center of the City University of New York, Iowa State University, Rutgers University, Florida International University, Wellesley College, Amherst College, City College of New York,

> Brooklyn College, Williams College, Mount Holyoke College, and Howard University, and they have competed for positions at Harvard, Yale, and the University of Wisconsin.

10. The New School continues to attract persons of national and international stature, including Dennis Wrong, Peter Berger, Thomas Luckmann, and Benjamin Nelson and, through the Theodor Heuss Professorship, scholars such as Jürgen Habermas, Renate Mayntz, Friedrich Tenbruck, Peter Ludz, and Niklas Luhmann.

11. The distinctive mission of the sociology program was not simply that of a "purveyor of European thought," as the Rating Committee argued, but a mission to train scholars to address macro-sociological problems against a thorough background of classical and contemporary European and American social theory, always with an historical and interdisciplinary thrust.

We did not address the Rating Committee's arguments that working students, who were learning something of the world of affairs while pursuing their studies, were *ipso facto* inferior students. Nor did we point out that sending well-trained students of sociology to teach in community colleges might be in the national interest.

In view of the Committee's assessment of our credentials, Lyman and I were obliged to conduct an exercise in self-promotion, instructing its members on our research and its reception, matters that they had apparently ignored. Lyman took particular aim at the Committee's attempt to portray him as a narrow specialist in race relations, a claim that he countered by a detailed account of publications in sociological theory, phenomenology, social psychology, deviance, symbolic interaction, and ethnomethodology, as well as works in race and ethnic relations, black studies, and Asian American studies. I took a somewhat different tack. The Rating Committee had noted in its report that "peer judgments on the quality and influence of a scholar's contribution are the most crucial determinant of standing in the discipline." I then presented "peer judgments" that lavishly praised *The New American Society* (1971) in the *American Journal of Sociology*, the *American Political Science Review*, and *Social Forces*. I also presented excerpts of favorable reviews of my volume edited with Joseph Bensman and Maurice Stein, *Reflections on Community Studies*. One review of that book had been written by a member of the Committee itself and had appeared in the *American Journal of Sociology*. Other favorable reviews of *Reflections* had been published in the *American Sociological Review* and the *American Anthropologist*. I also pointed out a favorable review of *Identity and Anxiety: Survival of the Person in Mass Society*, edited with Maurice Stein and David Manning White, that appeared in the *American Sociological Review*. I then revisited the critical acclaim that greeted the revised and expanded 1968 edition of *Small Town in Mass Society* in the *American Journal of Sociology*, the *Political Science Quarterly*, *The New Leader*, the *Times Literary Supplement*, and the *Sociological Review*. Finally, in response to the Rating Committee's claim that my productivity had declined after the original 1958 publication of *Small Town*, I pointed out that I had authored five books and thirty-two articles in the intervening years, served as an editor of two journals, and held several posts in various professional associations. I forgot to mention the two pieces that I published in the *American Journal of Sociology* on the controversy that followed the publication of *Small Town in Mass Society*. They were then (and they remain today) two of the most widely cited pieces on fieldwork in the discipline.[1]

We closed with remarks on our students at the Graduate Faculty and our relationships with them, detailed and favorable accounts that differed sharply from the general and condescending judgments of the Rating Committee. The Committee never answered our response. Then, suddenly and without explanation, Kai Erikson of Yale University, a former president of the American Sociological Association, made an appearance, visiting the department and interviewing faculty, students, and administrators. We never learned the purpose or outcome of his visit. The matter simply ended, and the sociology department survived. I should note that both the departments of political science and philosophy were also severely chastised in these reviews. Neither department responded with the same vigor that we demonstrated. At the time, I concluded that our department's determined and forthright response to the New York State assault brought the whole process to a halt.

This whole episode demonstrated to us the bankruptcy of the American graduate education establishment. However, it also forced us to think through and articulate our own conceptions of our work at the Graduate Faculty. In fall 1978, I wrote a position paper, "The

---

[1]   Editor's note: The pieces in the *American Journal of Sociology* are: Joseph Bensman and Arthur J. Vidich, "Social Theory in Field Research" and Arthur J. Vidich, "Participant Observation and the Collection and Interpretation of Data." *See also:* A. Vidich and J. Bensman, "The Validity of Field Data" published in *Human Organization*. All of these essays, along with "Ethical and Bureaucratic Implications of Community Research" and various rejoinders to criticisms made of *Small Town in Mass Society* may be found in the second (1968) edition and all subsequent editions of that book. *See also:* Arthur J. Vidich and Stanford M. Lyman, "Qualitative Methods: Their History in Sociology and Anthropology."

Place of the Graduate Faculty of Political and Social Science in Higher Education." I acknowledged the need for conventional institutions of higher learning to transmit established knowledge to new generations of students. But I stressed the need for programs designed both to create knowledge by focusing on major issues facing the world and to critically appraise what passed as established knowledge. I pointed out that the Graduate Faculty had done both for more than forty years in the United States and in the international arena.

By the mid-1970s, most American graduate programs in the social sciences and philosophy demonstrated virtually no interest in public affairs. The social tumult of the 1960s had quieted, and internal disciplinary concerns consumed most graduate programs. The postwar baby boom that fueled expansion of the education industry in the 1960s was over. However, the mighty organizational apparatus that universities had erected to capture those enrollments remained. The organizational legacy of the 1960s expansion included highly standardized curricula designed to service masses of students; a deep split between teaching and research, the latter bankrolled by government and foundation grants, the former relegated to second-class status; a concomitant split between graduate and undergraduate programs with a wholesale devaluation of undergraduate teaching; a deepening of disciplinary and departmental divisions, fueled in part as a response to the scholarly specialization encouraged by the flood of money pouring into social science research; weakened standards for granting tenure due to the 1960s sellers' market for certain kinds of professors, particularly those skilled in obtaining grants; and thus over-tenured departments in many disciplines, including sociology. In brief, universities across the country confronted a sharp contraction in demand for their services, but were burdened in responding to this new situation by inflexible and costly organizational structures.

I argued that there was no reason to think that universities could break out of this dilemma. Indeed, the larger and more centralized the universities, the more likely they were to reproduce the worst consequences of the over-expansion of the 1960s: narrow intellectual specialization, the bureaucratization of research, and the devaluation of teaching.

I concluded the paper by arguing that the Graduate Faculty's decentralized institutional form and its long-time commitments to iconoclasm, innovation, and free thinking presented a radical organizational alternative for sparking the kind of creativity and innovation essential to scientific endeavor. Only thinkers who can see the general implications of particular events, with eyes to both the past and the future, can penetrate, re-synthesize, and, at times, break down the fundamental canons of accepted theory. Only in this way can new perspectives be derived from received theory and new problems formulated. If this process of destruction and creation is not continuous, science stagnates. For four decades, I argued, the Graduate Faculty had been training the kind of generalists and theoreticians needed to define the critical problems facing modern society, problems unlikely to be defined by specialists or even perceived by those whose intellectual routines are governed by the constraints of large-scale organizations.

It's worth noting in passing that when the New York State Review Rating Committee issued its report, the American Sociological Association did not support us or intervene in any way on our behalf. The book that Stanford Lyman and I went on to write, *American Sociology: Worldly Rejections of Religion and Their Directions*, is a critique of the discipline of sociology born directly from the experience of the external review of 1978. We explored the practice of sociology at major universities, analyzing how their programs had influenced the development of the discipline. We prefaced the book with a quote from Harold Bloom's *The Anxiety of Influence*. It reads:

> 'Let the dead poets make way for others. Then we might even come to see that it is our veneration for what has already been created ... that petrifies us....' Mad Artaud carried the anxiety of influence into a region where influence and its counter-movement, misprision, could not be distinguished. If latecomer poets are to avoid following him there, they need to know that the dead poets will not consent to make way for others. But, it is more important that new poets possess a richer knowing. The precursors flood us, and our imaginations can die by drowning in them, but no imaginative life is possible if such inundation is wholly evaded.[2]

In our view, the major centers of sociology had forgotten the precursors of the discipline and all sense of the discipline's origins. In so doing, they had caused sociology to lose its way.

The University of Chicago in Exile

At the time of the external review, Joseph Greenbaum was replaced as Dean of Faculty by F. Champion Ward, with whom I had played tennis in Bogota. Ward was a 1932 graduate of Oberlin College who had served as the Dean of College at the University of Chicago from 1950-1956. He then went on to a career in the foundation business, principally with the Ford Foundation. After the Graduate Faculty survived the New York State review, Ward became the key broker in recruiting University of Chicago people to the Graduate Faculty.

---

[2] Bloom, 154.

The main events occurred in 1982 with the appointment of Jonathan Fanton as President of The New School. Fanton, who had been the assistant to President Hannah Grey of the University of Chicago, appointed another Chicago fixture, Ira Katznelson, chairman of its political science department, as the new Dean of the Graduate Faculty. Although I had no sense of this at the time, these two appointments inaugurated a new regime grounded in a new conception of what the Graduate Faculty should be.

Katznelson brought new faces to the faculty, new programs, and the prospect of new money. He appears to have been intent on forming a critical mass of scholars engaged in comparative work on the institutional conditions for state formation and development. The plan, it seems, was an exercise in market segmentation designed to mark the Graduate Faculty as the place to be for research in this area. From his old department at Chicago, he hired the Africanist Ari Zolberg, who worked in comparative politics and emigration studies. His wife, Vera, was also hired and given a professorship in the sociology department. Elizabeth Sanders and her husband, Richard Bensel, both comparative institutionalists and students of American political development, were hired as associate professors with tenure. The most prestigious appointment was Charles Tilly, whom I had not seen since my Fulbright year in London when he was a graduate student in the Department of Social Relations at Harvard. Tilly, who had directed a research center at the University of Michigan, was widely known for his studies on social movements and collective violence. He brought a number of assets to The New School: the cachet of a big name; a mobile grant, at the time rumored to be more than one million dollars that traveled with him when he relocated to New York; and graduate students who followed him from Ann Arbor. His wife, Louise, also a part of the Tilly appointment package, was hired as a tenured professor in sociology.

Katznelson transposed onto The New School the Chicago system of interdisciplinary committees in various research areas that cross-listed both courses and faculty from several of the university's departments. The most famous of these Chicago fiefdoms was the Committee on Social Thought, home at one time or another to Friedrich A. Hayek, Edward A. Shils, Saul Bellow, and Allan Bloom. New committees or "centers," all closely tied to Katznelson's appointees, quickly sprang up. Zolberg became head of the International Center for Migration, Ethnicity, and Citizenship. Louise Tilly chaired a committee on historical studies that promoted the macro-social historiography for which her husband was known. A center on studies of emerging democratic institutions in Eastern Europe provided opportunities for liberally funded travel. Participation in the democratization project, which was not linked to a specific research program or methodology, enabled The New School faculty members of the pre-Katznelson era to ally themselves with the new regime and prove their loyalty by embracing its interest in the development of civil society in Eastern Europe. Poland proved to be a favored site for research, or at least for travel to conferences, where The New School faculty members were able to network with Eastern European intellectuals. Fanton and Katznelson also recruited Janet Abu-Lughod, another University of Chicago graduate, then at Northwestern University. She too instituted the same kind of system putting students to work on "radical" investigations of New York City neighborhoods.

The centerpiece of this new system was Charles Tilly's Center for the Study of Social Change. Originally housed in the unprepossessing warehouse-like fourth floor of the Graduate Faculty building, it moved in 1984 to 64 University Place, where Tilly presided over the entire floor of an office building outfitted with the latest information technology and a team of graduate assistants. Along with the Tillys, Bensel and Sanders also left the Graduate Faculty for 64 University Place. The British historian Eric Hobsbawm was installed on a visiting basis somewhat later. A favorite of the *New York Review of Books*, Hobsbawn was chiefly known for his textbook syntheses of European history, each designated by some "age": *The Age of Revolution*, *The Age of Empire*, and so on. He also enjoyed a certain celebrity due to his longtime claim to communist credentials that he continued to maintain after the collapse of the Soviet Union and well into the 1990s.

From the standpoint of academic marketing, this system had obvious attractions. The variety of cross-listed courses in the Graduate Faculty catalog produced the illusion of a comprehensive and exciting social science curriculum unmatched by any other university. The business plan seemed fairly simple. Consider the Center for the Study of Social Change, "the Tilly industry" as some students called it. It was designed as a profit center for the Graduate Faculty. Tilly, with substantial seed money from his grants, recruited creative new faculty, authors of as yet unwritten prize-winning publications, in order to establish The New School as the leader in the scientific market niche of comparative state development theory. The Graduate Faculty, it was thought, would attract the best American and international scholars to conferences and workshops. The results of these meetings would be published in a series of working papers. Talented graduate students in pursuit of the next new thing and its leading proponents would follow. Success would beget success, and more grant money would flow into the Center. In short, the Center would demonstrate the operation of Robert K. Merton's "Matthew

Principle": to those who have shall be given. The enterprise would be self-sustaining. Unlike the Graduate Faculty departments of the pre-Katznelson era that drained resources from the university, the new centers and committees would produce revenue and reduce the cost of doing business.

For a time, this plan seemed to work, at least if one brackets all questions about the quality of what was produced. Conferences and workshops were held, and the results were duly published. The Tilly Center worked on the model of French and German research institutes in the social sciences: a factory system in which graduate students did research on problems generated by The Grand Scheme. With PhDs in hand and glittering letters of recommendation from faculty active in the Center, they generally found respectable jobs in other PhD programs that were envisioned as potential franchises or subsidiaries of The New School. Within a few short years, The New School became the University of Chicago in Exile.

As this account suggests, I was not an enthusiast of the new order or a part of its apparatus. I kept my distance and, on the whole, held my tongue, unlike Stanford Lyman, whose withering criticisms of the new committees and centers were a tiresome irritation for their advocates. Katznelson, a master academic administrator and tactician of bureaucratic maneuvers, easily found a way to arrange Lyman's self-propelled exit. When Lyman, who had been underpaid for years in spite of his publication record and reputation, spoke with Katznelson about a salary increase and the title of Distinguished Professor after Katznelson awarded that distinction to Stanley Diamond, he was advised to test the market and solicit job offers from other universities. The implication, as Lyman understood it, was that The New School would make a good faith effort to match these offers. When he won a competition for an endowed chair in the social sciences at

Florida Atlantic University, he rushed with the news to the Office of the Dean, expecting a generous increase in his salary and a new title. Katznelson warmly congratulated him on the chair, encouraged him to accept it, and wished him all success. In this manner, an adversary of the new regime was effortlessly dispatched.

In the mid-1980s, I experienced a stunning demonstration of the implications of the new order for my own position. As chair of the department, I went to a meeting with Katznelson to discuss a department proposal to hire Guy Oakes, a renowned Weberian scholar. To my surprise, I was greeted in the dean's office not only by Katznelson, but also by my much-junior departmental colleague Jeffrey Goldfarb, whom Stanford Lyman and I had shepherded through tenure during the 1978 external review crisis. Katznelson and Goldfarb, who was also a graduate of the University of Chicago, put me on notice that Oakes was not to be hired.

After that incident, I devoted my main energies to other scholarly ventures. In 1980, I had initiated the Dubrovnik Seminar, a biennial meeting of international scholars. I renewed my efforts to make that gathering both enjoyable and productive. In 1985, Stanford Lyman and I founded the quarterly journal *State, Culture, and Society*, later renamed the *International Journal of Politics, Culture and Society*. We edited the journal for many years before handing over the editorship, first to E. Doyle McCarthy and then to Guy Oakes. I should mention that it's useful to have a ready outlet for publication. On one occasion, Charles Tilly commissioned an essay from me on recent books about Robert K. Merton and Talcott Parsons for *Sociological Forum*, the journal of the Eastern Sociological Association. I wrote a substantial piece criticizing the work of both of these demi-gods of the profession. Tilly rejected the essay because, he said, it was too long. So I promptly published the piece in the *International Journal of Politics, Culture and Society,* where it got a good reception from our readers. In conjunction with our journal work, Stanford and I also started the Institute for the Study of Contemporary Society that met biennially at Marlboro College in Vermont for several years and helped stimulate good work by many graduate students, from The New School and other institutions as well. In 1990, Rick Tilman and I, with the assistance of Michael Hughey, established the International Thorstein Veblen Association. Its purpose, as we described it in our prospectus, was "to facilitate and revive, in a Veblenian spirit, a critical and historical attitude in the social sciences; to examine and evaluate Veblen's ideas and methods with respect to their applicability and utility for comprehending and analyzing the contemporary world order; to make explicit the attitudes, perspectives, and assumptions underlying Veblen's social, economic, political, and religious frameworks; to illuminate the relationship between Veblen's ideas and his linguistic, rhetorical, and poetic style; and to foster and facilitate communication among Veblen scholars throughout the world." Franco Ferrarotti of the University of Rome, whose 1949 translation of *The Theory of the Leisure Class* first brought Veblen to Europe, recruited several European scholars interested in Veblen's work—Georges Balandier, Michel Maffesole, Robert Cipriani, Gianfranco Corsini, and Mino Vianello, among others—and helped internationalize the Association. The Association's biennial conferences at The New School or Carleton College, which holds Veblen's archives, were lively and productive affairs, and the Association continued to foster work by a younger generation of Veblen scholars. Starting in 1995, Robert Jackall and I edited a series of eight books called *Main Trends of the Modern World*. The series included the following edited volumes: Arthur J. Vidich, *The New Middle Classes;* Stanford M. Lyman, *Social Movements*; Philip Kasinitz, *Metropolis;*

Robert Jackall, *Propaganda*; Alfred Tauber, *Science: The Quest for Reality*; Michael Hughey, *New Tribalisms*; Harry Dahms, *Transformations of Capitalism*; and Catherine Besteman, *Violence*. Finally, in 1994, Guy Oakes and I began the research that resulted in our 1999 book *Collaboration, Reputation, and Ethics in American Academic Life: Hans H. Gerth and C. Wright Mills*. All of these projects were rewarding collaborations with valued colleagues.

All the while, President Fanton remained determined to transform The New School for Social Research into a conventional American university. In some measure, he succeeded. Several wings of the already sprawling institution—the school for general study, the school for management and urban policy, the school of design, the school for liberal arts, and the schools for music and drama—were expanded and consolidated, forming them into what he called the New School University. He sought and found foundation support for this reconstruction of the institution and he steered most of the departments of the Graduate Faculty into the American academic mainstream of conventionality. As a result, the distance between 65th Fifth Avenue and Amherst, Ann Arbor, or Austin was much diminished.

However, the aspirations of the Fanton/Kaztnelson regime remained unfilled. This was largely the consequence of the discrepancy between programmatic aims and institutional resources. In the final analysis, it was about money: the centers were unable to achieve financial autonomy. Even Tilly's Center became dependent on the New School University's budget and eventually proved to be a financial albatross to the institution.

The leaders of the new New School did not remain in place to struggle with these problems. In the mid 1990s, Katznelson left for an endowed chair at Columbia. Charles Tilly, who could no longer expect the largesse to which he was accustomed, repaired to Columbia shortly thereafter. Shortly after leaving New School University despite the substantial support Fanton had provided him to fund his "historical studies" venture, Tilly stated in a biographical note in *Sociological Forum* that he had "resigned from The New School for Social Research in 1966 [*sic*] to protest cuts in The New School's graduate programs."[3] Louise Tilly and Janet Abu-Lughod retired.

The Graduate Faculty began as a place of refuge, and throughout its history, The New School has been a place of careers in transition, where academics practice a continuous assessment of transaction and opportunity costs. In 2000, Fanton made his own assessment and left his New School University for the presidency of the MacArthur Foundation in Chicago. After some fifteen years of grandiose plans, big ideas, long and heated discussions, and a furious pace of activity in which it was often difficult to distinguish genuine academic discourse from a kind of higher chatter, the grip of the University of Chicago in Exile on The New School eased, giving a new generation the opportunity to reshape the school according to its own insights.

An Active Retirement

I retired from the Graduate Faculty in 1991, remaining as an active emeritus faculty member. Although I still directed the sociology department's dissertation seminar for many years after retirement and continued to supervise several dissertations, the Graduate Faculty that I joined in 1960 had obviously disappeared. I took satisfaction in an announcement made by the new president, Bob Kerrey, in June 2005. Kerrey observed that after a "two-year, comprehensive study ...

---

[3]   Tilly, 687.

most of the world knows us as The New School." He went on to note: "The New School was founded on strong convictions. We began as a place that would embrace debate, safeguard intellectual and artistic freedom, and reinvent what it means to be a university. We remain true to our origin. This vibrant community is dedicated to rigorous academic inquiry, creative expression, and active citizenship. Our shared goal is to educate people who expect to make a difference in the world." Thus did Kerrey change the name of Fanton's New School University back to what it was and, in my view, should remain: The New School. It was a good start at recapturing one of the greatest and most daring legacies in American higher education.

Despite the travails of The New School that I've recounted here, I never seriously considered leaving it in spite of several opportunities to do so over the years. Since Hans Gerth first told me about the institution's remarkable history, I've felt a deep commitment to the idea of The New School. Most important, I've felt a profound connection to my many students at the Graduate Faculty over the decades. I've always encouraged my students to frame their own intellectual problems and shape their own long-term intellectual agendas. The New School provided me with plenty of independent-minded young men and women ready to tackle these challenging and self-altering tasks.

List of References

Compiled by Robert Jackall and Ina T. Liu

Adamic, Louis. *What's Your Name?* New York: Harper & Brothers, 1942.

Adler, Mortimer Jerome. *How to Read a Book: The Art of Getting a Liberal Education.* New York: Simon & Schuster, 1940.

Allen, Charlotte. "Spies Like Us: When Sociologists Deceive Their Subjects." *Lingua Franca* 7, no. 9 (November 1997): 31-39.

Anderson, Nels. *The Hobo: The Sociology of the Homeless Man.* Chicago: University of Chicago Press, 1923.

Arendt, Hannah. *The Origins of Totalitarianism.* New York: Harcourt Brace Jovanovich, 1951.

Arensberg, Conrad M., and Solon T. Kimball. *Family and Community in Ireland.* Cambridge, MA: Harvard University Press, 1940.

Ascoli, Max. *Intelligence in Politics.* New York: W. W. Norton & Company, 1936.

———. *The Power of Freedom.* New York: Farrar, Straus, 1949.

Bakke, E. Wight. *The Unemployed Worker: A Study of the Task of Making a Living Without a Job.* New Haven, CT: Yale University Press, 1940.

Barnes, J. A. *A Pack of Lies: Towards a Sociology of Lying.* Cambridge: Cambridge University Press, 1994.

Barnouw, Dagmar. *Weimar Intellectuals and the Threat of Modernity.* Bloomington, IN: Indiana University Press, 1988.

Barton, Roy Franklin, and Fred Eggan. *The Kalingas, Their Institutions and Custom Law*. Chicago: University of Chicago Press, 1949.

Becker, Howard Paul, Alvin Boskoff, and Franz Adler. *Modern Sociological Theory in Continuity and Change*. New York: Holt, Rinehart & Winston, 1957.

Benedict, Ruth. *The Chrysanthemum and the Sword: Patterns of Japanese Culture*. Boston: Houghton Mifflin, 1946.

Bensman, Joseph, and Arthur J. Vidich. *The New American Society: The Revolution of the Middle Classes*. Chicago: Quadrangle Books, 1971. Reprinted in a revised edition as *American Society: The Welfare State & Beyond*. South Hadley, MA: Bergin & Garvey, 1987.

Berger, Peter L. *Invitation to Sociology: A Humanistic Perspective*. Garden City, NY: Doubleday, 1963.

———. *The Noise of Solemn Assemblies: Christian Commitment and the Religious Establishment in America*. Garden City, NY: Doubleday, 1961.

Berger, Peter L., and Thomas Luckmann. *The Social Construction of Reality: A Treatise in the Sociology of Knowledge*. Garden City, NY: Doubleday, 1966.

Besteman, Catherine Lowe, ed. *Violence: A Reader*. In *Main Trends of the Modern World* book series, edited by Robert Jackall and Arthur J. Vidich. New York: New York University Press, 2002.

Bloom, Harold. *The Anxiety of Influence: A Theory of Poetry*. New York: Oxford University Press, 1973.

Bonilla, Frank. *The Failure of Elites*. Vol. 2 of *The Politics of Change in Venezuela*. Cambridge, MA: MIT Press, 1970.

Bonilla, Frank, and José Agustín Silva Michelena, eds. *A Strategy for Research on Social Policy*. Vol. 1 of *The Politics of Change in Venezuela*. Cambridge, MA: MIT Press, 1967.

Brecht, Arnold. *The Political Education of Arnold Brecht: An Autobiography, 1884-1970*. Princeton, NJ: Princeton University Press, 1970.

———. *Political Theory: The Foundations of Twentieth-century Political Thought*. Princeton, NJ: Princeton University Press, 1959.

Brew, John Otis. *Archaeology of Alkali Ridge, Southeastern Utah: With a Review of the Prehistory of the Mesa Verde Division of the San Juan and Some Observations on Archaeological Systematics*. Cambridge, MA: The Museum, 1946.

Buck, Peter H. [Te Rangi Hiroa]. "The Passing of the Maori." *Transactions and Proceedings of the Royal Society of New Zealand* 55 (1924): 362-75.

Calhoun, Arthur W. *A Social History of the American Family from Colonial Times to the Present*. 3 vols. Cleveland, OH: Arthur H. Clark, 1917.

"Candor Calls it Even." *Candor Courier*. July 4, 1958.

Chaplin, Charles. *City Lights*. Film. Directed by Charles Chaplin. United Artists, 1931.

———. *The Gold Rush*. Film. Directed by Charles Chaplin. United Artists, 1925.

———. *The Immigrant*. Film. Directed by Charles Chaplin. Mutual Film Company, 1917.

———. *Modern Times*. Film. Directed by Charles Chaplin. United Artists, 1936.

Childe, V. Gordon. *Man Makes Himself*. London: Watts & Company, 1937.

Clinard, Marshall Barron. *The Black Market: A Study of White Collar Crime*. New York: Rinehart, 1952.

Clissold, Stephen. *Whirlwind: An Account of Marshal Tito's Rise to Power*. New York: Philosophical Library, 1949.

Coser, Lewis A. *Refugee Scholars in America: Their Impact and Their Experiences*. New Haven, CT: Yale University Press, 1984.

Dahms, Harry F., ed. *Transformations of Capitalism: Economy, Society, and the State in Modern Times*. In *Main Trends of the Modern World* book series, edited by Robert Jackall and Arthur J. Vidich. New York: New York University Press, 2000.

Department of Sociology, Harvard University. "Sociology Dissertations 1932-2007." http://www.wjh.harvard.edu/soc/pdfs/sociology_dissertations.pdf . Accessed on July 3, 2009.

Diamond, Stanley. "Dahomey: A Proto-state in West Africa." PhD diss., Department of Anthropology, Columbia University, 1951.

Durkheim, Émile. *The Division of Labor in Society*. Translated by George Simpson. New York: Macmillan, 1933.

———. *The Elementary Forms of the Religious Life: A Study in Religious Sociology*. Translated by Joseph Ward Swain. New York: Macmillan, 1915.

———. *The Rules of Sociological Method*. Translated by Sarah A. Solovay and John H. Mueller. Edited by George E. G. Catlin. Glencoe, IL: Free Press, 1938.

———. *Suicide: A Study in Sociology*. Translated by John A. Spaulding and George Simpson. Edited with an introduction by George Simpson. Glencoe, IL: Free Press, 1951.

Durrell, Lawrence. *The Alexandria Quartet: Justine, Balthazar,*

Mountolive, Clea. New York: Dutton, 1962.

Embree, John F. *Suye Mura: A Japanese Village.* Chicago: University of Chicago Press, 1939.

Firth, Raymond William. *We, the Tikopia: A Sociological Study of Kinship in Primitive Polynesia.* New York: American Book Company, 1936.

Fison, Lorimer, and A.W. Howitt. *Kamilaroi and Kurnai: Group-marriage and Relationship, and Marriage by Elopement, Drawn Chiefly from the Usage of the Australian Aborigines. Also the Kurnai Tribe, Their Customs in Peace and War.* Melbourne, Australia: G. Robertson, 1880.

Forbes, Bryan, director. *King Rat.* Film. Columbia Pictures Corporation: 1965.

Fortune, Reo. *Sorcerers of Dobu: The Social Anthropology of the Dobu Islanders of the Western Pacific.* New York: E. P. Dutton, 1932.

Foss, Daniel. "The World View of Talcott Parsons." In *Sociology on Trial,* edited by Maurice Stein and Arthur Vidich, 96-126. Englewood Cliffs, NJ: Prentice-Hall, 1963.

France, Anatole. *The Red Lily.* Translation of *Lys Rouge* by Winifred Stephens. London: John Lane; New York: John Lane Company, 1914.

Gans, Herbert J. "Best-Sellers by Sociologists: An Exploratory Study." *Contemporary Sociology* 26, no. 2 (March 1997): 131-35.

Garfinkel, Harold. *Parsons' Primer.* Unpublished manuscript of Sociology 251: Topics in the Problem of Social Order, University of California, Los Angeles, 1959.

Genet, Jean. *The Maids: A Play.* Translated by Bernard Frechtman. New York: Grove Press, 1954.

Gerth, Hans Heinrich, and C. Wright Mills. *Character and Social Structure: The Psychology of Social Institutions.* London:

Routledge & Kegan Paul, 1954.

Gluckman, Max. "The Kingdom of the Zulu of South Africa." In *African Political Systems*, edited by Meyer Fortes and E. E. Evans-Pritchard. New York: Oxford University Press, 1940.

Goodman, Paul. *Growing Up Absurd: Problems of Youth in the Organized System*. New York: Random House, 1960.

Greffrath, Matthias, ed. *Die Zerstörung einer Zukunft: Gespräche mit emigrierten Sozialwissenschaftlern*. Reinbek: Rowohlt, 1979.

Gulachok, Michael. "Small Town in Mass Society Revisited." *Tioga County Courier*, January 27 and 28, 1988.

Halévy, Elie, E. I. Watkin, and Dalgairns Arundel Barker. *A History of the English People*. New York: Harcourt, Brace, 1924.

Harrington, Michael. *The Other America: Poverty in the United States*. New York: Macmillan, 1962.

Hayden, Tom. *The Port Huron Statement*. New York: Students for a Democratic Society, 1962.

Heilbroner, Robert L. *The Great Ascent: The Struggle for Economic Development in Our Time*. New York: Harper Torchbooks, 1963.

Hobsbawm, E. J. *The Age of Empire, 1875-1914*. New York: Vintage Books, 1987.

———. *The Age of Revolution, 1789-1848*. Cleveland, OH: World Publishing, 1962.

Homans, George Caspar. *The Human Group*. New York: Harcourt, Brace, 1950.

Howells, W. W. *Mankind So Far*. Garden City, NY: Doubleday, Doran, 1944.

Hughes, H. Stuart. *The Sea Change: The Migration of Social Thought, 1930-1965*. New York: Harper & Row, 1975.

Hughey, Michael, ed. *New Tribalisms: The Resurgence of Race and*

Ethnicity. In *Main Trends of the Modern World* book series, edited by Robert Jackall and Arthur J. Vidich. New York: New York University Press, 1998.

Jackall, Robert. "The Education of Barrington Moore, Jr." *International Journal of Politics, Culture and Society* 14, no. 4 (June 2001): 675-81.

———. *Moral Mazes: The World of Corporate Managers.* New York: Oxford University Press, 1988.

———. ed. *Propaganda.* In *Main Trends of the Modern World* book series, edited by Robert Jackall and Arthur J. Vidich. New York: New York University Press, 1995.

Jackall, Robert, and Arthur J. Vidich, eds. *Main Trends of the Modern World* book series. New York: New York University Press, 1995-2004.

Jonas, Hans. *The Imperative of Responsibility: In Search of an Ethics for the Technological Age.* Chicago: University of Chicago Press, 1984.

Kasinitz, Philip. *Metropolis: Center and Symbol of Our Times.* In *Main Trends of the Modern World* book series, edited by Robert Jackall and Arthur J. Vidich. New York: New York University Press, 1995.

Kirchheimer, Otto. *Political Justice: The Use of Legal Procedure for Political Ends.* Princeton, NJ: Princeton University Press, 1961.

Kluckhohn, Clyde. *Navaho Witchcraft.* Boston, MA: Beacon Press, 1944.

———. "Values and Value-orientations in the Theory of Action: An Exploration in Definition and Classification." In *Toward a General Theory of Action*, edited by Talcott Parsons and Edward A. Shils, 388-433. Cambridge: Harvard University Press, 1951.

Kluckhohn, Clyde, and Dorothea Cross Leighton. *Children of the People: The Navaho Individual and His Development.* Cambridge, MA: Harvard University Press, 1947.

Kroeber, A. L. "On the Principle of Order in Civilization as Exemplified by Changes in Fashion." *American Anthropologist* 21 (1919): 235-63.

Kroeber, A. L., and Clyde Kluckhohn. *Culture: A Critical Review of Concepts and Definitions.* Cambridge, MA: The Museum, 1952.

Krohn, Claus-Dieter. *Intellectuals in Exile: Refugee Scholars and the New School for Social Research.* Amherst: University of Massachusetts Press, 1993.

Landes, Ruth. *The Ojibwa Woman.* New York: AMS Press, 1938.

Lederer, Emil. *Die Privatangestellten in der modernen Wirtschaftsent-wicklung.* Tubingen: J. C. B. Mohr P. Siebeck, 1912.

———. *State of the Masses: The Threat of the Classless Society.* Translated from the German by Hans Speier. New York: W. W. Norton, 1940.

Lederer, Emil, and Jacob Marschak. "Der Neue Mittelstand." In *Grundriss der Nationalökonomie.* 1926. Translated into English as "The New Middle Class." The Works Progress Administration, 1937.

Leighton, Alexander H. *The Governing of Men: General Principles and Recommendations Based on Experience at a Japanese Relocation Camp.* Princeton, NJ: Princeton University Press, 1945.

Lowe, Adolph. *On Economic Knowledge: Toward a Science of Political Economics.* New York: Harper & Row, 1965.

Lowenthal, Leo, and Norbert Guterman. *Prophets of Deceit: A Study of the Techniques of the American Agitator.* New York: Harper, 1949.

Lowie, Robert Harry. *The History of Ethnological Theory*. New York: Farrar & Rinehart, 1937.

Luckmann, Benita. "New School: Varianten der Rückkehr aus Exil und Emigration." In *Exil, Wissenschaft, Identität: Die Emigration deutscher Sozialwissenschaftler*, Ilja Srubar, Hg., *1933-1945*, 353-78. Frankfurt: Suhrkamp, 1988.

Lyman, Stanford M., ed. *Social Movements: Critiques, Concepts, and Case Studies*. In *Main Trends of the Modern World* book series, edited by Robert Jackall and Arthur J. Vidich. New York: New York University Press, 1995.

Lyman, Stanford M., and Marvin B. Scott. *A Sociology of the Absurd*. New York: Appleton-Century-Crofts, 1970.

Lynd, Robert S., and Helen Merrell Lynd. *Middletown: A Study in Contemporary American Culture*. Foreword by Clark Wissler. New York: Harcourt, Brace, 1929.

MacDonald, Dwight. *The Ford Foundation: The Men and the Millions*. New York: Reynal, 1956.

Mannheim, Karl, Louis Wirth, and Edward Shils. *Ideology and Utopia: An Introduction to the Sociology of Knowledge*. New York: Harcourt, Brace, 1936.

Marcuse, Herbert. *One-dimensional Man: Studies in the Ideology of Advanced Industrial Society*. Boston: Beacon Press, 1964.

Martindale, Don. *Sociological Theory and the Problem of Values*. Columbus, OH: Merrill, 1974.

Matlin, Norman. *The Educational Enclave: Coercive Bargaining in Colleges and Universities*. New York: Funk & Wagnalls, 1969.

Matthiessen, F. O. *American Renaissance: Art and Expression in the Age of Emerson and Whitman*. New York: Oxford University Press, 1957.

Maynard, John. *The Russian Peasant and Other Studies*. New York: Collier Books, 1942.

Mayo, Elton. *The Human Problems of an Industrial Civilization*. Boston: Harvard University, 1946.

Mead, Margaret. *Coming of Age in Samoa: A Psychological Study of Primitive Youth for Western Civilization*. New York: W. Morrow, 1928.

———. *Growing Up in New Guinea: A Comparative Study of Primitive Education*. New York: Blue Ribbon Books, 1930.

———. *The Mountain Arapesh*. Garden City, NY: Natural History Press, 1938.

Mears, Helen. *Year of the Wild Boar: An American Woman in Japan*. Philadelphia: J. B. Lippincott, 1942.

Melville, Herman. *The Confidence-Man: His Masquerade*. New York: Norton, 1857.

Michels, Robert. *Political Parties: A Sociological Study of the Oligarchical Tendencies of Modern Democracy*. Glencoe, IL: Free Press, 1949.

Mills, C. Wright. "The Bureaucratic Ethos." In *Sociology on Trial*, edited by Maurice Stein and Arthur Vidich, 12-25. Englewood Cliffs, NJ: Prentice-Hall, 1963.

———. *The Power Elite*. New York: Oxford University Press, 1956.

———. *The Sociological Imagination*. New York: Oxford University Press, 1959.

———. *White Collar*. New York: Oxford University Press, 1951.

Mosca, Gaetano. *The Ruling Class*. New York: McGraw-Hill, 1939.

Murdock, George Peter. *Our Primitive Contemporaries*. New York: Macmillan, 1934.

Naegele, Philipp O. "Foreword." In *Health and Healing*, by Kaspar D.

Naegele, ix-xvi. Compiled and edited by Elaine Cumming. San Francisco: Jossey Bass, 1970.

Nash, Philleo. "The Place of Religious Revivalism in the Formation of the Intercultural Community on the Klamath Reservation." In *The Social Anthropology of North American Indian Tribes*, edited by Fred Eggan, 337-442. Chicago: University of Chicago Press, 1937.

Nelson, Benjamin. *The Idea of Usury: From Tribal Otherhood to Universal Brotherhood*. Princeton, NJ: Princeton University Press, 1949.

Nero, Karen Louise. "A Cherechar a Lokelii: Beads of History of Koror, Palau, 1783-1983." PhD diss., Department of Anthropology, University of California, Berkeley, 1987.

Nishihara, Kazumi. "Politics of Faith: Investigating Ethnographies about Modekngei." Master's thesis, Pacific Islands Studies, University of Hawaii at Manoa, 1998.

Nitobe, Inazo. *Bushido, The Soul of Japan: An Exposition of Japanese Thought*. Philadelphia: Leeds & Biddle, 1899.

Oakes, Guy, and Arthur J. Vidich. *Collaboration, Reputation and Ethics in American Academia: Hans H. Gerth and C. Wright Mills*. Champaign, IL: University of Illinois Press, 1999.

Orwell, George. *1984*. San Diego: Harcourt Brace Jovanovich, 1949.

———. *A Clergyman's Daughter*. San Diego: Harcourt Brace Jovanovich, 1936.

———. *Down and Out in Paris and London: A Novel*. New York: Harcourt, Brace, 1933.

———. *Homage to Catalonia*. London: Secker & Warburg, 1938.

———. *Keep the Aspidistra Flying*. London: Secker & Warburg, 1936.

———. "Shooting an Elephant." *New Writing* 1, no. 2 (1936): 1-7.

Pareto, Vilfredo. *The Mind and Society: Trattato Di Sociologia Generale.* Translated by Arthur Livingston. New York: Harcourt, Brace, 1935.

Parmentier, Richard J. "The Sacred Remains: Historical Anthropology of Ngeremlengui, Palau." PhD diss., Department of Anthropology, University of Chicago, 1981.

Parsons, Talcott. *The Early Essays / Talcott Parsons.* Edited and with an introduction by Charles Camic. Chicago: University of Chicago Press, 1991.

———. *The Social System.* Glencoe, IL: Free Press, 1951.

———. *The Structure of Social Action: A Study in Social Theory with Special Reference to a Group of Recent European Writers.* New York: McGraw-Hill, 1937.

———. "Towards a Common Language for the Area of Social Science." Harvard University Archives. Papers of Talcott Parsons, 1921-1979. HUGFP 42.64 Sociology and Social Relations Course Materials, 1931-1956. Box 1, SOC A.

Parsons, Talcott, and Edward Shils. *Towards a General Theory of Action: Theoretical Foundations for the Social Sciences.* New York: Harper Row, 1962.

Parsons, Talcott, Edward Shils, Kaspar D. Naegele, and Jesse R. Pitts, eds. *Theories of Society: Foundations of Modern Sociological Theory.* 2 volumes. New York: Free Press of Glencoe, 1961.

Piccone, Paul. "Postmodern Populism." *Telos* 103 (Spring 1995): 45-86.

Powers, Willow Roberts. "The Harvard Five Cultures Values Study and Post-war Anthropology." PhD diss., Department of Anthropology, University of New Mexico, 1997.

Radcliffe-Brown, A. R. *Structure and Function in Primitive Society, Essays and Addresses.* Foreword by E.E. Evans-Pritchard and

Fred Eggan. Glencoe, IL: Free Press, 1961.

Radin, Paul. *The Method and Theory of Ethnology: An Essay in Criticism*. South Hadley, MA: Bergin & Garvey, 1966.

Remarque, Erich Maria. *All Quiet on the Western Front*. Boston: Little, Brown, and Company, 1929.

Rieder, Jonathan. *Canarsie: The Jews and Italians of Brooklyn Against Liberalism*. Cambridge, MA: Harvard University Press, 1985.

Riezler, Kurt. *Man, Mutable and Immutable*. Chicago: Regnery, 1950.

Robinson, Forrest G. *Love's Story Told: A Life of Henry A. Murray*. Cambridge: Harvard University Press, 1992.

Rosenberg, Bernard. *The Values of Veblen: A Critical Appraisal*. Washington: Public Affairs Press, 1956.

Rutkoff, Peter M., and William B. Scott. *New School: A History of the New School for Social Research*. New York: Free Press of Glencoe, 1986.

Sakuma (Takeo Yano). "Hope and the Obstacle of Development." A paper submitted to the foreign administration of Palau. Date unknown.

———. "Our Hopes." Two separate papers with the same title delivered as lectures at the Korror School in Palau. Date unknown.

Salomon, Albert. *The Tyranny of Progress: Reflections on the Origins of Sociology*. New York: Noonday Press, 1955.

Sansom, Sir George Bailey. *Japan: A Short Cultural History*. New York: Century, 1931.

Saunders, Frances Stonor. *Who Paid the Piper? The CIA and the Cultural Cold War*. London: Granta, 1999. Republished as *The Cultural Cold War: The CIA and the World of Arts and Letters*. New York: New Press, 2000.

Schapera, Isaac. *Married Life in an African Tribe*. London: Faber and Faber, 1940.

Schutz, Alfred. "The Homecomer." *American Journal of Sociology* 50, no. 5 (1944): 369-76.

Seligman, Edwin R. A., ed. *Encyclopaedia of the Social Sciences.* New York: Macmillan, 1930-1935.

Shils, Edward. *The Present State of American Sociology.* Glencoe, IL: Free Press, 1948.

Shuster, Donald R. "Islands of Change in Palau: Church, School, and Elected Government, 1891-1981." PhD diss., Educational Foundations, University of Hawaii at Manoa, 1982.

Silva Michelena, José Agustin. *The Illusion of Democracy in Dependent Nations.* Volume 3 of *The Politics of Change in Venezuela.* Cambridge, MA: MIT Press, 1971.

Skates, John Ray. *The Invasion of Japan: An Alternative to the Bomb.* Columbia, NC: University of North Carolina Press, 1994.

Smith, Gerald L.K. *The Cross and the Flag, Monthly Periodical.* Glendale, CA: Christian Nationalist Crusade, 1942-1977.

Sorel, Georges. *Reflections on Violence.* London: George Allen & Unwin, 1915.

Speier, Hans. *From the Ashes of Disgrace: A Journal from Germany, 1945-1955.* Amherst: University of Massachusetts Press, 1981.

———. *German White-Collar Workers and the Rise of Hitler.* New Haven, CT: Yale University Press, 1986.

Spencer, Baldwin and F. J. Gillen. *The Native Tribes of Central Australia.* New York: Macmillan, 1899.

———. *The Northern Tribes of Central Australia.* New York: Macmillan, 1904.

Staudinger, Hans. *The Inner Nazi: A Critical Analysis of Mein Kampf.* Baton Rouge: Louisiana University Press, 1981.

Stein, Maurice. *The Eclipse of Community: An Interpretation of*

American Studies. New York: Harper Row, 1964.

Stein, Maurice, and Arthur Vidich, eds. *Sociology on Trial*. Englewood Cliffs, NJ: Prentice-Hall, 1963.

Stein, Maurice R., Arthur J. Vidich, and David Manning White, eds. *Identity and Anxiety: Survival of the Person in Mass Society*. Glencoe, IL: Free Press, 1960.

Steward, Julian H. *The People of Puerto Rico: A Study in Social Anthropology*. Champaign, IL: University of Illinois Press, 1956.

Stouffer, Samuel Andrew. *The American Soldier*. Princeton, NJ: Princeton University Press, 1949.

Sugiura, Kenichi. "Ethnology and Native Administration in Micronesia." In *Great South Seas: Its Culture and Its Soil*, 173-218. Institute of the Pacific. Tokyo: Kawade Shobo, 1941.

Tauber, Alfred, ed. *Science and the Quest for Reality*. In *Main Trends of the Modern World* book series, edited by Robert Jackall and Arthur J. Vidich. New York: New York University Press, 1997.

Tilly, Charles. "Invisible Elbow." *Sociological Forum* 11, no. 4, (December 1996): 589-601, 687.

Trewartha, Glenn Thomas. *Japan: A Geography*. Madison: University of Wisconsin, 1965.

Turner, Stephen. "The Origins of Mainstream Sociology and Other Issues in the History of American Sociology." *Social Epistemology* 8, no. 1 (1994): 41-67.

Veblen, Thorstein. *The Higher Learning in America: A Memorandum on the Conduct of Universities by Business Men*. New York: B. W. Huebsch, 1918.

———. "Hiroshima's Legacy: The Theodicy of Man-Made Hazards."

Anthropology Resource Center Newsletter 4, no. 3 (September 1980).

———. *The Theory of the Leisure Class: An Economic Study of Institutions.* New York: Modern Library, 1934.

Vidich, Arthur J. "The American Success Dilemma." Master's thesis, Department of Anthropology, University of Wisconsin, Madison, 1948.

———. "The Department of Social Relations and 'Systems Theory' at Harvard: 1948-1950." *International Journal of Politics, Culture and Society* 14, no. 4 (2000): 607-48.

———. "Interview with Arthur J. Vidich." Conducted by Charles Vidich. Middletown, CT. May 25, 2003. Unpublished.

———. ed. *The New Middle Classes: Life-Styles, Status Claims, and Political Orientations.* In *Main Trends of the Modern World* book series, edited by Robert Jackall and Arthur J. Vidich. New York: New York University Press, 1995.

———. "Participant Observation and the Collection and Interpretation of Data." *American Journal of Sociology* 60, no. 4 (January 1955), 354-360.

———. "The Place of the Graduate Faculty of Political and Social Science in Higher Education." Unpublished position paper. New York: Graduate Faculty, New School for Social Research, 1978.

———. *Political Factionalism in Palau, Its Rise and Development.* Washington, DC, Pacific Science Board, National Research Council, 1949.

———. "The Political Impact of Colonial Administration." PhD diss., Department of Social Relations, Harvard University, 1953. Published under the same title. New York: Arno Press, 1980.

———. "The Social Role of the Anthropological Advisor." *American Anthropologist* 59, no. 5 (October 1957): 878-83.

———. *Trujillo Bajo.* Unpublished manuscript.

Vidich, Arthur J., and Joseph Bensman. *Small Town in Mass Society: Class, Power, and Religion in a Rural Community.* Princeton, NJ: Princeton University Press, 1958. Reprint, Garden City, NY: Anchor Books, 1960. Reprint with supplementary materials, Princeton, NJ: Princeton University Press, 1968. Reprint in revised edition with a foreword by Michael W. Hughey and an afterword by Arthur J. Vidich, Urbana: University of Illinois Press, 2000.

———. "Social Theory and the Substantive Problems of Sociology." *International Journal of Politics, Culture and Society* 4, no. 4 (1991): 517-34.

———. "Social Theory in Field Research." *American Journal of Sociology* 65, no. 6 (May 1960), 577-584.

———. "The Validity of Field Data." *Human Organization* 13, no. 1 (Spring 1954), 20-27.

Vidich, Arthur J. and Maurice R. Stein, "The Dissolved Identity in Military Life." In *Identity and Anxiety: Survival of the Person in Mass Society*, edited by Maurice Stein, Arthur J. Vidich, and David Manning White, 493-506. Glencoe, IL: Free Press, 1960.

Vidich, Arthur J., and Stanford M. Lyman. *American Sociology: Worldly Rejections of Religion and Their Directions.* New Haven, CT: Yale University Press, 1985.

———. "Qualitative Methods: Their History in Sociology and Anthropology." In *Handbook of Qualitative Research*, edited by Norman K. Denzen and Yvonna S. Lincoln, 33-59. Thousand Oaks, CA: Sage Publications, 1994.

Vidich, Arthur J., Joseph Bensman, and Maurice Stein, eds. *Reflections on Community Studies*. New York: Wiley, 1964.

Vidich, Virginia Wicks. "Gerald L. K. Smith Speaks at 'Cross Roads': A Social Psychological Study in Public Opinion." Master's thesis, Department of Sociology, University of Wisconsin, Madison, 1948.

———. "Climatic, Public Health and Nutritional Correlates of Infant Mortality Variations among Cities in Columbia, South America, 1962." PhD diss., Department of Sociology, University of Connecticut, 1967.

Waller, Willard. "What Teaching Does to Teachers." In *The Sociology of Teaching*. New York: J. Wiley & Sons, 1932, 375-440.

Warner, W. Lloyd. *A Black Civilization: A Social Study of an Australian Tribe*. New York: Harper & Bros., 1937.

Weber, Max. *The Agrarian Sociology of Ancient Civilizations*. London: Verso, 1976.

———. *From Max Weber*. Translated, edited, and with an introduction by Hans H. Gerth and C. Wright Mills. New York: Oxford University Press, 1946.

———. *The Protestant Ethic and the Spirit of Capitalism*. Translated by Talcott Parsons. New York: Scribner, 1958.

———. *The Theory of Social and Economic Organization*. Translated by A. M. Henderson and Talcott Parsons. New York: Oxford University Press, 1947.

Wilson, Lynn B. *Speaking to Power: Gender and Politics in the Western Pacific*. New York: Routledge, 1995.

Wissler, Clark. *North American Indians of the Plains*. New York: American Museum of Natural History, 1912.

Wolfe, Tom. *From Bauhaus to Our House*. New York: Farrar Straus Giroux, 1981.

Wunderlich, Frieda. *British Labor and the War*. New York: New School for Social Research, 1941.

———. *Farm Labor in Germany, 1810-1945*. Princeton, NJ: Princeton University Press, 1961.

———. *Labor Under German Democracy, Arbitration 1918-1933*. New York: New School for Social Research, 1940.